ECONOMICS AND MARXISM

For my children

ECONOMICS AND MARXISM

Volume 2

THE DYNAMICS OF THE MARXIAN SYSTEM

Karl Kühne

Translated by Robert Shaw

St. Martin's Press   New York

St. Martin's Press, Inc. 175 Fifth Avenue, New York, N.Y. 10010
Printed in Great Britain
First published in the United States of America in 1979
LC 9–5149

ISBN 0–312–23437–6

Contents

Preface

It is with some hesitation that I make the book available to the public, for I am myself not completely satisfied with my efforts. All the same, I have here attempted to pay homage – long overdue – to Marx's achievements in the field of economics, and in so doing I have gone back to the statements of the leading writers on the subject since the beginning of the quasi-official controversy between Marxism and 'academic' economics. To that extent this work is based more or less on the history of economic doctrines. Many young Marxists may contemptuously dismiss it as dealing only with 'secondary literature' – a reproach with which I was faced in a debate at Berlin University in November 1972. Nevertheless, one should not underestimate the importance of literature that not only supports Marx to a great degree but also helps to overcome various deficiencies. Such literature is all the more important as Marx never had the opportunity during his lifetime to have his economic theses exposed to the chilling breeze of objective discussion. For the greater part of his work this was not possible in any case, since it appeared posthumously. That is why present-day Marxists should not shy away from criticism, as the criticism of some 'academic' economists is in many cases well meant and has made a fruitful contribution to enlarging the Marxian edifice of thought.

Although I am well aware of the many deficiencies in volume I of this work, and although I recognise similar shortcomings in this second volume, I do not like the idea of ultimately suffering the same fate as the Master (if the comparison is at all legitimate): that is, posthumous publication, perhaps in an unacceptable form, of sketches and drafts made during the previous twenty years. That is why I prefer to publish the text as it is, knowing that it is incomplete and capable of improvement. Besides, I hope, perhaps vainly, to provoke the criticism of other writers, in order to learn from it. There may then perhaps be the opportunity of publishing a more complete, revised edition at a later date.

This subjective decision to publish is based on objectively solid ground. Though the literature on Marx has been enriched of late by contributions from professional economists, there is still no comprehensive overview by which the chaff can be separated from the wheat and that does justice to Marx's structure of thought under dynamic aspects.

On the Marxist side important contributions have been made by Maurice Dobb, Antonio Pesenti, Oscar Lange, Paul Baran, Paul M. Sweezy and Ernest Mandel, but perhaps with the exception of the last-mentioned author none has tried to reinterpret the Marxian theory from the point of view of modern analysis and terminology. Unfortunately, the work of Mandel is much too concerned with historical, sociological, anthropological and political analyses. The creditable performance of Rosdolsky, which is the one that comes nearest to an attempt at an all-embracing presentation, is too strongly imbued with what has been called philosophical Marxism. In any case, Rosdolsky himself has stressed in the Preface to his great work that he is not in any way an economist, which makes it all the more astonishing that he could nevertheless produce such a book. This also explains why he was not able to do justice to the problems of modern economics. It has also to be recognised that the book is already somewhat out of date.

Modern attempts at an overall evaluation of Marx by non-Marxist economists have in general concentrated on a few central points. This is true of the works of Bartoli, and the study by the French Jesuit fathers Calvez and Bigo, and the studies by Wolfson and Balinky in the United States. Unfortunately, Balinky's study suffers from a lack of references to sources. There remains the work of Joan Robinson, one of the leading representatives of the neo-Keynesian Left. Her verdict on Marx is contained in numerous articles and in a short book, which still remains the most important work on Marx and does him full justice. Along with Joan Robinson's work we have to mention the analyses by Schumpeter, Blaug, Roll and Bronfenbrenner as the most profound, though they are contained in larger works.

In 1970 I published a study that took the form of an introduction to Marx's *Ökonomische Schriften* (Economic Writings) (Stuttgart: Kröner). Some favourable reviews of this held that in many respects I seemed to be a follower of the ideas of Schumpeter and Joan Robinson. This may be the right place to acknowledge that I am indeed attracted by their train of thought and their way of arguing, for it leads to a positive appreciation of Marx within modern economics. As regards Joan Robinson, the more humorous than sarcastic flavour of her writings, and her capacity for fair judgement, even where her interpretation is sometimes manifestly wrong, have impressed me greatly, and I think that Marxist writers, who are often prone to imitate the bitter irony of their Master, had better follow the example of her style. This does not mean that I consider myself a 'Robinsonian', though I consider Joan Robinson to be one of my teachers, together with Marx, Schumpeter, D. H. Robertson and Antonio Labriola.

I think that the time has come to bridge the gulf that separates Marxian and 'academic' economics. It is scarcely possible for the two systems to exist side by side without communication, just as the great powers, whether they trace their ideology back to Marx or to Adam Smith, can scarcely co-exist, in this world, the confines of which seem continually to shrink, without dialogue. Both must seek the answer to the famous puzzle confronting Shakespeare's Hamlet: 'To be, or not to be – that is the question'.

One need not necessarily be a follower of the theory of convergence to maintain that, between the thesis of 'capitalism' and the antithesis of 'revolution', the synthesis 'socialism', as envisaged by the great socialists of the nineteenth century, has not yet been found. Yet it must be found if the answer to the question is not to be a disastrous one. To put the question into the context of the present work: 'The question is whether one can be a socialist without being a Marxist and whether one can be a Marxist without asking the question of what are the odds on the continued existence of human civilisation'!

Towards the end of this book, a short section is devoted to the future development of the Marxian system, and in it reference is made to some other studies that deal with these problems in detail.

This volume – like its predecessor – has been pruned to a certain extent; it is thus the equivalent of a second edition. In particular, lengthy quotations from English-language authors have been paraphrased or condensed. Since the original texts are more easily accessible to the English reader, there was not so great a need for lengthy quotations as in the German and Spanish editions.

In order to shorten this rather voluminous work, a simplified method of quotation has been adopted which avoids footnotes: e.g. 'Joan Robinson, 1970, p. 100' refers to the page number in the respective publication as contained in the Bibliography.

Following up the effort of updating which has been made in this edition, the Bibliography also enumerates in an Addendum a few publications which appeared recently and could only be consulted cursorily. This applies to published works by Samir Amin, Stuart Holland, Joachim Adey, M. C. Howard and J. E. King, Gérard Maarek, Walter Steitz and Günter Herre, furthermore to the two volumes *Marx's Capital and Capitalism Today* by the team Cutler, Hindess, Hirst and Hussain, and finally also to the manuscripts of studies by Angus Walker and the Japanese author Kozo Uno.

Once more I wish to express my gratitude to all those who were of help to me, whom I have already mentioned in the Preface to the volume 1. Special thanks are again due to the translator, Mr Robert Shaw, to Mrs Gerda Kühne, who was responsible for the quotations and for the general presentation of this volume, and to Mrs Ranavalona Lise Iva, who typed it and prepared the bibliography. This book does not set out to be my last word on the subject, but seeks only to serve as an overview of the Marxian system, an overview meant to inspire young economists in their future work.

Brussels   KARL KÜHNE
April 1979

Part I
International Aspects

1 Marx's Theory of Foreign Trade and its Critics

The irony of history willed it that the economist whose international impact was widest and who was particularly bent on internationalism never had any chance to make a major contribution to the theory of international exchange, although he attributed the utmost importance to the international framework of capitalist development. This lacuna is corroborated by the fact that there are very few statements from 'academic' economists on Marx's theory of international trade.

The paradox does not stop there. It was perhaps just this lack of an adequate Marxian theory of international economics which prodded some Marxists into the attempt to make a politically oriented contribution to the analysis of the connexion between world economics and world politics, so producing the theory of 'imperialism'.

There are other paradoxes: in modern times, Rostow, in his – as he calls it (in a subtitle) – 'non-Communist Manifesto', has tried to disprove Marx's thesis of the development of capitalism. By using the term 'non-Communist Manifesto' he effectively demonstrated the profound impact that Marx's 'materialist' interpretation of history and his analysis of the origin of world capitalism have had on analysts of international problems.

Nevertheless, it must be admitted that comments on Marx's theory of international trade are rare, as rare as the passages in Marx's works referring to these problems. Besides, it is easy to explain why Marx had no fully-fledged theory of international exchange and why he reacted 'in a sort of vague and tacit agreement . . . with the Ricardian theory' (Emmanuel, 1969, p. 92). The reason is simply that his chief work remains incomplete. He actually intended to develop a theory of international exchange in one of the later chapters of *Capital*.

Blaug, who among academic economists comes nearest to doing Marx full justice, is one of the commentators who has dealt most extensively with the few Marxian passages on foreign trade. He thinks that in Marx's mind colonies were already a thing of the past, and believes that what was uppermost in Marx's mind – as, incidentally, had been the case with John Stuart Mill – was the idea that capital export forestalls a fall in the rate of profit in developed countries, because it absorbs redundant savings. This is a long way from maintaining that Marx's conception presupposes that markets would have to be conquered for capitalism to sell its superfluous

3

products, which would be a distortion of Marx's thought. Such a simplified version of under-consumptionist theory cannot even be attributed to Rosa Luxemburg. Strangely enough, this idea has been adopted by such a sophisticated author as Kindleberger (1962, p. 240), who perhaps took it over from Dupriez (1951).

Many other authors present distorted interpretations. For instance, Pohle, in a work revised by Halm, reached the astonishing conclusion (1919/1931, p. 2) that, according to Marx, 'capitalism means that commerce subjugates production'. There can be no greater misinterpretation: the exact opposite is true, as we have already shown in Volume I, Chapter 2, of this work. As a matter of fact, Marx starts from the premise that

> merchant's capital appears as the historical form of capital long before capital established its own domination over production. Its existence and development to a certain level are in themselves historical premises for the development of capitalist production. . . . Yet its development . . . is incapable by itself of promoting and explaining the transition from one mode of production to another. [i.e. from the feudal system to capitalism]. . . . Within capitalist production merchant's capital is reduced from its former independent existence to a special phase in the investment of capital. . . . It functions only as an agent of productive capital. . . . wherever merchant's capital still predominates we find backward conditions. This is true even within one and the same country, in which, for instance, the specifically merchant towns present far more striking analogies with past conditions than industrial towns. . . . The independent development of merchant's capital, therefore, stands in inverse proportion to the general economic development of society. . . . this monopoly of the carrying trade disintegrates, and with it this trade itself, proportionately to the economic development of the peoples . . . This is but a special form, in which is expressed the subordination of merchants to industrial capital with the advance of capitalist production. . . . In the pre-capitalist stages of society commerce ruled industry. In modern society the reverse is true.
>
> (*Capital*, III, ch. 20, pp. 327–30.)

It is obvious from this quotation that Pohle has completely distorted Marx's argument and turned it upside down. This is indeed a typical example of the carelessness that certain 'academic' economists have occasionally displayed in dealing with Marxian texts. Even a cursory reading of chapter 20 of volume III, where 'historical facts about commercial capital' are related, ought to have convinced Pohle, that his interpretation was the exact opposite of what Marx had said. The same goes for Halm, as reviser of Pohle's study.

In his great work on Marxian economics, which unfortunately is marred by the almost total lack of acknowledgement of sources, Balinky has correctly interpreted Marx's theory of foreign trade. It is true that even he harks back to the *Communist Manifesto*: for instance, he regards the 'hunt for markets' as an outstanding feature of this theory. On the other hand, as shown by the following statement, Balinky clearly recognises the connexion with the Marxian theory of the tendency of the rate of profit to fall: 'The real force behind the growth of foreign economic activity is given as the existence of differentials in the average rate of profit, reflecting differences in the order of the organic composition of capital, as between capitalist and underdeveloped economies.' Since Marx stated that 'the rate of profit is inversely related to the order of the organic composition of capital', which would be low in under-developed countries,

the average rate of profit [must be] higher in the under-developed. . . . the average organic composition of capital is at its lowest order in the least developed and at its highest order in the most developed economy. All other things being equal, therefore, the average rate of profit *is higher in the underdeveloped and lower in the developed economies*. As long as this disparity persists there will be a tendency on the part of capital to flow from the capitalist to the underdeveloped areas, and the more capitalists are driven to innovate (the higher the order of the organic composition of capital), the stronger is this tendency. When, and under what circumstance, will this process come to an end? When, as a result of this capital flow, the average order of the organic composition of capital and thus the average rate of profit are the same for all economies. (Balinky, 1970, p. 142.)

Balinky thus links the Marxian theory of international exchange to that of the tendency of the rate of profit to fall. At first sight, such a link may appear to be quite persuasive, especially with regard to certain phenomena in our world economic system. For instance, it would be possible to explain differences in interest rates between the United States and Europe by stating that capital-intensity is much higher in the United States. This fact would help to explain capital exports, direct investment and dollar flows towards Europe and other continents, would point to the tendency towards a 'neo-imperialist mopping-up' of fixed assets in the rest of the world, and would simultaneously establish a direct link with international monetary problems.

It must, however, appear somewhat doubtful whether such an interpretation can be accepted at face value. A difference in the level of interest rates is no proof of a difference in industrial profits. Besides, further discussion of the international situation has shown that it is not possible to assume *a priori* that capital profitability in underdeveloped countries is any higher than in industrial countries, except in some peculiar cases, such as those of certain plantation crops (for instance, rubber) and minerals (for example, oil and uranium).

In addition, such an interpretation smacks of the optimism of certain liberal schools of thought which set out from the assumption that the development of underdeveloped countries would follow in the wake of favourable private-investment opportunities.

Such an interpretation also ignores a number of important aspects, including the risk element and the modern tendency, where the necessary infrastructure and high-quality labour are to be found in consumption centres, for capital to move into congested areas, such as Western Europe. If capital really tended to move into underdeveloped areas, programmes of international aid within the framework of the World Bank would not be necessary. This criticism, however, cannot be directed against Marx, but only against Balinky.

Balinky considers that Marx emphasised other aspects of international economics. Profits are the proper driving force in the long-run expansion of international trade. Developed countries import raw materials and consumption goods, which are typically produced by third-world industries, while exporting manufactured goods, in the production of which they enjoy a comparative advantage. 'The question at this point is why and under what circumstances capitalists find it more profitable to sell their wares in the underdeveloped markets rather than domestically' (ibid., p. 143).

It must not be forgotten that things are complicated by the fact that some industrial countries, for instance the United States, also export raw materials.

Balinky points to the different degrees of mechanisation reached in developed and underdeveloped countries. In the developed countries, the continuous spread of innovations incorporated in new investment leads to a decrease in prices, which in turn induces a fall in the rate of profit. On the other hand, underdeveloped areas still apply the old methods of production, which are less capital-intensive, so that they cannot reduce their prices to the same extent.

This argument rests on the assumption that the quantity of consumption goods produced with the aid of new methods competes with a smaller quantity of similar consumption goods produced in underdeveloped countries. Thanks to exportation, capitalists escape the fate of reciprocal price-cutting, which lowers the long-run cost price within their countries. Here, as in other sectors of international economics, Marx moves away from value theory towards a comparison of prices of production.

In this way, the volume of world trade expands, a phenomenon which is strengthened by other factors. 'The principal ones are: (1) striking technological progress in the means of communication and transportation; (2) expansion of credit facilities; (3) periodic need for fresh foreign markets during periods of crisis' (ibid.). This last point indirectly touches upon the multiplier effect of foreign trade.

Rostow's book *The Stages of Economic Growth* (1971) does not so much contest the various theses developed by Marx in the realm of international trade as oppose the fundamental idea of the Marxian development scheme, in the sense that in the last resort it is not the development of productive forces that is decisive. He argues that national independence and a host of subjective, psychological and sociological elements are more important. In his chapter 10 (pp. 145ff.), Rostow deals with communism, as a political movement, under the heading 'A Disease of the Transition'!

2 Foreign Trade in Marx's Work

Right from the outset, foreign trade plays a decisive part in Marx's reasoning. The existence of a world market is for him the very condition for the development of a 'social value', i.e. of an abstract market value, dissociated from local and regional peculiarities:

> But it is only foreign trade, the development of the market to a world market, which causes money to develop into world money and *abstract labour* into social labour. Abstract wealth, value, money, hence *abstract labour*, develop in the measure that concrete labour becomes a totality of different modes of labour embracing the world market. Capitalist production rests on the *value* or the transformation of the labour embodied in the product into social labour. But this is [possible] only on the basis of foreign trade and of the world market. This is at once the precondition and the result of capitalist production.
>
> (*Theories*, III, ch. 21, p. 253.)

In view of this, it may appear surprising for Marx to argue that foreign trade does not itself create any 'value', but he has inherited this view from Ricardo. Marx applies Ricardo's view to commerce in general: 'whatever is true of foreign trade, is also true of home trade' (*Capital*, III, ch. 20, p. 325).

Here we touch upon one of the weak spots not only of Marx's work, but of classical economics in general, upon which Marx's system is based. We have already dealt with this problem in volume I of this work, in discussing 'productivity'. Marx himself expressly refused to identify productivity with the production of physically tangible objects. Basically, Marx adopts a notion of productivity linked to the existence of capitalism: any work is 'productive' which creates surplus value in the capitalist sense, no matter whether the product takes the form of physically tangible goods or that of immaterial values – for instance, a singer's song. (See Vol. I, ch. 18.)

It is true that Marx thinks that trade's function consists exclusively of promoting the exchange of commodities (*Capital*, III, ch. 20, p. 325). He does not recognise the generally accepted modern view that trade is the final stage in the provision of goods to the customer and therefore necessary – since the producer would have to carry out this function if it

8

were not executed by somebody else – and that it thus ought to be recognised as part of the production process itself. As soon as it becomes necessary for a fraction of the social labour to be reserved for this purpose, this fraction is contributing to the production of total value. If Marx seemed to imply that trade is unproductive, this is largely to be explained by his identifying the pure, commercial function with the (international) middlemen's activities since the late Middle Ages:

> as among the Venetians, Genoese, Dutch, etc., where the principal gains were not thus made by exporting domestic products, but by promoting the exchange of products of commercially and otherwise economically undeveloped societies, and by exploiting both producing countries. . . . [But] this monopoly of the carrying trade disintegrates, and with it this trade itself, proportionately to the economic development of the peoples, whom it exploits at both ends of its course, and whose lack of development was the basis of its existence. . . . [Parallel runs] the decline . . . of the predominance of the purely trading nations . . . [which ends in] the subordination of merchants to industrial capital. (Ibid., pp. 329–30, 328.)

Trade creates the 'production for the home and world-market. . . . The industrial capitalist always has the world-market before him, compares, and must constantly compare, his own cost-prices with the market-prices at home, and throughout the world' (ibid., p. 336).

Marx (and Engels) had already, in the *Communist Manifesto*, sung a dithyramb on the opening-up of the world market by the bourgeoisie – a process that reached beyond the economic sphere into the realm of politics and civilisation. They imagined, it seems, a more or less uniform extension of the capitalist system to the entire world, and did not yet envisage a division of the world into a group of exploited, poor countries (the 'third world') and a group of exploiting, rich countries, using classical 'imperialist' methods, 'neo-imperialism' or simple economic domination.

On the other hand, the author of *Capital* did deal directly, especially in chapter 24 and part of chapter 25 of volume 1, with the relationship between rich and poor countries. In chapter 25 he deals in particular with conditions in the recently developed countries of America and Australia.

At any rate, Marx assumed that, following the establishment of the colonial system, the gap between the standard of living of Indians and that of Europeans increased, through both an increase of the European standard and a reduction of the Indian one. For him, it was not the demographic factor which was decisive, but the annihilation of Indian home industry in a market reserved for British goods. Already, in his chapter on 'primitive accumulation', he had analysed the connexion between public credit, government debt, tax system, protectionism and so on by examining the examples of the British and Dutch East India companies and Luther's 'monopoly societies', which had been 'powerful levers for concentration of capital. . . . They also forcibly rooted out, in their dependent countries, all industry . . .' (ibid., I, ch. 31, p. 708). He is talking about the destruction of Indian domestic industry and the fact that every year one-fifth of British imports from India represented direct and indirect tribute from India to Britain (ibid., III, ch. 35, p. 630).

The idea of exploitation through commercial machinations is, however, fundamentally alien to Marx, who sees the essence of exploitation in the sphere of production. Indeed, he states that surplus value arises not in the sphere of distribution but in that of production – although it must ultimately be 'realised', i.e. sold or 'transformed into money', in the distribution sphere.

Marx is interested in foreign trade especially in the context of his development of the 'law of the tendency of the rate of profit to fall'. According to him, the first outcome of foreign trade is a cheapening of food for workers, which in turn means a lowering of 'variable capital', v (i.e. wage costs), provided that the 'sociological subsistence level' and therefore the level of real wages are not increased at the same time, perhaps because workers defend their money wages. If such a cheapening of wage goods occurs, the rate of surplus value (s) can be increased, provided the share of value added in total product remains the same. This would then counteract a possible fall in the rate of profit. An improvement in the rate of profit may also occur if imports reduce the cost of raw materials, so leading to a cheapening of 'constant capital', c.

So far we have dealt only with an increase in the rate of profit at home, on the assumption that food and raw materials become cheaper than before. In this case, therefore, the argument always concerns the situation of an industrial country that imports both. From the point of view of developing or less-industrialised countries, one may also add the possibility that cheaper investment goods are imported, which would again cheapen the 'constant capital' and thus improve the rate of profit. (see ibid., ch. 14, pp. 265 ff.)

According to the Ricardian 'law of comparative costs', productivity can in general be raised through foreign trade. This may also lead to a rise in the rate of surplus value, provided that it is not inhibited by an increase in real wages. Marx mentions the Ricardian law only *en passant*; he talks of 'the variety of use-values and the volume of commodities' or of 'Ricardo's theory' according to which 'three days of labour of one country can be exchanged against one of another country' (a point *not* noted by Say). (*Theories*, III, ch. 24, German ed. Dietz, p. 439.)

This remark by Marx has given rise to an entirely new neo-Marxist doctrine, that of 'unequal exchange', which we discuss in the next chapter. Marx, however, had already warned that the difference between 'labour days of different countries' is 'similar to that existing between skilled, complex labour and unskilled, simple labour within a country'. It is no longer quite clear what Marx's ground is for assuming that 'the richer country exploits the poorer one, even where the latter gains by the exchange' (ibid., p. 105). The mere criterion of unweighted labour time cannot in this case suffice.

It is true that one cannot speak of a fully developed Marxian theory of foreign trade. Marx most nearly approaches such a theory within the framework of the 'reproduction schemes' of volume II of *Capital*, where he states (ch. 20, p. 470) that 'foreign commodities must be imported to realise the money-surplus in I. . . . conversely, commodities II (articles of consumption) will have to be exported to realise the depreciation part of II_c in means of production'. In this context foreign trade does no more than facilitate the absorption of surplus income generated in the country or the sale of surplus consumption goods. One can scarcely see in this an anticipation of the foreign-trade multiplier of Keynesian theory.

It is true that Marx repeats his statement that capitalist production could not possibly exist without foreign trade; but he does not see in foreign trade an essentially new element within the framework of 'normal annual reproduction', for 'one also assumes that foreign commerce only replaces home products by articles of other use or bodily form, without affecting value-relations'. From this he concludes that 'the involvement of foreign commerce in analysing the annually reproduced value of products can therefore only confuse without contributing any new element'. He therefore assumes no case of 'gold mines in a country with capitalist production'. (ibid., p. 474.) With this assumption he avoids analytical complications.

So much for 'simple reproduction'. In treating of 'extended reproduction' Marx does not again refer to the problems of foreign trade, which remain, therefore, somewhat apart from his dynamic reasoning. One of his rare references to the subject, and one that may be interpreted as containing in outline the theories of Rosa Luxemburg on the necessity of international or 'third person' sales outlets, occurs in the following statement: 'During its first stages of development, industrial capital seeks to secure a market and markets by force, by the *colonial system* (together with the prohibition system)' (*Theories*, III, Addenda, p. 470). One could easily conclude from this formulation that 'prohibitive' protectionism would prevail only in the early stages of capitalism.

In his discussion of the rate of profit in foreign trade, Marx returns to the subject of the Ricardian law of comparative costs. He says (ibid., III, ch. 14, p. 238) that a country 'may offer more materialised labour *in kind* than it receives, and yet thereby receive commodities cheaper than it could produce them'.

In this context he takes up another idea, which was later to inspire the theory of 'unequal exchange': 'Capital invested in foreign trade can yield a higher rate of profit, because . . . there is competition with commodities produced in other countries with inferior production facilities' (ibid.).

Here he looks at the country with greater productivity and a lower level of costs in the same way as at an oligopolistic entrepreneur who enjoys a cost advantage: he can easily undercut other firms, thus depriving them of a part of their markets, and yet still earn higher profits than they can, so long as competition does not bring his prices down to the level of costs. Marx's argument with regard to international trade is analogous: the country that has the lower cost level conquers the markets of competing countries and earns extra profit into the bargain.

It is quite a different question what the more productive country will gain in real terms from the exchange.

> In so far as the labour of the more advanced country is here realised as labour of a higher specific weight, the rate of profit rises, because labour which has not been paid as being of a higher quality is sold as such. The same may obtain in relation to the country to which commodities are exported and to that from which commodities are imported; namely, the latter may offer more materialised labour *in kind* than it receives, and yet thereby receive commodities cheaper than it could produce them. (Ibid.)

In the first case, the country that enjoys the more favourable cost level conquers markets and simultaneously obtains a higher rate of profit. By reinvesting its profits, it is able to improve its technical equipment still more, so as to obtain a still greater superiority on the world market. The second case actually concerns the same phenomenon, but in a different garb: after all, 'qualitatively higher labour' means nothing else but that workers are better equipped. The latter situation boils down to a more favourable cost situation. It remains a moot point whether the export industries of a country that is thus favoured might not be able to pay higher wages as well. Marx, however, assumes that in this case the 'general rate of profit' in the exporting country would have to increase. But, on the other hand, he also says that 'capitals invested in colonies . . . may yield higher rates of profit for the simple reason that the rate of profit is higher there due to backward development, and likewise the exploitation of labour, because of the use of slaves, coolies, etc.'

This argument contradicts the preceding one. If the rate of profit in the 'more progressive country' is higher, because of greater 'production facilities' (in other words, higher productivity because of better technical equipment and a higher level of training), it is not quite logical to conclude that it ought also to be higher in colonial countries where such productivity conditions do not exist at all. It seems that Marx here fell an easy prey to a confusion which is still rampant today, in that he confounds low wages with high profits. He does not seem to be fully aware of the fact that higher productivity in more progressive countries allows for lower costs in spite of higher hourly wages. Such a slip is all the more astonishing as Marx, in discussing in the same volume the differences in profit rates between countries, actually assumes a higher degree of mechanisation for Europe.

Incidentally, in comparing profit rates in this way, Marx seems to assume that the rate of profit in an Asiatic country which has a lower 'organic composition of capital' may well be higher. This follows from the assumption that the high degree of mechanisation in the more progressive country does not increase the rate of surplus value to a multiple of 'variable capital'. He did, however, make this assumption in the context of his theory of the tendency of the rate of profit to fall. Furthermore, Marx assumes the price of the product to be higher in the Asiatic country than in the European one. His example runs as follows.

The rate of surplus value (s) is 100 per cent in the European country and 25 per cent in the Asiatic one; at first sight, this looks plausible.

Let $84_c + 16_v$ be the composition of the national capital in the European country, and $16_c + 84_v$ in the Asian country, where little machinery, etc., is used, and where a given quantity of labour-power consumes relatively little raw material productively in a given time. Then we have the following calculation:

In the European country the value of the product $= 84_c + 16_v + 16_s = 116$; rate of profit $= 16/100 = 16\%$.

In the Asian country the value of the product $= 16_c + 84_v + 21_s = 121$; rate of profit $= 21/100 = 21\%$. (Ibid., ch. 8, p. 150.)

Essentially, Marx assumes in this context that competition has already run its course in the European country, and that the 'surplus profits' which might be realised there have been competed away. Again, it seems that reasoning in value terms misled him. Indeed, if higher productivity in the European country means that, for example, twice as much product, expressed in 'use values', is produced for the same product value, i.e. labour input, as in the Asian country, this double quantity could be sold at a total price of 232 and the sum of the profits realised by the European country would be not 16 but 132, i.e. $132/100 = 132$ per cent, or six and a half times the rate of profit in the Asian country!

Marx, in his discussion of merchant capital, sees the essential reason for international exchange as lying in the 'differences in production prices of various countries', which are exploited by merchant capital, which at the same time works to eliminate such differences. It must be admitted that Marx discusses this point in the context of

'undeveloped societies', in which merchant's capital appropriates an overwhelming portion of the surplus-product partly as a mediator between communities which still substantially produce for use-value . . . partly, because under those earlier modes of production the

principal owners of the surplus-product . . . the slave-owner, the feudal
lord, and the state (for instance, the oriental despot) represent the
consuming wealth and luxury which the merchant seeks to
trap. . . . Merchant's capital, when it holds a position of dominance,
stands everywhere for a system of robbery . . . directly connected
with plundering, piracy, kidnapping slaves, and colonial
conquest . . . (Ibid., ch. 20, pp. 330–1.)

Marx sees the logical continuation of the merchant mentality in the old
exploiting companies of the colonial period, notably the East India
companies: 'The behaviour of merchant's capital wherever it rules over
production is strikingly illustrated not only by the colonial economy (the
so-called colonial system) in general, but quite specifically by the methods
of the old Dutch East India Company' (ibid., p. 329).

Marx's analysis of the phenomenon of speculation is not quite
satisfactory, although he admits that commerce brings about an equalisation of the prices of production. (It must be emphasised that he does not
reason in 'values' in this context!) At any rate, commodity circulation
tends to bring about an equalisation of rates of profit. This would speak in
favour of Balinky's interpretation. For · Marx, the main interest of
merchant capital appears to lie in increasing the rate of turnover, though it
must be said that the relevant passage (ibid., ch. 18, pp. 313–4) is
somewhat ambiguous:

> From the standpoint of merchant's capital, therefore, it is the turnover
> which appears to determine prices . . . [which leads to] its internal
> connection with the production of surplus-value being entirely
> obliterated . . . [so] that profit made on the turnover of a given
> commodity-capital is in inverse proportion to the number of times the
> money-capital turns over this commodity-capital. . . . Small profits
> and quick returns. . . .

It is little wonder that, in view of the unsatisfactory condition of Marx's
theory of foreign exchange, there have been several attempts to reconstruct
it. These attempts have been made in three different directions.

First there is the approach suggested by some remarks in volume II of
Capital, where Marx points out that foreign trade can have an equalising
effect, *via* exports and imports, in realising domestic production or in
absorbing an excess of domestic income. This approach ends up as a theory
of growth which considers foreign trade as an equilibrating mechanism
which helps to prevent sales difficulties that might otherwise threaten
capitalism. This is the starting point for Rosa Luxemburg's theory of
capitalist development.

Secondly, these considerations quite naturally lead to a theory of
conquest and protection and to the idea that capitalism was forced to take

over the sources of raw materials in dependencies. This goes beyond Rosa Luxemburg's analysis and leads to Lenin's theory of imperialism.

Thirdly, a few, widely scattered comments of Marx on the exploitation of dependencies provided a starting point for Emmanuel's modern theory of 'unequal exchange'.

The first two theories mentioned above cannot really be considered Marxian in origin, since Marx sharply rejected an under-consumption theory and viewed military conquest as important only in the early days of a capitalist system. The third theory, however, is conceived in the true spirit of Marxian economic analysis and draws our attention to value relationships. It assumes a certain degree of exploitation, similar to that encountered in the sale of individual labour power, and it also assumes strict observance of the rules of the capitalist game.

As the theories of imperialism strictly speaking go beyond Marx's work, they are not discussed in the present publication (though a chapter dealing with these theories was contained in the German edition of 1974).

3 The Modern Theory of International Exploitation

Owing to the diminution in the degree of world domination by the old European colonial powers, the neo-Marxist theory of imperialism has lost some of its plausibility. A newer thesis, which emphasises the indirect economic exploitation of the rest of the world by the industrial nations, is gaining more and more ground. This is the theory of 'unequal exchange', which has won popularity especially in Latin countries. It derives from two sources: the Ricardian 'law of comparative costs', and Condillac's objectivist philosophy, according to which there can be no exchange of equal values. This dichotomy has been expressly recognised by Emmanuel, the leading protagonist of the new theory, who considers himself (1969, pp. 23 and 290) a direct heir to Marx.

For him, the epoch of direct imperialism is over: 'From the moment that the big powers felt certain that the doors were wide open for their business, they saw no virtue in incurring the cost of direct administration' (ibid., p. 216).

In addition, he stresses (ibid., p. 288) that one begins 'intuitively to realise that, in a world which as a whole is poor, the enrichment of a minority would have been impossible without the impoverishment of the broad mass of the rest of the world'. He refers to Singer's finding that average incomes in the 'third world' were higher around 1900 than they are today. In view of demographic factors, this is not altogether improbable.

Here we touch upon a whole range of problems, which extend from 'neo-Malthusianism' to statistical questions of international income levels and income distribution. Among the authors who have addressed themselves to these problems are Kuznets and Sukhatme. They have pointed out the difficulties and uncertainties of comparisons of income levels, which do not always take account of consumption in kind, climatic and cultural elements, collective consumption, and so on.

The theory of 'unequal exchange' was first developed by Emmanuel in a paper presented at the Sorbonne on 8 December 1962. It concentrates on the problems of international exchange and places particular stress on indirect exploitation under the guise of 'unequal exchange', as opposed to direct exploitation based on imperialist power.

The transition towards this new theory of international exploitation is furnished by Perroux's thesis of the 'domination effect'. A 'dominant nation' or 'dominant economy' is defined as

> a large nation which . . . is able to exercise asymmetrical and irreversible actions against key nations of the world, and this holds with regard to developed economic systems as well as developing nations. Instruments of this superiority are industries which enjoy certain advantages, which lead to monopoly positions, to monopolistic freight and information policies, and to a unique position in the world . . . .
>
> (Perroux, 1969, pp. 25–6.)

Emmanuel is influenced by Perroux only in part. In the first place, he follows in the footsteps of the Ricardian theory of comparative costs and asks the reasons for the differences in productivity of the various countries participating in international exchange. He makes the point that the conditions which give rise to a higher level of productivity in industrial countries could be transferred to an underdeveloped country without transferring the 'sociological minimum' wage which prevails in the richer country: 'It is the ability of underdeveloped people [*sic!*] to use the instruments of our time while being far from voicing the demands of our times which in the last resort is the origin of the super profit resulting from the unequal exchange' (Emmanuel, 1963).

Ultimately, this analysis boils down to a determination of the unequal rates of surplus value in countries participating in the exchange. In richer countries, the sum of variable capital, or wages, has increased in real terms as the minimum standards of living have increased. This may explain the constancy of the rate of surplus value in spite of an increasing degree of monopoly. On the other hand, the underdeveloped countries would in theory offer the possibility of a higher rate of surplus value so long as the wage claims of the workers are kept low.

Emmanuel's argument thus becomes nothing more than a new version of the old thesis of higher profitability from investment abroad or even from 'wage dumping', for one can imagine, instead of increased rates of surplus value from foreign investment, under-cutting in domestic markets through the sale of goods produced in underdeveloped countries. Against the thesis of 'wage dumping' it has always been maintained by economists that the lower productivity in underdeveloped countries would not permit such under-cutting. It is, however, the heart of Emmanuel's reasoning that, in principle, productivity would be the same in underdeveloped as in developed countries, at least in certain sectors. Here Emmanuel adopts a view held by de la Charrière (1964, p. 131): 'At best, it may be a coincidence of quasi-Western productivity with wages that still remain at an exotic level!'.

A DOUBTFUL APPEAL TO MARX

Before delving in detail into these problems, which touch upon some basic questions of international exchange, we must examine how Marx dealt with them, for Emmanuel believes that he is able to provide a new foundation for Marxian theses.

It is true that Marx, in volume III of *Capital*, assumes that foreign trade may offer a higher rate of profit or a 'surplus profit'. In one passage, he justifies this assumption by reference to the 'exploitation of slaves and coolies', which leads to a 'higher degree of exploitation of labour' – i.e. apparently a higher rate of surplus value than in developed countries.

Palloix has tried further to refine Emmanuel's thesis. He points (1969, p. 65) to another passage where Marx talks about an increase in the rate of surplus value: 'Since foreign trade partly cheapens the elements of constant capital, and partly the necessities of life for which the variable capital is exchanged, it tends to raise the rate of profit by increasing the rate of surplus-value and lowering the value of constant capital' (*Capital*, III, ch. 14, p. 237).

Here the rate of surplus value to which Marx refers is not specifically that from foreign trade, but, in the general economic system of the industrially developed country, it increases because of the cheapening of the means of subsistence for workers, which in turn leads to lower or at least relatively low money wages. This, according to Marx, must entail the further consequence that the share of surplus value in value added will increase.

It is a moot point whether the rate of profit in foreign trade will be increased, and Marx thought 'its special nature . . . beyond the scope of our analysis' (ibid., p. 238). Nevertheless, he later (ibid., p. 237) proffered the suggestion, which was taken up by Bettelheim, that a higher rate of profit could result from 'the more advanced country [selling] its goods above their value even though cheaper than the competing countries'. In other words, within the framework of a kind of oligopolistic competition between nations, the more industrialised country enjoys a cost advantage; it keeps slightly under-cutting other oligopolists on the world market, but it nevertheless earns an additional 'extra profit'. The 'terms of trade' work in its favour, for it 'realises the specifically higher productiveness of the labour [it] employs as surplus-labour' (ibid., p. 238).

In the same context Marx mentions (ibid.) the idea that 'the labour of the more advanced country is here realised as labour of a higher specific weight'.

THE GIST OF THE THEORY OF 'UNEQUAL EXCHANGE'

This idea clearly contradicts the simplified formulation of 'the theory of international exploitation' as developed by Palloix, for he says (1969, p. 76).

> Let us hazard an extrapolation of Marx's ideas on this subject by showing that the exchange of equivalent amounts in circulation is apt to camouflage an inherent inequality: one day of formal labour is not exchanged for a labour day, but the exchange value of labour in one system is exchanged for the exchange value of labour in another system; these exchange values are at the root of inequalities. . . . If . . . in the capitalist system . . . the labour necessary for the worker's subsistence amounts to four hours . . . and surplus labour also to four hours . . . , exchange conditions under the capitalist system require that the exchange value of the product of one day of labour correspond to eight hours, or to the subsistence cost of maintaining two workers (four hours plus four hours). When, now, a traditional system (in a developing country) is opened up to foreign trade . . . , it must take over the capitalist product of one working day at an exchange rate which is equivalent to the subsistence cost of two workers in the capitalist system. But considering that this traditional system is less productive, it can furnish the equivalent only with sixteen hours' work, which represents the subsistence cost of two workers in the traditional system. . . . There is indeed an equivalence of labour exchange values, but this equivalence is simply apparent and covers deep inequality.

This reasoning appears to be basically wrong. The same arguments could as well be applied to relationships within a single capitalist system where one industry is less productive than another. According to Marx, it is not labour time as such that is decisive, but *socially necessary* labour time. With regard to the exchange operations referred to by Palloix, we may quote Marx's statement that 'The favoured country recovers more labour in exchange for less labour, although this difference, this excess is pocketed, as in any exchange between labour and capital, by a certain class' (*Capital*, III, ch. 14, p. 238).

Looked at from the vantage point of world economics, the longer labour time required for the production of a particular commodity in under-developed countries does not represent a higher value than the shorter labour time required for the production of the same commodity in developed countries, for, 'although the man works for himself for 12 hours, he hardly produces as much as a worker under more favourable conditions of production does in 8 hours. This is the same relationship as that of the hand-loom weaver who competes with the power-loom' (*Theories*, II, ch. 8, p. 38).

With regard to this example, Marx expressly states (ibid., I, Addenda, p. 394) that twelve hours labour of a hand-loom weaver is no longer represented in a value of twelve hours . . . if the weaving of a yard with the power-loom requires only half the labour-time required with the hand-loom . . . but in one of six [hours], since the *necessary* labour-time has now become six hours. The hand-loom weaver's twelve hours now [represent] only six hours of social labour-time, although he still works twelve hours as he did before.

The measuring rod for the 'correct' level of productivity is the labour time which is 'necessary' from the international standpoint.

One might object that this is not a matter of comparing more and less rationalised methods of production for one particular commodity, but one of the exchange of two different commodities. In this context, however, we must refer to the fundamental considerations underlying the Ricardian law of comparative costs. Both the more and the less developed countries reap an advantage from a situation where each saves labour. This is even true when one of the countries is more productive in absolute terms in all industries!

Theoretically, it would be perfectly possible for the developed country itself to produce the commodity in which the underdeveloped country specialises. If we take up Ricardo's example of wine and cloth, the developed country renounces the cultivation of wine, because in its own case it requires eight hours' labour to produce one unit of cloth but twelve to produce one unit of wine. It is true that the underdeveloped country would have to expend sixteen hours of labour for one unit of wine, but it sells that for a unit of cloth, which costs the other country eight hours and which would have cost the underdeveloped country twenty hours.

In this context it does not appear justifiable to talk of 'exploitation'. According to the law of comparative costs, which has remained basically valid in spite of all objections and modifications, the exchange operation is advantageous to both sides, since in its absence both countries would have been obliged to use their labour in relatively less productive activities.

Emmanuel's reasoning is subtler than that of Palloix. He starts from the Ricardian law of comparative costs and states that it is predicated upon the immobility of factors of production as between countries. If capital moves freely, but not labour, profit rates will be equalised at the international level, but wages will not be. According to Emmanuel, this is the case that seems best to reflect the reality of the relationship, at least between continents.

For Emmanuel, the 'unequal exchange' is to be explained by the fact that, although the share of value added in the total price is the same for both of the commodities exchanged, in the richer country the largest part of value added represents wages, while in the poorer one it represents surplus value. In international exchange, an 'equalisation' of profit rates takes place. Neither the richer nor the poorer country obtains the volume of surplus value which would have been due to it had there been no exchange, but both obtain the same rate of profit, calculated on 'capital employed', or constant plus variable costs. This leads to a much higher production price for the richer country's commodity, for this price includes not only the higher sum for wages but also the total profit the poorer country receives. This means that the poorer country must renounce part of its surplus value, which then accrues to the richer country. (Emmanuel, 1969, pp. 108–10).

> Unequal exchange consists in the relation between the equilibrium prices, which result from the equalisation of profits between regions where 'institutionally' differentiated rates of surplus value prevail; and these 'institutional differences' mean that, for one reason or another, these rates escape the competitive equalisation process in the market for factors of production and are independent of relative prices.
>
> (Ibid., p. 111.)

Basically, this yields a theory according to which underdeveloped countries have to give up part of their surplus values.

In Emmanuel's example we find (ibid., p. 110) the figures presented in Table I, which are drawn from volume III of *Capital*, where they occur in the context of the transformation problem. With regard to these figures a number of fundamental objections can be raised.

TABLE I

	(1) Capital stock	(2) Constant capital	(3) Variable capital	(4) Surplus value	(5) Sum of values	(6) Production costs	(7) Rate of profit (8/1)	(8) Profit	(9) Price of production
Country A	240	50	100	20	170	150		60	210
Country B	240	50	20	100	170	70	25%	60	130

First, it is not clear how the capital stock (1) has been calculated, and this is crucial for the calculation of the sum of profits (8). In addition, it is not possible to calculate speed of turnover from the figures for production costs (6) and capital stock (1).

Secondly, there is no explanation of why the cost per unit of production should be so much lower in underdeveloped countries.

Thirdly, the thesis that the rate of surplus value is much higher in underdeveloped countries than in developed ones contradicts the Marxian argument as well as any rational analysis. Indeed, as we saw in the previous chapter, Marx indicates (*Capital*, III, ch. 8, p. 50) a rate of surplus value of 100 per cent for a European country and 25 per cent for an Asian one.

Emmanuel might have argued that he postulated the equalisation of the rates of profit at the international level. He thus assumes a much higher rate of surplus value for the underdeveloped country, and this contradicts not only Marx's statements on an equalisation at the international level, but also historical logic. A high rate of surplus value means that the country in question has reached a relatively high level of productivity, so that each worker can earn his living by working relatively few hours and still produce a large surplus for the ruling classes – an unlikely state of affairs under quasi-feudal conditions! The theory can be applied only to individual businesses and never to entire underdeveloped countries.

The theory of unequal exchange is in its present form somewhat unsatisfactory. In particular, it omits a thorough analysis of the modern theory of international exchange. It is not even adequate from the point of view of classical Marxism, which after all dealt with foreign trade only very cursorily. Even so, in volume I of *Capital* (ch. 17, p. 492) Marx had already examined the problem of the impact of differing labour-intensities on foreign trade: 'But still, even then, the intensity of labour would be different in different countries, and would modify the international application of the law of value. The more intense working-day of one nation would be represented by a greater sum of money than would the less intense day of another nation.'

Not only the superior equipment, but also the degree of intensity of labour plays its part. In fact in many underdeveloped countries the whole social climate is against maximum productivity. These and other factors lead to a higher level of productivity in developed countries, even if identical equipment and production methods are exported to the under-developed countries. For this reason workers in underdeveloped countries are not up to the average standard of productivity of workers in developed countries, because their general and specific development is not the same and their working rhythm is far from being the same. There are facts to which Varga points when he says (quoted in Emmanuel, 1969, p. 289), in what is tantamount to a rejection of Emmanuel's theory, 'In the same way as in the dictatorship [of the proletariat] the individual worker's share is measured not by his needs but by the results of his work, one must in the international exchange of goods take into account the higher product of labour.'

It therefore seems difficult to deny the inherent advantages that developed countries enjoy under this 'unequal exchange'. It is true that the exchange is unequal as measured by the working hours spent in the production of the goods involved, but these working hours do not constitute a measure of the inequality of economic performance, which is inversely related to working time.

The supporters of the theory of unequal exchange attempt to establish a contradiction between the theories of Marx and Ricardo. For instance, Palloix comments (1969, p. 83) on the theory of comparative costs, 'For

Marx, comparative advantage essentially consists in the difference in level of economic development, which reflects the productivity of workers. . . .' This is undoubtedly true, in so far as Marx delved more deeply into these problems than did Ricardo, who touched only rather superficially upon these productivity differences and did not investigate the underlying reasons for them.

But neither do the advocates of 'unequal exchange' go deeply enough into these problems, because they neglect, for instance, the complex of 'human investment' in education and training which conveys to the workers of developed countries their superiority and capacity to work with a higher intensity.

Palloix tries to justify his thesis of inequality (what is meant is rather injustice) of exchange by quoting (ibid., p. 79) passages from the Grundrisse, where Marx says that a trading nation acquires wealth by importing more labour time than it exports. He sees in these passages a recognition of the exploitative character of such transactions:

> The most developed nations have an instrument of privilege at their disposal: the law of comparative costs. . . . One of the basic contributions of Karl Marx lies in the fact that he stressed that international exchange found its formal motivation in the law of comparative costs, the gist of which is that both partners gain from the point of view of increased consumption at the level of use values, while the less developed country is exploited at the level of exchange values. . . . International investment, which is seeking out higher profit rates, is working in the same sense. . . . [The law] shows on the one hand the inequality of exchange and on the other the inequality of development . . . and guarantees at the same time the profitable realisation of the capital of developed economic systems . . . .   (Ibid., pp. 81–3.)

AN UNEQUAL COMPARISON

The law of comparative costs hides a great number of problems, which concern not only general differences in the productivity levels of various countries, but also specific cost advantages created by the exchange operation itself. These advantages arise wherever the optimum size of plant and enterprise cannot be attained so long as production remains limited to the internal market, but instead require operation on the world market. This was seen by Marx when he said that foreign exchange allows for an increase in the internal rate of profit by facilitating 'production on a large scale' – i.e. with increasing returns owing to the increasing size of plant.

There arises the question of whether these increasing returns accrue only to the producers, i.e. in this case to the exporting countries, or also to the consumers, i.e. to the importing countries. The same question would have to be answered in examining exchange between two socialist countries. In practice, the answer depends on the degree of monopoly that the exporting countries have in the commodities that they export.

In this context, it must be mentioned that it was just this aspect of increasing returns and mass production that furnished the starting point for Rosa Luxemburg's analysis (1913). She raised the question of sales potential in the home market. In the last resort this can be judged only by examining the relevant demand elasticities or the degree to which the market for the products concerned has become 'saturated'.

It is true that Rosa Luxemburg was interested not in individual products but in macroeconomic aspects or in total production. She saw in exportation the possibility of 'realising' surplus goods, which would otherwise be without a market. Under this reasoning, trends towards under-consumption can only be avoided in capitalism if 'third persons' in non-capitalist sectors or countries can offer enough purchasing power to warrant the opening of sufficient sales outlets. From this point of view, 'unequal exchange' would actually constitute a disadvantage for industrial exporting countries, which are the more easily spared sales crises the lower their prices are and the more they can sell.

In a way, the Luxemburg thesis represents a revival of the Malthusian theory, which Marx condemned out of hand. Malthus had thought that a lack of effective demand could be made good by 'unproductive consumers'. In this form, the Luxemburg thesis has been rejected by many Marxists, including Bukharin (1926) and Sweezy (1942), in that it flatly contradicts the fundamental principles of Marxian reproduction schemes.

Preiser has pointed out (1950; 1965, p. 286) that there is a grain of truth in Rosa Luxemburg's theory, for surpluses on foreign trade induce multiplier effects and serve as an engine of growth, in the Keynesian sense. To this extent, one could almost talk of a reversal of the conditions of the theory of unequal exchange; for if, according to this theory, developed countries take more away from poor countries than they give them, this must lead to (real) import surpluses, which could have a paralysing effect on developed countries. In the long run this could lead to a narrowing of the gap between the two groups of countries.

The theory of unequal exchange does not take into account such side effects on employment and growth. It concentrates on the 'exploitation effect', under which, though one labour hour ought to equal another, the labour hour of the developed countries represents a higher value on the world market than that of the less developed countries. The fact is, however, that such a situation would still prevail between rich and poor countries even if capitalism were to disappear.

Marx repeatedly refers to the general problem of the relationship between richer and poorer countries. For instance, in the *Theories of Surplus Value* he points out (III, p. 106), referring to John Stuart Mill, that it is quite possible that 'the richer country exploits the poorer one, even where the latter gains by the exchange'. He admits again and again that, in terms of Ricardian comparative costs, the poorer country gains too.

We must not forget that Marx never considered one working hour to be the same as another, but always assumed that market conditions would allow for comparability between skilled labour and less skilled labour. Skilled labour used to produce export products in developed countries would always have to be expressed as a multiple of less skilled labour in underdeveloped countries. Again and again Marx emphasises, the importance of the degree of skill, or level of qualification. Otherwise 'exploitation' could be said to appear not only in foreign trade, but also, though differing levels of skill, in exchange transactions within one and the same country. The exploitation of workers by capitalists would then lose some of its importance, in view of the exploitation of less by more highly skilled workers – a strange situation indeed for Marxists who give priority to the class struggle!

Marx actually forestalls such a misinterpretation by saying (*Capital*, III, ch. 14, p. 238) that 'the labour of the more advanced country is . . . realised as labour of a higher specific weight'. He did not, therefore, see anything wrong in the 'unequal exchange' of more working hours of less skilled labour for fewer working hours of skilled labour, because the yardstick of labour time does not indicate the relative values of the two kinds of labour, and because the allegedly wronged party actually draws a very real advantage from the exchange operation.

Marx compares the relationship between a developed and a less developed country to the situation that exists where 'a manufacturer who employs a new invention before it becomes generally used undersells his competitors and yet sells his commodity above its individual value' (ibid.). This means in practice that the notion of a 'temporary monopoly', which Marx applies in his analysis of technical progress, is extended into the sphere of foreign trade.

In the same way as entrepreneurs whose firms work with an inferior level of technology have to lower their prices 'below the individual value of their commodities' (i.e. to a lower level than would correspond to their more extensive use of labour), countries with backward technology and labour organisation simply do not succeed in obtaining full remuneration for their high labour values. They are thus, as it were, 'exploited' by foreign entrepreneurs whose firms enjoy a higher standard of technology, and 'temporary' (but in practice permanent) monopolistic cost advantages.

Marx uses exactly this notion of monopoly in his speech *Free Trade* (1847, published New York, 1921, List of Marx's Works, No. 15). He points out (p. 42) that some branches of industry are superior to others and guarantee domination of the world market to the nations that develop them.

The proponents of the theory of unequal exchange ought to have discussed the problem of the underlying reasons for differences in the level of development of different nations, regions and industries, as reflected in world market relationships. It is true that some economists who write on development economics have tried to tackle the problem, but it is only comparatively recently that Marxists – for instance, Gunder Frank (1967) and Stuart Holland (1978) – have begun to do so.

Frank argues that profits made in underdeveloped areas are not reinvested there; this implies two consequences. First, the transfer of profits means that in practice the poor countries finance the rich ones. Secondly, in poor countries a process of 'development of underdevelopment' takes place, which is to say that a backward economic and social structure is fostered and maintained. In this case, international aid serves only to guarantee private profit transfers at the expense of public funds.

MARXIST CRITICISM OF THE THEORY OF UNEQUAL EXCHANGE

Emmanuel's theory has met with considerable criticism in Marxist circles. To begin with, his teacher, Bettelheim, has attacked his theses in a postscript to Emmanuel's book. Bettelheim thinks that it is against Marxist tradition to derive exploitation from exchange instead of from the sphere of production. It should be remembered, however, that even Marx spoke of exploitation through trade, as practised by the Genoese, the Venetians and the Portuguese, though he speaks of it as a 'racket' superimposed upon the fundamental exploitation occurring in the production sphere.

Bettelheim supports his criticism by referring to Marx's statements on differences of labour skill. Furthermore, he even points to similarities between the theory of unequal exchange and certain ideas dear to Rosa Luxemburg; and he warns us not to assume that the elimination of such forms of exploitation would be fatal to capitalist countries. After all, they are each other's best customers!

Finally, he argues that it would be easier to explain the misery of the 'third world' by referring directly to the imperialistic attitudes of the large nations. This brings us back to the theory of imperialism, which, owing to certain world events, became fashionable again after the Second World War. (Bettelheim, in Emmanuel, 1969, pp. 297 ff.)

Emmanuel claims that his theory derives from Marx and reminds us that Marx was pessimistic with regard to the future trend of prices of industrial products on the world market. Emmanuel sees this attitude as harking back to Ricardo's fear that the prices of primary products must rise.

It seems doubtful whether Marx really followed Ricardo who took refuge in 'organic chemistry' to prove his theses; and quite a number of passages can be quoted to show that Marx thought that increased industrialisation could raise productivity even in agriculture and in the production of primary materials. However, it would seem that the fundamental point at issue here is the evolution of the 'terms of trade' between the poor and rich countries of the world.

As it happens, the proponents of the theory of unequal exchange would have done better to start at this level. In this context, the dominant hypothesis is that in the long run the 'terms of trade' of the poor countries are progressively deteriorating. This hypothesis is controversial and, strangely enough, Emmanuel opposes it, though it would favour his own ideas. He thinks it over-simplified, because people 'identify only too easily exports from rich countries with exports of industrial products and exports from poor countries with exports of primary products' (ibid., p. 49).

It is indeed not easy to pass a final judgement on this issue. *A priori* there is much to be said for the assumption that concentration tendencies in industrial countries lead to a higher degree of oligopoly in export industries and, therefore, to cartelisation and high prices. On the other hand, concentration is even stronger in certain primary sectors – oil, uranium, natural gas and iron ore are cases in point – and the governments of producer countries operate stabilisation schemes for organic primary materials and food. Even so, many underdeveloped countries can be said to *suffer* from monoculture.

Emmanuel rightly remarks that monoculture is a consequence of the working of the law of comparative costs, which condemns the poor to eternal poverty in exchange for a temporarily improved living standard, which would not have been possible on the strength of their own efforts and without excessive specialisation. Incidentally, many Marxists see in international aid an instrument by which rich countries keep the poor permanently in the position of dependent suppliers of primary materials.

Studies by MacBean and others (see especially MacBean, 1962, p. 73), have given rise to doubt as to whether instability of export prices is really at the root of the backwardness of poor countries. In addition, Leontief's studies show that, contrary to expectation, the labour-intensity of some leading United States export goods is greater than that of some important import goods. These indications suffice to show how complicated matters are in this field.

In Emmanuel's work, two quite different fundamental concepts are in conflict with each other. On the one side, there is the assumption that the rate of surplus value in developed countries tends to decrease, thanks to the pressure of the working class, the 'institutionalised class struggle' of the trade unions, the resulting increase in the 'sociological minimum' standard of living, and the secular shortage of labour as capital becomes relatively abundant. On the other side, there is the hypothesis that underdeveloped countries have succeeded, thanks to the input of capital, in raising the productivity of their labour to the same level as that prevailing in developed countries, while at the same time avoiding a rise in the 'sociological minimum' standard of living, thus holding wages down to about the subsistence level. This hypothesis seems to rest on a fundamental error, for it is not the individual productivity of workers in the progressive industry which matters, but the average productivity of the country which decides the real level of progressive wages.

Another Marxist, Salvati, has demonstrated (1971, pp. 478 ff.) that Emmanuel's theses boil down to the problem of how the wage difference between rich and poor countries is to be explained:

> If one removes all [unnecessary and erroneous] complications from this argument, it boils down to a hunch which has already been developed by Arthur Lewis [1954] and which has been taken up by many others. If one looks at competition between capitalists at the world level and takes as given the tendency towards the equalisation of profits, international commodity prices depend essentially on labour costs, and naturally, also, on the price of raw materials, on the organic composition of capital and on the average rate of profit.
>
> The components of labour costs are wages and the level of productivity. If for any reason money wages remain low, while productivity increases, labour costs will be lowered, and prices will also decrease continually with a constant organic composition of capital and constant rates of profit. This train of events occurs in underdeveloped countries. In developed countries, on the other hand, money wages will remain high and will continue to increase in proportion, or more than in proportion, to productivity. This means that the advantages of increased productivity will be exported from underdeveloped countries to be appropriated by the developed countries through lower prices, and that increased productivity of the commodities exported from developed countries will not find its expression in lower prices . . . .

This argument may be reduced to the statement that the 'terms of trade' have moved against developing countries, a tendency reinforced by the fact that oligopolistic or monopolistic elements also work in favour of the rich countries.

Salvati raises the essential question: why do the two groups of countries differ as regards their level of development and dynamics? One may offer a number of answers. First of all, there are differences in average productivity levels. Secondly, the organisational strength of the working classes varies. Thirdly, the size and strength of the 'industrial reserve army' vary, depending on the speed of rationalisation, the capital available to carry this out, the relative rate of growth of the capital stock and labour resources, and thus also demographic factors. All these are important elements. Some Marxist authors, such as Furtado (1968), have followed Lewis and addressed themselves to these matters.

The contributions of Emmanuel, Palloix and others would appear to provide only a partial clarification, for the entire problem is much more complex than most Marxist authors are prepared to admit.

What is particularly laudable in Emmanuel's approach is that he has fought to free himself from the value scheme and has tried to approach reality by basing his reasoning on prices of production. Bettelheim comments in his theoretical postscript to Emmanuel (1969), that to accept Emmanuel's claim that 'value theory . . . does not apply to the capitalist form of production' would be to contradict the theoretical basis of Marx's work, for Marx derives prices from values. Bettelheim admits that Engels, in the preface to volume III of *Capital*, states that value theory applies merely to pre-capitalist conditions, but he contends that this is not justification enough, and that Emmanuel falls prey to the illusion of reasoning in terms of 'factors of production', thus being beguiled by the 'trinitarian formula'. This would appear to be a grave sin for an orthodox Marxist.

Emmanuel replies to this criticism by saying (1969, p. 344) that he is not relying on Engels, but he indirectly warns us not to swallow too much 'Hegelianism', which Engels too sought to avoid. Emmanuel also warns us (ibid., p. 345) not to confound 'materialised values' and 'socially necessary values', which cannot yet be crystallised, because they are values of the future! This controversy leads us too far astray, but it is significant in showing how modern Marxists are trying to rid themselves of the fetters of value theory.

A STATISTICAL VERIFICATION: CHANGES IN THE TERMS OF TRADE

In support of his argument that the terms of trade have moved against developing countries, Emmanuel (1969, p. 42) quotes various sources:

> Series published by the United Nations show that, between the end of the nineteenth century and the Second World War, the terms of trade of countries producing primary products deteriorated by some 40 per cent . . . .
> The terms of trade of primary products compared to industrial products were 137 (1938 = 100) in 1913 and 147 in 1876–80, while the terms of trade of the United Kingdom were also 137 in 1913, but 163 in 1876–80 (this is the inverse ratio import prices/export prices). (Source: *Relative Prices of Exports and Imports of Underdeveloped Countries* (United Nations) p. 22.) . . .
> These series confirm others, compiled by Schlote, Silverman, Imlah and the Board of Trade. These cover a shorter period, 1880–1913, over which they show a deterioration of some 20 per cent.

Emmanuel then goes on to quote (ibid, pp. 48–9) a number of predictions
by eminent economists which would have led us to expect the opposite.
Ricardo, Marshall, Bukharin, Colin Clark, Moret, and Aubrey are
examples. They all more or less took for granted a relative increase in the
prices of primary products, as neo-Ricardians are still prone to do.

Emmanuel thinks that Marx too may have shared the pessimism of the
Ricardian school, which imagined that the terms of trade would shift
against industrial products and in favour of primary producers.

However, Emmanuel partly contradicts his own theory by stating
(ibid.) that 'the deterioration in the terms of trade of primary products is
an optical illusion . . . the result of an exaggerated identification of
exports from rich countries with manufactured products and of exports
from poor countries with primary products'.

Kindleberger, who conducted perhaps the most detailed study of this
subject, draws much more sophisticated conclusions (1956, pp. 263–6).
From the point of view of underdeveloped countries, the terms of trade
with Europe improved between 1872 and 1913, but then deteriorated
sharply until 1938, and remained at a much higher and much more
unfavourable level than in the nineteenth century till the early 1950s.
(1913, 100; 1872, 112; 1938, 176; 1952, 155.)

In examining the terms of trade between industrial products and raw
materials, Kindleberger reaches quite different conclusions: 'there is no
long-run tendency for the terms of trade to move against primary products
in favour of manufactures'. On the contrary, because the quality of
industrial products certainly has improved over the past eighty years,
'the terms of trade may have turned against manufactures. . . . Since
primary products and underdeveloped countries are generally closely
associated, this situation may be regarded as paradoxical.'

Kindleberger finds three main reasons for this situation. First, the
deterioration in the terms of trade did not occur between the poorer and
richer countries of Europe, but only between the developing countries of
the rest of the world and Europe. Secondly, there has been hardly any
change in the terms of trade for Europe as a whole relative to the 'young
nations' of America and Australia, which in spite of their development
have continued to supply raw materials. Thirdly, it is often very difficult to
obtain a statistical identification between products and world trade
regions.

Kindleberger offers the suggestion that, 'though developed and underdeveloped countries both produce primary products, those produced by
the latter, and particularly the densely populated underdeveloped
countries, are not the products in "dynamic" (income-elastic) demand'.
However, he thinks that the evidence does not allow one to reach this
conclusion. For each primary product, there are different conditions in
different parts of the world: 'Wheat is income-inelastic in developed
countries, income-elastic in densely populated. The obverse is possibly true
of petroleum products.'

On balance, Kindleberger sees the main explanation for a possible differentiated evolution working to the detriment of underdeveloped countries in

> differences in long-run monopoly power. . . . this is the key to the development of the long-run terms of trade between developed and underdeveloped countries and between primary products and manufactures. It is likely that potential competition is . . . smaller, on the average, for developed economies and manufactures than for underdeveloped countries and primary production. . . . attempts at cartels and commodity price interference [are less successful] in affecting price over time. (Ibid., p. 251.)

Recent developments such as the OPEC cartel seem to contradict this interpretation; but it may nevertheless remain valid in the longer run, considering that already the real price of oil and of many other international commodities has again started on a downward course.

We should probably also take account of the fact that European concerns derive considerable intermediary profits from the sale of certain primary products on the world market. In so far as they succeed in obtaining a monopoly in such products, the developed countries, through their multinational companies, and indirectly even through cartels such as OPEC, pocket the bulk of the profits. This is .a further reason for maintaining that regional statistics do not reflect the real situation.

Generally speaking, one may say that the 'unequal exchange' relates to the stronger monopolistic position of developed countries and their multinational companies. It would then be nothing but a by-product of concentration at world-market level. If one considers that a similar situation is developing in the case of American multinationals operating on European markets, one might wish that Marxist authors dealing with these matters had concentrated on examining the reasons for differences in the degree of monopoly.

INTERNATIONAL EXPLOITATION AND THE EXTERNAL PROLETARIAT IN HISTORICAL ANALYSIS

It now becomes clear that the connexion between exploitation and 'imperialist' tendencies is more complex and indirect than used to be the case in the past, or than it appears in the current theories of imperialism. The real importance of imperialist and neo-imperialist tendencies may reside in the fact that they assist in making it possible for monopolistic firms to act freely on the world market; i.e. they help keep open a safe 'hunting ground' for them.

The struggle of the big powers to safeguard the political and ideological bases of their satellite regimes therefore, is in the case of the capitalist powers, to be explained by a desire to keep the doors open to big business in the widest sense, and less by a tendency to exploit such countries directly, as in colonialist days. Once access is guaranteed, big business penetrates these countries with impunity, in the wake of what is called 'market forces'.

The colonial empires of the past were partly inspired by the vested interests of the middle classes in metropolitan areas, which found in the colonies employment and business opportunities. Nowadays, it is only big business which matters. It calls for state intervention only when there are upheavals in countries in which it has interests or that are strategically important to it. Here may be found the fundamental relationships for a modernised theory of imperialism.

The positive features of the theory of unequal exchange are to be found in the fact that in a certain sense it leads us back to the sources of Marxian theory. For instance, it harks back to Ricardo, who provided a starting point for the Marxian system, but whose theory of comparative costs found little favour with Marx, though it has now been taken up from a different viewpoint by Emmanuel and his followers. This is all the more justified as the theory was originally developed with the methodology of the labour theory of value.

A second source of inspiration may be found in Condillac, who, in his controversy with Le Trosne in the times of the Physiocrats, advanced the theory that there could be no exchange of equal values. (See Bettelheim, Emmanuel, 1969, p. 23).

A further positive feature of the theory of unequal exchange lies in the fact that it provides Marxism with a way out from the politico-military aspects which threaten to supplant the proper content of the theory of imperialism, whether one sees this as providing an outlet for capitalism's difficulties in marketing its products or as stressing the tendency to monopolise primary products. For this theory, the epoch of direct colonial imperialism and of its scramble to divide the world is over. As Emmanuel says (1969, p. 216): 'From the moment that the big powers were certain that the doors were open to them for trade, they had no longer the slightest desire to bear the costs of direct administration.' Thus the accent is again transferred to purely economic considerations, as was emphasised in Marx's main works.

Marxists are thus obliged to consider what Toynbee called the 'external proletariat' of a given civilisation: Celts and Germanic tribes in the Roman Empire, Huns, Miao–Man and Tai in ancient China, and foreign immigrants nowadays. 'One begins intuitively to recognise that in a world which is at the same time poor and indivisible the enrichment of a minority would be impossible without the impoverishment of the broad masses in most countries' (ibid., p. 288).

Emmanuel refers to Singer's calculations that average incomes in many countries of the 'third world' were higher prior to 1900 than they are today. Marx points to a similar situation when he alludes to the eradication of Indian artisans in the nineteenth century. On the other hand, he saw in the British Raj a precondition for the liberation of India from a thousand years of stagnation (see Melotti, 1972, p. 180).

We find in Colin Clark's monumental work further indications of the deterioration in living standards in India since the eleventh century, i.e. the heyday of Hinduism. They reached their lowest point in about 1895, when the skilled worker's wages were about one-third of what they had been early in the seventeenth century. (Clark, 1940/57, pp. 206–7.)

In the background hovers the idea, which has been particularly cherished by Maoism, that the real proletariat is indeed the 'external' proletariat, and that World Revolution will and must start from the under-developed countries (as Aron agrees, if not Toynbee!). This seems to represent a return to the theme of Marx's 'original accumulation' and at the same time an aggressive reply to all those who criticise Marxism because the revolution it prophesies has come not in the rich countries but in the poor ones.

The reasons why wages are low in many countries and do not exceed the minimum subsistence level are complex; demographic factors cannot be neglected. Bettelheim reproaches Emmanuel for neglecting 'neo-imperialist' tendencies. These may be of some importance to monocultures, for it may be that for the countries concerned their only chance of prosperity lies in diversification of production, since industrialisation may prove very difficult.

The discussion of this subject is not yet over, but we may here draw a provisional conclusion. It is most welcome that in this case Marxists do not rely on emotional appeals but try to base their analyses on a sober examination of the facts, supported by the most modern theories. Whatever criteria we may choose to apply, they seem to indicate that the exploitation of the 'third world' continues, but there is not yet a fully satisfactory theory to prove it beyond any doubt.

In principle, such an analysis can hardly be based on the idea that higher rates of surplus value prevail in developing countries. On the other hand, the notion of exploitation seems to hinge on a slow shifting of the terms of trade against developing countries. The discussion cannot be pursued further at this juncture, nor can the problem be considered as solved, all the less so as Marx himself offers few clues for a profound analysis of international trade.

The debate on imperialism has been continued into present times. This is not the place to enter into a detailed discussion of the contributions to it, since, after all, it is only indirectly related to Marx's theories.

A detailed study of the situation of underdeveloped countries has been offered recently by Samir Amin in his analysis of what he calls 'peripheric Capitalism' and accumulation at world scale (1970, p. 159).

Part II
Accumulation and Growth

4 Marxian Accumulation and Growth Theory from the Viewpoint of 'Academic' Economics

The rediscovery of classical macroeconomic analysis, which leads to growth theory, cannot by-pass Marx. It is true that one of the fathers of modern growth theory, Harrod, did not directly refer to Marx in his early works on this subject, but he spoke of him indirectly in stressing 'how important this dynamic theory was in the corpus of doctrine then known as Political Economy'. He also expressed the view that 'the idea that Keynes is more dynamic than Ricardo is the exact opposite of the truth'. (Harrod, 1948, pp. 28–9.) To the extent that Marx builds on Ricardo, one can say that a reference to Marx is here implied. Harrod directly, but rather cursorily, refers to Marx in his 'Second Essay' (1960, pp. 277 ff.).

The other father of growth theory, Domar, puts greater emphasis (1946, pp. 137–8) on the role played by Marx:

> The relation between capital accumulation and employment . . . has been discussed in economic literature a number of times, the most notable contribution belonging to Marx. . . . The idea that the preservation of full employment in a capitalist economy requires a growing income goes back (in one form or another) at least to Marx.

A few years later he writes (1952, p. 480),

> In economic literature, growth models, interpreted broadly, have appeared a number of times, at least as far back as Marx. Of the several schools of economics the Marxists have, I think, come closest to developing a substantial theory of economic growth, and they might have succeeded had they given less time and effort to defending their master's virtue. Some highly elaborate and interesting growth models did, however, appear in Soviet literature.

Domar devoted a study (1957, pp. 223 ff.) to the growth model that the Soviet economist Feldman published in 1928. Feldman's work was based on a number of preliminary studies undertaken in the early days of the Gosplan office by Groman and his disciples, above all Basarov. The abrupt termination of these studies is to be explained by the general climate of the Stalin era, when too detailed an economic calculus appeared to be undesirable, because it was feared that this might delay measures to transform the entire economic system. Even so, these early Russian studies represent the only real attempt by Marxists to go beyond Marx's growth theory. Admittedly, some attempts in this direction were made by Otto Bauer, Rosa Luxemburg and Grossmann, but their interest centred on the problem of equilibrium.

It can be said with some justice that Marxists did not continue the most essential and original approach of Marx's work, in that area where the future growth of capitalism was at stake. On the other hand, 'academic' economics received a stimulus from this side, although this was not always openly recognised. In a sense, this is even true of the way in which Cassel handled the problem of the 'evenly progressing economy'. We have already noted, in volume 1 of this work, some affinities with Marx in Cassel's notion of the 'disposition of capital'. It is true that he does not, in the context of his growth theory, quote directly from Marx, but, since he often refers to him elsewhere, it seems reasonable to assume that he was somehow inspired by the Marxian schemes of 'extended reproduction'. (Cassel, 1918; 1923, pp. 27 ff.)

Another pioneer of growth theory, Ramsey, does not, in his 1928 study (repr. 1970, pp. 493 ff.), directly refer to Marx, but in referring to the accounting system of socialist states he shows that he is fully aware of the influence of Marxian thought on it.

Oparin's 1930 study, which merits being mentioned alongside Ramsey's study, is founded on a process analysis with a constant rate of growth and thus is based on the models of Marx and Cassel. Oparin assumes a 'secular growth rate', an equilibrium rate around which the short-run growth rate oscillates. The rising trend is to be explained by the fact that the exhaustion of natural resources is made good by technical progress. (Oparin, 1930, pp. 120–3, 407–8.)

Curiously enough, after these first attempts and in what can be considered the middle period in the development of growth theory, direct references to Marx become rarer. Perhaps to bring about a return to the first formulations of growth theory, which may be found in Marx's work, would have required that the predominantly 'neo-neo-classical' theory lost some of its impetus and direction.

When in 1937 von Neumann produced his famous mathematical model in which consumption goods in effect occur only as inputs for processes the output of which is 'labour', he virtually went back to Marx's methods, for Marx's 'values' in the process of production constitute only inputs, as will be shown below. Von Neumann uses his model to arrive at a maximum rate of proportional growth, but even such a well-meaning critic as

Koopmans, who fully appreciates von Neumann's model, nevertheless calls it (1964, p. 356) 'rather poor economics'.

A similar kind of implicit reasoning is used by Joan Robinson. Having dealt with Marx and his growth theory in a separate book and a large number of articles, she apparently did not think it necessary, in her major work on accumulation, *The Accumulation of Capital* (the affinities of which are evident from its title), to underline the links between her analysis and Marxian theory. It is true that such an acknowledgement was not absolutely essential, since the close relationship between her categories and Marx's was quite obvious, and she had acknowledged her debt to Marx elsewhere. (Robinson, 1956, and 1952, pp. 145 ff.)

Thus it may be concluded that Marx's importance was recognised from the outset in growth theory, but that references to his work became rarer in the 1950s, as growth theory became more and more dominated by neo-classical authors, or 'neo-neo-classicists', as they were dubbed by Joan Robinson. These authors did not see that their essential thesis, that of the variability of the capital–output ratio, had already been anticipated by Marx, although in a somewhat one-sided form, for he expected the 'organic composition of capital' to increase, though with periodic reversals.

At any rate, in the 1950s there came the parting of the ways for 'the neoclassical (consumer-oriented) and the Marxian (accumulation-oriented) points of view'. From the Marxian point of view, it is characteristic that 'firms behave according to certain independent objectives that are not reducible to consumer decisions' and that they 'act so as to *maximize* the rate of increase in net worth at every moment of time. This is indeed a Marxian postulate.' (Cass and Yaari, 1967, p. 259.)

The importance of the reproduction schemes in volume II of *Capital* was spelled out in 1932 by Burchardt, in an essay that unfortunately did not attract much interest. In it Burchardt examines (1932, pp. 116, 171) the significance of these schemes of the stationary circular flow for the growing economy. He also links the schemes to business-cycle theory by laying his finger on 'lags which constitute obstacles to adjustment'.

Shortly after the Second World War, Mangold conducted a reappraisal of Marx's analysis of Quesnay's famous 'Tableau Economique' and expressed his regret that 'Marx, as an economist, receives so little attention'. Even Marxist theoreticians never really took up Marx's theory of the circular flow (Mangold, 1953; pp. 52–61). With reference to the business-cycle problem, Mangold expressly states (ibid., p. 57) that 'an interpretation of the Marxian schemes shows that the "residue of commodities", which is supposed to be unsaleable in the case of extended reproduction, need not exist'. This takes away the ground from beneath under-consumption theories.

Erich Schneider too has paid homage (1958, I, pp. 134–7, 139–40) to the Marxian concept of the circular flow in the economy, and the rapidly increasing literature on growth problems has recognised that 'Marx introduced certain ideas into the theory of economic development that have been there ever since. . . . He indicated the slenderness of the tightrope which an economy must walk for steady growth' (Higgins, 1959, pp. 119–20).

'Economic development . . . is the keynote to all Marxist theory' says Brenner, (1966, p. 104), and Lewis, in his *Theory of Economic Development* (1960), gave (p. 288) general recognition to the importance of Marx's business-cycle theories for development analysis. Finally, the Keynesian Joan Robinson, 'in her far-reaching synthesis [1956], not only established a merger of growth and distribution theory, but also created a new unity in the spheres of production and circulation, through the incorporation of the production function into the growth model', as Güsten has said (1960, p. 9).

Current 'academic' theory holds that Marx's theory of evolution boils down to a theory of the collapse of capitalism (Stavenhagen, 1951; 1957, p. 154). This 'theory of collapse' seems rather to be an invention of the revisionists. At any rate, as Roll states (1953, p. 281), 'The prognosis of the development of capitalism which arises from his analytical concepts is the most spectacular part of Marx's work and . . . has had a far more dramatic appeal than the . . . analysis of the theory of value'.

THE MARX–DOMAR EQUATION

As it is, the Marxian growth model, in the framework of an essentially unstable economy, has anticipated the important conclusions of the Harrod–Domar analysis. It is nowadays cast more and more in the role of an antithesis to neo-classical analysis, although, paradoxically, both conceptions regard the variability of the capital–output ratio as a key magnitude. The Marxian model, as it happens, largely relies on linking the potentially stable with existing unstable growth processes, as Joan Robinson has shown (1952, pp. 91–2):

> Now we have to consider whether the situation is such that this state of affairs [i.e. the golden age] will maintain itself as time goes by. This is, in essence, the problem that Marx treated by means of the famous 'Schema' in volume II of *Capital*, which have '(sic!)' recently been revived in modern dress . . . by Harrod and Domar. . . . Marx showed that it is not logically impossible to conceive of steady accumulation taking place indefinitely, but he held that 'in the crude conditions' of capitalist production it would do so only by an accident. Indeed, as we shall see, the conditions which steady accumulation requires are such as never to be found in reality. . . .

The doyen of British economists, Robertson, referred to this statement of Joan Robinson when he recognised (1954; 1956, pp. 236 ff.) that modern growth theory had indeed been anticipated by Marx: 'Mrs. Robinson, for all I know, may well be right that [the "Domar equation"] had lain for years wrapped up in the tangled phraseology of Marx before being brought to light by Domar and Harrod.'

Robertson characterises the 'Domar equation' in the following terms:

Let there be a society in which output is increasing by a fraction *r* of itself in every year, and in which the proportion of capital equipment to the annual stream of output which it helps to produce is fixed inexorably at *q*. Then if this state of affairs is being smoothly maintained, without the generation of inflationary or deflationary pressures, we can be sure that the proportion of their real income which the members of the society desire to save is equal to *rq*. For if, and only if, this is so, the sums saved in each year will just suffice to buy the new batch of capital equipment created in that year, and the additional sum spent on consumption in each year will just suffice to buy the additional batch of consumption goods for which that new batch of capital equipment is responsible.

This is the Marxian scheme of extended reproduction in an academic nutshell. It contains, as opposed to the theory of the tendency of the rate of profit to fall, a constant capital–output ratio and a constant saving ratio for capitalists. The former finds its expression in Marx's ratio between constant capital and value added $(v + s)$, and the latter in the accumulation rate based on the rate of surplus value (which is thought of·as constant, i.e. as the constant share in value added which accrues to capitalists).

In a concrete example the 'Domar equation', which should properly be termed the 'Marx–Domar equation', looks as follows: if the capital–output ratio is 2 and the growth rate $^1/_{10}$, $^1/_5$ of income (i.e. the incomes of capitalists and workers in aggregate) must be saved, i.e. $2 \times {}^1/_{10} = {}^1/_5$.

Shortly after Robertson's 1954 essay (originally an address in the previous year), Lewis made some pronouncements which showed little understanding of Marx's economic theorising and in which he repeated almost all the old objections to Marxian sociology that we have criticised in Volume 1 above. Lewis (1955; 1960, pp. 297–8) discusses the Marxian theory of growth in connexion with the theory of the tendency of the rate of profit to fall, distinguishing two stages in the growth process:

in all that phase of economic growth where labour can be drafted into the capitalist sector of the economy from other sectors at a constant real wage . . . once the accumulation of capital has caught up with the 'surplus' labour . . . wages grow with capital accumulation. . . . In the early stage . . . there is no tendency for the rate of profit to fall. In the later stage, when labour becomes scarce, the rate of profit would fall if innovation did not constantly provide new opportunities for investing capital.

Lewis then goes on to refer to the numerous economists who 'have expected the rate of profit to fall rather than to rise at this stage (Smith, Ricardo, Marx, Keynes, and most others)', and continues, 'most of them, contrary to present fashions, expected this to check rather than to stimulate investment'.

Lewis does not, however, discuss the central question of whether the exhaustion of the labour flow from pre-capitalist reservoirs or from the 'industrial reserve army' will raise wages and thus give rise to a tendency towards predominantly labour-saving progress. This would in turn exercise pressure on the wage bill, or rather on its increase, if capital is all the time increasing. If the division of the social product is not changed, the rate of profit must fall.

Lewis instead develops another theory:

> there seems to have been no secular decline of the rate of profit over the past hundred years. Here again account must be taken of the behaviour of governments. If they have a secular tendency it is to tax profits and to stimulate consumption, but whether this checks or stimulates invest-ment in 'mature' economies we must leave to the debate.

Marxian growth theory was not properly appreciated before the 1960s. As Hicks has noted (1965, p. 77), Marx's influence on the general trend of ideas has been in impelling thought away from what has been called the 'method of temporary equilibrium' and towards the analysis of disequilibria.

Since it cannot be denied that the initial inspiration to develop growth models stemmed from Marx's schemes, as recognised by Domar, why, given that the approach of Harrod and Domar came very close to Marxian theory, in both its method and its conclusions, did so few subsequent growth models pursue the Marxian line?

The answer is difficult, and here it is possible only to suggest the outlines of it. As Cass and Yaari have indicated (1967), there has been a split between more consumer-oriented and more accumulation-oriented models, and the predominance of the former is to be explained on grounds of economic and political reality. Following the restrictions of the war years, the supply of consumer goods remained of paramount importance in all countries, and, in the wake of the buyers' market, accumulation seemed automatic. It was only when the growth forces subsided and were called into question that models which gave priority to accumulation came into prominence.

THE MARXIAN THESIS: CAPITALISM IS DYNAMICS WITH AN INBUILT DETONATOR

In 'academic' circles, it is increasingly recognised, as, for instance, by Bombach and von Weizsäcker (1968, p. 377), that growth theory owes much to Marx. Von Weizsäcker, one of the leading neo-classical growth specialists explicitly says (1962, pp. 78–9),

> Marx was the first to see with acuteness the close link which exists between economic growth and capitalism. His theory is openly anti-capitalist and attempts to understand capitalism, to fight it and overcome it. If non-socialist economic theory since Marx and parti-cularly the great neo-classical schools in Austria, Lausanne, England and America have learned so little from Marx, it is probably owing to this bias.

This is only part of the explanation. On the other hand, it can safely be said that the neo-classical schools derived part of their inspiration from their antagonism towards Marxian theses; even 'neo-neo-classical' tendencies have profited from this antagonism. Von Weizsäcker (ibid.) has very pertinently pointed to a cardinal weakness in neo-classical reasoning in connexion with growth theory: 'If one can correctly maintain that a capitalist system can remain workable only as a growing economy [this is one of the central theses of Marx], all theories of interest which have grown up on the basis of neo-classical theory do not reach to the heart of the phenomenon of interest.' Indeed, 'the essence of interest under capitalism is understandable only . . . if one considers its dependence on economic growth. Growth, however, means in most cases a qualitative modification of the structure and system of the economy'.

This last remark could almost be considered a Marxist one. Here the veil which generally lies over the relationship between Marx and modern growth theory is lifted. Growth theory has never been conspicuous for its homage to Marx, whose name remains anathema, but the further evolution of his fundamental ideas permeated growth theory – not only the Marxophile versions, but also the neo-classical version, which gained new strength from Solow's analysis.

Von Weizsäcker's analysis further shows (ibid., pp. 26–7), again in conformity with the Marxian version, that capitalism and a positive rate of profit are possible only where growth is high:

> Provided there is always a certain readiness to accumulate, technical progress or population growth is a necessary condition for a profit-oriented capitalist system of a liberal stamp. . . . In a stationary or pre-stationary economy, a positive level of interest and profit can prevail in the long run only if capital accumulation stops. . . . If one supposes that

there are always people who are willing to improve their income and social status by accumulating property, there are only three possibilities in a stationary or pre-stationary economy . . . .

Either . . . accumulation will be effectively prohibited, a measure which must work in favour of property-owning classes, or there must exist a group of people or an institution that is capable of over-accumulating, and is willing to do so, to the extent that other people save. . . . If these two paths are not chosen, the rate of interest and the rate of profit will go on falling to zero . . . .

In other words, if Marx can be said to be successful in showing that there are under capitalism forces working in the direction of a radical slowing down of growth or of the rhythm of technical progress, this would be an indication of the end of capitalism, for a slowing of the growth process must inexorably usher in 'a qualitative modification of the structure and system of the economy'.

The Marxian version of the Hegelian 'cunning of Reason' attributed to over-investment or at least to the relative growth of gross capital formation, the task, *via* a fall in the rate of profit or at least a tendency in that direction, of putting the brakes on growth – an operation which, as von Weizsäcker demonstrates, may, in theory, kill off capitalism altogether.

We thus see that Marxian daggers are hidden under neo-classical garb. We need not be astonished if recently some attempts have been made to bridge the gulf between neo-classical and Marxian thinking. This tendency found eloquent expression in a seminar organised by the Massachusetts Institute of Technology in 1965–6.

Marglin introduced his paper to the seminar by saying (1967, p. 141) that the assumptions he makes – of an elastic supply of labour, of the total allocation of consumption to wages, of productivity increases through capital expansion – represent a theoretical simplification of the growth framework reaching back at least to Karl Marx.

At the same seminar, Cass and Yaari presented what they called a 'mixed neo-classical–Marxian model', in which the neo-classical component was the consumption relationship and the Marxian an orientation towards accumulation and 'the Marxian postulate of a maximized growth rate of net value' (Cass and Yaari, 1967, p. 259).

In Germany, Ott has stated (1963) that Marx was one of the most important precursors of the theory of economic growth, and in 1967 he attempted to reach a larger economically-literate audience through an article in the review Der Volkswirt (1967, pp. 637–8). It was also Ott who devised a classification of the kinds of technical progress, permitting greater precision in the Marxian analysis of the character of that progress.

TECHNICAL PROGRESS AND 'RELATIVE SURPLUS VALUE' IN THE 'ACADEMIC' CRITICISM OF MARX

The dynamic element in Marxian theory rarely receives proper appreciation. This is particularly true of 'extra surplus value', which appears within the framework of 'relative surplus value' and alongside 'absolute surplus value', and can be reaped by an individual entrepreneur through the introduction of improved production methods or machinery. This is a subject that has become popular only through the work of Schumpeter, and even those authors who recognise that Marx dealt with it are primarily conscious, in this regard, of what they take to be contradictions in his reasoning. Thus Alexander Gray writes (1946, p. 312),

> though doubtless the introduction of machinery reduces the amount of surplus value, nevertheless the employer who takes this course secures for himself a bigger whack of what is going. . . . There is something whimsical in the suggestion that, in order to increase surplus value, the capitalist thus cuts down that part of capital which yields surplus value, replacing it by that part of capital which can yield none.

This should be corrected in line with the following. The increase in constant capital, in the form of machinery, creates individual extra surplus value or relative surplus value, but only as long as other entrepreneurs do not follow suit by introducing new machinery as well, for then the 'socially necessary labour time' and thus the 'value' of the commodity would decrease. Piettre, however, recognises (1957; 1962, p. 56) that what happens with regard to the equalisation of profit rates resulting from absolute surplus value may perhaps be less important than individual extra surplus value within the framework of what Marx calls relative surplus value:

> It is of course quite clear that every entrepreneur, taken as an individual, will try to produce as cheaply as possible by increasing the productivity of his workers through the application of technical progress. He then receives extraordinary surplus value or extra profit. By so doing, he obliges others to introduce the cheapest method of production, thus reducing the 'socially necessary labour time' . Doing an extraordinary about-turn, Marx reverts to what has been hallowed by experience, namely the fact that technical progress, contrary to what has been said before, constitutes for those firms that are best equipped a source of 'extra profits'.

The whole question revolves around the issue of what attracts more capital: a high surplus value with labour-intensive production, giving considerable scope for mechanisation; or capital-intensive production, where the technical progress that has already been made may not or may still leave much scope for further technical refinement, so that intra-marginal profits could look more promising than absolute surplus value?

Irma Adelman recognises (1962, pp. 70–1) that Marx sees gross investment as the vehicle for technical progress: 'it is only when new pieces of capital equipment are introduced or when old machinery is replaced that changes in the proportions of capital to labor employed are at all possible. The rate of innovation is consequently governed by the gross rate of addition to the capital stock of the economy.'

At this juncture we have four different aspects of Marxian theory, which have been duly recognised by thoughtful observers. First, accumulation takes place, according to Marx, primarily out of internal funds (i.e. self-finance), so that the direction in which newly created capital flows – into firms and industries which realise 'extra profits' (i.e. very probably those which are capital-intensive) is determined largely from the very outset. Secondly, the most dynamic firms enjoy, at least in practice, a 'temporary monopoly', thanks to the cost advantage they reap from progressive production methods. Thirdly, the success of those firms means that the process of concentration progresses, either because of concentrated self-financing (Marxian 'concentration') or through mergers with, and takeovers of, other firms (Marxian 'centralisation'). Fourthly, there is the tendency of the (average) rate of profit to fall, which is brought about by technical progress in firms which fulfil a pioneer role for society.

The first aspect, which concerns the interdependence of technical progress and self-financing in big business has received careful attention from the analysts of modern development theory – for instance, Higgins (1959, p. 109):

> Marx laid a good deal more stress on technological progress as the 'motor' of capitalist growth, and by the same token, assigned a more important role to the entrepreneur. He saw more clearly than his predecessors – and most of his contemporaries – that there is a two-way relationship between investment and technological progress. Certainly investment is needed to take advantage of technological progress, but technological progress also provides the opportunities for profitable investment.

The complementary role of external funds was clearly seen by Marx in his analysis of the credit system, in connexion with the modern joint-stock company and the concentration of the credit system on banks. This constitutes an additional advantage for big business, the development of which opens the way for a smooth elimination of capitalism while raising production to new heights. (See Fritsch, 1968, p. 120.)

5 Simple Reproduction and Analysis of the Circular Flow

In Volume I we examined the fundamental idea underlying the scheme of 'simple reproduction' developed in volume II of *Capital*. On the inevitability of the circular flow Marx says (*Capital*, I, ch. 23, p. 531),

> The conditions of production are also those of reproduction. No society can go on producing, in other words, no society can reproduce, unless it constantly reconverts a part of its products into means of production, or elements of fresh products. All other circumstances remaining the same, the only mode by which it can reproduce its wealth, and maintain it at one level, is by replacing the means of production – i.e., the instruments of labour, the raw material, and the auxiliary substances consumed in the course of the year – by an equal quantity of the same kind of articles. . . .

Having given a general outline applicable to all systems of society, Marx goes on to depict 'reproduction in its capitalist form'. Here reproduction appears 'but as a means of reproducing as capital – i.e., as self-expanding value – the value advanced'.

This is the famous formula money–goods–money: money is turned into more money *via* the commodity. For this it is first necessary that capital remains intact, as would be necessary in a stationary economy without any growth.

Marx repeatedly emphasises that such a system is not typical of capitalism, but, rather, in contradiction to its essence, although such apparent equilibria may temporarily appear in the course of the business cycle at the upper and lower turning points. Beyond that, in the phenomenology of capitalism, there is a world of outward appearances: 'As a periodic increment of the capital advanced, or periodic fruit of capital in process, surplus-value acquires the form of a revenue flowing out of capital' (ibid., pp. 531–2).

Apart from this increment, which is the very essence of the production process from the point of view of capitalists, reproduction appears in two forms: first, in the reconstitution and maintenance of human energy (in the widest sense); and, secondly, in the restoration of the material means of production.

The reconstitution of human energy is brought about by spending 'variable capital', i.e. wages. Wages are generally paid in advance, before execution of the production process. This leads to a telescoping of periods, and macroeconomically it presupposes the existence of a stock of consumption goods prior to the beginning of the process of production. This is the grain of truth in the theory of the 'wage fund', and only in this sense can one say that Marx, who opposes the theory, had some affinities with it.

> The capital given in exchange for labour-power is converted into necessaries, by the consumption of which the muscles, nerves, bones, and brains of existing labourers are reproduced, and new labourers are begotten. Within the limits of what is strictly necessary, the individual consumption of the working-class is, therefore, . . . the production and reproduction of that means of production so indispensable to the capitalist: the labourer himself.   (Ibid., p. 537.)

Thus Marx draws the picture of consumption as an input into production, a view which was to be taken up in the 1930s by von Neumann. Consumption has, so to speak, priority over the other inputs, which serve only for the reproduction of real capital (installations, raw and ancillary materials) and the production of the final output, which cannot take place without labour.

Marx's analysis of simple reproduction is a model of economic circulation within a stationary system, where there is no enlargement or improvement of the means of production and no growth. In modern theory, however, this model can be linked with a theory of 'disembodied' technical progress, and in this case growth of production without net investment would indeed be possible, though Marx was far from assuming this. Modern analysts of Marxian theorems (for instance, Zinn, 1972, p. 123) sometimes refer to this possibility. The model of the circular flow is then turned into a model of intensive growth.

MARX'S ANALYSIS OF THE CIRCULAR FLOW

Owing to his use of the Physiocratic system, Marx used semi-feudal conditions to illustrate the circular flow, though the introduction of money goes beyond purely feudal conditions. In Quesnay's system, the farmers (the producers in the Physiocratic scheme) are assumed to have accumulated savings from their former activities, so that the circular flow can start. Under such circumstances, the labouring class finances the ruling class, and the latter receives its income solely from legal titles, i.e. rights to landed property, from which the largest part of surplus value derives.

In his *Theories of Surplus Value* Marx presents an almost humorous dialogue between capitalist and worker, in which he purports to explain the 'circular flow of money' between the classes. As he is quick to point out, under capitalism it is not, as in Quesnay's semi-feudal agricultural system, the worker who finances the appropriator of the surplus value, but the capitalist who finances the worker.

Could the reverse not also apply under capitalism? This question has also been raised by various authors, including Samuelson. Marx, however, replies with a definite 'No', for otherwise 'the whole relationship between wage-labour and capital' would be overthrown, and this would

> destroy the economic justification of surplus value. The result of the process is in fact that the fund from which the capitalist pays the wage-labourer is nothing but the latter's own product, and that therefore capitalist and labourer *actually* share the product in aliquot parts. But this actual result has absolutely nothing to do with the transaction between capital and wage [labour]. . . .
>
> What the capitalist buys is the temporary right to dispose of labour-power. . . . But the labour *belongs* to the capitalist after that transaction, which has been completed before the actual process of production begins. The *commodity* which emerges as product from this process belongs entirely to him. . . .
>
> The capitalist's surplus arises precisely from the fact that he buys from the labourer not a commodity but his labour-power itself, and this has less value than the product of this labour-power. . . . But now, in order to justify profit, its very source is covered up. . . . [If the assumption is made that the worker is the proprietor of the product . . . then this would mean that] the labourer has sold his share in the product to the capitalist, *before it has been converted into money*.
>
> So the capitalist is no longer owner of the product, and thereby the whole process through which he has appropriated another's labour *gratis* is invalidated. . . . If – turning the actual relationship upside-down – wages are to be derived from the discount on the part of the value of the total product that belongs to the workmen – that is, from the fact that the capitalist pays them this part in advance in *money* – he would have to give them very short-term bills of exchange, such as for example he pays to the cotton jobber, etc. The workman would get the largest share of his product, and the capitalist would soon cease being a capitalist. From being the owner of the product he would become merely the workmen's banker. (*Theories*, 1, ch. 6, pp. 315–16 and 320–1.)

The theory of the circular flow thus serves Marx as a means whereby to demonstrate his theory of surplus value. One could of course object that it is the very essence of the capitalist's business, as contrasted with the semi-feudal landowner's, that he pays the worker in advance but has to shoulder the risk of selling the commodity. It would thus appear that the capitalist's profit is to be explained by the function of risk-bearing. Marx objects (ibid.),

> just as the capitalist takes the risk of selling the commodity below its . . . value, he equally takes the chance of selling it above its value. The workman will be thrown out onto the street if the product is unsaleable; and if it falls for long below the market-price, his wages will be brought down below the average and short time will be worked.

Here Marx moves from the macroeconomic to the microeconomic level. He wants to point out that if the worker had only to pay interest (as is here implicit) to the capitalist, who acts as a banker, the worker would be able to pocket the 'pure' profit himself and would become independent of the loan or advance from the capitalist. This would mean that the ideal of 'associated producers' in the producers' society would be realised.

Could Quesnay's farmer have liberated himself in a similar way from his landowner? In fact, it seems that in Ricardian Britain the process of purchasing feudal ground rights followed this pattern. Farmers accumulated from the part of surplus value that they retained – since the landowner did not finance anything in advance and thus did not claim any interest beyond his ground-rent – sufficient means to be able to purchase the capitalised ground-rent. Marx seems to have imagined that this would be impeded by the particular semi-feudal conditions of landownership (in Prussia, for instance, family entails). All the same, in Quesnay's scheme the transition of agriculture to capitalism is foreshadowed.

That part of the *Theories of Surplus Value* from which we have quoted above dates from around 1862–3, and the essential thing to note about it in this context is that it contains a presentation of the circular flow. In Quesnay's analysis, neither the process of reproduction nor even growth is in the foreground. Quesnay was chiefly interested in distribution. As it happens, he was quite revolutionary, both in his presentation and in his conclusions, as Marx pointed out in the *Grundrisse* (II, p. 330) in 1857–8:

> The capitalist does not want to give the use of his capital for nothing; the landowner, similarly, does not want to give land and soil over to production for nothing. They want something in return. This is the way in which they are introduced, with their demands, as historical facts, but not explained. Wages are actually the *only economically* justifiable, because necessary, element of production costs. Profit and rent are only *deductions* from wages, arbitrarily wrested by force in the historical process by capital and landed property, and justified *by law*, not economically.

These revolutionary conclusions, which Marx sees as drawn both by Quesnay and the Physiocrats and by the early 'Ricardian' socialists, he does not himself share. Paradoxically, the Physiocrats, while reaching these conclusions, also glorify feudal landownership, for to them the soil is the only source of productivity, and commercial capital has no such use.

Here one could almost establish it as a law that each type of society glorifies the outward forms of earlier ones. Even Marxism does this, for the 'labour theory of value' would appear to show a hankering after (pre-feudal and pre-capitalist) 'simple commodity production'. In the Physiocrats' scheme, however, the formal obeisance to ground capital is accompanied by a rather materialistic afterthought:

> An over-abundance of agricultural products (grain, cattle, raw materials) is therefore the true form of general wealth. From the economic viewpoint, therefore, *rent* is the only form of wealth. Thus it is that the first prophets of capital conceive only the non-capitalists, the *feudal landed proprietors*, as the representatives of *bourgeois* wealth. . . . agriculture . . . is therefore the only *productive labour*, for they have come so far that . . . *only labour which creates surplus value is productive* . . . . (*Grundrisse*, II, pp. 328–9.)

This is analogous to modern capitalism recognising labour as the only productive factor, in order to tax wages alone. This is very nearly what happens with value-added tax, which principally affects earned income, and which some of its most fanatical supporters wish to see established as the single tax on all expenditure. This would almost imply a resurrection of the *taxe unique* of the Physiocrats in a new garb.

In this context, Marx is chiefly interested not in the problems of distribution, but in a presentation of the macroeconomic circular flow. In establishing his scheme of 'simple reproduction', he actually follows the Physiocrats' method of presentation; and he praises their achievement, since in their 'Tableau Économique' they were the first to analyse the circular flow (*Capital*, I, ch. 22). Marx quotes Mirabeau's assertion, 'There have been since the world began three great inventions. . . . The first is the invention of *writing*. . . . The second *is the invention of money*. . . . The third is the *economical table*, the result of the other two, which completes them both' (*Theories*, I, ch. 6, p. 343).

It must be emphasised that the 'Tableau Économique' contains in a nutshell the later Marxian distinction between constant capital (i.e. from a microeconomic point of view, purchases and self-provision of material; and, from a macroeconomic point of view, depreciation of society's capital stock, work in progress, and reserve stocks of material) and value added (in the German *Wertschöpfung* – 'value creation'; i.e. variable capital, or sum of wages, plus surplus value, or sum of profits). This distinction undoubtedly represents a great advance on some of the muddled thinking of the earlier classics, and it was Marx who fully clarified it.

The Physiocrats also anticipated Leontief's input–output analysis, which we consider in Chapter 8 in relation to the Marxian schemes.

THE CATEGORIES OF SIMPLE REPRODUCTION

In the Marxian schemes of reproduction, both department I (means of production and basic products) and department II (consumption goods), have an internal and external circular flow, the latter constituting the exchange between them. There is no class of external 'consumers only', like the landowners in Quesnay's scheme; nor is there any intermediate class, like Quesnay's farmers in their semi-feudal dependency, between workers and capitalists. On the other hand, the income of the capitalists, to whom the surplus value accrues, has no real input character, since Marx leaves out of account the capitalists' managerial role in their own firms (which role he analyses very thoroughly elsewhere, in volumes I and II of *Capital*). All employees, up to and including managers, are counted as workers, which contradicts the general Marxist assumption that managers are remunerated out of surplus value. If one drops this assumption, capitalists' income in the schemes would partly have the character of an input, while if taken by itself it would resemble Quesnay's rent. (*Capital*, II, ch. 20.)

The turnover of both departments consists of constant capital c, variable capital v, and surplus value s. From the point of view of department II, the turnover of I, including s, constitutes 'purchases'. In detail, the significance of the various categories for department I (means of production, raw and auxiliary materials, energy) is as follows.

c_1 Replacement of machinery, buildings and other fixed installations and equipment. These are produced within department I itself, the various firms of this sector buying from and selling to each other. (In this case and that of c_2, the monetary circulation necessary for exchange within the department is not shown).

c_2 Raw materials, auxiliary materials, and primary (coal, gas, oil, etc.) and secondary energy supplies. Again, firms supply each other within the industry.

v Sum of wages. Wages are paid in money, which is used to buy consumption goods from department II; this money derives from the 'hoard' that the department I capitalists control, or from the sale of a sum of means of production produced by department I and corresponding to the sum of wages paid by it.

s Sum of profits earned from sales to department II, less wages paid by I.

Department II covers consumer goods in the widest sense – including housing, for instance. For department II, c_1 signifies machinery, c_2 raw and auxiliary materials bought from department I, to which the price paid for both represents wages and surplus value.

VII is the sum of wages paid to workers in consumption industries which they use for buying their industries' goods.

SII is the sum of profits earned from sales of consumption goods which are supposed to be entirely spent on consumption goods produced by those capitalists.

The gross social product is therefore

$$(\text{I } c_1 + \text{I } c_2 + \text{I } v + \text{I } s) + (\text{II } c_1 + \text{II } c_2 + \text{II } v + \text{II } s),$$

while the net social product or national income is $(\text{I } v + \text{I } s) + (\text{II } v + \text{II } s)$.

The gross social product can be conceived in terms of values as well as of prices. In value terms it is the sum of 'socially necessary' labour time required to produce fixed capital equipment and raw materials c, wage goods v and capitalists' consumption goods s.

There is no difference between values and prices if the 'organic composition of capital' or the ratio $c{:}v$ is the same in both sectors. In the examples chosen by Marx, this rule is observed, for the ratio is everywhere $4{:}1$. (Ibid.)

THE CIRCULAR FLOW IN SIMPLE REPRODUCTION

Analogously to Quesnay, Marx represented the process of simple reproduction schematically. Ott, who has presented the schema in a more lucid form (1967, p. 637), says it is probably the only diagram by Marx in existence. It and Marx's comments upon it are contained in a letter of 6 July 1863 to Engels. What Marx calls departments I and II in *Capital*, he numbers the other way round in this schema, but here, to avoid confusion, we shall keep the same numbers as in *Capital*.

In his letter to Engels, Marx describes how the workers use their wages to buy consumption goods from the capitalists in department II. These capitalists and those of department I buy consumption goods from department II. The department II capitalists retain some part of their product to be exchanged with the capitalists in I.

The capitalists in I can buy from the capitalists in II only as much as can be covered by their surplus (which they are supposed to consume), while the capitalists in II buy from those in I the machinery and raw materials needed to replace used constant capital, which the capitalists in I replace from their own production.

The workers in I spend their money on consumption goods, as capitalists of both departments do; besides, both categories of capitalists are left with an excess of goods, which they use or exchange to replace that part of their real capital that has been used up.

In chapter 20 of volume II of *Capital*, Marx presented these conditions in a more detailed form, thoroughly examining the role of money, the tendency to hoard, and so on.

The simple reproduction scheme, i.e. that of the circular flow without net investment, looks as follows:

$$\text{I} \quad 4000\ c + 1000\ v + 1000\ s$$
$$\text{II} \quad 2000\ c + 500\ v + 500\ s$$

Furthermore, Marx assumes that a money capital of 5000 exists in department I and one of 2500 in department II. The process of production starts with an advance of 500 granted by the capitalists in II to their workers and the purchase by these capitalists of 2000-worth of the means of production from I. Thus the capitalists in I are enabled to buy consumption goods to the value of 1000 from II, which corresponds to exactly half the use of the means of production by department II. The other half is accounted for by the consumption goods that workers of department I buy from II. II has thus sold its entire output. Its own workers and capitalists consume 2×500, and the workers and capitalists of department I buy the remaining 2000 with money they earned by selling production goods to the capitalists in II. As a matter of fact, department II only requires a money capital of 2000 to buy 2000-worth of means of production from I, and for department I an advance of 1000 might suffice to enable its workers to buy consumption goods from II.

The scheme itself is thus relatively easy to understand. If equilibrium is to prevail, II c must equal I v + I s. In other words, the capitalists and workers of I must buy consumption goods from II to the same value as entrepreneurs of II spend on means of production and raw materials from I.

Marx formulates this thus (*Capital*, II, ch. 20, p. 406): 'It follows that, on the basis of simple reproduction, the sum of the values of $v + s$ of the commodity-capital of I . . . must be equal to the constant capital II$_c$, which is likewise taken as a proportional part of the total commodity-product of department II; or I $(v + s) = $ II$_c$.'

As Fritsch has pointed out (1968, p. 90) one of the conditions of the scheme is this: 'Marx considers the two departments and their various productive activities as one vast industry, i.e. as completely integrated.'

Furthermore, this formula is a sort of *perpetuum mobile*, an eternal circular flow based on an apparent 'stationary equilibrium'.

From this stationary-equilibrium model some authors have sought to draw certain conclusions, which are repeated in the case of the 'extended reproduction' scheme. They think that Marx was suggesting the possibility of perpetual equilibrium in the capitalist system – which he clearly was not. The mere fact that, even in the case of simple reproduction, disturbances are possible, proves that Marx assumed that any equilibrium in capitalism would in principle be unstable.

With regard to raw materials and intermediate products, two different interpretations of the scheme can be imagined. First, one could assume that both departments produce their own raw materials and intermediate products (though perhaps not auxiliary materials and energy), by means of machinery supplied by 1. There would then indeed be vertical integration in Fritsch's sense in both departments. This interpretation, however, is not relevant, since Marx assumes that raw materials are supplied by department 1.

This raises the problem that has been examined by Burchardt (1932, pp. 150 ff.), who demonstrates that, if one transposes the scheme onto the macroeconomic level, raw materials as such can no longer appear, since they are the product of the combined employment of equipment, plant and the labour force. Burchardt, however, considers auxiliary materials and energy as part of the production of department 1. Since raw materials (coal, oil, natural gas, etc.) have a growing importance in the production of energy, it would appear reasonable to treat them in the same way.

If one acknowledges Burchardt's objections, this would lead to a shortened version of the formula for the social product as expressed in 'values'. In it would be included labour hours spent on the production and maintenance of machinery, other equipment, fixed capital, buildings and services (transport, etc.), and 'surplus labour hours':

$$(\text{I } c_1 + \text{I } v + \text{I } s) + (\text{II } c_1 + \text{II } v + \text{II } s)$$

Compared with the 'orthodox' Marxian formula, this shortened version avoids double counting and seems to correspond to the value concept in its purest form.

If one were to count labour hours expended on the production of raw materials and auxiliary materials, including energy, this would be to neglect that these hours are already taken into account in the total amount of labour required for replacing the means of production and consumption goods. After all, raw and auxiliary materials are produced by using means of production and labour. Here a difference appears between a value scheme and a price scheme: in the latter, all products have a price, but only the value added in the industries producing raw materials and suchlike appears as part of the social product.

In a value scheme, once the labour hours expended on means of production and consumption goods have been counted, there is no justification for counting separately 'costs' for the use of both. Nor is there any justification for counting separately labour hours expended on the production of raw materials and auxiliary materials, for as soon as means of production exist and consumption goods to feed the labour force (and dependants) are available, our only concern is the use to which these commodities are put.

There is no further hidden value, for it is purely a matter of using resources which have already been created, i.e. crystallised 'socially necessary' labour hours. Burchardt was the first to point this out in a value scheme; the problem does not exist at a macroeconomic level.

Intermediate products, which we call original basic materials, are produced without presupposing the existence of unfinished goods, through the mere application of finished means of production and labour to a given state of nature. . . . [They] contain as cost elements only the consumption of finished goods. . . . In period analysis of a static economy, we cannot count alongside finished goods any intermediate products. . . . [Their] reproduction . . . is identical with the reproduction of the departmental products, for their transformation into finished goods, i.e. their metamorphosis, represents their exhaustion . . . .

For two reasons, then, intermediate products must not be inserted into the circular flow of a period: (1) their unit values depend on the number of stages of production, which is arbitrarily determined; and (2) their inclusion would involve 'double counting', for their annual production dissolves into p (profits) and v (wages). . . . Marx sees clearly that the sum of values of intermediate products is not determined, i.e. it depends on the vertical organisational structure of the economy. . . . (Marx, *Theories*, 1, p. 248.)

Also, the incorporation of raw materials is not compatible with the basic equation of departmental equilibrium. . . . In this sense, the scheme presented in *Capital* must be amended in accordance with the findings of the *Theories* and one must seriously conceive of a 'combination of all branches of production in one giant industry'. . . .

Dickinson states the argument concisely (1956–7, p. 124):

[One must] subsume the organic composition of capital under the durability of variable capital. Since this involves the disappearance of constant capital as a separate category, it will probably arouse great opposition from orthodox Marxian economists. . . . One firm's constant capital is resolved into other firms' variable capital. If we consider the economy as a whole, the distinction between constant and variable capital is meaningless: all capital is variable. . . .

These considerations lead to the conclusion that it is necessary to eliminate raw and auxiliary materials (1 and II c_2) from Marx's gross social product formula. If one wants to avoid this, one can do so by assuming, contrary to Marx, that each department supplies its own materials and is thus vertically integrated: department I would have its own iron ore and coal mines, oil deposits and refineries, department II its own cotton plantations, latifundia and so on, and both would in addition supply their households and industries with energy and auxiliary materials.

In this vertically integrated world, each department would with its own labour and (either self-produced or purchased) means of production produce its raw materials and auxiliary materials. Thus the presentation would be simplified and the danger of double-counting in the value scheme would be avoided.

In this case, Fritsch's statement (1968, p. 90) that 'Marx considers the two departments and their various productive activities as one vast industry, i.e. as completely integrated', which strictly speaking is not true of Marx's vertical scheme, would appear justified. Fritsch is here referring to Marx's statement (*Capital*, II, ch. 20, p. 399) that 'All the various branches of production pertaining to each of these two departments form one single great branch of production. . . .'

Unfortunately, the passage from which this is taken does not say anything about the problem of vertical integration backwards to the stage of raw materials. Shortly afterwards, Marx speaks of raw and auxiliary materials, semi-finished products and suchlike as part of the constant capital that department II buys from department I in exchange for consumption goods. One could thus conclude that he thought raw materials would be supplied by department I. Other passages seem to confirm this.

The alternative is that the equilibrium formula should be $\text{II} c_1 = \text{I} v + \text{I} s$; in other words, department II would buy only machinery and fixed equipment and not raw materials. It is true that it might then be appropriate to include in II a separate category v_2 to remind us of the labour which produces raw materials with part of the means of production supplied by I.

THE ROLE OF MONEY IN THE CIRCULAR FLOW

One could consider the theory of 'simple reproduction' simply as an exchange system: department I exchanges its means of production, without the intervention of money, for the consumption goods of department II. In such a natural barter economy, the wage system as such would disappear, except – emphasising the real character of surplus value (as a surplus of 'corn' which serves as circulating and fixed capital, in so far as it is not consumed by workers) – in the Ricardian sense of wages in kind.

Marx did not choose this way, principally because the Physiocrats had already introduced money into their system, and it was on this that he built his structure. Marx did not wish to identify simple reproduction with capitalism, for the latter was for him essentially dynamic and growth-oriented; nevertheless, he did not want to renounce monetary circulation, to which he devotes many pages.

There are now two questions to be asked. Where does the money come from that is needed for circulation? Does the supply of money suffice for the total circulation?

Older Marxists always took the first question very lightly, pointing to the production of gold, which Marx, who wanted to view the capitalist world as a whole, in order to exclude foreign trade from his circular-flow scheme, treats in various passages and especially in the last paragraph but one (xii) of *Capital*, volume II, chapter 20. Marx then raises the question, 'Where does the money come from . . . to turn the surplus-value into money?' (ibid., p. 477).

We have already tried to answer this question in Volume I. Suffice it here to say that if department I pays its workers wages, or if its capitalists take money out to live, and if both buy consumer goods from department II, II has the wherewithal to buy means of production from I. This, however, presupposes that II has a stock of commodities before the production process in I starts, and that capitalists I hold a stock of money.

Marx, in the paragraph cited above, assumes that department I itself produces the 'money material'. This hypothesis does not seem to be a happy one, for in this case 'money' would be part of $1\,c$, which represents materials produced for self-consumption in department I. It would not then be quite clear how it could be transformed into $1\,s$ or $1\,v$, which, in money form, represent the equivalent of $11\,c$, so as to give department II the means to enable it to buy up to this amount from I's production, after which the money would flow back to I.

Earlier Marx had emphasised (ibid., p. 404) 'A certain supply of money, to be used either for the advancement of capital or for the expenditure of revenue must under all circumstances be assumed to exist beside the productive capital in the hands of the capitalists, as we have shown above.' This means that surplus value was hoarded at an earlier stage, i.e. it had not been consumed. This, however, makes simple reproduction appear absurd: how can there have been accumulation at the very outset – 'original accumulation'?

One would have to add that if workers and capitalists are to live during the process of production, and if this process is to start at all, the money stock must be matched by certain quantities of commodities (machinery, raw materials and consumption goods), which would allow them to hold out until the production process yields more goods. The 'money hoard' must be matched by corresponding stocks.

This is the old problem of which came first, the chicken or the egg? The money supply may stem from a hoard accumulated in feudal or pre-capitalist times, or it may be the result of credit creation, which would, however, be inseparable from growth processes.

The second question concerns the quantity of money. Will it be adequate? Marx points to the adaptability of the effective quantity of money through a variation in the velocity of circulation, but a minimum amount must be available corresponding to ordinary transaction requirements. This has been discussed above, in Volume I, Part IX.

At any rate, Marx speaks (*Capital*, II, ch. 17, pp. 330, 349) of compensation 'by a greater velocity of money currency . . . by a greater . . . balancing of purchases and sales . . . by greater economy in the use of the circulating quantity of money . . . or by the transformation of money from the form of a hoard into that of a circulating medium'.

A few additional remarks may be useful. In the case of variable capital, or wages, paid by the producers of consumption goods, we are dealing with circulation within the confines of department II; the money flows back to the same capitalists, who can therefore hold their cash stock at a minimum level in that sector.

Wage payments made by the capitalists of department I take a more roundabout route. They first go into the pockets of the capitalists in II, who in turn use the money to buy means of production from I. One may therefore expect that the capitalists in I would have to hold more cash in relation to the same circulating capital, because the velocity of circulation is slower in this case. This is all the more relevant as the capitalists in II sell consumption goods to each other, and the department as a whole will hold less cash for consumption purposes. Capitalists of department I are not put at a disadvantage in this respect. They too must buy their consumption goods from other capitalists, i.e. those of department II. There is therefore little need for increased cash-holding for the consumed surplus value of I.

Marx assumes that, under conditions of simple reproduction, capital intensity is the same in both departments. This in itself would not lead to a higher cash stock for liquidity purposes, unless the larger volume of capital in department I implies that its fixed capital is replaced in larger 'lumps' or 'humps' of investment. For instance, it might be that the installations and equipment of department I, because of their indivisibility, have to be replaced once at the end of the year, while those of department II may be replaced in small amounts over the course of the year. In this case, there would indeed be a reason for a higher cash holding in department II. However this may be, the fact that variable capital in department I has to take a longer road justifies higher cash-holding.

This problem certainly was envisaged by Marx, who says (ibid., p. 454),

the form of this renewal . . . may vary. The new purchases . . . may take place at more or at less prolonged intervals, then a large amount may be invested at one stroke, compensated by a corresponding productive supply [as with stocks of machinery]. Or the intervals between purchases may be small; then follows a rapid succession of money expenditures in small doses, of small productive supplies.

Under conditions of 'simple reproduction', Marx says,

> A large amount . . . [of fixed capital will be replaced] at one stroke. . . . But the money proceeds realised from the sale of commodities . . . settle down beside the productive capital and persist in the form of money. . . . This money then serves to replace the fixed capital . . . in kind. . . . The formation of this hoard is thus itself an element of the capitalist process of reproduction; it is the reproduction and storing up – in the form of money – of the value of fixed capital, or its several elements, . . . until [at the end of the depreciation period] the fixed capital has ceased to live and in consequence has given off its full value to the commodities produced and must now be replaced in kind.

Towards the end of the same chapter, Marx says (p. 477),

> We see, then, . . . that even simple reproduction, excluding accumulation proper, namely reproduction on an extended scale, necessarily includes the storing up, or hoarding, of money. And as this is annually repeated, it explains the assumption from which we started in the analysis of capitalist production, namely, that at the beginning of the reproduction a supply of money corresponding to the exchange of commodities is in the hands of capitalist classes I and II.

Following the above argument, he ought to have said that the cash should principally be in the hands of the capitalists in I, since their advances to their workers return to them only after a detour _via_ department II. At this juncture, Marx does not think of what is now called the Lohmann–Ruchti or Eisner–Domar effect, i.e. capacity enlargements through the use of depreciation funds, which means that there will be no formation of idle cash balances, because the money will be continuously reinvested. In so far as he did not deal with a growing economy, Marx did not, in this context, need to take note of the Lohmann–Ruchti effect, which is applicable only to growing firms, in which net investment can be financed largely out of funds set aside for depreciation.

On the other hand, hoarding means a decrease in the velocity of circulation of money, the amortisation of debts and, therefore, a reduction in the effective quantity of money, such as would occur in a recession. Indeed, simple reproduction, which does not seem to be compatible with capitalism, appears as a snapshot of the economy at the upper turning point of the business cycle, when an interruption in the circular flow leads to hoarding or the destruction of money, so that a part of effective demand disappears. Conversely, simple reproduction can appear as a picture of the stagnation of the economy at the bottom of a recession.

In this way we are already linking the phenomenon of business cycles to the condition of simple reproduction. Before dealing more extensively with this point, we must stress that Marx gives a double answer to his question about the origin of the money required to finance the circular flow. First, in the *static* sense, with regard to cash holding, he writes (ibid., p. 482),

> Therefore the quantity of money which circulates the annual product exists in society, having been gradually accumulated. It does not belong to the value produced during the given year, except perhaps the gold used to make good the loss of depreciated coins. This exposition presupposes the exclusive circulation of precious metals as money . . . although money can function also as a means of payment, and has actually done so in the course of history . . . and though a credit system and certain aspects of its mechanism have developed upon that basis.

Secondly there is Marx's *dynamic* answer (ibid., p. 480): 'Every industrial capital . . . throws at one fling money into circulation . . . which it recovers but gradually, in the course of years.' Here we touch upon the phenomenon of distribution, which we have examined in Volume I.

SIMPLE REPRODUCTION AND BUSINESS CYCLES

For Marx, capitalism is in the long run incompatible with simple reproduction. In a capitalist system, which is inseparably linked to growth and synonymous with 'extended reproduction', it can appear only temporarily. Marx declares right at the outset (*Capital*, II, ch. 20, p. 399) that 'the absence of all accumulation or reproduction on an extended scale is a strange assumption in capitalist conditions. . . . However, as far as accumulation does take place, simple reproduction is always a part of it, and can therefore be studied by itself, and is an actual factor of accumulation'.

Rosa Luxemburg found (1913; 1966, p. 134) a striking formulation for this phenomenon: 'Simple reproduction on a capitalist basis is an imaginary unit in theoretical economics, a scientifically justified and indispensable unit, like $\sqrt{-1}$ in mathematics. . . .'

As far as it does exist in capitalism, Marx thinks that simple reproduction has the role of a constant minimum – somewhat comparable to the 'under-employment equilibrium' of Keynes, but going beyond it. Such a temporary equilibrium can also occur at the upper turning point of the business cycle, but there it is inherently unstable. Simple reproduction would be a stationary state resembling the economy of the medieval artisan – an intermediate stage between 'simple commodity production' and capitalism – in which, as compared with its predecessor, there is only one new phenomenon: that equilibrium need not prevail.

Marx's formula for simple reproduction – II $c = $ I $v +$ I s – contains the

possibility of disturbance. This can occur when, for instance, 'the total
production of I for II_c remains unchanged'. It then happens that 'the
greater part of fixed capital II_c . . . flows to I. . . . So there is a greater flow
of money to I', which 'acts only onesidedly in the function of a means of
purchase. . . . A greater portion of I_s . . . would not therefore be convertible into commodities II, but would persist in the form of money . . .'
(*Capital*, II, ch. 20, p. 471).

In essence, Marx is here describing an inflationary process. The demand
for means of production increases and cannot be satisfied from current
production. Department I realises profits because its prices must rise. Marx
did not expressly admit that such a process creates the conditions for
extended reproduction. Department I can invest its profits, attracting
resources even from II, and thus create the additional means of production
to make good the worn-out assets of II_c and perhaps to increase the total
capacity of the economy, which would lead us to extended reproduction.

Marx, however, aims at something else, although he deals with this new
aspect only laconically: 'The opposite case, in which the reproduction of
demises of fixed capital II in a certain year is less and on the contrary the
depreciation part greater' [this means that the production in I, i.e. $I v + I m$,
which serves to cover depreciation costs in II_c, is too high] 'needs no further
discussion' (ibid., p. 472).

Marx is evidently thinking here of the case in which department II pays
less than hitherto for the constant capital it purchases from I. In this case,
part of the product of I remains unsold, either because the economic life of
assets in II is longer than was foreseen, or because rationalisation measures
lead to a better use of resources and to savings of raw and auxiliary
materials (Marx here considers II c only from a microeconomic point of
view). Both cases are clearly exposed in Marx's reasoning.

> There would [then] be a crisis – a crisis of over-production – in spite of
> reproduction on an unchanging scale [i.e. even without a preceding
> growth process]. In short, if under simple reproduction and other
> unchanged conditions – particularly under unchanged productive
> power, total volume and intensity of labour – no constant proportion is
> assumed between expiring fixed capital (to be renewed) and fixed
> capital . . . the total production I would have to grow [so that
> department I could supply the missing parts of constant capital to II to
> allow it to replace its assets, but then the lid would have been blown off
> simple reproduction, and extended reproduction would take place!]
> or . . . there would be a deficit in reproduction. (Ibid., p. 472.)

This would be the case where department I does not produce enough. 'In
the other case, if the size of fixed capital II [is] to be reproduced in
kind . . . then . . . [this would mean] either decrease in aggregate pro-

duction of 1, or surplus . . . and surplus that is not to be converted into money' (ibid.).

Here we have two aspects. First there is a boom in certain industries, setting off inflationary processes and destroying the framework of the stationary economy and sending it sliding willy-nilly into growth. Secondly, there is in department 1 a sectoral crisis, caused by technological conditions or rationalisation, which leads to a recession and to a departure from stationary equilibrium. In other words, the stationary situation is not immune from disturbances. Thus Marx states (ibid., p. 473),

> This illustration of fixed capital, on the basis of an unchanged scale of reproduction, is striking. A disproportion of the production of fixed and circulating capital is one of the favourite arguments of the economists in explaining crises. That such a disproportion can and must arise even when the fixed capital is merely *preserved*, that it can and must do so on the assumption of ideal normal production on the basis of simple reproduction of the already functioning social capital is something new to them.

Here Marx succeeds in simultaneously proving two things. First, he shows that business cycles need not be a by-product of growth processes. Secondly, he shows how it is that the upper turning point can, at the very moment when industrial production stagnates at a high level, lead over into a recession. These are original ideas to which we shall return in the next chapter.

In this context, we need only, in order to disprove the idea that business cycles are nothing but an offshoot of the growth process, point out that Kaldor tried to give a similar demonstration some eighty years later. Kaldor's 'static model' has no trend:

> [This] shows that it is not necessary to assume economic growth or dynamic change in order to account for the existence of fluctuations. . . . It strongly suggests therefore that economic growth, as well as other dynamic and erratic changes, should be treated rather as the cause of aberrations from the pure rhythm of the static cycle than as a *sine qua non* without which the basic phenomena would not be accounted for.   (Kaldor, 1954, p. 61.)

6 Extended Reproduction and Growth Theory

At first sight, the examples Marx gives of his famous schemes of extended reproduction or growth are far from clear. Rosa Luxemburg has complained of this, and we shall come back to her criticism later. In modern times, this complaint has been echoed by Krelle, who in three essays pays homage to Marx's work on growth, but remarks (1970, p. 93):

> The greatest part of the analysis is verbal or consists of numerical examples. As we are concerned with a dynamic analysis in which it is well-nigh impossible to find a general solution in verbal terms or by numerical examples, Marx again and again breaks off his calculations and tries new ones without reaching a definitive result. It therefore is not easy to follow his demonstration. Marx himself did not think that his work was ripe for publication. . . . His text is thus not easily readable, and this is probably the reason why the Marxian growth theory of the second volume [of Capital] has not influenced economists and has not found the recognition it merits. Modern growth theory started afresh at the end of the 1930s, independently of Marx and at a lower level.

Capitalists of department I always 'accumulate' (i.e. save and invest) 50 per cent of their surplus value. On the other hand, capitalists of department II have had to experience a number of corrections to their original rate of accumulation, in order to preserve the identity of the formula $I\,v + I\,s = II\,c$ as postulated by Marx, and in order to meet the requirements of I through new investment in consumption goods. Furthermore, Marx combines at each stage two phases: the current one, in which goods are produced and income generated; and the next one, in which savings and investment take place.

The Gordian knot of the schemes, which are not clearly set out in the tables but are in the text, may be untied only if one examines them point by point from one year to the next.

SCHEME NO. 1

FIRST YEAR

Marx starts from the following situation, in which it is particularly striking that the 'organic composition of capital' is different for each department (in I, 4 : 1; and, in II, 2 : 1):

TABLE II

$$
\begin{array}{rl}
\text{I} & 4000\ c + 1000\ v + 1000\ s = 6000 \\
\text{II} & 1500\ c + 750\ v + 750\ s = 3000 \\
\hline
\text{Social product} & 9000
\end{array}
$$

Of a total of 3000 units of consumption goods produced, only 2850 are consumed: 1500 by workers and capitalists in department I and 1350 by workers and capitalists in department II, for the capitalists in II save 20 per cent, i.e. 150-units worth, of their surplus value.

In the same year, 6000 units of the means of production are produced, but only 5500 are consumed: 4000 in department I, 1500 in II. The capitalists in I save 50 per cent of their income, i.e. 500 units. The first year thus begins with uniform rates of surplus value (100 per cent in Marxian terms, i.e. 50 per cent of value added), but with different saving rates (I, 50 per cent; II, 20 per cent). The rates of profit are also unequal: 20 per cent in department I (1000/5000) and $33\frac{1}{3}$ per cent in department II (750/2250).

If Marx had not postulated that each group of capitalists could invest only in its own department, this divergence would have led to a flow of capital from I to II, seriously disturbing the prospects for further development.

SECOND YEAR

In the second year, input grows by the amount saved in the first year. The 150 units of consumption goods 'saved' (which would be the counterpart as a stock of goods to the 150 money units saved) can now be used to employ additional workers. 100 units are employed in department I and fifty in department II. These workers work not only for their own remuneration, but also provide 'surplus labour time', which represents 150 units of surplus value: again, 100 units in department I and fifty in department II.

Of 500 units of means of production 'saved' in department I, 400 are sold within the same department, and 100 are sold as a counterpart to 100 units of consumption goods (always against money) to department II.

The production results for the second year are thus:

TABLE III

$$
\begin{array}{rl}
\text{I} & 4400\ c + 1100\ v + 1100\ s = 6600 \\
\text{II} & 1600\ c + 800\ v + 800\ s = 3200 \\
\hline
\text{Social product} & 9800
\end{array}
$$

Thus the departments have grown at different rates – department I by 10 per cent and department II by only $6_2/3$ per cent. This results from the chosen point of departure and from the conditions of accumulation: department I saves again 50 per cent of its surplus value, and department II more than before, i.e. 30 per cent. Thus the capitalists in II retain for consumption only 560 units of surplus value, i.e. less than in the first year, when they could still consume 600 units!

Rosa Luxemburg is right in saying that this is 'in any case a very strange result of accumulation'. One could explain it by assuming that these capitalists wanted to make a particularly large, once-and-for-all investment effort. This realistically conveys something of the nature of an investment boom.

Rosa Luxemburg has emphasised, however, that this investment effort is to the detriment of the capitalists in II. In her words, this process shows 'drastically how Marx pushes through accumulation in I to the detriment of II' (this is reminiscent of the theory of the German economist Arndt, who says – 1966b, II, p. 188 – that dominant enterprises eat up the reserves of the weaker ones).

SUBSEQUENT YEARS

For the subsequent years, we follow the commentary of Rosa Luxemburg, who forthrightly depicts (1913; 1966, p. 94) the confusing complexity of the Marxian calculations:

Marx deals as unkindly with the capitalists of department II in the following years. In the third year, following the same rule, he lets them accumulate 264 s and consume 616, this time more than in both preceding years. In the fourth year, he allows them to capitalise 290 and to consume 678. In the fifth year, they accumulate 320 and consume 745. On this Marx says, 'If the affair is to be settled normally, accumulation in II must proceed more rapidly than in I, because the part of I $(v+s)$ which has to be transformed into commodities II_c, would otherwise grow more rapidly than II_c, against which it can only be exchanged.'

The numbers indicated not only show no faster accumulation but in fact show fluctuating accumulation in department II. The rule is as follows: Marx persistently advances the process of accumulation, by letting department I produce on a larger scale; accumulation in department II appears only as a consequence and condition of accumulation in I . . . First, in order to take up the surplus means of production, and, secondly, to supply the necessary surplus consumption goods for the additional labourers. The initiative in movement lies all the time with department I, to which department II is a passive adjunct. Thus capitalists in II can each time only accumulate and consume as much as is required for accumulation in I . . . .

In reading these words of Rosa Luxemburg, one is almost tempted to suppose that Marx intuitively anticipated the reasoning of the Russian Bolsheviks, who preached the primacy of heavy industry. Rosa Luxemburg's judgement (ibid., p. 95) is harsh:

> There is no evident order in this accumulation in department I. That the absolute figures of the scheme in each equation are arbitrary is a matter of fact and in no way reduces its scientific value. What matter are the ratios, which are supposed to express exact relationships. The accumulation ratios in department I are dictated by clear regularity, but this seems to be purchased at the cost of a completely arbitrary construction of the conditions in department II . . . .

It is paradoxical that a Marxist of Rosa Luxemburg's standing should pass such a harsh judgement on Marx's scheme no. 1, while modern growth analysts such as Ott and Krelle derive from the same scheme their conviction that Marx is the father of modern growth theory.

These authors are much more forgiving towards Marx's inconsistencies than the Marxists are, for they round off his figures. For instance, Krelle says (1970, p. 93),

> Marx, who (as he himself regretfully states) had inadequate mathematical instruction, could unfortunately not proceed analytically, but had to content himself with numerical examples. It is not difficult, however, to indicate the general solution to his problem. Marx's theory is a two-sector model, a type of model which has only recently been tackled by economics – which shows how far in advance of his time Marx was in this part of his work. One must admire all the more what has been achieved by Marx with inadequate means . . . .

What has been particularly criticised is that the rate of profit – according to the Marxian method of calculation, $s/(c+v)$ – in department I is permanently below that in department II, i.e. 20 per cent, as compared to $33 1/3$ per cent in II. If one calculates this rate of profit as a percentage of turnover, it is $16 2/3$ per cent in I and 25 per cent in II. Marx may have been thinking of this difference in the rate of profit when he remarked, 'If the affair is to be settled normally, accumulation in II must proceed more rapidly than in I . . . .' Rosa Luxemburg justly makes the criticism that this does not happen at all. Marx's remark cannot be applied to the process of accumulation as such, for I constantly accumulates 50 per cent of surplus value and II only 30 per cent (in the first year only 20 per cent!). Neither does the remark apply to the share of investment in turnover: this amounts on average to 8·33 per cent in I and to 7·5 per cent in II.

It is interesting to note that these very inequalities, which are the reason for the scheme's built-in disequilibria, are what make it from the very outset unusable for a theory of harmonic development. Was this intentional?

If there is nevertheless steady growth of 10 per cent from the second year onwards, this is to be explained by the fact that what can be called the 'quasi capital–output ratio', $c/v + s$, remains constant in both sectors, at 4 and 2 respectively. This difference in the rate of profit ultimately reflects a difference in the share of value added in the departmental gross product, and this also explains why department II does not sooner experience a decline in its share in the total gross social product, despite the higher rate of saving and accumulation of department I.

Joan Robinson thinks (1951) that this difference in the rate of profit is simply a mistake, in view of the Marxian theory that profit rates tend to be equalised. One could perhaps explain this difference by the existence of stronger monopolistic tendencies in the consumption-goods sector. One could also ask whether it was not Marx's intention, by means of this 'trick', to justify his postulate, which Rosa Luxemburg criticised as unfulfilled, that II would have to accumulate faster than I.

One must also ask whether the difference in the rate of profit was not perhaps introduced to illustrate further possible disequilibria. If there were no monopolistic barriers, or if they could be overcome, capital would normally flow from department I to department II.

Monopolistic barriers could also perhaps be explained by the hypothesis, which appears in the works of several modern authors (for instance, Solow and Seton) that means of production are produced by artisans, while consumption goods are produced by large-scale industrial concerns. This, however, is contradicted in Marx's model by the high capital–output ratio in department I. If this coefficient were the same in both departments, as it is in Marx's scheme no. 2, the hypothesis would be more plausible. If one assumes that such monopolistic barriers exist, Kaldor's reasoning (1954, p. 60) would seem to apply: 'If . . . entrepreneurial expectation in the capital-goods industries were more sluggish than in the consumption-goods industries [and it must be, if profits lag behind those of department II for years!] it is quite possible that the capacity of the capital-goods industries was maintained at too low a level to secure full employment in boom periods . . . .'

In this case this seems to be true. Indeed, the postulate that labour must be constantly available means, after all, that full employment is never reached. One must then ask oneself whether such a situation can in the long run really be considered one of equilibrium.

It is true that the growth process is measured in 'values' in Marx's schemes, not in output or volume. Thus labour productivity cannot be measured directly and must be considered to remain constant. It would only be possible to measure the real growth of the social product

(1) if we assume that the increase in v does not signify that additional

labour is being hired, but that it means a rise in real wages for a constant number of labourers;

(2) if therefore the ratio of c to the *number* of labourers were to rise, which in turn would mean that their productivity had risen through the increasing use of fixed capital (one could simultaneously assume with Burchardt that c, macroeconomically speaking, does not include raw and auxiliary materials as such, but is made up of fixed assets, machinery, and so on);

(3) if the investment of parts of s in v means that higher wages are paid for the same number of labourers, i.e. relatively more labour is being used for wage goods (investment of parts of s in c means then that fixed capital is being created at the same pace as real wages rise).

THE PROBLEM OF VALUE IN THE GROWTH SCHEME

In the case of simple reproduction there were no difficulties of the kind discussed in the previous section, because Marx postulated one level of 'organic composition of capital'.

In Volume I, we spoke of a 'second transformation problem', which occurs as soon as growth processes and price rises occur. In this case, the value calculation seems to leave us in the lurch as soon as the situation is reached where labour input remains the same (computed as 'socially necessary' labour time) but prices per unit of output do not decrease proportionately to increasing productivity. It seems paradoxical that a value theory which in the end is to serve anti-capitalist tendencies has to use as a counterpart the ideal of neo-liberal competitive capitalism, which contains within itself the Utopian hope of conquering the bacillus of inflation, and which assumes that it is possible continually to pass on to consumers the benefits of increased productivity, in the form of reductions in price. In a world of imperfect competition, such a hope looks Utopian indeed.

Samuelson remains unduly fascinated by the 'first transformation problem', which gave rise to a debate with Baumol and Morishima as late as 1974. Baumol blames Samuelson for having wrongly attributed to Marx a labour theory of value. He reminds him that Stigler demonstrated, with regard to Ricardo, that the classical economists used the labour theory of value only for expository purposes. He goes on to say that Marx was by no means hankering after a substitute for a theory of price, but tried to find an answer to the question of how non-wage incomes were produced and distributed. Marx measures the contribution of each industry to the social product by its labour input, while what each industry takes out of the fund of surplus value as 'profit' is measured by the quantity of capital it uses. According to Baumol, 'transformation theory' tries to answer the question, 'under what circumstances will a given industry withdraw more than it has contributed?'

Samuelson objects that Marx's analysis of distribution trends, business cycles and growth has been hamstrung by his newfangled value analysis. Samuelson goes on to argue, especially in his contribution to a symposium of essays in honour of Metzler, that this was an unnecessary detour. In a postscript, he refers to Wolfstetter, who maintains that for normative planning in a socialist system it is prices, not values, that are of paramount importance.

Morishima stresses that decisions are taken by individuals and firms in terms of prices, since values represent only the technocratic requirements for labour input. All three authors seem, nevertheless, to overlook the particular problems which arise for value theory within a dynamic framework. (Baumol, Samuelson and Morishima, 1974, pp. 32–3, 69, 71, 76.)

We here encounter a formidable problem in value theory. A growing mass of 'use values' with possibly rising prices appears nowhere at all in a calculation which in effect measures not output but only inputs.

Values incorporate only the 'socially necessary' labour time expended for production, and this is expressed in money in Marx's analysis. The increase in 'use values' is nowadays measured by volume indices, i.e. at constant prices based on a particular year; and, though this movement in the physical volume of production is not reflected in value analysis at all, it is the essence of growth analysis to show the increase in production volumes. Here we encounter a glaring contradiction. The increase in the volume of the social product cannot be measured by values if they represent only the same social labour time. In other words, if twice as much can be produced with the same average social labour time, the sum of values remains the same, while the real social product doubles. For this reason, the concept of values is ill adapted to measure growth processes.

'EFFICIENCY UNITS' AND THE PROBLEM OF AN 'INVARIABLE' MEASURE OF VALUE

The schemes of extended reproduction show a continuous increase in inputs. The sum of values increases only as far as new labour and new means of production are engaged in the production process. Labourers work for constant wages and supply, over and above the labour time required to cover their wages, a quantity of surplus labour time, which leads to an increase in surplus value proportionate to the increase in labour input. Constant capital also keeps growing in proportion to the additional use of labour. The principle of identity between the sum of values and the sum of prices over time can be maintained only if one uses a concept of 'efficiency units'. In this case, the increasing productivity of a constant quantity of physically measured 'socially necessary' labour hours would find its expression not in the notion of a 'decreasing sum of values', but in that of an increasing sum of efficiency units.

Such a conception could be happily reconciled with that simplification of Marxian reasoning which is to be found early in volume III of *Capital*, where Marx simply identifies value with wages (i.e. 'socially necessary' labour time multiplied by current average wages). This also bears a resemblance to Fourastié's attempt to declare as a measure of value for a period the average real wage of a manual worker, such as a hairdresser, who does not rely on a large amount of fixed capital. Finally, it could be compared to similar experiments made by the somewhat bizarre *Valoristie* school, founded by Michelet in the mid-thirties, which flourished in the 1950s. Michelet tried to make the varying 'value' of the average hour of labour a yardstick for each period (see Michelet, 1936).

These would indeed be variable yardsticks that could represent only a kind of typical social average, and they would come near to what Keynes proposed as a wages standard. It is true that several quite different conceptions seem to merge harmoniously in this new notion, but it remains a fact that 'value' would no longer be a single yardstick but would change each time productivity changes; i.e. 'value' would grow proportionately to what it purports to measure!

Incidentally, such a solution would vindicate Ricardo's statement in *Principles of Political Economy* (1817; 1951, p. 27) that an 'invariable standard measure of value . . . is impossible . . . because there is no commodity which is not itself exposed to the same variations as the things the value of which is to be ascertained'. Ricardo always upheld this thesis – for instance, in letters addressed to McCulloch (in 1820 and 1823) and Malthus (in 1823).

Marx did not explicitly state that, in a dynamic capitalist world, labour loses the characteristic of an invariable yardstick; this applies also to his notion of labour power and its emanation 'socially necessary' labour time. From Marx's own logic and his postulate of a constant value of money, which one cannot explain away by distinguishing between 'constant value of money' and 'constant value of gold', in von Bortkiewicz's sense, it inexorably follows that these propositions will have to be defined. To this extent, we must admit that Peter was right in saying (1934, II, p. 38),

> It was tempting for the old theoreticians of labour value to try and introduce labour as an arbitrary yardstick. Since we have defined the 'allergic economy' [Peter's term for dynamic capitalism!] precisely by the statement that the law of labour value does not apply to it, we shall of course refrain from opening the back door to the wrong price theory . . . .

Marx argues in the same way as Peter, for he admits (*Capital*, III, ch. 10,

p. 177) that the simple labour theory of value cannot apply to capitalism: 'The exchange of commodities at their values. . . thus requires a much lower stage than their exchange at their prices of production.'

One might be tempted to leave it at that and to state simply, with regard to dynamic conditions, that we reason only in prices of production, leaving the value problem aside. In so doing, we should after all, act in the same way as Marx in volume III of *Capital*, and as many of his commentators have done. There are, however, two difficulties.

First, we cannot appeal to the assumption, which Samuelson recognised as potentially disarming, that the 'organic composition of capital' (the capital:wage-bill ratio) is the same in all industries. Marx did indeed introduce this simplification in his second scheme of extended reproduction. In the first he does not make this assumption, and to that extent one can say that the reasoning in volume II of *Capital* is not based on the labour theory of value. After all, this would not be admissible in an analysis of dynamic conditions.

Secondly, we must not forget that modern theory has produced what amounts to a refined version of Marxian value theory: Sraffa's theory of 'dated labour' (see Harcourt and Massaro, 1964, pp. 715ff.). Such parallels have not yet been fully exploited by modern Marxists.

There are two ways in which one might try to escape from these difficulties. First there is the view, advanced by de Cindio (1967, pp. 101ff.), that the monetarily interpreted values in Marx's works are nothing but prices, where profits are proportionate to the wage bill or to the share of wages in the total sum of costs; this would be, as it were, a sort of mark-up on wages. Such an interpretation is hardly tenable, since Marx did not accept the mark-up theory.

Secondly there is the thesis, supported chiefly by Mandel (1972, p. 269), that Marxian 'prices' are not market prices at all, but rather values in the proper sense of the word, i.e. 'socially necessary' labour hours valued in money terms. Mandel thinks that when Marx speaks of prices he means only to indicate that within these magnitudes surplus value is corrected in such a way that it is proportionate not to variable capital but to constant capital: 'As a matter of fact, such production prices in Marx's terminology are not "prices" in the current sense of the word, but only the result of the redistribution of social surplus value among the various industries.'

If we accept this interpretation, the confrontation of values and prices in the Marxian sense would have nothing to do with the opposition between the principle of profit calculation on the basis of labour inputs and that of price formation in the market, but would simply be a matter of the modification of the method of exposition within the framework of the same Marxian value scheme.

However this may be, it cannot be denied that the notion of 'socially necessary' labour time remains somewhat nebulous, given that technical progress leads to a continual reduction in such labour time for a given product. In practice, decreasing 'costs' in the sense of the labour value ought to lead to decreasing market prices. Monetary evolution leads to a secular rise in the global price level, and this constitutes an additional objection at least to the practical applicability of the labour theory of value for longer periods and *a fortiori* for the analysis of secular growth processes.

THE DICHOTOMY BETWEEN VALUE THEORY AND INFLATION ACCORDING TO HOFMANN

The problem of the applicability of value theory therefore becomes particularly acute in periods of growth, which go hand in hand with inflationary tendencies. Such an eminent Marxist as Hofmann, in a book he wrote in collaboration with Abendroth, saw in these inflationary elements the really decisive objections to value theory. He rejected the current objections to value theory. If one says that value theory neglects the demand side, one forgets that demand is contained within the notion of 'socially necessary' labour time, and that Marx wanted to criticise precisely the fact that capitalism neglected use values, as opposed to exchange values. Marx is criticised for ignoring the productivity of capital and land, but he surely recognises their *physical* productivity in use values. One can only make the criticism that the value concept does not permit a numerical presentation of such use values, but this is equally true of the pure capitalist accounting system, which reckons in money units.

Furthermore, it is said that labour values are generally immeasurable. Hofmann agrees, but he reminds us that this is equally true of subjective values such as 'marginal utility' and 'disutility of work', and that purely theoretical concepts have been applied by many economists, including Keynes, Fisher and Hawtrey. However, Hofmann accepts as valid (1971, pp. 117–18) two other criticisms:

> In so far as labour value is regarded as the 'fundamental' basis of price movements, the theory cannot be defended against one theoretical and one empirical objection. . . . The level of socially necessary labour time is given by the state of technology. . . . But the level of productive technique (actually applied) depends on the interest managers show in technical development . . . and therefore on the volume of research and investment in improvements, etc. Given conditions of pricing and profit opportunities enter into the development of technology and determine the way capital is distributed over different industries and is used (for investment in rationalisation or simple 'capital widening') . . . .

In other words, the labour value or the pace of its decrease per unit of output depends on the capitalists' propensity to invest, to rationalise, and to favour research. This touches upon the problem, mentioned above, of efficiency units.

The second valid objection that Hofmann mentions (ibid., p. 116) concerns inflation:

> In our epoch of secular inflation, there can be no question of theoretical values moving in step with actual market prices. Labour productivity has increased vastly during this century, and the 'labour value' of the average commodity would, therefore, have to be considered as having been considerably reduced, but in spite of that the price level for all commodities has increased to an extraordinary extent in all industrial countries. . . . The trend of prices has evidently been completely dissociated from the trend of theoretical values, so that there is no longer any cyclical evening out of prices, which would result in a decreasing level of average prices. Under these circumstances, there can be no question of prices being determined by the [long-run] evolution of labour values. Such a constant distortion of the price level cannot be neutral with regard to the global economic process; it must have far-reaching repercussions on net production, on the expansion of physical assets and on the volume, proportion and structure of production . . . .

If we consider these repercussions on the expansion of the productive system, we reach the conclusion that the use of 'values' cannot be considered feasible for extended reproduction or for economic dynamics in general. Yet, though Hofmann goes on to say, 'There is no evidence that Marxist theory has succeeded, in our times, in interpreting the phenomenon of "secular inflation" on the basis of labour values, or that it even made an attempt to do so', a courageous attempt in this direction has in fact been made by Mandel. Mandel speaks (1972, pp. 373ff.) of an attempt in Marx's work 'to overcome the dualism, as Ricardo saw it, between the labour theory of value, which purports to determine commodity values, and the quantity theory determining the "value of money"'.

In a pure value calculation, the additional hours of labour, which find their expression in surplus value, can appear in the second period only in a 'crystallised' form, as stock of goods and machinery to be used as soon as additional labour is hired for the production of additional means of production and consumption goods. A certain quantity of (crystallised) labour hours is not consumed by capitalists in the first period, when accumulation starts. For the moment, we leave out of consideration the fact that capitalists in department I could not have consumed this surplus value (or these surplus labour hours), crystallised in the form of a certain stock of the means of production, because there were not enough consumption goods in stock in department II as the counterpart of this surplus value.

In the second period, the 'accumulated' (or 'saved') stocks of the means of production and consumption goods are used. Department I obtains from II in exchange for its accumulated means of production the consumption goods it needs in order to hire additional labour. Department II uses the means of production it gets from I, together with a part of its accumulated consumption goods, to hire labour, in order to increase the production of consumption goods. Department I combines hired labour, paid with the goods it draws from II, with its accumulated means of production, to increase the latter. This is the situation if we maintain the fiction that each department relies on barter; but, following Marx, who from the outset used money in his reproduction schemes, we do not assume this.

The introduction of money raises a number of peculiar questions which must be clarified.

CAPITAL AND MONEY IN THE GROWTH PROCESS

Various passages in *Capital* lead us to assume that Marx developed his theory of value on the assumption that the value of money would not change. This assumption is mere wishful thinking in the face of increasing productivity; lower costs, if translated into lower prices, mean a higher value of money, unless offset by its increased quantity or velocity. We may suppose that Marx's assumption is more or less based on the conditions of his times, for between 1863 and 1867, when volumes III and I of *Capital* were written, the general price level was indeed remarkably stable. Sauerbeck's index (in Schlote, 1938, pp. 179–82) shows between 1862 and 1867 a variation of only 2 or 3 per cent around the 120 mark (1913 = 100). According to this index, there was almost complete price stability from 1854 to 1867. A sharp decrease in prices began in the middle of the 1870s and lasted until the 1890s, with the lowest point being reached around 1894–7, with the index at 72 or 73. This might indeed have been considered as evidence of decreasing 'values', i.e. of productivity increases being reflected in decreasing prices. In these circumstances it would be impossible to uphold the thesis of a constant value of money. Thus the problem of money assumes great importance in the framework of the growth process.

Another basic Marxian postulate derived from the value concept contradicts the idea of a constant value of money, for Marx assumed (*Capital*, III, ch. 9, pp. 159–60) that, if one considered the social product as a whole, the sum of 'prices of production' ought to equal the sum of values: 'in society – the totality of all branches of production – [it] is equal to the sum of their values'. This postulate then conflicts with that of a constant value of money, if values decrease with rising productivity. This shows that the value concept is full of pitfalls, if we consider growth processes.

Indeed, from the concept of a constant value of money it would follow logically that prices per unit of commodity or for a representative basket of commodities would fall with increasing productivity. On this Marx is unmistakable (ibid., ch. 13, p. 230):

> the price of the individual commodity may fall as a result of greater productiveness of labour and a simultaneous increase in the number of this cheaper commodity if, for instance, the increase in productiveness of labour acts uniformly and simultaneously on all the elements of the commodity, so that its total price falls in the same proportion in which the productivity of labour increases . . . .

Thus Marx implicitly drops the assumption of a constant value of money. There is no knowing whether this was directly owing to the fall in prices during the 1870s, though we do know that the bulk of the manuscript of volume I of *Capital* was written later than that of volume III.

De deux choses une, say the French. On the one hand, if the value of money remains constant, then with increasing productivity and output the sum of prices must grow, since the price per unit of output does not vary. If, though the sum of prices has risen, the sum of inputs, i.e. labour hours, remains the same, the sum of values does not increase and values and prices fall apart.

On the other hand, if we accept Marx's postulate that the sum of values must equal the sum of prices, then, with increasing productivity and the same sum of values, price per unit of output must fall, so that the sum of prices and values remains equal. In this case the value of money increases!

This was indeed what happened from the 1870s to the end of the nineteenth century, and it was to repeat itself in the 1930s. Ever since, prices have been on the increase, and this fact of secular inflation is at odds with value theory. As it happens, growth appears to be more or less synonymous with a price level that rises in the long run. Extended reproduction, which was for Marx synonymous with capitalist growth, can not, therefore, be very well analysed within the framework of value theory.

Peter has argued (1934, II, p. 37) that Marx tried to do away with the problems arising from inflationary and deflationary tendencies by a heroic assertion: he simply decreed that the value of money should be invariable in the system considered.

> Marx underlines this point, even if summarily, for the transformation problem . . . and the problem of a progressive economy. This is wrong in both cases, but for different reasons. In the case of transformation, we had to deal with a comparison of two models and not with a real process. Here the yardstick for the price of money was modified at the same time as the measures for other commodities were.

Even, therefore, in the case of the transformation of values into prices, the value of money in no way remains constant, least of all if – following von

Bortkiewicz – it is assumed that the commodity value of money is represented by gold. (Marx still maintains this assumption, at least for simple reproduction!) Peter goes on to say (ibid.): 'Here [i.e. in a progressive economy] we encounter real modifications in the value of gold, which coincide with modifications in the value of other commodities.'

The problem of money, therefore, appears in the framework of extended reproduction, because of Marx's working assumptions. These, contrary to his normal reasoning in matters of dynamics, temporarily divert attention from the credit system. This is not really practical, because Marx needs money in his system, since the exchange between departments I and II is by no means founded on barter. A flow of money appears parallel to that of commodities and is the very condition of it. Money is by no means a 'veil' for Marx, as it is in Say's law, which Marx in fact rejected for this reason, in the same way as he refused to accept the conclusions that Ricardo drew from it. Indeed, in his *Theories of Surplus Value* he repeatedly rejects the idea of the 'veil of money', which had been so dear to the classical economists: 'Money is not only "the medium by which the exchange is effected" . . . . but at the same time the medium by which the exchange of product with product is divided into two acts, which are independent of each other, and separate in time and space' (*Theories*, II, Ch. 17, p. 504).

This passage, especially in the Kautsky edition, is of great importance, for it settles what actually happens in the Marxian reproduction schemes. It is not a question of a barter operation (product for product) between department I and II, but of purchases and sales, in which money plays its part. We must also take into account that in both stages there may be a telescoping of phases within each 'year'. We see in Marx's polemics against Say, James Mill and Ricardo that it may even happen in simple reproduction that department I buys from II, paying in money, but II does not buy from I or *vice versa*. Money introduces a source of disturbance. This fact is proof enough that it would be a fundamental mistake to suppose that Marx intended that his schemes should illustrate a sort of prestabilised harmony in capitalist development.

The Marxian postulate of no changes in the value of money can certainly be accepted as a working hypothesis. It must not, however, be linked to the further assumption, held for much of volume II of *Capital*, that we deal with 'values' and not with prices of production.

In the same context Marx mentions (*Capital*, III, Ch. 21, p. 497) that 'these potential capitals within the credit system, by their concentration in the hands of banks, etc., become disposable, "loanable capital", money-capital, which indeed is no longer passive and music of the future, but active capital growing rank'. This is one of the few places in which Marx mentions growth. It is particularly interesting because he seems to have been fully conscious of the fact that even the 'hoards' of liquid financial means accumulated by a particular firm or industry could form the basis for credit creation and growth in a wider context.

Nevertheless, he goes on to say (ibid., p. 505) that he provisionally eliminates credit problems for his analysis of the reproduction schemes, so as to ensure that 'the matter appears in primitive form instead of the later, reflected form . . . under the credit system . . . .'

THE EXTENSIVE GROWTH SCHEME AND MODERN THEORY

We must repeat that the Marxian schemes are conceived in 'values', i.e. in 'socially necessary' labour hours expressed in money. The growth process is thereby measured in (growing) inputs. Indeed, it is not the quantity of goods which appears, but only the increased input of labour hours (of equal efficiency) required to produce that quantity.

If one takes this into consideration, it appears that the Marxian schemes represent a purely extensive conception of growth. They presuppose that there is not full employment, and that labour resources are inexhaustible. Rosa Luxemburg's 'third persons' appear in this context not as consumers but as (foreign?) workers.

In modern analyses such as that of Ott, the extensive character of the Marxian schemes is explicitly recognised. For instance, Ott says (1967, pp. 637–8): 'In his growth theory, Marx works with investment, which is of a "widening" nature and is not linked to technical progress. It requires a constant input relationship between capital and labour and a constant productivity of capital and labour.'

This has tempted some authors, such as Samuelson, into assuming that Marx constructed his theory on the assumption that the capital–output ratio is invariable. Nothing could be further from the truth. Marx himself, in his theory of the tendency of the rate of profit to fall, laid great stress on such variability and on substitution effects, although it is true that he regarded the latter as being biased towards labour-saving processes.

On closer inspection we must, however, qualify the view that the Marxian scheme of extended reproduction is a purely input-based growth scheme. In Marx's eyes, the input 'labour' has a peculiar quality within value analysis: the labour hours worked are not limited to those required to produce the value equivalent of wages, but extend to the extra hours required to create surplus value for capitalists. Every newly hired worker immediately creates surplus value, even if the increased production or capacity leads to lower prices and therefore to the destruction of 'values' in the capitalist sense.

Even if we regard the Marxian schemes as purely value constructions, they are not quite limited to extensive growth reflecting the expansion of inputs. On the contrary, a certain real growth process takes place in so far as every new worker by definition increases the sum of surplus value, and this happens in both departments.

Now, nothing obliges us to interpret the schemes in value terms only.

One may even be tempted to ignore value problems altogether. There is, however, one difficulty. In Marx's scheme no. 1 (*Capital*, 11, ch. 21), which we have already set out in detail, 'organic composition of capital' and the rate of profit are neither of them the same in both departments, so that the value and price schemes fall asunder and an equalisation process for profit rates ought to take place. The rate of profit amounts to 33⅓ per cent in department II and only 20 per cent in department I, but there is no capital flow from I to II.

We cannot here delve into the intricacies of capital theory, which has already received exhaustive analysis, especially by Harcourt (1972). We shall, however, attempt to translate the reproduction schemes into some of the current notions of 'academic' economics. This must not be interpreted as an acceptance of neo-neo-classical notions, particularly as the author is positively inclined towards the analysis by Joan Robinson, who is considered by Harcourt (ibid., p. 18) and Nell (1970, pp. 41–4) as a leader of the neo-Marxists rather than of the neo-Keynesians. Instead this attempt should be seen as one at translating some Marxian terms into notions that are currently in use and are readily intelligible to industrial economists. The translation is to be carried out in terms which, to quote Harcourt (1972, p. 93), are 'concerned with aggregation and approximation and [relate] to the empirical implications of saving and investment decisions'.

Here our discussion of capital theory must be restricted to what Solow calls 'lowbrow theory', as opposed to 'highbrow theory', in which Sraffa's approach and the Ricardo-based Marxian conception are foremost. The latter, however, can hardly be used to explain statistical and empirical data, since there are very few attempts on the Marxist side to make Marxist theory accessible to a broader public, and those that have been made have not found wide favour. Thus it may be justifiable to expound the problems of capital theory in non-esoteric language.

Nowhere is the incomplete character of the torso that *Capital* represents, so painfully evident as in this area, and nowhere else have Western Marxists so palpably failed. In its intellectually most dynamic period, through the endeavours of Groman, Basarov and Feldman, the Soviet Union has made a contribution to growth theory; but otherwise Marx's schemes have been left largely in their extensive state, although Marx elsewhere in his work gives some hints that might have proved helpful in developing them further. The introduction of technical progress would have given them an intensive and dynamic character. However, the predominance of inputs in value theory largely inhibited this, for in this theory technical progress could be expressed only as a reduction of inputs and not as a more than proportional increase in output in the process of growth.

Thus technical progress was not introduced. Yet, in his theory of the tendency of the rate of profit to fall, Marx had provided a starting point for its introduction. This in turn led to Otto Bauer's schemes and to an exaggerated interpretation by Grossmann. Generally speaking, Marxists did not dare go beyond the framework drawn by their master – a framework which did not foresee a long-run downward trend in the 'organic composition of capital', or quasi capital–output ratio.

The basic element of technical progress, i.e. the essential characteristic of capitalism, was not taken into account within these schemes. The principal sin of Marx's successors seems to have been not so much their acceptance of the cumbersomeness of the value scheme, as their failure to attempt to correct this. Not only did the field of growth theory become the province of the neo-Keynesians, but the latter even reformulated in detail the Marxian reproduction schemes, beginning with their assumption of fixed coefficients.

Thus the road was paved for a neo-neo-classical counter-offensive, which introduced into the debate the variability of the capital–output ratio, the importance of which Marx had been the first to enunciate. Yet, though Marx reached the conclusion that capitalism was fundamentally unstable, neo-neo-classical theory drew just the opposite conclusion. It was precisely the variability of the capital–output ratio that was supposed to give it stability!

THE MARXIAN SCHEMES IN MODERN (PRICE) TERMS

Let us now try to translate the terms used in the Marxian schemes of extended reproduction into modern notions such as social product, national income, saving and (fixed) investment. In this case it will be necessary, as has already been pointed out, to leave the value scheme completely out of the picture – as is now frequent in discussions of the Marxian schemes. We start from the hypothesis that 'Marx, as a general rule, assumes that an identity of values and prices prevails', and this means that

> his 'laws' can only be reasonably understood as referring to price theory. The rate of profit is in Marx's works ascertained on the basis of prices. Therefore . . . a detailed preoccupation with Marxian value theory is not necessary. Constant capital is identical with real capital use valued at the prices of its elements, variable capital corresponds to labour input valued in wages, and profit is equal to the difference between the price of the output and the price of the factors of production which entered into the process . . . .

This statement by Schmitt-Rink (1967, p. 137) specifically concerns the law of the tendency of the rate of profit to fall, but one may argue that it is generally applicable to the reproduction schemes, especially as Marx did not assume a change in the 'organic composition of capital' in the course of time and thus the development of the rate of surplus value and of the rate of profit does not change. Unfortunately, in his schemes of extended reproduction Marx assumed different 'organic compositions of capital' for departments I and II (4:1 in I and 2:1 in II), so that for this economy values and prices do not coincide. It is true that the rate of surplus value (100 per cent) is the same in both departments, but the rate of profit (20 and 33⅓ per cent) is not. As a first approximation we may leave aside these difficulties, in order to start from Schmitt-Rink's working hypothesis.

There is, however, a further complication: Marx deals at each stage with two aspects – the social product resulting from production, and its use. Surplus value is produced, in the form of means of production and consumption goods, but it is not necessarily consumed in the same 'year', or period, and is at least partially consumed in the next. This is 'saving' (or, in Keynesian terms, 'investment'). At this point, difficulties arise, because two different phases are represented by one set of figures. There is no attempt to introduce separately a Robertsonian period analysis for a 'supply' of commodities produced and a (monetary?) 'demand'.

The figures of Marx's scheme no. 1 of extended reproduction come to life if we employ modern terminology, as in Tables IV.1–IV.3. Following this approach, scheme no. 1 appears as in Table IV.4.

Broadly speaking, the conclusions that can be drawn from Table IV.4 are as follows. Except over the first to second year, depreciation, value added (i.e. national income) and social product (GNP) all grow by 10 per cent per annum. This ratio also applies to fixed capital formation but not to total investment, for the stocks of consumption goods increase quite irregularly: from the first to the second year, they increase by 60 per cent, only to grow by a regular 10 per cent per annum from the third year

TABLE IV.1

(1) Year	(2) Social product (GNP), $c+v+s$	(3) National income $(v+s)$	(4) Net savings	(5) $(4)/(3)$ $\times 100$	(6) Gross savings	(7) $(6)/(2)$ $\times 100$
1	9000	3500	650	18·6	6150	68·3
2	9800	3800	790	20·8	6790	69·3
3	10780	4180	869	20·8	7469	69·3
4	11858	4598	955	20·8	8215*	69·3
5	13043	5058	1052	20·8	9040*	69·3
6	14348	5564	1157	20·8	9939*	69·3

*

TABLE IV.2

| Year | Growth rate (%) of | | |
	social product (GNP)	national income	consumption
2	8·88	8·57	5·6
3	10	10	10
4	10	10	9·97
5	10	10	9·96
6	10	10	9·99

TABLE IV.3

Year	Consumption goods : means of production	Marginal capital-output ratio (increment in investment and structures : increment in national income)	Average capital-output ratio $(c+s(\text{acc.}):v+s)$
1	3000:6000 (50%)		6150:3500 (1·76)
2	3200:6600 (48·5%)	500:300 (1·67)	6790:3800 (1·79)
3	3520:7260 (48·5%)	600:380 (1·58)	7469:4180 (1·79)
4	3872:7986 (48·5%)	670:418 (1·60)	8215:4598 (1·79)
5	4259:8784 (48·5%)	725:460 (1·58)	9040:5058 (1·79)
6	4686:9662 (48·5%)	799:506 (1·58)	9939:5564 (1·79)

TABLE IV.4

Year	Depreciation	Value added	Total product	Fixed capital formation	Investment Stocks of consumption goods	Total
1	5500	3500	9000	500	150	650
2	6000	3800	9800	550	240	790
3	6600	4180	10780	605	264	869
4	7260	4598	11858	665	(290)*	945
5	7985	5058	13043	735	(320)*	1055
6	8784	5564	14348	805	(350)*	1155

* Figures in parentheses are not directly stated by Marx, but are derived from his argument. We assume that in department II 30 per cent of the surplus value is accumulated, as in the second and third years; in the first year, the quota was only 20 per cent.

onwards. If we start from Schmitt-Rink's hypothesis, i.e. if we consider the reproduction scheme as a price scheme, it can be analysed in the following way: in the first year, the social product increases. The surplus value (= profits) accumulated in department I is invested by entrepreneurs in the form of stocks of means of production, and the surplus value of department II in the form of stocks of consumption goods. These stocks will be carried over to the second year and will then enter into the process of production, i.e. using them up will turn them into cash receipts. The entrepreneurs of department I either employ the means of production kept in stock in their own plants or sell them to entrepreneurs in department II. In turn, the entrepreneurs in II either use their stocks of consumption goods to hire workers or sell them to I. Production in I grows by 10 per cent, and in II by 6·67 per cent.

Thus the profits 'saved' (and physically embodied in stocks) in period 1 will be turned into 'inputs' in period 2, creating a larger social product. This is basically because not all the increased production in period 1, or all the income saved in period 2, will be consumed in the latter period as means of production or consumption goods.

In Marx's example, the social product will grow by 800 units in year 1, and of this 500 units are owing to 'saving' by the capitalists in I and 150 to 'saving' by the capitalists in II. The growth is thus owing to disinvestment (the running-down of stocks). The genuine increase in the social product in year 1 – the part that cannot be explained by this disinvestment – is 150 units. Over year 2, the capitalists in II make a particular effort, for they have to raise the share of their income devoted to investment from 20 to 30 per cent. It follows that their consumption decreases from 600 to 500. They are thus enabled to save 240 units of consumption goods, 60 per cent more than before. The capitalists in I save 550 units of the means of production. These savings appear as stocks, which are thus increased. Production grows in both departments by 10 per cent.

'GENUINE' GROWTH IN THE MARXIAN SCHEME

The increase in income in year 3, which can be explained by the using-up of stocks accumulated in previous periods thus amounts to 790, but the total increase of production in this period is 980. Thus the 'genuine' growth amounts to 190 units.

From year 4 onwards, things develop more smoothly, as may be seen from Table iv.5. The figures in column (8) represent real growth, which accrues entirely to capitalists. Practically speaking, these amounts correspond to the increase in the total income of capitalists (I and II) each year (see column 6), because Marx assumes that the division of value added (national income) will remain at 50:50 and that capitalists' income will thus grow every year by the same amount as the wage bill.

TABLE IV.5

(1) Year	(2) Social product (GNP)	(3) Depreciation	(4) Net invest- ment	(5) National income	(6) Increment in (5)	(7) Increment in (2)	(8) Genuine growth*
1	9000	5500	650	3500			
2	9800	6000	790	3800	300	800	150
3	10780	6600	869	4180	380	980	190
4	11858	7260	955	4598	418	1078	209
5	13043	7985	1052	5058	460	1185	230
6	14348	8784	1157	5564	506	1305	253

* col.$(7) - (t-1)$ col. 4

This increase is owing to Marx's value concept, which we take for granted in this context. It represents just that 'social dividend' which is not determined by the renunciation of consumption in the previous period. It is thus, in this economic system, the only 'genuine' increase in output, which is not to be explained by inputs. It is only with regard to this growth of less than 2 per cent in social product and about 4·5 per cent in national income that we can speak of 'genuine' growth. These are, after all, quite realistic figures – apart from the inflated values of the social product.

Incidentally, it may be noted that, if one leaves aside the basic depreciation of 5500, as representing 'double counting', i.e. intermediate goods, one could conclude that, from the second year onwards, the ratio between gross investment in the previous year and the increment in social product is 1·4 (e.g. in the third year $600 + 869 = 1469:1078$ in the fourth year $= 1·4$). This might be called an investment–output ratio'. Net investment compared to net increase would yield 2·1.

This calculation, however, is somewhat dubious, for the marginal capital–output ratio is often considered to be somewhat shaky, since, as has been pointed out by Helmstädter (1969), there is no evident connexion between investment and growth in the social product in the next period.

GROWTH PER HEAD IN MARX'S WORKS: A 'SCHEME FOR IMMIGRANT WORKERS'?

If one assumes that the population remains constant, growth in the national income of about 10 per cent per annum would mean a corresponding growth of income per head, i.e. a genuine growth process. In an extreme case, this would be the result if at the outset there were as many capitalists as workers and the former were transformed into the latter in the wake of the process of concentration.

The other extreme would be where to begin with there were only a few capitalists and the workers came from outside the system. In this case there would be almost no growth per head (taking employed and unemployed workers together).

Reality may be found somewhere between the two extremes. If one assumes that labour is drawn from a pool of 'external proletarians', i.e. through immigration (temporary or otherwise), while the number of capitalists is large and remains so, growth will be moderate. One may postulate that each wage unit represents a worker, and that there are 500 capitalists. Then the situation outlined in Table IV. 6 results.

TABLE IV.6

Year	No. of workers	No. of capitalists	No. of income receivers Absolute	Index	Index of national income Global	Per head
1	1750	500	2250	100	100	100
2	1900	500	2400	106·7	108·6	101·8
3	2090	500	2590	115·1	119·4	103·7
4	2299	500	2799	124·4	131·4	105·6
5	2529	500	3029	134·6	144·5	107·4
6	2782	500	3282	145·9	158·9	108·9

Under this assumption, national income grows at first by about 2 per cent per year and then more slowly, since each increase in the wage bill (at constant real wages on the assumption of constant prices) means that additional income accrues to capitalists, through the surplus work being done by the additional labour. Since we assume a constant number of capitalists, the 10 per cent rise in income per capitalist must correspond to the growth in the labour force and in surplus work, and this must result in an increase in national income per head, which will be smaller the smaller is the proportion of capitalists to workers. If the number of capitalists is insignificant, there will be practically no increase in national income, for the growth of the labour force (10 per cent per annum) corresponds to the growth rate of income. The labour force, total population and income grow at practically the same rate.

Conversely, under the assumption that the distribution of income remains unchanged, the larger is the (constant) number of capitalists in proportion to the labour force, the longer will it take for the increase in the growth rate of the population to reach a significant level in relation to the growth of national income, so that the part of the population which does not grow loses in relative importance. Under these circumstances, income per head must grow more slowly in later years, because the growth of population will catch up with the growth of income. This is true where additional labour comes from abroad.

If the number of capitalists remains constant, while the labour force increases, growth in income per head, assuming a constant distribution of income, will be faster than it would be if the number of capitalists grew. If concentration leads to a decrease in the number of capitalists, distribution will become more unequal. If, in the extreme case, the number of workers increases *pari passu* with the decrease in the number of capitalists, average income per head will grow *pari passu* with total income, by 60 per cent in six years, since the combined number of workers and capitalists would always remain the same. The growing sum of surplus value would accrue to an ever-smaller group of capitalists, whose income per head would grow exponentially, while workers' wages per head would remain constant.

In such a system, one would have to assume that the rate of accumulation does not remain constant, as in Marx's model, but increases. The relative decrease in capitalists' consumption would then lead to an increased share of investment-goods industries in the social product.

This would in turn lead to an increase in the 'organic composition of capital', i.e. in the capital–output ratio, for, under our assumption that as the labour force cannot grow faster than the capitalist class loses members, the increase in the labour force hits a ceiling, and accumulation and growth can be maintained only by capital-intensive methods of production. If technology is not able to employ more fixed capital per worker, there will be a recession. Constant capital-intensity means a crisis.

Here we see a connexion with concentration processes, the decline of small businesses, distribution problems and growth frictions, which can be indirectly deduced from Marx's schemes. The schemes, however, do not say whether the number of capitalists increases or whether it is large or small in relation to the number of workers. Furthermore, the latter does not appear directly, but occurs only in the form of its 'shadow', variable capital.

This analysis presupposes that we identify growth with an increase in total product per head of population. This is the definition accepted by modern Marxists, such as Meissner (1972, p. 12). In the Marxian scheme, this condition will be observed only if the number of capitalists is relatively large at the outset; in our example (ignoring families), capitalists account for 22·5 per cent of total population in the year 1. The increase in production per head must necessarily slow down in this scheme from year 3 onwards (1·9, 1·7, 1·6 per cent of the initial value), because we assume that the number of workers will grow in proportion to production. The labour supply is replenished from unlimited labour reservoirs abroad, while the number of capitalists remains constant. The rate of increase of national income will slow down, since the capitalist group remains constant and loses weight, because of the increase in the number of workers, so that the rate of growth of the population corresponds more and more to the growth of income. This Marxian scheme is of course based on the assumption that capitalists do not work. We can therefore explain the increase in national income per head by the mere fact that the share of the employed population increases (leaving aside their families). If we assume that unemployed workers are progressively brought into employment, the share of the employed in the total labour force increases as well.

It would seem that the assumption that capitalists too may work is alien to the Marxian concept of surplus value. Marx elsewhere considers this possibility, but then part of wages would simply represent 'the rewards of the entrepreneurs', and part of surplus value could be described as capitalists' (or, rather, artisans') self-exploitation.

The alternative would be to assume that capitalists work but receive their remuneration out of surplus value. This would be absurd from the point of view of the Marxian assumption that for every working hour embodied in variable capital (the remuneration of workers) there must correspond a surplus value. If one were to assume that working capitalists are indeed remunerated out of surplus value, one would reach the absurd conclusion that, with the expropriation of these capitalists and the conversion of them into proletarians in the wake of the concentration process, they would go on doing the same work, but, whereas before it had no effect on (or even served to reduce) surplus value, it would now increase it. Clearly, the only logical assumption is that capitalists do not work.

Our analysis has hitherto been based primarily on the assumption that additional workers are drawn from reserves outside the capitalist sector, or, rather, immigrate temporarily or permanently from abroad. Alternatively, it would from the outset be possible to calculate national income per head on the basis of the final figure of 2782 workers and 500 capitalists, i.e. the total population would remain constant, and the re-employment of the unemployed would simply lead to a proportional increase in national income and in total income per head. In a neo-classical accounting system, about 80 per cent of this increase would be attributable to the increase in labour input, some 20 per cent would be attributable to capital, and nothing at all would be left for technical progress. The expansion would be purely extensive.

In both cases, the constancy of the number of capitalists has an effect: the growth rate per head depends on the ratio of the number of capitalists to the number of workers. If one starts with a certain number of workers, which is increased by immigrants, and if one assumes that full employment is reached in the last year and that the number of capitalists is very low, there will be almost no growth in national income per head, because income rises by one-half and so does the number of earners. If the number of capitalists is and remains quite high, there will be genuine growth in income per head, because the number of income earners grows more slowly than national income; while, if the number of capitalists is quite large and workers immigrate (from outside the capitalist sector or from abroad), income per head will grow more slowly. In principle, where the number of capitalists is constant, growth will be maintained, because the rate of growth of surplus value will exceed the rate of growth of income receivers; but the difference between the two growth rates diminishes the more the percentage of capitalists in the total population declines. It is not entirely justified to calculate income per head, for by definition income increases only for capitalists. The underlying principle is this: if one calculates income per head in a society in which the unemployed are progressively absorbed, the number of capitalists is of no importance, for growth per head is largely extensive, being caused by an increase in the labour input. If one counts only workers who are employed, assuming the 'industrial reserve army' to be external, the growth rate per head will be low if the percentage of capitalists in the population is small. It will be relatively high if the percentage of capitalists is high and their numbers constant, because in this case the growth of total population will be slower. Thus one might conclude that a rapid process of concentration, which destroys the middle class, must depress the real growth rate per head of such a system!

THE REALISM OF THE MARXIAN SCHEME: THE UNADJUSTED AND ADJUSTED WAGE SHARES AND THE CLASS STRUGGLE

In adding the criterion of the number of income receivers in the two classes, the Marxian growth scheme becomes quite instructive, for it reflects a certain distribution theory. As a rule, Marx assumes the unadjusted share of wages or the 'rate of surplus value' to be constant. Since, however, the number of workers is rising while the number of capitalists remains at least constant, the share of the individual worker in the national income must decrease, while that of the individual capitalist must rise. This is equivalent to saying that the adjusted share of wages keeps decreasing. Some authors have defined this development as a 'relative increase in poverty' (see Volume I, Part VI).

Now, in real life, at least since the end of the Second World War, there is a tendency in the opposite direction. The unadjusted share of wages rises slowly while the adjusted share seems to remain constant (EEC Commission, 1967, pp. 30ff.). We cannot examine these conditions in detail. It might be useful, however, to extend the Marxian system in a realistic sense by combining simple growth analysis with an investigation of the class relationship. Such an analysis is sadly lacking in most works on growth, which measure the growth of income not for different classes but for the entire population.

To some extent it can be said that the Marxian schemes, under certain assumptions, approach reality in spite of maintaining generally a rather high degree of abstraction. This realism prevails as far as Marx tackles the problem of distribution in principle. In other respects, however, the schemes are deficient in macroeconomic realism. Marx more or less identifies technical progress with a rising 'organic composition of capital', yet in his schemes the 'organic composition' remains constant. This is a major drawback, for it means that there is no technical progress involved. It could of course be assumed that the 'real growth of production', the existence of which we have pointed out, represents technical progress, but this is not directly implied in Marx's reasoning.

The constancy of the 'organic composition of capital' on which the Marxian schemes of extended reproduction are based has also the following consequence, as Peter (1934, II, p. 60) draws to our attention:

> If the economy is to progress in such a way that the ratio w [the ratio of constant costs to labour costs, i.e. virtually the 'organic composition of capital'] remains always the same, though all units grow by the same percentage from one period to another, additional means of production will have to be produced in each period, which will in turn lead in the following period to their increased use. Thus department I must be larger in a growing system than in a stationary one, provided the ratio w always remains the same.

GROWTH EQUILIBRIUM

Marx ensured this by choosing larger initial values for department I and by allowing the capitalists in I to accumulate more (50 per cent) of their surplus value than the capitalists in II (20 per cent in the first year, 30 per cent thereafter). Thus department I grows progressively faster than II, because each group of capitalists keeps investing only in its own sector.

Rosa Luxemburg has stigmatised this as the dependency of department II on I, and other critics have considered as severe shortcomings in this scheme not only the relative magnitudes, but also the constancy of the 'organic composition' and the gross divergencies in the rates of accumulation. Marx's scheme no. 1 is interesting just because of these irregularities, since they lead to the consequences that Peter points out. That the ratio is not more heavily biased in favour of I is simply owing to the fact that new workers, who have to be nourished, are continually being recruited. This implies that part of the accumulated surplus value of I must be transferred to II, and the consumption of capitalists increases because more 'surplus' work is being done.

Thus, despite the different rates of accumulation, surplus value does not grow very much faster in I than in II: from the first to the sixth year, it rises in I from 1000 to 1610, i.e. by 61 per cent, and in II from 750 to 1172, i.e. by 56 per cent.

Now, the equilibrium formula for undisturbed growth is $I\,v + I\,s = II\,c$. Expressed verbally this means that the wage bill paid by I, which is wholly consumed, together with the surplus value consumed by the capitalists in I, must equal the sum of the means of production sold by ɪ to ɪɪ. Now, in Marx's scheme no. ɪ, this would no longer be the case from the second year onward if Marx did not also throw in the surplus value of ɪɪ. As soon as ɪ v + ɪ s exceeds ɪɪ c, the capitalists in ɪɪ will have to renounce part of their surplus value (as embodied in their stocks of consumption goods) and hand it over to ɪ.

To this extent Rosa Luxemburg's criticism is justified, but it is just this that makes Marx's example attractive; for it does not show, in contrast to what many commentators claim, the smooth growth of capitalism, but on the contrary a growth process which is continually being disturbed and an equilibrium restored only intermittently by additional bursts of investment!

The capitalists in ɪɪ as a group are acting as a *deus ex machina*. One is tempted to compare their stand-by function with modern business-cycle policy; without this 'compensatory finance', the growth process would simply falter, because it is poised on a 'knife edge'.

From the third year onwards, the scheme develops more regularly, since the capitalists in ɪɪ now save about 30 per cent of their surplus value, as opposed to 20 per cent before, while the growth rate of national income stabilises at 10 per cent.

Rosa Luxemburg therefore is not quite right. Her complaints are vindicated if we look at the rather passive adaptation of savings and investment in ɪɪ. She is also right when she points out that the consumption of capitalists in ɪɪ develops irregularly and with little plausibility. Her argument, however, differs from modern analyses, which emphasise not so much the development of the two separate departments as overall development, which is not so irregular.

THE CAPITAL–OUTPUT RATIO, THE CAPITAL STOCK AND THE PROBLEM OF DOUBLE COUNTING

What is particularly unrealistic in the Marxian scheme is the fact that depreciation looms so large. It would appear that Marx assumed that raw and auxiliary materials play a part in the calculation of depreciation in national accounting systems.

As Burchardt has pointed out, this assumption would be tantamount to double counting. The Marxian scheme is quite correct as long as it remains confined to a microeconomic comparison of the two departments, but it suffers from an inherent defect as soon as it is to be understood macroeconomically. Raw and auxiliary materials are produced by labour and means of production and cannot appear once again under the heading of depreciation. In other words, the Marxian category c, constant capital, has been devised at the microeconomic level and cannot be transposed without further ado onto the macroeconomic plane. This explains the vast difference between gross social product and national income in Marx's examples.

The calculation of a capital–output ratio becomes an awkward task, in view of this gross distortion of constant capital. Nevertheless, the calculation is necessary if we want to compare the Marxian scheme and the equilibrium condition in the Harrod–Domar model. If we start from the Burchardt assumption (1932, p. 166) that 'raw materials do not enter into the total product', because 'the total product decomposes into used-up fixed capital, auxiliary materials and labour', and if we leave out auxiliary materials and energy (for instance, by assuming that each enterprise is self-sufficient – as in coal-mining, with its own electricity generation), the scheme will be reduced to means of production, in the guise of installations of machinery, and consumption goods.

In the Marxian schemes, there are two hidden aspects, as Mandel, for instance, has recognised (1962, 1, p. 397): the schemes express, first, the production of goods and, secondly, the generation of income from this process, i.e. supply and demand. In the case of the means of production consumed in department 1, we encounter own-consumption.

Surplus value presents a difficulty. It is not an input at the production level, but only an output. We do not want to neglect the twofold character of surplus value in the Marxian scheme, i.e. as a product of 'exploitation' and as the source of internal finance, so in order to escape the difficulty we do not split up value added.

Thus we encounter only two categories on the supply side, means of production and consumption goods, and again two on the demand side, investment (including replacement) and consumption. Anything which is not consumption automatically represents investment in the Keynesian sense; it has only to be clarified whether it is voluntary investment (in stocks of production or consumption goods) or involuntary investment, i.e. such stocks as are built up because of a recession. If one now wants to analyse the Harrod–Domar equation in Robertsonian terms, to free it from the 'tangled phraseology' of Marx, one comes across a major difficulty, i.e. how to define a capital stock in a scheme representing flows.

In the first year 18·6 per cent of personal income is saved, and in the second 20·8 per cent. The growth rate in the second year is 8·57 per cent and thereafter 10 per cent. Thus the capital–output ratio is around 2·0 from the third year onwards, and is higher only in the second year: a somewhat daring calculation gives exactly 2·2, then 2·08, 2·06, etc.

If one wants to verify these figures on the basis of capital stocks, one must try to identify these stocks. In so doing, one can first use the sum of c in both departments, adding annual savings, which are embodied in stocks of means of production and consumption goods. We then obtain the figures in Table IV.4. Such a calculation would imply a cumulation of net and replacement investment, as is usual in calculating the capital–output ratio. For instance, Helmstädter says (1969, p. 53), 'In most empirical calculations, the capital–output ratio has been represented as the ratio of cumulative net investment to net social product.'

The difficulty with this is that there is no real cumulation in the Marxian examples, because Marx assumes a capital–turnover coefficient of 1·0 per period, assuming that the means of production are consumed and replaced in the very same year. If, say, one were to consider as the 'capital stock' in the third year the sum of constant capital in both departments and the means saved by them and serving as net investment, one would reach a ratio of $7459:4180 = 1·79$.

This method would result in an almost constant capital–output ratio of 1·76–1·79 over the whole period, which would approach the theoretical ratio (savings quota : growth rate) of about 2·0. One could also consider as the capital stock a mean value of depreciation and savings, because in a flow analysis where consumption is distributed equally over the year about one-half of the quantities can be considered as a stock. We should then reach a capital stock of about half the figure in Table iv.3 (fourth column, left hand side). The resulting ratio would be below 1·0, which would appear absurd.

It would appear more reasonable to base calculations on the gross social product. If we consider the savings share to consist of depreciation plus savings out of surplus value, we shall end up with an enormously high ratio of 68·9 per cent, because Marx used enormously high values for constant capital. In modern societies, total depreciation amounts to 8 to 10 per cent of the gross social product. Marx's high figure is to be explained by what Burchardt called the double counting of the microeconomic elements auxiliary and raw materials. The same objection applies to the above calculations of national income, but there the figures are more realistic, because the high figures for c as 'stocks' appear quite plausible. As soon, however, as c affects the savings quota, the figures are no longer realistic.

We therefore assume that only 10 per cent of the gross social (or national) product represents genuine depreciation. This leads us to the adjusted figures set out in Table iv.7.

If one now follows the Domar formula, dividing the savings ratio by the growth rate, which amounts to 10 per cent for the gross social product as for national income, one reaches exactly the capital–output ratio for total output presented in Table iv.3 (fourth column).

It thus looks as if Marx's 'tangled phraseology' contained, as Robertson thought, the secret of the Domar formula, but Marx's figures must be adjusted to avoid double counting and to introduce the notion of stocks. What is problematical in our account is that we use c as a clue to capital stock, which has no place in Marx's reasoning, and thereby reduce the share of depreciation to around 14 per cent. Such a hypothesis seems to be quite realistic, for it means that fixed capital will be renewed in about seven years, which is almost the period covered by Marx's analysis.

Another method of finding a capital–output ratio on the basis of

TABLE IV.7

Year	Depreciation of fixed assets	Savings	Total	Total as % of gross social product (Table IV.5–(2))
1	900	650	1550	17·2
2	980	790	1770	18·1
3	1078	859	1937	18·0
4	1186	945	2131	18·0
5	1304	1052	2356	18·1
6	1435	1127	2562	17·9

Marxian flows would be to proceed as follows, again considering the Marxian growth schemes in money terms (i.e. in constant prices). Saving in the first two years leads to accumulation of a stock of means of production of 600 and of consumption goods of 150. Although Marx deals only in flows, a stock can thus be seen to appear. On the basis that in each period saving and investment replace the stocks of the preceding period and still add something, investment in one period can be regarded as equal to the capital stock at the beginning of the next period minus the capital stock at the beginning of the previous period. If we compare these stocks with the growth in output in the period, we arrive at 'marginal' capital–output ratios in the modern sense, and these, at around 0·8, are abnormally low (650:800, 790:980, etc.). If we choose to consider this as the capital–output ratio, the Domar formula would give us as the average growth rate of the gross social product 0·1. The capital–output ratio from the third year onwards would be 0·8 and the savings ratio would then be 0·1 × 0·8 = 0·08 or 8 per cent. Indeed, of the gross social product from the second year onwards (see Table IV.1, column 4 divided by column 3 × 100), some 7.8 per cent is saved (790:9000), but between the first and second year the savings ratio of the capitalists in II rises from 20 per cent of their surplus value to 30 per cent, and this makes up the difference. Thus it is clear that Robertson was right in assuming that the Domar formula was hidden in Marx's obscure terminology.

THE NOTION OF INVESTMENT IN MARX

In Marx's scheme no. 1 the savings ratio amounts to 18·6 per cent of national income in the first year, and 20·8 per cent from then on, if one assumes that the consumption goods saved that will accrue to the workers are to be consumed only in the next period. Consumption increases in the second year by 5·6 per cent and thereafter by 10 per cent a year.

Marx's periods telescope in a spiral manner, as Utta Gruber pointed out in a debate between Tsuru and Bettelheim. In each period, the stocks of means of production and consumption goods produced in the preceding period are 'exhausted'. Thus the largest part of the increment in the social product in each period does not represent genuine growth. The real growth rate, if one deducts stocks consumed, adds up to no more than about 2 per cent; in year 2, it is 1·66 per cent, in year 3, 1·8 per cent, in year 4, 1·9 per cent, and in years 5 and 6 about 2 per cent.

Utta Gruber comments (1961, p. 325) on Marx's procedure that 'Marx solves the problem of delimiting periods by considering individual periods as telescoping circuits, the end of the first circuit being the starting point of the second'. Indeed, Marx says (*Capital*, II, ch. 4, p. 104), 'In a constantly revolving circle every point is simultaneously a point of departure and a point of return'.

Utta Gruber continues (1961, pp. 325–6),

> This idea of a rotating circuit contradicts, in its final outcome, the traditional way of delimiting periods, where each 'event' must be unmistakably ascribed to one or other period. . . . In the Marxian circular scheme, these 'events' are to be marked by phases of the cycle. . . . The convention of the usual period analysis of today is to consider all events in a period as happening simultaneously . . . .

If one wants to explain Marx in modern terms, it cannot be denied that the schemes present particular terminological and analytical difficulties, which most commentators either ignore or sublimely disdain to consider. It is owing to Utta Gruber's painstaking analysis that the differences between modern and Marxian terminology can be made clear. These differences concern on one side the delimitation of periods and on the other the notion of investment. Utta Gruber examines

> the contradiction which is to be found in the fact that the realisation of surplus value s, if one considers society as a whole, already presupposes that it is spent on s_v, s_c and s_k [i.e. on wages, on purchases of means of production and on capitalists' consumption], for s_v, s_c and s_k are ways of spending surplus value . . . .

She speaks of 'a contradiction which consists in asserting that the level of profits will be determined only if the utilisation of profits is', but she admits that such a contradiction could also occur in modern analysis. Then she asserts that one could escape these difficulties by assuming 'that not only net investment, but also capitalists' consumption could be financed in advance by credit operations'. She then, however, chooses to assume that transactions will take place, so that 'the investment and consumption of capitalists includes the spending of realised surplus value. Thus the contradiction that the realisation of surplus value presupposes its use is eliminated.'

Marx's notion of investment is to be distinguished 'from the related notion of investment in use today' by the fact that 'it includes investment in variable capital' and that 'increases in stocks . . . are not in every case considered to be real investment'. Utta Gruber also thinks that one cannot clearly determine under what conditions Marx would consider stockbuilding to be equivalent to accumulation. She then goes on to say,

> First of all, it is certain that increases in stocks of consumption goods for capitalists cannot be considered as investment according to Marx. It is also certain that, as in modern theory, not all unintentional stockbuilding is considered to be investment. The situation is different with regard to consumption goods for unemployed workers . . . .
>
> (Ibid., pp. 328–31.)

In fact the Marxian telescoping of periods can only be interpreted in such a way that the meaning of 'accumulation' is as follows. In the first period, means of production and consumption goods are produced which accrue to capitalists as part of their surplus value; these capitalists do not realise their surplus value, by consuming it or (in the case of the capitalists in II) by selling consumption goods to the capitalists in I or (in the case of the capitalists in I) by selling means of production to the capitalists in II. On the contrary, they retain the goods, which thus provide a voluntary increase in stocks. It is only in the next period that the goods are sold and the surplus value of the first period is transformed into cash.

It must be considered to be an advantage of the Marxian notion of investment that it does not, as the Keynesian concept did before Robertson's delimitation of periods, consider involuntarily formed stocks, which reflect a recession, to be equivalent to investment. On the other hand, such involuntary stockholding does not in fact occur in Marx's schemes of extended reproduction, though he hints at its existence when discussing the impact of hoarding on simple reproduction. Utta Gruber explains this convincingly (ibid., pp. 332, 345–6):

> What is decisive for the investment process is not the increase in stocks as such, but the fact that the investment decision has been taken. That Marx explicitly recognised this shows that his investment notion is by no means as antiquated as it appeared to be at first sight, and that it is able to radiate fertile impulses even for modern investment theory. . . .
>
> The situation is that, completely independent of the periodicity, the hiring of additional workers, according to Marx and Tsuru, implies an increase in the capital stock. . . . Marx's notion of investment, as opposed to that of Keynes, takes into account the dual aspect of investment, i.e. its employment effect and its capacity effect. . . . This

dual aspect is also a central problem of modern growth theory, which, however, does not draw the logical conclusions from the formulation of the investment notion, but takes over, in most cases without qualification, Keynes's concept of investment, which is based on a short-run outlook. . . . If the concept of investment employed by Keynes includes multifarious economic actions which differ in their productivity effects, this is owing to the fact that it is primarily used to define the effect of the multiplier in short-run analysis. Over and above, we must note that the Keynesian notion of investment is 'system-neutral', and therefore applicable to all economic systems, while the Marxian notion reflects the peculiarities of the capitalist system.

It here becomes evident that Marx, in his effort to discover the laws of motion of the capitalist economy, succeeded better than Keynes. Furthermore, Marx is superior to Keynes in that he included from the very outset the capacity effects. These effects were not explicitly taken into account in modern economics until Domar analysed them.

CAPITAL STOCK AND TECHNICAL PROGRESS

On the other hand, it is true that there is a basic flaw in Marx's attempt to deal with the capacity complex, for he does not work with real capital stocks, but only with their 'shadows', as it were, in the form of depreciation flows (c). Here we hit upon the paradox pointed out by Utta Gruber, who makes reference to Tsuru. This is that the capacity increase is reflected by the appearance of additional workers, who also are only 'reflected' by their 'shadows', i.e. additional payments from surplus value for the goods they consume. This is the double appearance of the term *sav* (average propensity to save), criticised by Bettelheim, in Tsuru's equation system. Formal discrepancies are thus turned into factual differences. This explicitly shows that the Marxian scheme was better suited to long-run growth theory than was the Keynesian system. *Habent sua fata libelli* – destiny has willed it that the less perfect system has, *via* Harrod, had the greater influence on subsequent thought – although, as we have seen, Domar was fully conscious of Marx's work.

Strangely enough, in Marxist literature, we find hardly any hints regarding the connexion between the savings ratio and the capital stock, although Luxemburg and Bukharin formulated the equilibrium equation. With the sole exception of Gillman, who broke with the tradition, Marxists have not calculated capital stocks but have rather slavishly followed Marx's method. The master contented himself with analysing flows and simplifying the calculus by assuming a velocity of turnover for fixed capital equal to $1 \cdot 0$. This made it impossible to calculate a capital–output ratio on the basis of a capital stock and an increment in production.

Some hints of an awareness of this problem are to be found in Otto Bauer's works. In his criticism of Rosa Luxemburg, Bauer writes (1913, 1, pp. 833 ff.),

If the equilibrium between accumulation and population growth is to be preserved, the growth rate of accumulation must remain in a fixed ratio to the rate of increase in the population and the capital stock. . . . Anyone accustomed to reckoning in abstract values will easily find the equation which expresses this ratio in general terms.

Bauer thus introduces another aspect of what was later to become known as the Domar equation, i.e. that of the natural increase of population. In Robertson's simplified formula and in our calculation above it is assumed that there is no such increase, although the recruitment of additional labour can be interpreted as an increase of population or at least in the labour force. What is essential is that Bauer sees a connexion between the rate of accumulation and the rate of growth of constant capital, i.e. broadly a capital–output ratio. He does not, however, mention the growth of output and equates the savings rate with the rate of investment. To boot, Bauer even leaves the calculation of such a ratio to the reader!

The main sin of Marxist epigones lay, however, in the fact that they omitted to introduce technical progress into the Marxian scheme, which properly speaking considers only extensive investment. Wherever Marxists tried to use and develop the schemes, they either ended up, like Rosa Luxemburg, in the blind alley of a relatively crude under-consumption growth theory, or, like Bauer and Grossmann, arrived at a rather one-sided theory of the tendency of the rate of profit to fall, in which they identified, even more than did Marx, technical progress with capital deepening. In the face of this one-sided identification, the neo-classical school then extolled the autonomous role of technical progress – 'investment is unimportant!' – in direct contradiction to Marx and his followers and successive generations of 'academic' economists, who had believed that 'investment is all-important'.

If today one reads the dithyrambs on technical progress and science in Marx's *Grundrisse*, one may well ask if the publication of this work fifty years earlier (for it has become widely known only since 1953!) might not have changed the entire course of development of Marxist theory, especially in economics. The Marxists could have developed a growth model of their own, based on technical progress, before growth economics became the domain of neo-classical model builders. To do so, they would have had to steer clear of the peculiar secular version of the theory of the tendency of the rate of profit to fall, which might have proved a blind alley if taken too literally.

As it was, however, the fundamental laws of motion of capitalism remained largely a closed book to Marxists. The inherent dynamics of the system required dynamic analysis, but instead Marxists treated capitalism mainly from a static point of view, as if it could not, through technical progress, escape from the doldrums of recessions and depressions. Samuelson once said that technical progress gave capitalism its resilience, in the same way as plucking the strings of a violin helps keep it in tune.

Furthermore, Marxists concentrated mostly on the social aspects of unemployment, and they failed to see what the 'industrial reserve army' meant for the dynamics of the system. For them, the enlargement of the reserve army, as opposed to the disappearance of it, was the destabilising factor for capitalism. In reality the reverse has been the case: it was precisely the temporary exhaustion of labour reserves which effectively menaced the profit system. This exhaustion, together with the existence of strong trade unions, whose rise Marx had foreseen, became the real stumbling block for the capitalist system.

Recent Marxist theories, such as that developed by Glyn and Sutcliffe, have indeed concentrated principally on this phenomenon. They argue (1972, pp. 73ff.) that the downfall of capitalism will be brought about not by mass unemployment and mass misery in periods of depression, but by a combination of the disappearance of labour reserves and of strong unions in a long-lasting upswing, because this would cause profits to be eroded from the side of costs. In this context, it is desirable to discuss the rôle of inflationary excess demand, which might save the rate of profit, and the further question of the ultimate function of technical progress.

As it happens, such an interpretation comes very close to an implicit assumption upon which the reproduction schemes are based. Marx points out that frictionless growth presupposes an inexhaustible reservoir of labour. On the other hand, this interpretation flatly contradicts Keynesian wage theory and the 'Marxist Keynesianism' of Kalecki.

7 Reproduction Schemes and Equilibrium

At first, Marx's reproduction schemes provoked astonishingly little response from Marxists and their enemies. Characteristic was Oppenheimer's remark that it would be best if they were quickly to fall into oblivion. Almost no one recognised that here were laid the foundations of the imposing edifice that is modern growth theory.

Rosdolsky (1968, vol. II, p. 541ff.) was doubtless right in saying that the 'reproduction schemes of the second volume of *Capital* went almost unnoticed in German Marxist literature for about two decades', apart from some remarks made by Kautsky in his review of volume II written in 1885. Rosdolsky says that it was 'only the German translation of 1902 of the book by the Russian professor Tugan-Baranowsky' that drew 'the attention of German Marxist theorists to Marx's analysis of the social reproduction process'.

FROM THE EARLY RUSSIAN DEBATE ON GROWTH TO HILFERDING

In Russia in the 1890s, however, a group of Russian Marxists, the so-called 'Legal Marxists', under the leadership of Peter von Struve and Mikhail Tugan-Baranowsky, had emphasised the importance of the Marxian reproduction schemes. This they had done in reaction to an attack by the 'Populists', whose leaders were Wassily Worontsow (pseudonym 'W. W.') and Nikolai A. Danielson (pseudonym 'Nikolai-on'). Danielson translated the works of Marx. The Populists denied that capitalism had any chance of prospering in Russia: it could not thrive on domestic consumption because it would lead to the pauperisation of the masses, and capitalists themselves would not, in view of their limited (and decreasing) numbers, be able to consume enough. On the other hand, export markets would be inaccessible to Russian capitalism. (Lenin, 1893; 1937).

Even the 'Legal Marxists' did not use Marx's schemes to develop a growth theory as such, for they brandished them only to prove the viability of capitalism and show that capitalism might indeed develop without a great extension of consumer markets! In other words, they implicitly accepted the theory of a 'relative increase in poverty' (which, as we saw in

Volume I, Part VI, is alien to Marx) and the idea that under capitalism there would be limits to consumption. They did not deny that there was a tendency towards under-consumption inherent in capitalism, but they contested the conclusion that business cycles and disturbances to growth must necessarily follow from such a tendency. Tugan-Baranowsky especially had a curious role to play. It was he who gave prominence to the Marxian reproduction schemes, but at the same time he disagreed from the very beginning with the orthodox interpretation by denying the validity of the theory of the tendency of the rate of profit to fall, and he went so far (1915, p. v) as to rebuke Marx for not having adequately developed Quesnay's method in his theory of markets:

> Quesnay's method found no (genuine) successor. The 'Tableau Économique' was a puzzle to economists for a long time, and nobody was interested in solving it. It was only much later that Marx reverted in volume II of *Capital* to Quesnay's method in presenting his schemes of the reproduction of social capital. These schemes are rather isolated within the general context of Marx's system, and Marx himself does not make any use of them in his analysis of the capitalist system as a whole . . . .

Tugan-Baranowsky's argument goes beyond growth theory, into business-cycle theory. It boils down to the view that under capitalism production could in principle proceed without disturbance, provided that all sectors of industry grew in proportion, or that the capital-goods industry grew in proportion to the growth in capitalists' purchasing power. Tugan did not, however, draw the conclusion that such a process of undisturbed growth was inevitable. He proved to be Marx's heir to the extent that, despite his 'revisionist deviations', he embarked on an analysis of fluctuations in the investment-goods sector, which was to be the starting point for modern business-cycle analysis.

We cannot examine in detail the controversy between the 'Populists' and the 'Legal Marxists', on whose side Lenin was to be found. This controversy has been presented in detail in *Rosa Luxemburg's Accumulation of Capital* (1913, chs 18–23), somewhat cursorily in Grossmann's principal work (1929) and again in detail in volume II, chapter 2, of Rosdolsky's monumental work (1968). Rosdolsky rightly says that among the 'Legal Marxists' Bulgakov (1897, pp 199ff.) – unlike the 'wildly optimistic' von Struve – presented the future prospects of capitalism in a sober way and sought to develop the Marxian theories further.

Bulgakov's work centres on two main theses. On the one hand, he protests against a theory expounded by the 'Populists' and taken up by Rosa Luxemburg: the 'fantastic dogma according to which capitalist production has an absolute need of foreign markets'. Bulgakov stresses the simple fact that foreign trade is by no means a 'bottomless pit', and that exports are counterbalanced by imports. He also stresses that 'the only market for the product of capitalist production is . . . this production itself', and therefore 'the only barrier to an increase in production is to be found in capital and in the necessity for its growth'.

As to the schemes themselves, Bulgakov raises a question concerning the growth process as such:

> The main difficulty in the analysis of extended reproduction processes resides in explaining how an expansion of production can come about in I and II, given that the first department produces only constant capital and the second only variable capital. This difficulty can be overcome by I accumulating constant capital for itself and for II, while II accumulates variable capital for itself and for I. The difficulty arising from accumulation is thus reduced to an exchange of those parts of their products which each department accumulates for the other.

In thus analysing investment in stocks of means of production and consumption, which is what is meant by the notion of 'accumulation' in this case, Bulgakov came very near to formulating a Marxist growth theory. Rosdolsky is wrong in his criticism that this is only an abstract solution and in his accusation that Bulgakov came near to adopting Say's Law and the teachings of 'Neo-Harmonism'. Even Lenin is subjected to such criticism by Rosdolsky, who thus joins the chorus of critics, including also Plekhanov and Rosa Luxemburg, of Lenin's early economic writings. As a matter of fact, Lenin, Bulgakov and Tugan-Baranowsky are all condemned outright, because they seemed to espouse the thesis that 'reproduction knows no barriers, and crises are to be explained simply by disproportionality in the means of production' (Rosdolsky, 1968, II, pp. 556ff.).

As it happens, the young Lenin, writing under the pseudonym 'Vladimir Ilyin', developed, in his debate with the 'Populists', a remarkable insight, which raises his early economic works above the common run of political polemics. In his study 'On the So-Called Question of Markets', written in response to Krassin's *The Question of Markets* (in Russian), which used Marx's reproduction schemes and put forward a theory of the non-existence of markets for capitalism in Russia, Lenin even employs a rudimentary input–output scheme, as well as making a whole series of realistic and perceptive remarks on prospects for the future. For him, 'the development of capitalism appears not only to be feasible, but absolutely necessary'. This development 'will of necessity bring about an increase in the standard of living ["level of requirements"] of the entire population and of the working proletariat'. Lenin even speaks of a 'law of increase in the standard of living', which has found its expression 'in the history of Europe', especially in France and Britain, but even in Russia. Here as well, the living standards of the peasantry had risen. 'This undeniably progressive phenomenon is an asset of Russian capitalism. . . . This is shown by the fact that peasants in industrial areas live much more "decently" . . . .' (Lenin, 1893; 1937). Meek has emphasised (1962 p. 14, note 321) that this perception of the historical increase in living standards was 'extraordinarily profound' for a Marxist of that time.

The satisfaction of this rising demand is brought about by technical progress, which Lenin (in the same way as Marx) sees (1893; 1937) as being linked to investment and to the relative growth in department I (means of production): 'The work of man is pushed further and further into the background by the work of the machine. . . . Capitalist society uses a larger part . . . of the year's supply of labour to produce means of production . . . .' It cannot, therefore, 'exist without accumulating'; also, 'that part of the social production which is devoted to consumption goods must of necessity increase'. There will be crises, for 'equilibrium between production and consumption will come about only through a series of oscillations'. Foreign markets are indispensable for the international division of labour. Lenin is superior in his realism to many Marxists of his time and ours. . . .

A few years later Lenin returned to the subject, directly referring to the work done by Tugan-Baranowsky and Bulgakov. He unmistakably pronounces himself in favour of the latter: 'In our view . . . truth is entirely on Bulgakov's side'. Bulgakov had rebuked Tugan-Baranowsky for turning too far away from Marx's schemes, thus forgetting their main purpose; the gist of the matter, according to Lenin, is to be found in the distinction between gross and net social (national) product. Lenin criticises Tugan-Baranowsky by stressing that 'a certain level of consumption is one of the conditions of proportionality' and concludes that 'the domestic market . . . grows more than in proportion to the means of production. . . . It follows that department I . . . can and must develop more rapidly than department II . . . .' (Lenin, 1898).

Rosdolsky in turn criticises Lenin's statement by saying that 'in fact Marx's schemes show nothing of the sort. We have shown, however, in our analysis of the schemes, that Marx's scheme no. 1 contains the germ of a slow growth in the dominance of the investment-goods industry. Lenin, who never lost sight of the business-cycle problem, recognises in any case the limits to the schemes, which, he says, 'in themselves cannot explain anything; they can only illustrate a process'. (Lenin, Oeuvres, Vol. IV Paris/Moscow 1959, 'Note sur la Théorie des Marchés' (1898), p. 62).

Hilferding, by contrast, attributed a much greater explanatory value to the schemes. He started from simple reproduction and showed (1909; 1947, p. 332) that at this stage possibilities of disturbance already existed:

If simple reproduction is to go on undisturbed, that part of fixed capital which decays annually must equal that which is to be replaced. . . . A disequilibrium may occur in the production of fixed and circulating capital even if fixed capital is simply replaced, when, as happens in real life, the proportion of annually consumed fixed capital changes in relation to what needs to be replaced.

We see clearly that Marxists emphasised the importance of depreciation for financing purposes at a time when this had not yet been fully appreciated by 'academic' theory. On the other hand, Hilferding does not succeed in presenting a fully-fledged theory of replacement cycles, although it had already been indicated by Marx.

Instead, in analysing accumulation, i.e. the schemes of extended reproduction, Hilferding puts the chief emphasis on (ibid., p. 338) 'the many points where money is withdrawn from circulation only to crystallise in numerous individual hoards, i.e. in potential money capital'. This is a somewhat crude way of looking at things, for it boils down to assuming a tendency for the velocity of monetary circulation to slow down, or to assuming a straightforward destruction of money (analogous to its creation) in the banking system.

In his analysis of the production schemes, however, Hilferding did not think primarily of the growth process, but stresses the business-cycle aspects. He uses the schemes in a manner similar to that of the Russian 'Legal Marxists', to fend off under-consumption theories, which he considers incompatible with the Marxian system. Indeed, from his point of view (ibid., p. 344),

the schemes prove that in capitalist production both simple and extended reproduction can proceed without disturbance, provided that proportionality is preserved. . . . It does not, therefore, at all follow that the crisis must have its origin in under-consumption by the broad masses, a feature which is endemic under capitalist production. Any rash expansion of consumption would in itself lead to a crisis, in the same way as stagnation of or reduction in the production of investment goods. Nor does it follow from these schemes as such that there is a possibility of general over-production. . . . [On the contrary,] it is possible to show that any sort of expansion is feasible, provided it takes place within the capacity framework of the existing means of production.

It is true that Hilferding did not construct a growth theory, as he might have done by enlarging upon this statement. For him, the schemes simply prove the under-consumption theories wrong and serve as a starting point for the introduction of the proportionality principle as an explanation of the business cycle.

ROSA LUXEMBURG'S CRITICISM: THE PROBLEM OF VALUE AND TECHNICAL PROGRESS

Rosa Luxemburg, who published her main work shortly after Hilferding, is outspokenly critical, and also probes more deeply into these matters. She thinks that 'the initiative remains all the time with department I. It is true that Marx's way of presenting his schemes conveys this impression, for he seems to ascribe to the capitalists in II the merely passive role of adjusting their investment. To this extent the scheme somewhat resembles Röpke's nightmare world of a planning system where all adjustments fall upon the provision of consumption goods, with the difference in this case that adjustment takes place in order to restore conditions of equilibrium.

With regard to this process, Oscar Lange formulated a significant phrase (1965; 1969, pp. 27–8): 'In a planned economy, accumulation takes place primarily in Division 2 and is invested mainly in Division 1.' Even in Lange's work, a critical note is evident about the hypothesis that profits are always invested in the same branch. Recently, Morishima has called this (1973, p. 119) a 'very peculiar investment function' and emphasised in the same way as Rosa Luxemburg the 'adjustment function' of the capitalists in department II. Indeed, Rosa Luxemburg (1913; 1966, p. 99) found it impossible to swallow the assumption that 'accumulation in department II depends entirely on and is dominated by accumulation in I . . . , that the whole accumulation movement which is introduced and actively prosecuted by I is followed passively by II.

Rosa Luxemburg may be motivated by the fear that Marx, in introducing such a hypothesis, may have prepared the ground for Tugan-Baranowsky's merry-go-round of investment for investment's sake. On the other hand, she may also have implicitly postulated (as Kautsky and Hilferding undoubtedly did) that the initiative ought to be with the consumption sector, and that the investment-goods sector ought only to react to consumers' demand (through the accelerator, as we are wont to say in modern times!).

Rosa Luxemburg was not content with this criticism, but pointed to the two main weaknesses of the schemes: the absence from them of technical progress, and the fact that they are built upon values and therefore do not reflect real growth in 'use values', whether in absolute terms or per head of population. Rosa Luxemburg's criticism is expressed as follows:

Above all, the scheme does not take into account the growing productivity of labour. From one year to another, it continues to show the same composition of capital despite accumulation, i.e. the same technical basis to the production process. If, however, one considers the progress being made in the productivity of labour, it follows that the material mass of the social product, investment goods as well as consumption goods, grows still more rapidly than the mass of values as shown in the scheme . . . .

Rosa Luxemburg's 'material mass' is nothing but the quantity of goods, which does not appear at all in value accounting, which registers only the increase in inputs. Thus she basically anticipates the truism that value theory is ill adapted to deal with the growth phenomenon as such. On the other hand, even she identifies technical progress with an increase in the 'organic composition of capital', a question that we discuss later.

Rosa Luxemburg's interpretation of the reproduction schemes has been sharply criticised by Rosdolsky. It is thus all the more remarkable that he recognises her merit in pointing to the absence of technical progress from the schemes, though he goes on to rebuke her for having overlooked the fact that the second Marxian scheme shows regular growth and that even 'in the first Marxian scheme . . . accumulation is by no means so unsteady and irregular' as she says it is. It is indeed true that Rosa Luxemburg made some minor arithmetical mistakes and believed that the rate of accumulation for II declined in the third year from 30 to 29 per cent. This is not correct, for the great jump actually occurs in the second year. (See ibid., p. 305.)

BUKHARIN'S EQUILIBRIUM FORMULA

In order to prove that in the Marxian schemes growth is of an equilibrium nature, Rosdolsky sets Rosa Luxemburg's reasoning against Bukharin's formula. Bukharin (1926, pp. 11ff.) divides surplus value into three parts:

α = the share of surplus value consumed;
β_c = the share of surplus value invested in constant capital; and
β_v = the share of surplus value spent on variable capital.

Thus in Bukharin's presentation the two Marxian Schemes appear as in Table v.

Bukharin then goes on to derive from these schemes the following equilibrium formula, which must be satisfied if extended reproduction is to proceed without interruption:

$$c_{II} + \beta_{c_{II}} = v_I + \alpha_I + \beta_{v_I}$$

Rosdolsky tries to exploit this equation in a formal way, with the help of the American mathematician Chester. Rosdolsky (1968, II, pp. 526ff.) explains that in this formula, 'a strict correlation between the rate of accumulation and the organic composition of capital in both departments' seems to be given. Hence, 'the rates of accumulation in both departments must grow in

TABLE V

Year	Dept	c	v	s		
				α	β_c	β_v
(a) Scheme no.1						
I	I	4000 + 1000 + 500 + 400 + 100				
	II	1500 + 750 + 600 + 100 + 50				
2	I	4400 + 1100 + 550 + 440 + 110				
	II	1600 + 800 + 560 + 160 + 80				
3	I	4840 + 1210 + 605 + 484 + 121				
	II	1760 + 880 + 616 + 176 + 88				
4	I	5324 + 1331 + 666 + 532 + 133				
	II	1936 + 968 + 677 + 194 + 97				
(b) Scheme no. 2						
I	I	5000 + 1000 + 500 + 417 + 83				
	II	1430 + 285 + 101 + 153 + 31				
2	I	5417 + 1083 + 542 + 452 + 90				
	II	1583 + 316 + 158 + 132 + 26				
3	I	5869 + 1173 + 587 + 489 + 98				
	II	1715 + 342 + 171 + 143 + 28				
4	I	6358 + 1271 + 636 + 530 + 106				
	II	1858 + 370 + 185 + 155 + 30				

an inverse proportion to the rates of the organic composition, or, expressing this in an equation:

$$\frac{\beta_I}{s_I} : \frac{\beta_{II}}{s_{II}} = \frac{v_{II}}{c_{II}+v_{II}} : \frac{v_I}{c_I+v_I}$$

In Marxian scheme no. 1, this ratio was 50:30 per cent = $^1/_3 : ^1/_5$.'

Rosdolsky concludes from this that even in the first year the scheme follows a strict rule – provided one disregards the irregularity which occurs in the transition from the first to the second year, but it is to just this irregularity that Rosa Luxemburg refers in talking of the 'jerkiness' of accumulation.

Rosdolsky thinks it possible to disprove Rosa Luxemburg's allegations, and he affirms that in Marx's first scheme,

accumulation in department II is not so jerky . . . for, if one disregards the first year, the result is that department I in this scheme always accumulates 50 per cent and department II 30 per cent. This is of course no mere accident, but is an inevitable result of the difference between the departments in the 'organic composition of capital'.

While the 'organic composition' strictly defined $(c:v)$ is $4:1$ in department I and $2:1$ in department II, Rosdolsky construes, with the aid of Chester and on the basis of Bukharin's formula, another version of it, i.e. $v:(c+v)$, which works out to $1:3$ (department I) and $1:5$ (II). The ratio of I to II is here the inverse of the ratio of their accumulation rates, $50:30$ per cent.

Now, it does not appear to be quite logical for Rosdolsky to try to establish a connexion between the share of savings in profits and the inverse relationship between the wage bill and total costs in the two departments. It would seem more logical to construct an inverse rate of profits, by relating the sum of investments $c+v$ to the sum of profits (surplus value). One would then get a ratio of $5:1$ for department I and $3:1$ for department II, and this could be related to the ratio of the rates of accumulation, $50:30$. This would mean that 50 per cent or 30 per cent of profits would have to be accumulated to re-establish this ratio – (investment:sum of profits in I) / (investment:sum of profits in II).

In fact, this ratio need not give rise to a complicated analysis in the Rosdolsky–Chester fashion, for the profit rates of the two departments determine the growth rate of the entire system. The rate of profit of department I is 20 per cent, that of department II $33^1/_3$ per cent, related to 'cost price' (sum of costs). If I accumulates 50 per cent of 20 per cent, this means that 10 per cent of total costs are accumulated. The same is true if II accumulates 30 per cent of $33^1/_3$ per cent. Since Marx assumes that surplus value (or the sum of profits in each department) always grows in the same way as the wage bill, and since the latter grows in proportion to constant capital (given that the 'organic composition of capital' remains the same), the entire system must grow by 10 per cent per annum – a simple outcome.

ROSA LUXEMBURG'S ANTICIPATION OF BUKHARIN'S EQUATION

It must be said that Rosdolsky misses the point of Rosa Luxemburg's criticism. Her criticism stems from the fact that Marx, instead of saying clearly that from the second year onwards II accumulates 30 per cent of its surplus value, expresses himself in a much more sophisticated manner: he allows just as much surplus value to be accumulated by capitalists II as is necessary to cover I v and one half of I s, the amount consumed by workers and capitalists in I through sales of constant capital to II. This amounts to 50 units more constant capital than II bought in the first year. The further decisions on accumulation taken by the capitalists in II do not look at all spontaneous but bear the mark of a kind of technological constraint –

namely, that the old ratio $v:c$ be maintained. Thus the capitalists in II are constrained to capitalise 110 s which they cannot consume (i.e. consumption goods kept as stocks). So it continues. Indeed, the proportion of its surplus value that department II accumulates is not owing to its own propensity to invest, but, rather, is a corollary of what happens in I.

In his criticism of Rosa Luxemburg, Rosdolsky has also overlooked the fact that she anticipated Bukharin's equation when she gave it as a rule that 'Accumulation can only occur in both departments simultaneously, and on the condition that the supplier of the means of subsistence [department II] enlarges its constant capital by as much as the capitalists of the investment-goods department [I] enlarge their variable capital and their personal consumption fund.'

This she translates into the equation

$$\Delta \text{ II } c = \Delta \text{ I } v + \Delta \text{ I } s_k$$

In Bukharin's terminology, which Rosdolsky prefers, this would be

$$\beta_{c_{II}} = \beta_{v_I} + (\alpha_I \text{ year } 2 - \alpha_I \text{ year } 1).$$

This equation differs from Bukharin's equilibrium equation in that c_{II}, on the left-hand side, and v_I and α_I, on the right-hand side, are omitted. These units correspond to each other, for in the first year

$$c_{II} = v_I + \alpha_I$$

(i.e. constant capital II corresponds to workers' and capitalists' consumption in I). Thus Rosa Luxemburg not only anticipated Bukharin's equation, but also found a simplified version of it!

This does not, however, change one regrettable fact, that she undoubtedly erred in the very heart of her growth theory, for she assumed, in a manner similar to the Russian 'Populists' and the German Cunow, that capitalism could not keep growing on the strength of its own resources. As we shall see later, she has been proved wrong on this point by other Marxists, such as Otto Bauer, Bukharin and later Sweezy, and by the great post-war boom of 'late capitalism'. This boom lasted into the 1970s and clearly demonstrated that industrial countries, and not semi-feudal states or under-developed 'third persons', are the best customers of industrial countries.

Her fundamental error on the strength of capitalism's resources does nothing to detract from Rosa Luxemburg's acuity on other matters. She discovered *en passant* such things as the foreign-trade multiplier as Preiser (1950/65, p. 286) was quick to point out, and it was she who first analysed in depth the growth aspects of the Marxian schemes, while criticising their weaknesses in a way which could have been fertile if only other Marxists had followed in her footsteps.

Instead, she was subjected to a stream of what was often sharp, unjust criticism. Even Rosdolsky says, of her most spirited critic, that 'the modern reader of Bukharin's essay . . . often feels uncomfortable in the face of the violent and sometimes frivolous tone of his polemics against Rosa Luxemburg, who had fallen victim to fascist murderers a few years earlier'. Rosdolsky himself, however, did not do full justice to Rosa Luxemburg, as his treatment of, above all, the equilibrium formula shows.

Finally, Rosa Luxemburg attempts to remedy the weakness caused to the schemes by the absence from them of technical progress, and to this end introduces 'rising organic composition'. In so doing, she emphasises (1912; 1966, p. 311) the element of disturbance which technical progress represents: 'However we may envisage the technical transformation of the mode of production within the framework of continuing accumulation, it cannot be introduced without disturbing the basic conditions of the Marxian scheme.' Rosdolsky comments (1968, II, p. 584) that she

> is undoubtedly right in saying so . . . . Her criticism has also a cogent aspect, about which her critics are in most cases silent . . . that the Marxian schemes of extended reproduction ignore all modifications to the mode of production which are caused by technical progress . . . namely the rising organic composition of capital, the increase in the rate of surplus value and the rising rate of accumulation. . . . As soon as these alterations are introduced into the schemes, the equilibrium conditions of reproduction are disturbed . . . .

Marxists ought to have concentrated their attention on this point, though in so doing they would to begin with have ended up in a blind alley, since they identified technical progress with 'capital deepening'. Several authors tried to tackle the problem. Eckstein (1923/70) combined a rather superficial criticism of Rosa Luxemburg's under-consumptionist ideas ('it is precisely the schemes which show who buys the products') with an emphasis on monetary aspects. Otto Bauer stressed that 'in capitalist production, there is a tendency to adapt the accumulation of capital to population growth'. Bauer disproved Rosa Luxemburg's thesis of the indispensability of the non-capitalist sector, and he came very near to developing a genuine growth theory, but he chiefly concentrated his attention on business-cycle aspects. Furthermore, his method of calculation, which incorporates a slightly rising 'organic composition', gave rise later to Grossmann's theory of capitalist collapse. (Bauer, 1913, pp. 833, 863ff.) In more recent times, Mandel thought (1971, pp. 11ff.) that Rosdolsky had proved that 'the schemes as developed by Marx do not suffice for the purpose . . . of explaining the laws of motion of capitalist production'. He maintains that it would be impossible to demonstrate the final collapse of capitalism by means of these schemes and sees

> a definite objective in Marx's analysis of capitalism: that [the schemes]
> should explain why a system based upon the pure anarchy of the
> market . . . does not remain in permanent disequilibrium and con-
> tinuous collapse, but may attain a periodic equilibrium. . . . The task of
> the reproduction schemes remains always the same: to show that
> periodic equilibrium is possible, and what the general conditions for it
> are.

He then goes on to conclude that the reproduction schemes 'are ill
adapted, by their very character, to contribute towards an analysis of these
laws of motion', for they 'inevitably imply disequilibria'.

We believe, on the contrary, that the schemes actually afford indications
of why, in capitalism, equilibrium rests on a knife edge. Mandel overlooks
the fact that Marx succeeded in showing that business cycles would be
possible even under simple reproduction. This is analogous to Kaldor's
analysis in modern times. Furthermore, the importance of Marx's
discovery of basic disequilibria is reinforced by the fact that Marx's 'spiral
analysis', contained in his reproduction schemes, anticipates Robertson's
period analysis.

RECENT MARXIST ATTEMPTS AT DYNAMICS

Since the Second World War, several attempts have been made by
Marxists at introducing a dynamic element into the reproduction schemes.
Among the most important attempts at this have been those of Nemchinov,
who provides a refreshing example of a Russian author alive to new
impulses. In 1958 he established a new equilibrium equation for extended
reproduction:

$$Q = \frac{s_c}{(v_\mathrm{I} + s_\mathrm{I}) - c_\mathrm{II}}$$

Equilibrium prevails whenever $Q = 1$. If Q is smaller than one, only part of
the accumulated means of production will be used: investment is not active
enough. If Q is larger than one, inflation will set in. Nemchinov tried
(1958; 1959) to calculate this coefficient for Great Britain. Unfortunately,
he does not manage to avoid double counting, because in his case, the
difference between gross and net social product is made up not only of
depreciation (on equipment and stocks), but also of raw materials
consumed. He thus ignores the work done by Burchardt, Dickinson and
others.

It is regrettable that Oscar Lange did not deal with the problem of double counting in his book on the theory of reproduction, published in 1965. As it is, this book represents a remarkable attempt to analyse the schemes and render them useful from a modern point of view. In doing so, Lange discusses the ratio $P_I:P_{II}$ between the social products of the two departments. He emphasises (1965; 1969, p. 35) that this ratio must change if 'a transfer is made to less durable means of production. . . . This is explained by the fact that each year more means of production have to be produced for replacement . . . .'

According to Lange (ibid., p. 37), the condition for extended reproduction free from disturbance is $v_I + s_I > c_{II}$, which 'surplus . . . can be called the accumulation of means of production (it is the net supply of means of production, i.e. the surplus production of means of production over replacement requirements).'

Lange refers to Domar's calculation that 42 per cent of depreciation in the United States and 89 per cent of depreciation in the Soviet Union is devoted to net investment, in the dynamic sense of the Lohmann–Ruchti (or Eisner–Domar) effect. Lange corrects Domar's figure for the Soviet Union to 78 per cent and stresses (ibid., p. 32) that 'in the case of extended reproduction . . . the proportion between the value of production in Division 1 and Division 2 depends not only on the input coefficients . . . but also on the accumulation coefficients'. There is an essential difference between the two: in the first case, it is a matter of technical coefficients, and the second is concerned with the outcome of economic decisions.

In this context, Lange (1965/69, p. 32) discusses the question of an increase in the 'organic composition of capital' (W_1 and W_2), which he distinguishes from the ratio of total production in department 1 to total production in department II: this is P_I/P_{II}. He refers to the work of Minc, who denied that this ratio must constantly increase. Lange refers briefly to the various attempts made since Tugan–Baranowsky's time to use the schemes to analyse development potential under capitalism. He comes to the conclusion that 'the schemes of production equilibrium do not suffice for solving the problem'.

The Japanese economist Morishima, who seems to be well disposed towards Marxism, chose a rather daring approach in trying to use the schemes to solve the problem of the stability of equilibrium. However, he wants the value scheme to be ignored, not only because of the difficulties of measurement to which we have referred, but also for other reasons. He states (1973, p. 159) that 'it is extremely important in Marxian economics to distinguish those theories which are independent of the labour theory of value from those which cannot dispense with it', and he reckons the reproduction schemes among the former.

ANALOGIES TO THE VON NEUMANN MODEL IN MORISHIMA'S VIEW

Morishima identifies Marxian extended reproduction with a von Neumann growth path: 'He assumed . . . that the labour force could be expanded at a rate which was higher than the maximum rate of growth of capital, or at least that the supply of labour could adjust itself quickly and smoothly to demand' (Morishima, 1973, p. 117). It had already been pointed out by Koopmans (1964; 1970, p. 296) that von Neumann assumed,

> contrary to all experience about economic growth, . . . that all production and consumption activities grow in time all at the same proportional rate. Worse than that, it seems quixotic to ignore completely the historically given capital stock available at the beginning of the time period under consideration, and to assume instead that out of some fourth dimension one can at time $t = 1$ pull forth a capital stock of precisely that composition that enables proportional growth to take place at a maximal rate and through a continuing competitive equilibrium.

Koopmans then goes on to say that 'subsequent developments have fully vindicated the intuitions that led von Neumann to make these drastic and arbitrary-looking simplifications'. The same reasoning can actually be applied to the assumptions upon which the Marxian schemes are based.

Up to a point, Koopmans confirms Tugan-Baranowsky's old assumption in saying that in this model

> consumption is not treated as in any way an end in itself. Consumption goods occur only as inputs to processes that have labor . . . as outputs. . . . This implies that the only labor-producing processes that will be utilized are such as to absorb in some sense the minimum consumption input needed to produce the required labor output . . . with possibly some scope for incentive goods . . . .

Morishima has postulated an identity between von Neumann's model, as summarised by Koopmans, and the Marxian schemes. In so doing, however, he overlooks the fact that Marx, in his general theory of development (see Volume I, Ch. 24), starts from the notion of a sociological minimum level, which is historically determined and which periodically brings an increase in the absolute standard of living and, therefore, in the minimum level of inputs it requires. All the same, the identification of the von Neumann model with Marx's reproduction schemes is probably justified. It is indeed true that Marx postulates constant wages in this context, but Morishima has no hesitation in saying (1973, p. 167) that Marx's

> analysis of the process of reproduction does him great credit, because it may be considered as a seedling of the von Neumann-type growth theory. If Marx had been more mathematical and had thought of the von Neumann golden rule, he could have developed the whole of the von Neumann model independently and a huge short cut might have been made in the history of economic theory.

In quoting the 'golden rule', Morishima also refers to the treatment of depreciation in von Neumann's work: the latter regards investment goods inherited from the previous period as having been newly produced; thus the depreciation problem is practically circumvented.

From his analysis Morishima cannot be dubbed a Marxist, but he could claim that nowadays similar ideas are gaining ground even with Marxist authors – for instance, the Hungarian Marxist Brody, who wants to reformulate the theory of surplus value. Morishima, however, does not believe, as Brody (1970) does, that growth can be adequately represented in labour values. He starts from the assumption (1973, p. 157) that 'no capitalist makes a decision about accumulation in terms of the surplus value measured in labour time'. He says that even Marx recognised 'that capitalists made their decisions on saving and investment in terms of money. Then the rate of accumulation a Marx assumed in his reproduction theory must be founded on the actually observable propensity to consume s_c [i.e. capitalists' propensity to consume].'

Here we must enlarge upon Morishima. We have pointed out that the quantity of 'use values' grows more rapidly than the sum of labour values; but it cannot be assumed that prices per unit of use value fall as rapidly as their quantity grows, to ensure an identity between money sums. We have also pointed out that the sum of surplus value per capitalist grows in all probability more rapidly than average income. If the capitalists' propensity to consume remains the same, while their numbers decrease, the rate of accumulation cannot remain constant but will have to grow – although it may grow more slowly if capitalists' propensity to consume increases.

This again means that the volume of accumulation must grow more rapidly than national income and that small entrepreneurs are being squeezed out. This remains true no matter whether we reckon in value or in price units. The share of 'saving' or investment would, according to this scheme, have to increase, and, following the Harrod–Domar equation, the 'warranted' rate of growth would increase too, provided that the capital–output ratio remains the same. As soon as this rate diverges from the 'natural' or effective rate, the disturbances that Harrod expects would arise.

In the Marxist system, this would find an even simpler explanation. The 'organic composition of capital', which is identical with increasing productivity, would rise, and the volume of use values would increase even faster. In this case, paradoxically, the deviation between growth expressed in values and growth expressed in terms of personal income would increase to an ever-greater extent.

Four conclusions may be drawn from this reasoning.

(1) Formally speaking, the exposition in values is less representative of the real growth process the more productivity and the (real) growth rate increase.

(2) The rate of accumulation must show a tendency towards continual increase; otherwise, growth will cease.

(3) Technical progress must proceed ever faster, which would either lead to a current decrease in the capital–output ratio (which would permit an increase in the growth rate with an unchanged savings rate) or to a 'rising organic composition' in the Marxian sense, with faster progress in the consumption-goods sector, which would be more than offset by the contrary development in the capital-goods sector.

(4) In the latter case, the capital-goods sector would have to expand relative to the consumption-goods sector.

Lenin, unlike the many Marxists (for instance, Rosdolsky) who fought shy of the spectre of Tugan-Baranowsky, was aware of this last point. Marx himself indicated such a possibility by reckoning with a higher rate of accumulation for department II in the transition from the first to the second year.

Now, it is difficult to deny what Morishima calls the very peculiar character of the Marxian investment function. He almost repeats Rosa Luxemburg's criticism in saying (ibid., p. 119) that 'capitalists of department II have been assigned the role of adjuster'. In the same context, Morishima states that the growth rates of the two departments differ only in the transition from the first to the second year: 10 per cent for I, 6·67 per cent for II, while from the second year onwards it is 10 per cent for both. He emphasises (ibid., pp. 119–20) that the transition from disequilibrium to equilibrium growth comes about much more quickly in the Marxian scheme than in neo-classical models: 'In Marx's economy there prevails a tendency towards balanced growth, which is much stronger than the convergence claimed by neo-classical economists such as Solow, Meade, and Uzawa, because any state of unbalanced growth will disappear in Marx's economy in a single year'.

In this way, what appeared to be a simple arithmetical correction is elevated by Morishima into a matter of principle, for he sees it not as an accident, but as a special consequence of Marx's peculiar investment function, i.e. that the capitalists in II have an adaptive investment function.

He then modifies Marx's example by assuming uniform rates of saving and profit. Along with Marx, he assumes that the rate of surplus value is the same in both departments, since the same assumption is made about 'organic composition'. For, if we regard a constant 'organic composition of capital' as a quasi capital–output ratio, identical rates of saving out of surplus value, which in turn imply identical rates of saving out of personal income (since we postulate that there are no workers' savings), lead, according to the Domar equation, to identical growth rates, if the 'organic composition' is the same in both departments. Morishima's analysis thus provides a further proof that the Domar equation was, as Robertson says, hidden in Marx's 'tangled phraseology'.

Here we need only note that Morishima attributes decisive importance to the 'organic composition' with regard to the stability problem: if it is greater in department I, there will be a 'monotonous deviation from an equilibrium growth path', and, in the reverse case, a series of 'explosive oscillations around an equilibrium growth path'. In any case, Morishima considers the equilibrium growth path to be inherently unstable: if a deviation occurs, it will tend progressively to increase.

Rosa Luxemburg, Otto Bauer and other Marxists introduced into the Marxian schemes an increasing 'organic composition', which meant in the end that they postulated a decreasing marginal efficiency of investment, expressed in values. The value scheme is particularly annoying in this respect, for, as long as one does not know how the hidden mass of 'use values' (or the volume of personal income), which accompanies the value figures like a shadow, actually grows, one cannot really measure the efficiency of investment in modern growth terms.

In view of the importance that Marx attributes, in volume III of *Capital*, to the rise in the 'organic composition', the extended reproduction schemes seem to cry out for the introduction of such a coefficient of 'capital deepening', which for Marx and his followers was synonymous with technical progress. This would be easy if one assumed that capitalists did not reinvest their savings in both c and v, but only in c, and used raw materials so sparingly that they required only an increase in fixed capital. Certain statements in Kalecki's later work could be interpreted in this way.

We should then have to ask what happens in such a model to the growth of income and consumption, which, after all, is the purpose of all economic activity. If the wage bill no longer grows, the sums of surplus value would no longer grow either, unless one drops the hypothesis of a constant rate of surplus value. It seems one would be thrown back onto Tugan-Baranowsky's famous merry-go-round so severely condemned by Hilferding and Lenin.

Such reasoning would neglect the fact that the Marxian schemes are set out in values. If indeed the increase in the 'organic composition of capital' leads to an increase in productivity, the net product (value added or personal income), while remaining constant in values, would nevertheless grow in volume (expressed in constant prices), even if only as a reflection of the value scheme. Growth in the modern sense, i.e. growth in the volume of goods and services per head of the labour force, occurs in the value scheme 'behind a veil', as it were.

Furthermore, if there is to be by definition no increase in v or in the labour force, workers must be transferred from department II to I, since the latter must increase relatively more if capital equipment is to increase in proportion to the wage bill. In value terms the growth of I will then be the very engine of total growth, and in volume terms its relative growth must be even faster, provided real productivity grows equally fast in I and II.

DISEQUILIBRIUM IN THE SCHEMES ACCORDING TO HARRIS

The Marxian schemes have in the meantime received increasing attention outside the circle of Marxist authors, owing to their consequences for the growth process. At about the same time as Morishima, the American economist Harris drew attention to the elements of instability that he finds in the schemes, even in that of simple reproduction. To demonstrate this, Harris transforms the equilibrium condition $c_{II} = v_I + s_I$ by dividing it by v_{II} and by introducing 'organic composition' k and rate of surplus value ε.

$$\frac{v_I}{v_{II}} = \frac{k_{II}}{1 + \varepsilon_I}$$

According to Harris (1972, pp. 510–11), this

> is the only relation which ensures that the capitalists in each department realise an amount of surplus value at the appropriate rate on the value of the wages advanced. . . . It is, so to say, the equilibrium condition of the system and determines a unique allocation of labor between the two departments. . . . There is, however, no guarantee that the capitalists, taken together, would advance just the right amount of wages and in the right proportions. There is therefore no guarantee that the system could achieve equilibrium.

This is undoubtedly an important extension to the Marxian thesis that cyclical instability is possible in a stationary state. But Harris does not simply refer to hoarding tendencies, as Marx does, but lays his finger on the problem of proportionality in the ratio of wage bill I to wage bill II.

This is the starting point for the formulation by Harris of an analogous condition for the schemes of extended reproduction. Here he introduces the notion of the rate of accumulation a. The equilibrium condition then becomes

$$\frac{a_{II}}{a_I} = \frac{\Delta v_I}{\Delta v_{II}} = \frac{1 + k_{II}}{1 + k_I}$$

Only if this equation holds will there be equilibrium growth for both departments, on condition that capitalists always reinvest in their own department. Harris then goes on to say (ibid, p. 513), 'Equilibrium for the system as a whole requires that the amounts invested in hiring labor in the two departments be proportional. . . . But since a_i and k_i are independently determined parameters, there is nothing to ensure that this condition would, in fact, hold. An equilibrium therefore might not exist.' Herein a_i is the (non-specific) proportion of their surplus carried over from the previous period which capitalists invest, and k_i is (non-specific) organic composition of capital regarded as a given constant' (Harris 1972, p. 511 and 508).

Harris then analyses the profit rate. Uniformity of the rate in both departments is meaningless, as long as one reckons in labour values, if the rate of profit is to be related to capital stocks. At the same time, a uniform rate of profit presupposes a flow of capital between industries, which would be equivalent to abandoning the hypothesis that capitalists always invest in their own industry. If so, the equilibrium condition is then simplified to read $a_{II} = a_I$.

According to Harris (ibid., p. 517), an equilibrium is possible only if the hypothesis of pure self-financing is given up. One might be tempted to conclude that modern monopolistic systems, which rely predominantly on self-finance, are prone to instability. The reason seems to be that in a scheme based on prices

> some of the surplus value appropriated is redistributed between departments by the price mechanism. . . . This transfer of surplus between the capitalists compensates for the difference in the value of their capital. For growth to be balanced, it is then only necessary that the capitalists reinvest the same proportion of their profits.

Harris thinks (ibid., pp. 518–19) that the Marxian system does not answer the question of what factors bring about the correct rate of accumulation (net investment). He is of the view that Marx thought that the pressure of competition would be a sufficient reason, for it obliges capitalists incessantly to modernise through investment. This begs the question, for it is by no means certain that net investment is required. Harris adds that Marx found no evidence of a minimum level of profits, and he refers to certain passages in 'Wages, Price and Profit' where Marx seems to hint at the notion of the factor-price frontier.

By contrast, Eagly took up Charasov's idea of a minimum profit rate below which the capitalists' propensity to invest would cease. He goes on to introduce the problem of business cycles, when he says (1972, pp. 533–4): 'As long as capitalists automatically reinvest all surplus value they receive, the likelihood of a business cycle is considerably reduced, if not eliminated entirely.' Only external shocks could start such cycles. As soon, however, as we assume that the propensity to invest varies, the endogenous cycle becomes possible.

KALECKI'S GROWTH THEORY IN PRICE TERMS

In his late work on growth theory, Kalecki tries to answer the question of whether net investment or even an increase in the capital–output ratio is indispensable for an improvement in productivity. He denies that it is and asserts that productivity could well be increased, without additional capital input, through organisational improvements, reduced wastage and economies in raw-material consumption (this reminds us of a similar enumeration in *Capital*). Kalecki then tries to measure such improvements by introducing a coefficient u. He then proposes using this coefficient to measure the marginal utilisation of productive equipment. He even sees in an appropriate interpretation of u the basic difference between the capitalist and the socialist systems. The former is marred by continuous fluctuations, while the latter would be characterised by full utilisation of fixed assets. In the case of the capitalist system,

> u is not an independent coefficient . . . but reflects changes in the degree to which it is possible to find a market for the output of the existing productive facilities. It is only in the socialist economy, where utilisation of productive capacity is safeguarded by the plan . . . that the coefficient u begins to reflect solely the effect of organisational and technical improvements which do not require significant capital outlays . . . .
> (Kalecki, 1963; 1970, p. 12.)

Kalecki only cursorily touches upon the problems of the Marxian schemes of extended reproduction, but the chapter in which he does so (12) is one of the highlights of Marxist growth theory.

One may well ask whether Kalecki does not overwork his coefficient u by applying it to both the problems of technical progress and those of business-cycle analysis. These matters are discussed in detail in subsequent chapters.

It should be noted that Kalecki ignores the value scheme and starts from a price scheme. His attention is mainly devoted to the question of how to increase the growth rate. In his model, he starts by assuming a kind of 'natural rate of growth' in Harrod's sense: labour supply grows by 1·5 per cent per year, and technical progress increases production by 5·5 per cent each year, which adds up to a 'natural growth rate' of 7 per cent. The share of investment is (like Marx's figure for department 1) 26 per cent. If, now, the growth rate is to be raised by 1 per cent, the investment share will have to be raised to 29 per cent. This denotes a capital–output ratio of 3·0. Kalecki sets all this out in essentially algebraic terms. He expands the Marxian model – which exclusively relies on additional labour and capitalists' savings – through the introduction of autonomous technical progress and of a capital stock, which is reflected in the investment coefficient.

He then goes on successively to examine the possibilities of raising the growth rate by increasing the investment (capital) coefficient and by accelerated depreciation (essentially the more rapid modernisation of equipment), taking into account the difficulties which might arise from accelerated growth for external equilibrium.

In his discussion of Kalecki's book, Feiwel arrived at the conclusion (1971, p. 815) that 'Kalecki tends to conclude that growth acceleration has probably no major practical significance in conditions of unlimited supply of labour' – i.e. just the case on which Marx based his model.

Kalecki's conclusion flatly contradicts the analyses of such authors as Dobb (1960) and Sen (1960), who thought that an increase in the capital–output ratio would be worthwhile even in the case of an unlimited labour supply. Even so, Kalecki's conclusion appears plausible at first sight, for, as long as labour is abundant, less capital–intensive methods would appear to be justified. To that extent, Marx's case seems to be more appropriate for less-developed countries. Kalecki bases his justification primarily on the argument that, in the period of transition towards a higher capital–intensity, unemployment must occur, even if in the long run positive results are forthcoming – which he doubts. He particularly examines the possibility of raising the growth rate by curtailing consumption and shows the limits to this process. He had already pointed out in earlier works the danger that an optimal investment rate might be so high that in the short run the population would be starved to death. While he thinks a small productivity gain may result from increasing growth, he believes that if real wages are to be kept constant such an increase is only temporarily possible. He thinks, however, that a permanent increase in the growth rate of personal income may well be possible under conditions of capital-using technical progress.

ACCUMULATION, INVESTMENT AND THE IMPULSE TO GROWTH

Marx's schemes of extended reproduction are based on the hypothesis that growth follows upon investment (in value terms). To that extent, the schemes are analogous to certain simplified practical concepts, especially in countries of the Eastern bloc.

Bombach (1960) points out that the popularisation of growth theory, which we consider in the next chapter, has led to the adoption of such simplified devices: for instance, that stemming from the assumption that the capital–output ratio remains constant over a long period. By way of further simplification, we start by identifying this ratio with the Marxian notion of the 'organic composition of capital', but we shall see later that this Marxian term is more complex.

According to Bombach (ibid., pp. 45–6), the 'prediction of the growth rate boils down to a prognosis of the investment rate. This is a scheme of thought that can of course also be applied for planning purposes. One can say what the investment share ("the instrumental variable") will have to be, if a certain growth rate ("the objective variable") is sought.' In Marx's scheme no. 1, the share of accumulation (50 per cent in I and 30 per cent in II in terms of surplus value and 25 or 15 per cent in terms of national income) is the 'instrumental variable'.

It is no accident that Bombach's simple planning scheme draws its inspiration from the schemes of extended reproduction, in which growth and investment are effectively synonymous. This comfortable scheme is jeopardised as soon as Marx's other idea, namely the change in the 'organic composition', enters the debate. Bombach goes on to say,

> If . . . the capital–output ratio grows along with the increasing growth rate, these calculations collapse, at least in their over-simplified form. There are in fact real grounds for assuming that the growth rate and the capital–output ratio are linked in a certain manner. To each growth rate there corresponds a certain structure of the economy, and this structure . . . determines the magnitude of the capital–output ratio.

Here we return to Marx's theory of the tendency of the rate of profit to fall, which implies structural problems. It is only in the context of this theory that we can deal in detail with the problem of the capital–output ratio. At this juncture, however, we merely hint at the statistical problem and add a brief comment on the connexion between technical progress and net investment. As we shall see in detail, it is hardly possible to affirm that the capital–output ratio is constant. Most statistical series seem to indicate a slow rise during the nineteenth century and until shortly after the First World War, since when the contrary tendency has prevailed. Such a sceptical observer as Hickman believed that following the end of the nineteenth century there was a tendency at least for the investment–output ratio to fall, but he believed that this trend slowed down in the 1920s and 1950s and that since the late 1950s it had actually been reversed. He tries to explain this by saying (1965, p. 202) that 'a falling gross investment share was compatible with a rising net capital–output ratio until World War I because depreciation was a small share of gross investment in those early years when the capital stock was still comparatively small', while the bulk of depreciation occurred much later.

Now, objections have been raised to the use of the investment–output ratio. Helmstädter, for instance, categorically denies (1969, p. 36) a connexion between investment and the increase of production in a given period. A decreasing share of gross investment in gross social product leads us to conclude that net investment will also be of less importance, if faster technical progress calls for an increased share of depreciation, which seems more and more to be the case in modern times.

In modern economies, technical progress can hardly result from rising depreciation alone. It is much more likely that it requires, as Marx postulates, not only gross investment but also increasing net investment, as would be the case when fixed assets which are renewed or modified can only partially be adapted to the most up-to-date processes. Replacement generally does not take the form of completely new installations – as it would, as a rule, need to, if modern technology is fully to realise its potential – but is carried out piecemeal.

These microeconomic facts do not, at the macroeconomic level, irrevocably justify the postulate that net investment is absolutely necessary. It is possible to imagine that old equipment is scrapped at the same pace as the new is constructed. In that case, disinvestment and new investment would to some extent cancel out, and no net investment would appear at the macroeconomic level. A final answer to these questions can only be found in a combination of technological and economic reasons.

Dieterlen has indicated (1957, p. 104) three main conditions for growth: innovations, in the widest sense; the will to apply them (on the entrepreneurs' side); and 'a sufficient mobility of factors and needs, a malleability of structures'. Modern plants are increasingly being designed according to narrow specifications, so the last condition is in most cases unlikely to be fulfilled. If it were, this would speak in favour of Marx's assumption that net investment and growth are linked, although it was Marx himself who pointed to the importance of depreciation and gross investment as a vehicle for innovations. By and large, his conception of growth seems to be rooted more in new investment and new installations in the widest sense.

8 Modern Growth Theory and Marxian Analysis

In this chapter we seek to point out some of the affinities between the Marxian theory of extended reproduction and modern growth theory, but without pretending to delve into the latter deeply.

ORTHODOX CRITICISM FROM THE STANDPOINT OF THE THEORY OF REPRODUCTION

We must first deal with the work done by the Gosplan group in the early years of the Soviet Union. This work marks the transition from Marxian growth analysis to modern growth theory. This group, centred on the old Menshevik Groman and his disciples Bazarov and Feldman, has, curiously enough, not yet received its due acclaim in modern Soviet analysis; nor has this analysis as yet recognised modern growth theory as a logical continuation of the Marxian reproduction schemes. Very often, an artificial contrast is drawn between 'reproduction' and growth theory. For instance, Meissner, one prominent East German commentator on growth theory, tries to distinguish between them as follows (1972, p. 17):

> Reproduction theory deals with production and reproduction of the total social product, its circulation between spheres of production and between classes. It must take into account the material composition and the value composition of the product. On the other hand, bourgeois growth theory is not interested in the circulation and distribution of the total product to the different classes nor in the problem of the material and value composition of the product. It centres on a few production relations which are relevant for the growth of the total product . . . without considering the process of production and reproduction of social capital in all its aspects and contradictions, i.e. without satisfying the requirements of reproduction theory . . . .

This authoritative Marxist comment deliberately ignores the fact that creative modern Marxists such as Oscar Lange and Kalecki have tried to develop growth theory precisely for a socialist society, for which it should prove particularly fruitful. Thus, at a meeting of German-speaking growth theorists at Ottobeuren in 1971, Gahlen pointed out (Gahlen and Ott, 1972) that it is 'funny that in multi-sector growth models in particular it is obvious that, if any implications can be drawn from these theories, they will be relevant to a totally planned economy'. It thus looks as if countries of the socialist bloc are fighting shy of adopting the techniques of modern growth theory, although it first blossomed in the Soviet Union. This is the same attitude as is witnessed in the case of Leontief's input–output system, which was conceived in Russia in the 1920s and has only recently and reluctantly been taken over; or in the case of cost–benefit analysis, which has been developed in the West and will probably take some time yet to be accepted, although it is undoubtedly useful for planned systems in particular.

Nevertheless, Meissner's criticism contains some grains of truth. 'Bourgeois' growth theory certainly ignores many real factors and especially instability elements, which we examine later. On the other hand, it is manifestly absurd to accuse authors such as Kaldor and Pasinetti of neglecting the problems of distribution and class. A left-wing economist, Riese, has expressly stated (Gahlen and Ott, 1972, pp. 381) that authors such as Abramovitz, Kuznets, Lewis and even Rostow have endeavoured to take account of historical, geographical, sociological and psychological elements within the framework of a general theory of economic growth.

Another aspect of Meissner's criticism is certainly fully justified. Growth theory has often been too closely identified with a pure analysis of equilibrium conditions, while Marx, Adam Smith and Schumpeter, albeit that their instruments were imperfect, sought to explain empirical growth processes. The refined instruments of modern theory ought to be applied to the goals pursued by the great theoreticians of the past.

AFFINITIES TO MODERN GROWTH THEORIES

Peter asked at an early stage (1934, II, p. 63) what precisely is the significance of the reproduction schemes for growth theory:

> When working with these schemes, one must reflect very carefully upon what conclusions one may draw from them. The schemes are enormously overrated by some authors, while others wrongly consider them to be worthless. One is well advised to define their limits pedantically on the basis of the methodological assumptions under which they are to be construed.

He particularly examines the problem of the capital stock, which is not explicitly covered by the schemes. He refers to 'the fiction that the period for capital turnover in the schemes is always and everywhere equal to one . . . which makes the schemes extraordinarily unwieldy. . . . As soon as the turnover period is no longer everywhere equal to one, turnover and gross social product differ . . . .'

If one considers the embittered controversy that rages between the neo-classicists and the British Cambridge School with regard to the concept and measurement of capital, one may ask oneself whether the absence of a concept of the capital stock in Marxian theory is not rather to be considered an advantage.

Marx wanted to discover the laws of motion of capitalism. Since capitalism was for him essentially dynamic, this entailed an analysis of growth processes. In this sense, one may interpret Marx's entire work as a gigantic attempt to develop a theory of growth. Indeed, for Marx the growth of institutions and of the social structure was nothing but a reflection of economic growth processes, which still remain topical even in the decline of capitalism, for socialism will have to develop on the basis of the foundations laid in the dying social system.

There is a fundamental difference between what Joan Robinson calls the neo-neo-classical version of growth theory and the Marxian conception. For the latter, Irma Adelman has emphasised (1962, pp. 70–2) that evolution and growth are by their very nature disequilibrium phenomena, while the former concentrates on equilibrium conditions.

Paradoxically, there are formal similarities between the two, antagonistic positions. According to Schmitt-Rink (1967, pp. 145–6),

Marx's argument shows [within the framework of the tendency of the rate of profit to fall] certain affinities to neo-classical growth theory, such as the substitution of capital for labour, decreasing capital productivity, and increasing labour productivity. These consequences occur in the neo-classical system only if technical progress proves unable to compensate for the substitution effect, no matter whether the progress, as in older work, is considered to be entirely autonomous, as a residual, or whether, as in more recent models, it is introduced partly under the guise of 'embodied technical progress'. Marx, however, did not deal with the analysis of an 'imaginary world, where capital accumulation occurs without giving rise to an accumulation of technical knowledge' [Joan Robinson, 1955a, p. 67]; for him, investment and technical progress were inseparably connected. . . . There is a second point on which Marx's argument differs from that of neo-classical growth theorists. In the neo-classical model, rising real wages, which reflect slow growth of population as compared to investment, induce the substitution of capital for labour. In Marx's model, on the other hand, population growth is not a constructive element on its own, but exercises only a modifying influence: increasing real wages accelerate the fall in the rate of profit; decreasing real wages slow down its pace . . . .

On the other hand, it has been argued that Ricardo and Marx have something in common partly with neo-classical authors and partly also with Harrod: 'the idea that a steady process of accumulation can act as an engine of economic growth only if the capital–output ratio as well as the rate of profit remains constant. From the constancy of both results the constancy of the profit share, from which derive the impulses towards steady capital accumulation' (Hemmer, in Gahlen and Ott, 1972, p. 132).

THE PECULIARITIES OF MARXIAN GROWTH THEORY

A further paradox is that Marx, who was the first to sketch the conditions for steady growth, was also the first to perceive the elements of instability in this process. Technical progress was for him no vehicle of steady, frictionless development, but the carrier of ever-recurring disruptive and convulsive forces. This is the second difference between Marx and the neo-classical authors.

Some considerable difficulties have arisen for Marxian growth theory owing to the fact that it was conceived in value terms, which means that basically the Marxian schemes show inputs. It follows that a capital–output ratio cannot be construed in the Marxian system, because output appears only as a shadow of its 'value', so that its volume cannot be quantified; furthermore there is no stock, as opposed to flow, of capital. When productivity increases, the increase in the real social product is not visible. On the other hand, it cannot be overlooked that Marx wanted to analyse essentially the same problems as modern growth theory seeks to tackle using a capital–output ratio. Marx wanted also to understand the relationship between capital and labour inputs and the character of technical progress.

Here again is one of the instances where Joan Robinson's dictum is justified: modern economics will have to try to solve the problems which Marx could not tackle with his imperfect instruments. These problems require the refined instruments of modern economics. It cannot be the other way round, although some Marxists affirm that the Marxian instruments, which they regard as sacred, are preferable. After all, his questions still remain relevant today, together with some of his tentative attempts to answer them; it may appear doubtful whether modern research has made much headway since his time, or whether there has been any improvement on his conceptualisation of the essential problems. On the other hand, it would really be astonishing if progress had not been made in economic technique in the course of a century, and recourse still had to be made to instruments that should now be of mainly historical interest.

The heart of the matter is that Marx's schemes show two principal defects. The first consists in their remaining pure input schemes which do not show the growth in the volume of goods, and the second is that Marx assumed, within the framework of the theory of the tendency of the rate of profit to fall, that technical progress was invariably accompanied by a rise in outlays on constant capital, as opposed to wage payments. Even if we accept the Marxian point of view at face value, it remains a shortcoming that, in contrast to the case of modern growth analysis, the idea of technical progress plays no part in the schemes at all – at least not in its specifically Marxian garb, as 'capital deepening'.

All this may perhaps be explained by the fragmentary nature of the manuscripts from which Engels compiled volume ii of *Capital*. Perhaps Marx would have introduced a scheme with a rising 'organic composition of capital', had he had the time to finish the volume himself. Among further peculiarities of the Marxian schemes can be mentioned the existence of an inexhaustible supply of labour, in the form of an 'industrial reserve army', which nourishes the growth process. This army may consist of the unemployed, of the expropriated or ruined 'petty bourgeoisie' of shopkeepers and artisans who slide down into the ranks of the proletariat, and of an inflow from an 'external proletariat'. Hence there is in Marx's reasoning an element strongly reminiscent of Rosa Luxemburg's 'third persons', except that for Marx they are not purchasers, but suppliers of labour – their own. Marx therefore speaks (*Capital*, ii, ch. 21, p. 518) of 'a development of all the circumstances which produce a relative surplus-population among the working-class', and goes on to talk about the 'conversion into new capital', 'the purchase of additional labour-power', and 'the articles of consumption of this additional labour-power'.

Thus the Marxian growth theory employs an extensive scheme: the 'industrial army', fed from an inexhaustible pool, and capital, which the constant rate of saving by capitalists keeps fed, both keep growing continuously in the same proportion. This may seem reminiscent of the Cobb–Douglas function, but Dobb rejects the likeness.

EARLY ATTEMPTS AT MODERN GROWTH THEORY IN THE SOVIET UNION

It is curious that economists in socialist countries are still fighting shy of modern growth theory, just as they did with Leontief's input–output matrices. Yet in the case of growth theory they have every reason to claim priority, as they are prone to do, with less reason, elsewhere. This is not so much because of Marx's paternity as because of the work of certain of his followers.

There are no obvious reasons why the theory of reproduction should be considered more comprehensive than growth theory. After all, it is dominated by the idea of renewal and reconstruction, while growth, by definition, goes beyond renewal of what was originally invested.

Of Eastern-bloc economists, only the Poles and Hungarians have fully accepted growth theory. Wholesale adoption would have been all the more justified, as undoubtedly growth theory offers the classic instrument for long-run planning. Furthermore, it was originally conceived by Russian economists in the 1920s, some fifteen years before its formalisation by the Western economists Harrod and Domar.

As a matter of fact, the first attempts to establish input–output matrices, which represent an intermediate stage between Marxian theory and growth analysis, were made, as Solow (1953–4, pp. 74ff.) has pointed out, by a group of Soviet economists centred on Groman, who first stimulated Leontief. Groman's part has been preserved from oblivion by Jasny (1962, pp. 51ff.):

> V. G. Groman [was] a Menshevik who stayed behind the Iron Curtain to fight Stalinism from within until he was deprived of his position in the Gosplan USSR in about 1928 and ultimately condemned in the Menshevik trial in 1931. . . . the name of Groman was abused (usually together with that of V. A. Bazarov, his closest collaborator) almost every time there were pronouncements on the balance of the national economy (see, for example, J. Stalin's speech of 27 December 1929, in Stalin, *Problems of Leninism*, eleventh Russian edition, p. 294, and in A. Kursky, *The Planning of the National Economy of the USSR* [in Russian] (Moscow, 1949) p. 127).
>
> Early in that year V. G. Groman made a report on it to the statistical–economic section of the Gosplan. . . . In November 1923 Groman read an extensive paper on the 'balance' before an extraordinary meeting of the Chief Board of the Gosplan. . . . Indeed, in the meeting, which took place on 21 November 1923, Groman presented a draft balance of the national economy for the year ending 30 September 1923. The draft was not only crude, . . . it was also very inaccurate (S. G. Strumilin declared the figures 30–50 per cent too low). Yet the draft seems to have contained the most important ingredients of a balance (gross output of large-scale and small-scale industry and gross agricultural production with subdivision into means of production and means of consumption and showing the consumption of means of production by each sector; next was shown the utilisation of the produced goods with subdivision into farm and industrial products, and into urban and rural, total and *per capita* consumption; urban consumption was furthermore subdivided into bourgeois and proletarian). The calculation was of necessity in pre-World War I prices with distinction between farm and retail prices.

Between 1923 and 1927, Groman's group undertook further studies. Bazarov published intermediate results in 1927. A committee presided over by Trachtenberg worked out the results, which in 1928 were made available in a study by Falkner. It was only after this preparatory work that the group's efforts culminated in the first larger study by Feldman, whose comprehensive growth model was published at the end of 1928.

Harrod may have been ignorant of this work. The other 'father' of modern growth theory, however, knew of this work in its original language, as his detailed article of 1957 on the Feldman model proves (Domar, 1957, pp. 223ff.). If one bears this fact in mind, along with Domar's various remarks on Marx's achievements, it is not too much to say that impulses for modern growth theory have been derived from both sources: from Marx himself, and from Groman's group, who were inspired by the spirit of Marxism.

It is all the more astonishing that some contemporary economists in socialist countries try to fob us off with the assertion that all subsequent work in growth theory, derived from these foundations, is nothing but 'bourgeois growth theory'; and that they fail to ask themselves whether these achievements could be exploited for the purposes of their own planning system.

It still remains to be seen whether the pioneer work of Oscar Lange and Kalecki will be fruitful in this field. In the case of input–output analysis, which originated in Russia, the technique has now been readopted after a detour abroad.

Input–output analysis was further developed by Leontief in 1941 in the United States. He had already published an article on the subject in Russia in 1925 and one in the *Weltwirtschaftliches Archiv* of Kiel, where he worked for some time in the Economic Institute, having emigrated from the Soviet Union. Curiously enough, Leontief seems to have completely forgotten his own contribution in Russian. When he was reminded of it in 1960, he acknowledged the priority of the work of the Groman group. Things were no less curious on the other side of the fence. In the Soviet Union the work had effectively been halted since before 1930. It was only when the American successes in these fields (for wartime planning) became known that studies of the same kind were undertaken in the Eastern bloc – first in Yugoslavia (1957), then in Hungary (1959) and later in 1959 in the Soviet Union as well, in the guise of a publication of the Central Directorate for Statistics (Dyabushkin, 1960, p. 399).

Leontief himself has repeatedly pointed out that there are connexions between his input–output tables and the Marxian schemes. It was Oscar Lange who, in the Indian review *Samkhya* in 1957, analysed the direct relevance of the schemes of extended reproduction in this context. The fate of this article is significant. It was reprinted in Moscow with an introduction by academician Nemchinov and made a decisive contribution to the resumption of the work which had been interrupted under Stalin.

How was it that the first steps in input–output technique and in growth theory – taken, on a Marxian basis, in the Soviet Union, so early and with such promise – came to nought? The Belgian economist Nagels thinks (1970, pp. 241–2) that the principal explanation may lie with the conservatism of the majority of planners in Stalin's time. To this, he notes, must be added the lack of technical and statistical data. There were no staff, calculating machines, computers, and so on. Furthermore, there was a confusion between 'planning in kind . . . [and] an artificial price policy which prevented a transformation of the tables that contained physical figures into numerical values'.

Perhaps the explanation may be summarised as follows: Stalin feared a detailed economic appraisal, which would have revealed the vast squandering of productive forces that followed as an inevitable consequence of the precipitate pace of industrialisation during the early Five Year Plans. Stalin ordered a number of economists to be shot – first and foremost the 'father of socialist accumulation', Preobrazhensky – in order to be able to use their blueprints, unmolested by their criticisms. One of the economists shot was the discoverer of 'long waves', Kondratieff, who was accused of being a protagonist of a peasants' party! It was only when the practical foundations had been laid that the Soviet Leadership could again afford precise economic analysis.

MARX AND THE CLASSICAL ECONOMISTS IN RELATION TO HARROD AND DOMAR

Kindleberger says (1958; 1965, p. 45) that from Marx to Harrod and Domar is a 'great leap'; indeed, the problem of economic growth has cropped up only since the Second World War, as a by-product of the Keynesian revolution and as a consequence of the preoccupation with under-developed countries.

This is somewhat paradoxical. Growth theory is concerned with the long term and tries to assess the relation between capital and labour and also the capital–output ratio. Keynes, however, who inspired Harrod, explicitly dealt with the short term, in which capacity does not alter. Finally, the refined problems of a reciprocal substitution of capital for labour are of only a very limited relevance to developing countries, with their poverty and their abundant supply of cheap labour. On the other hand, the classical economists were right from the outset interested in growth problems. The relationship between investment and growth was studied first by Adam Smith and later by Ricardo. Kindleberger has provided (ibid., p. 42) an excellent résumé of the classical position:

Like Smith, Ricardo believed that growth resulted from 'accumulation', or capital formation. . . . Adam Smith's theory of growth was interesting in a number of other respects beyond his attention to accumulation: the importance of 'internal economies of scale' as illustrated by increasing returns in pin making in his famous illustration of the division of labor; the extent of the market, which limited the division of labor; and the invisible hand, which guided resources into the most efficient

lines under *laissez faire*. . . . But [Ricardo thought] accumulation in
turn was a function of profits, which depended on wages, which
depended on the price of food, which depended on the availability of
land or food imports . . . .

If Kindleberger then says that Marx's theory of the inevitable decline of
capitalism rests on the labour theory of value and on the tendency of the
rate of profit to fall, without paying attention to rent theory, one must
say that he is here almost completely wrong. First, Marx devoted whole
chapters to rent theory. Secondly, neither the theory of the tendency of the
rate of profit to fall nor the thesis of the decline of capitalism depends
wholly on the labour theory of value. What is true is that 'In [Marx's]
system, capital piles up as surplus value is reinvested, until the rate of profit
falls' (ibid., p. 44). This is also the content of Domar's theory of
accumulation, which stresses the effect of competition between new
investments. This is a capacity effect with no part in Keynesian theory and
denoted by Domar denotes as σ.

For Smith as for Marx, growth is based on net investment or
'accumulation'. This is similar in Harrod's and Domar's analysis:

> But Harrod observed that the full-employment income in period t would
> not be sufficient in period $t+1$ because of the additional capacity
> created by investment in period t. How much more spending would be
> needed in $t+1$ could be determined by the relationship between capital
> and output, i.e., the capital/output ratio. . . . growth can be increased
> by expanding the savings ratio or by lowering the capital/output
> relation. . . . savings lead to an increase in investment, which leads to
> an increase in income (through the incremental capital/output ratio),
> which leads to more savings, more investment, more income
> etc. . . . (Ibid., p. 46.)

This is in certain respects a replica of Marx's 'extended reproduction', i.e.
it 'is a process of growth which Rostow likens to compound interest' (ibid.).

Marx was fully aware of the problems implied in this model. First of all
we must ask ourselves whether it was not an advantage that Marx kept the
problem of the realisation of surplus value, i.e. of the effective transformation of saved funds into investment, neatly apart from the concept of
saving, which in his schemes implies investment. This is expressly contrary
to the spirit of Keynes, who saw saving as the outcome of investment!

On the other hand, Marx repeatedly warned against simple identification of the notion of compound interest with the process of growth.
Although he says (*Theories*, III, ch. 21, p. 298) 'In fact, however, capitalist
accumulation is nothing but the reconversion of interest into
capital. . . . Thus it is compound interest', he goes on to declare that such
a notion of uninterrupted exponential growth is a chimera:

I have explained the decline in the rate of profit in spite of the fact that the rate of surplus-value remains the same or even rises, by the decrease of the variable capital in relation to the constant. . . . Hodgskin . . . explains it by the fact that it is impossible for the worker to fulfil the demands of capital which accumulates like compound interest. . . . In its general sense, this amounts to the same thing.

Marx then sees the contradiction:

Thus it should be noted first of all that Hodgskin's view only has meaning if it is assumed that capital grows more rapidly than population, that is, than the working population. If the population grows at the same rate as capital, then there is no reason whatsoever why I should not be able to extract from 8 × workers with £800 the [same rate of] surplus labour that I can extract from x workers with £100. . . . Eight times 100 C makes no greater demand on 8 times x workers than 100 C on x workers. Thus Hodgskin's *argument* becomes groundless. ("C" in this quotation stands for "K" "Capital"; in the current sense).

This is the same as Marx's extended reproduction, under conditions of which a regular supply of labour represents the engine which drives steady growth. Nevertheless, such regular growth of the employed labour force can be explained only if there is a surplus or reservoir of labour, or if population growth outstrips that of capital, which means that labour-augmenting or labour-saving progress prevails.

On the subject of surplus labour Marx says (ibid., pp. 298–300): 'Even if the population grows at the same rate as capital, capitalist development nevertheless results in one part of the population being made redundant, because constant capital develops at the expense of variable capital.' Here again we encounter a paradoxical situation: the apparently smooth growth of capital and labour in the reproduction schemes is attributable to the abundance of the production factor, labour, consumption of which increases but can always be met from a reserve pool, which is replenished by 'releasing' labour. The mechanism by which labour is released does not directly feature in the Marxian schemes, which ignore technical progress by not providing for increasing 'organic composition of capital'. From where will the labour pool be replenished? Logically, there are only two possible sources: the artisan and peasant classes, through their destruction (in his schemes, Marx mentions neither class); and the 'external proletariat'.

If one ignores the latter problems, the Harrod and Domar model bears a considerable resemblance to the Marxian model, for both are based on a fixed capital–labour ratio. In Marx's case this was in the nature of an editorial oversight, for he did not have time enough to introduce into his model a change in this coefficient, though in other parts of his work he described such a change as axiomatic for capitalist development.

On the other hand, one can consider the Harrod–Domar theory as an inversion of Marxian concepts:

> it relies largely on a capital theory of value, in contrast to the Ricardo–Marx labor theory of value. Labor can be introduced into the system, but only at a constant capital/labor ratio. Such a ratio is likely in reality only if labor accidentally grows at the same rates as capital, or if labor is redundant at any and all rates of capital expansion, so that as much labor as needed can be found at very low wages.

This is Kindleberger's pertinent comment. This criticism of the Harrod–Domar model is somewhat similar to that of Marx's model of extended reproduction. Kindleberger presents this criticism (ibid., p. 48) in simple terms:

> If labor and capital grow at different rates under the Harrod–Domar model, either labor or capital must be less than fully utilized. In the second place, the Harrod–Domar model ignores all possibility of change in technology. Thirdly, the Harrod–Domar model fails on empirical grounds. Growth as observed in concrete situations proceeds faster than can be accounted for by the rate of inputs of capital with a constant capital/output ratio.

Thus the similarities between the Marxian and the Harrod–Domar model are to be found chiefly in their weaknesses. However, Marx's model at least has the merit of having tackled at an early stage what Ott says (1967, p. 638) modern growth theory has only recently dared to take up: the analysis of a two-sector model. Apart from that, in considering the growth conditions of individual classes, Marx also tackled the problem of distribution.

The main difficulty in the Marxian growth scheme lies in the fact that it is in character exclusively extensive. This could be remedied by transforming it into an intensive scheme, but this has not been attempted so far. It could be done by interpreting the increasing units of variable capital not simply as units of consumer goods, but as a reflection of an increased production of such goods per worker employed, i.e. as an expression of increased labour productivity. A constant number of workers produce an increasing volume of goods – because of, for instance, better education and better 'know-how' – without an increasing 'organic composition of capital', or capital–output ratio. There is then no increase in the physical volume of labour, but 'neutral' (in Harrod's sense) labour-augmenting technical progress. We thus approach the 'golden age' of modern growth theory, 'wherein capital and output grow at a rate equal to the population growth rate plus the rate of labor-augmenting technical progress' (Wan, 1971, p. 75).

A FORMAL COMPARISON WITH THE HARROD–DOMAR MODEL

Klatt has proposed starting the Marxian schemes from the second year. We should then escape two difficulties: first, the growth rate would be at 10 per cent for each year considered, instead of starting at 9 per cent in the first year; and, secondly, we should avoid the difficulty that the accumulation rate of department II is in the first year only 20 per cent, jumping later to 30. If we follow Klatt's proposal, the model outlined in Table VI results (see Klatt, 1960, p. 240).

Klatt starts from the basic equation of the Harrod–Domar model, which presents the relations between savings, changes in the capital stock and income growth as follows (the so-called Domar equation):

$$\text{growth rate} = \frac{\text{savings quota}}{\text{capital–output ratio}}$$

Klatt prefers a more complicated equation:

$$E_t = E_0 \left(1 + \frac{s}{k'} \right)^t$$

in which E_t = income (or social product) of period t;

$\quad E_0$ = income in the initial period;

$\quad s$ = the average propensity to save; and

$\quad k'$ = ratio of a change in capital stock ($\Delta k \cong 1$) and the resulting change in real income (ΔE), i.e. the marginal capital–output ratio.

Joan Robinson has declared (1952, p. 90) that Harrod and Domar have done nothing more in their famous formula than fit out in modern garb Marx's reproduction schemes outlined in volume II of *Capital*. Elsewhere (1952; 1964, pp. 42, 74) she has described what the various models have in common:

[They] all have their origin in a simple piece of arithmetic. When a constant proportion of income is added to capital every year and capital bears a constant ratio to income, then income expands continuously at a constant proportional rate. Thus, when 10 per cent of net income is invested every year, and the stock of capital is 5 years' purchase of net income, then the stock of capital, the rate of investment per annum,

TABLE VI
Marx's Two-Sector Growth Model in Klatt's Presentation

Year	Department I (capital goods) (accumulation rate 50%)			Department II (consumption goods) (accumulation rate 30%)		
	c	v	s	c	v	s
0	4400	1100	550 (440 in c) (110 in v)	1600	800	560 (160 in c) (80 in v) (240)
1	4840	1210	605 (484 in c) (121 in v)	1760	880	616 (176 in c) (88 in v) (264)
2	5324	1331	665·5 (532·4 in c) (133·1 in v)	1936	968	677·6 (193·6 in c) (96·8 in v) (290·4)
3	5856·4	1464·1	732·05 (585·64 in c) (146·41 in v)	2129·6	1064·8	745·36 (212·96 in c) (106·48 in v) (319·44)
4	6442·04	1610·51	805·255 (644·204 in c) (161·051 in v)	2342·56	1171·28	819·896 (234·256 in c) (117·128 in v) (351·4)
5	7086·244	1771·561	885·7805 (708·6244 in c) (177·1561 in v)	2576·816	1288·408	901·8856 (257·6816 in c) (128·8408 in v) (386·5)

(Figures in brackets: surplus value reinvested)

consumption per annum and net income per annum all expand cumulatively at 2 per cent per annum.

In his model, Klatt first of all examines the ratio of constant capital in periods o and t, and he arrives at the following (growth) formula:

$$c_{1,t} = c_{1,0} \left(1 + \frac{1}{10} \right)^t$$

This shows already a certain affinity to the Domar equation. Klatt then calculates the share of saving in the surplus value of department 1 $(v+s)$. This works out to 25 per cent. For department II, the corresponding share is 15 per cent (from year 2 onwards). Klatt next devises a new equation, $f = (s+v)/(c+v)$, which he calls the 'factor coefficient'. The result is that the growth rate in Marx's system is $g = s/f$, i.e. the growth rate (g) is derived from the saving quotient (s) and the factor coefficient (f). The formula closely resembles the Harrod–Domar formula. If we now insert the figures just cited, dividing the savings quotient by the factor coefficient, we reach $0.25/2.5$ for department 1 and $0.15/1.5$ for department II, or a growth rate of 10 per cent for both. Klatt repeats the operation using marginal figures and reaches the same result.

He then explains the peculiar character of his factor coefficient, which neglects capital stocks, and which he says (1960, pp. 245–7) can conveniently be compared to an input–output model (which has only two sectors).

'What seems decisive to us is the comparison of input and output, which . . . finds its parallel in Marx's model. The input–output model consequently constitutes the link between the growth-theory element in Marx's accumulation theory and recent growth models'. . . . 'In this interpretation, Marx's numerical example bears similarities to the input–output model, and the factor coefficient resembles [Marx's] technical production coefficients. Since, on the other hand, there is a relationship between growth models of the Harrod–Domar type and Leontief's input–output model, . . . there is more than a formal resemblance and, indeed, there is an indirect, inner relationship between growth models and accumulation theory'.

Klatt even sees a certain superiority in the Marxian model: 'One could, for instance, reproach Domar's construction for ignoring the factor "labour" and relying exclusively on the factor "real capital".' (Klatt, 1960, p. 243–247).

He then refers to a study by Power, who tried to place alongside Domar's formula one containing the marginal labour coefficient $l':/g = s/l'$. In this case, the analogy to Marx's model is evident, because growth is traced back to capital and labour. (Power, 1955, pp. 197 ff.)

Klatt concludes by saying (1960, p. 248), 'The growth relations between savings, real assets and real income which are expressed by equations in recent models are in principle by no means new discoveries; they already exist in a comparable guise in Marx's works.'

Ott drew the same conclusion seven years later when (1967, p. 638) he compared Marx to Harrod and Domar: 'Marx's growth rate coincides . . . with the growth rate of Harrod and Domar. This means nothing less than that Marx anticipated the main result of post-Keynesian growth theory, the condition of equilibrium growth . . . .' Ott indicates that, on the condition that saving equals investment (here arises Marx's 'realisation' problem!), post-Keynesian growth theory expresses the growth rate as

$$g = \frac{\text{investment (or savings) rate}}{\text{marginal capital–output ratio}}$$

Ott now makes short shrift of what Klatt prudently called the factor coefficient. He postulates that $(c+v)/(v+s)$ is the capital–output ratio, although essentially it expresses the ratio of costs to value added.

According to Ott, the growth rate in Marx's model corresponds to the ratio of accumulated surplus value to the sum of costs, $c+v$. The savings ratio in turn is described in the Marxian model as

$$\frac{\text{accumulated surplus value}}{\text{value added (national income)}} = \frac{a}{v+s}$$

The Harrod–Domar equation would then be written as

$$\frac{\text{Savings ratio}}{\text{capital–output ratio}} = \frac{a}{v+s} \bigg/ \frac{c+v}{v+s} = g$$

Ott now points out that in both departments the growth rate from the third year onwards is always 10 per cent of the preceding year's values. These growth rates are calculated for both departments as the ratio of accumulated surplus value to the sum of costs, i.e.

$$\frac{a_\text{I}}{c_\text{I}+v_\text{I}} \text{ or } \frac{a_\text{II}}{c_\text{II}+v_\text{II}}$$

Thus there results for both departments the same growth rate, written in Marxian terms, as results from the Harrod–Domar equation.

Shortly after the publication of Klatt's article, Utta Gruber offered a criticism, which can be extended to Ott's presentation. She concentrates on the weakness that the two interpretations have in common: namely, the notion of the capital–output ratio. She underlines (1960, p. 394) the fact that Marx was fully aware of the notion of the capital stock. In her opinion, accumulated quantities must be seen as stocks, since, for instance, 's_c (the accumulated sum, in the guise of constant capital which has been reinvested out of surplus value) fully represents an increase in the stock of constant capital of the next period, but not necessarily constant capital which will be completely exhausted in the next period.' For her, s_c/c is a key magnitude. This ratio can be derived for department 1 from the following data:

$$\frac{s}{v} = 1, \qquad \frac{c}{v} = 4, \qquad \frac{s_c}{s} = 0.4$$

Thus

$$\frac{s_c}{c} = \frac{(s/v) \times (s_c/s)}{c/v} = \frac{1 \times 0.4}{4} = 0.1$$

This is then the growth rate for the entire Marxian system. Utta Gruber then constructs stock magnitudes by linking the accumulated constant capital c of one period to the stock of constant capital in the same period. This stock she denotes by capital letters and thus reaches the following equation for period 1 as related to period 0:

$$C_1 = C_0 + s_{c_0} = C_0 \left(1 + \frac{s_{c_0}}{C_0} \right)$$

The fraction s_c/c remains the same for all periods, since the growth rate remains the same. This ratio must be smaller than the growth rate of the entire system ($= 0.1$), because it was assumed that $C > c$! (Ibid., p. 395.)

Utta Gruber also criticises the use by Klatt of the so-called factor coefficient. He had derived the following growth formula for constant capital:

$$c_t = c_0 \left(1 + \frac{s}{f} \right)^t$$

Here s is the average savings rate, which, as Ott had already stressed (1967, p. 638), coincides with the marginal one, since 'technology is supposed to remain constant in the Marxian equilibrium model'. This average savings rate is then written in Marxian symbols as the amount accumulated out of surplus value which is spent on c and v, in relation to value added, i.e. $(s_c + s_v)/(s + v)$.

On the other hand, f is the ratio of the sum of costs to value added, $(c + v)/(s + v)$, just as in Ott's essay.

The result is

$$\frac{(s_c + s_v)/(s+v)}{(c+v)/(s+v)}$$

or, more briefly,

$$\frac{s_c + s_v}{c+v}$$

Now Utta Gruber says (1960, pp. 397–8),

> This formulation of s/f and the comparison with the formula $c_t = c_0$ $(1 + [s_c/c])^t$ show immediately that the quotient s/f can only be introduced into the general formulation of the growth equation provided the following condition is fulfilled:
>
> $$\frac{s_c}{c} = \frac{s_v}{v}, \text{ for only then is } \frac{s_c}{c} = \frac{s_c + s_v}{c + v}$$
>
> This condition must be satisfied if growth conditions are to be expressed
>
> by the formula $c_t = c_0 \left(1 + \frac{s}{f}\right)^t$

In other words, 'The general formulation of growth equations with the aid of the quotient s/f presupposes that the accumulated surplus value will be divided in the same proportion between constant and variable capital as that which has governed the relation between c and v up to now.'

We are thus led to discuss the 'organic composition of capital', which does not undergo any change in Marx's schemes of extended reproduction. Utta Gruber is not wrong in pointing out that this represents 'a certain deviation from Marx's basic ideas'. In this context, the introduction of an increasing 'organic composition' would entail that 'none of the growth rates could any longer be formulated with the aid of the savings ratio and the factor coefficient'. This would mean that s_c/c and s_v/v are no longer equal. Utta Gruber admits (ibid., pp. 398–9) that 'in spite of a variable ratio c/v, the ratio s_c/c can remain constant, because the ratios s_c/s, s_v/s, s_k/s [the last denotes capitalists' propensity to consume out of their surplus value] change, and/or the rate of surplus value s/v changes. . . . Under certain circumstances, s_v/v can at the same time remain constant.' Thus we are at the very heart of the problems which concern the Marxian law of the tendency of the rate of profit to fall, which we shall discuss in the next chapter.

At this juncture, it is enough to say that for Marx the increase in the ratio c/v was synonymous with technical progress, which is absent from the models we have so far considered. If technical progress is for Marx indissolubly linked to investment, we shall have to see how well modern growth theory (which we have tried to show possesses a formal identity with the Marxian model) fits into this framework.

What has been ascertained so far may be summarised in the words of Klatt (1960, p. 241): 'It is true that growth models of the Harrod–Domar type do not go beyond Marx's work. Their basic components exist, although in a wilful arrangement, in the Marxian model of extended reproduction. The first dynamic growth model, which at the same time includes a circular flow, was produced by Marx.'

This statement must be elaborated by reminding the reader that the identity goes very far, for both model-types work with fixed capital–labour coefficients. On the other hand, this is the very flaw that diminishes their dynamic character.

DISCUSSION OF THE GROWTH SCHEMES WITHIN THE GLOBAL FRAMEWORK OF THE MARXIAN SYSTEM

The American author Irma Adelman and two German economists, Krelle and his collaborator Gabisch, have discussed the Marxian growth models within the framework of a global analysis of the entire Marxian system. As regards growth aspects, the following comments may be made.

Irma Adelman's concept of the Marxian growth process is dominated by the idea that production coefficients are not fixed in time, but change with changing production conditions. Thus she does not discuss the peculiar character of the Marxian schemes of extended reproduction, which provoked, for instance, Samuelson's quite opposite criticism of them as based on 'fixed coefficients'. For Irma Adelman (1962, p. 72), 'the organic composition of capital is an increasing function of the rate of gross capital formation'.

With regard to the reproduction schemes she states (ibid., p. 93),

Marx's scheme for expanded reproduction provides a basis for a useful analysis of the interrelation between long-run development, savings, and investment as monetary and real flows, a line of study which was later taken up independently by both Harrod and Domar. The inherently dynamic nature of Marx's models provides an excellent example of the power and importance of dynamic analysis.

She also mentions that it was Leibenstein in particular who reformulated and re-emphasised (1957) the relations between disequilibrium systems and internally generated growth and between equilibrium systems and stagnation.

Krelle indicates the general lines of his discussion of the Marxian model in a paper he delivered early in 1968 at Münster. Here he describes the

Marxian model and transposes it, since 'Marx regretted not being a good mathematician', from numerical examples into a homogeneous difference equation of the first degree. 'The result of the Marxian analysis is this: the growth rate w_i of the sector i is proportional to the investment share s_i of capital owners in this branch and proportional to the mark-up factor $r_i/(1 + k_i)$ on costs, which is applied by entrepreneurs' (Krelle, 1969, p. 24).

Krelle here develops an idea which would have been anathema to Marx, who abhorred the very idea of defining profit as a mark-up. Krelle thinks that the constant rate of surplus value, which reflects in Marx the division of value added or of the social product, 'boils down to an assumption that all entrepreneurs apply the same, fixed mark-up or, what would be the same, that profits remain a fixed percentage of turnover'. This cannot be considered to be correct, if one analyses several industries.

Krelle further says (ibid., pp. 23–4),

> The larger the surplus value . . . and the greater the propensity of capitalists to invest, the greater is the growth rate of output and the greater also the growth rate of employment with the same wage rate; the two growth rates coincide. And this growth can continue indefinitely, provided sufficient labour is available. . . . Marxian growth theory was far ahead of the economics of its time; it has only been overtaken by the dynamic input–output analysis of the 1940s and the post-classical growth theories of the 1950s. The dynamic input–output analysis developed by, in particular, Leontief and his disciples can be considered as an extension of the Marxian model into n sectors, although the development of demand is exogenously given, a feature which represents a step backward compared to Marx. . . . After all, in the history of economic thought, Marx is the last classical economist proper.

He then proceeds to give a general survey of neo-classical growth economics and compares this to Marxian growth theory. His results (ibid., pp. 28–9) are presented in Table VII, and he concludes, 'If one considers the overall result, one will admit that neo-classical growth theory is more comprehensive than its Marxian equivalent. After all, it would be strange if recent developments in economics lagged behind Marx . . . .' Krelle does not examine the work of the Cambridge School, the major opponent of the neo-classicists, nor does he discuss the stability problem.

In his later works, he repeats this analysis in part, but he also makes an ambitious attempt to prove that in Marx's works there are two different theories of the evolution of capitalism. It would go beyond the scope of this chapter to offer here a detailed exposition of these two theories. Krelle outlines them in his paper of 1968 (published 1969) and discusses them more fully in an article published in *IFO Studien* in 1970.

The first of these theories, he says (1969, p. 21), sees elements of disturbance everywhere:

TABLE VII
Differences and Similarities between Marxian and Neo-classical Growth Schemes

Aspect	In Marx	In neo-classical analysis
Differences		
Share of profit		
Share of savings	Assumed constant	Derived from the production function on the basis of the maximisation of profits
'Organic composition of capital'		
Technical progress	'Behind the scenes'	Visibly effective
Employment	Derived from savings share	Used to derive the rate of savings
Development of wages	Not directly covered	Determined by model
Rate of interest Optimal growth		
Similarities		
Growth rate	The higher the greater the share of savings	Independent of the share of savings, but this determines the level of the growth path
Profit margin (= rate of interest)	The higher the greater growth rate	The higher the growth rate, the higher the rate of interest
'Organic composition of capital'	Determines the growth rate (The higher the 'organic composition', the lower the growth rate)	Determined by the growth rate

An increase in the organic composition of capital, relative over-population, increasing poverty of workers, the concentration of capital, a decreasing rate of profit; in the end comes the collapse of capitalism, the expropriation of the expropriators and world revolution.

The second theory has only been designed as part of a study of the process of the circulation of capital. It arrives at the conclusion that a capitalist system leads to steady proportional growth; there is no question of any contradictions which might lead to a collapse of capitalism.

In his 1970 essay, Krelle expounded in detail the first of these theories. Strangely enough, he says (1970, p. 39), in discussing the theory of value, one 'must change Marx's notions from stock magnitudes to flow magnitudes'. This remark is all the more curious as it is just the absence of stock magnitudes which is so annoying to other interpreters of Marx! Similarly, in discussing the 'organic composition of capital', Krelle says (ibid., p. 91), 'Marx did not indicate any reason why . . . population should grow faster than employment'. It is strange that he thus ignores all Marx has to say on the 'industrial reserve army', which is constantly replenished as a result of technical progress. Krelle and Gabisch have tried to prove in their *Wachstumstheorie* ('Growth Theory') of 1972 (see pp. 16–20) that technical progress can very well come about without any rise in the 'organic composition'. In this way, they complete Krelle's thesis, stated in his 1968 paper, that technical progress is present 'behind the scenes' in the Marxian schemes of extended reproduction.

In his 1970 essay (p. 97), Krelle emphasises that in Marx's schemes 'organic composition' is not the same in both departments, that additional wage payments are included in the notion of investment, and that over the first year the growth rates of the two departments diverge (10 per cent for I; 6·6 per cent for II), which is bound to lead to disturbances.

Marx corrects this in scheme no. 1 by changing the share of accumulation from the year 2 onwards in department II, so that $S_{II} = 0.3$, which in turn means that the growth rate is the same as in department I. This would appear to confirm the neo-classical thesis that the rate of investment affects not the growth rate but the level of the growth path, for, in spite of different rates of accumulation, both departments grow at the same speed, because of the figures chosen.

> The result is that each department grows at the rate $\lambda_i = s_i r (1 + k_i)$. The growth rate is higher the higher the rate of surplus value, r, and lower the lower the organic composition of capital, k. This is a result that strongly recalls the growth theories of Harrod and Domar at the end of the 1940s. . . . (Krelle, 1970, p. 96.)
>
> In retrospect, one can even say that his theory represents the beginning of modern growth theory. . . . It is true that the text is not easily readable, which is probably the reason why the Marxian growth theory in volume II [of *Capital*] has not enjoyed the influence and recognition it deserves. Modern growth theory only appeared at the end of the 1930s, independent of Marx and at a lower level.   (Ibid., p. 96.)

In their 1972 joint study, Krelle and Gabisch ask whether the Marxian presentation permits of any equilibrium at all. They reach the same conclusion as Klatt and Gruber did: 'The . . . economy is in equilibrium whenever output and wage income in the two sectors grow at the same rate.' The growth rates of the two departments become, after the correction of the initial investment rate from 20 to 30 per cent in department II, $(0.5 \times 1)/(1+4)$, for I; and $(0.3 \times 1)/(1+2)$, for II. Therefore

$$\frac{v_I}{v_{II}} = \frac{1+r-o_I w_I}{o_{II}(1+w_{II})}$$

In this equation, $o = c/v$ and r is the ratio of the rate of profit to the total wage bill. Finally, Krelle and Gabisch declare that it is remarkable that, after Marx's daring attempt to tackle a growing two-sector economy, it was not until the early 1960s that another attempt was made, in line with neo-classical growth theory. (Krelle and Gabisch, 1972, pp. 123–4.)

Incidentally, we may be allowed to say here that Krelle's distinction of two contrasting Marxian theories is simply erroneous. In discussing simple reproduction, we have already pointed out that Marx's analysis of it served to demonstrate (as Kaldor later realised) that business cycles can appear in capitalism even without growth. *A fortiori* this must be the case under the more complicated conditions of extended reproduction. In his scheme no. 1, Marx found, perhaps intuitively, that, by assuming an initial saving rate of 20 per cent, instead of (as is required if equilibrium is to prevail) 30 per cent, disturbances were possible. Krelle also recognises this case. Thus Marx proves through his reproduction schemes how precarious equilibrium is: as Harrod sees it, capitalism is continually poised on a knife-edge.

GROWTH FACTORS IN MARX AND IN MODERN THEORY

Technical progress, which still remains to be examined, appears to Marx in the guise of the increasing 'organic composition of capital'. This is a complex notion, which cannot simply be identified with the capital–output ratio, or capital coefficient. It must be remembered that Marx thought of technical progress as being furthered by investment. As we should say today, he took it to be 'embodied' in capital equipment.

In the meantime, modern growth theory has been seeking out a number of growth factors which are not synonymous with 'embodied' technical progress. In general, 'disembodied' technical progress includes economies of scale, education and training in the widest sense ('investment in human capital'), progress in knowledge through practice ('learning by doing'), managerial ability, and managerial knowledge or 'scientific manage-ment'. Factors of this type can be found in Denison and Poullier (1967, p. 279), Kindleberger (1965, p. 54), and so on.

Marx had considered these other factors. This can be seen from certain remarks in the *Grundrisse*, which unfortunately did not find their way into Engels's edition of volumes II and III of *Capital*. This is a sin of omission that distorted Marx's image for several generations!

> Such an increase of the force of production, a piece of machinery which costs capital nothing, is the division of labour and the combination of labour within the production process. This assumes, however, work proceeding on a large scale. . . . Another productive force which costs it nothing is scientific power. . . . [Capital] calls to life all the powers of science and of nature, as of social combination and of social intercourse, in order to make the creation of wealth independent (relatively) of the labour time employed on it. . . . The development of fixed capital indicates to what degree general social knowledge has become a *direct force of production* . . . . (*Grundrisse*, pp. 765–6.)

Earlier (ibid., pp. 704–5) Marx says,

> But to the degree that large industry develops, the creation of real wealth comes to depend less on labour time and on the amount of labour employed than on the power of the agencies . . . whose 'powerful effectiveness' . . . depends rather on the general state of science and on the progress of technology, or the application of this science to production.

This recognition of science and of technical know-how as a particular factor of production need not be seen as being in contradiction to Marx's famous statement (ibid., pp. 711–12) that, in the last resort, it is the purpose of all progress to reduce human labour:

> Real economy – saving – consists of the saving of labour time (minimum – and minimization – of production costs); but this saving [is] identical with development of the productive force. . . . The saving of labour time [is] equal to an increase of free time, i.e. time for the full development of the individual, which in turn reacts back upon the productive power of labour as itself the greatest productive power. From the standpoint of the direct production process it can be regarded as the production of *fixed capital*, this fixed capital being man himself.

One might be tempted to call this the theory of 'learning by not doing anything' or of the mobilisation of forces through creative rest; the idea of 'human investment' appears quite clearly in this context.

At any rate, Marx's schemes of extended reproduction exhibit only extensive growth. In this case, growth and investment are identical, for continuous growth is predicated upon continuous saving, provided that this is invested. If investment ceases, the growth process will peter out. This would also happen if no additional labour were available; Marx here took the notion of investment in the labour force seriously. As long as fixed coefficients exist between the quantities of capital and labour, a continuation of saving and investment would only lead to over-capitalisation and ensuing depression, because newly created capital would remain unused for lack of complementary labour.

Things would turn out differently if a shortage of labour could be offset by 'capital deepening', i.e. by an increase in the quantity of capital per worker with a corresponding (or more than proportionate) increase in productivity. This was the basic idea behind Marx's thesis of the tendency of the rate of profit to fall. It remained an open question to what extent the increase in production brought about by capital deepening would be more than proportional. In the value system it does not appear, as we have pointed out; the increase in productivity appears as a shadow of use values.

The neo-neo-classicists, for whom technical progress drops like manna from heaven, removed investment from its throne: 'In the golden age of the supply-oriented theory, the growth of the social product is completely independent of the rate of investment', as Oppenländer puts it (in Gahlen and Ott, 1972, p. 247). The same author characterises neo-classical theory in the following way (ibid., p. 255):

> The growth model determines the growth path towards which the system converges, whenever the parameters n (growth rate of the labour potential), s (average rate of saving) and a' (autonomously given technical progress . . .) . . . remain constant over time. . . . Under these conditions, the growth of the social product remains independent of the investment rate. The latter need only be positive . . . .

Krelle expresses this concisely (1964, p. 6): 'In the last resort, the growth rate cannot be in anyway influenced by the investment rate.'

GROWTH WITHOUT NET INVESTMENT?

This idea found some sympathy even among economists of Marxist leanings: an extension of investment, or 'extended reproduction' in the Marxian sense, would no longer be required for a continued growth in use values. Long before the neo-classical theories of Solow had gained widespread acceptance, this idea had been recognised by Peter, who thought (1934, p. 69) that 'a technical improvement . . . could so work that a larger net product could be produced with the same input of means of production and labour, or the same net product with less material input'. More recently, a similar formulation is to be found in the writings of Zinn, who admits (1972, p. 123) that in the wake of technical progress 'a technically growing capital stock can be financed from depreciation. . . . The idea, which had been dominant until the 1930s, that technical progress is normally connected with net investment has had to be corrected in the meantime.'

At the microeconomic level, we have seen that it was Marx who was one of the first, if not the first, to suggest that it was possible to finance progress out of depreciation. In his case, however, it is properly a matter of financing net investment out of funds which are intended to replace worn-out assets, but which are not yet required for replacement. It is net investment, however, the necessity for which is contested by Peter and Zinn. Moreover, things look different from a macroeconomic angle. Here one cannot juxtapose certain fixed assets and the corresponding reserves; what alone matters is the profits out of which additional investment will have to be financed. Therefore, a reference to Marx's early discovery of the dynamic financing of depreciation is not quite to the point.

Then we must ask what is the purpose of investment activities as such. If one were to accept this argument, it would be possible in the extreme case for technical progress to lead to an increase in production with a physically shrinking capital stock, i.e. in the face of negative investment or disinvestment.

Zinn re-examined the logic of simple reproduction in order to define a genuinely stationary state. Among the conditions he mentions is (ibid., p. 94) that one 'must leave aside technical improvements in replacement investment', for otherwise, under the above conditions, the state of simple reproduction would give rise to disguised extended reproduction. One must add to this argument that such improvements must take place with regard to neither machinery nor fixed assets: one must not think of savings in these sectors, and this applies also to auxiliary materials and energy. In a genuine stationary state, labour efficiency must not be improved either, whether through training or through 'learning by doing'. If this happened, the increased efficiency of equipment or improved utilisation of raw and auxiliary materials and labour or both would bring about a 'relative' or 'extra surplus', and it would then be a matter of dealing with a disguised growth process.

Dieterlen went even farther than Zinn in a similar argument. He thinks it possible (1957, p. 33) that technical progress can occur without the exhaustion of depreciation funds:

No doubt new investment will always be necessary, but the costs of such new investment may very well be lower than those of an asset which had been installed before . . . i.e. a *de facto* disinvestment occurs, of which we must take account. In this case, economic progress has indeed led to gross investment, but also to net disinvestment . . . .

In other words, one may well imagine the replacement of one machine by one that costs half as much and produces twice as much. Then disinvestment would occur to the extent of half the amount of depreciation, and production would still double. The case need not be so extreme. It is essentially a matter of principle: gross investment abdicates in the face of technical progress.

Dieterlen has expanded this thesis of the regression of investment in his theory (1954, p. 90) of the 'relation of dissatisfaction', although in an analysis of genuine shrinkage. In this context, a few remarks are justified. First, Dieterlen carries the process of microeconomic valuation proceedings into the field of macroeconomics. Secondly, such growth processes within the production sphere despite shrinking gross investment would be equivalent to what would appear a fantastically rapid decrease in capital–output ratios. Thirdly, if the theory of technical progress without net investment were accurate, rapid progress and high growth rates should be possible at the top of the cycle, with fully utilised capacity. This contradicts all experience. As a general rule, real growth rates tend to shrink in such a situation. The high point for the introduction of innovations seems to occur neither at the bottom of a trough or recession nor at the top of a boom, but to be situated in between. As Mansfield states (1960, p. 107), 'innovation was discouraged by the meagerness of profits and the bleakness of future prospects at a trough and by the lack of unutilised capacity, where changes could be made cheaply and without interfering with production schedules, at a peak.'

Zinn is right in saying (1972, pp. 95–6) that 'The stationary economy is not a true replica of the capitalist system of competition. On the contrary, competitive pressure enforces the application of surplus value to cost-reducing and capacity-increasing net investment.' If one considers Marx's global conception from this point of view, one should not confuse matters by introducing neo-classical growth 'without investment', which does not exist for Marx.

Incidentally, it may be said that Marx's simple reproduction has two aspects. On the one side, there is a (mediaeval?) economy without growth, in which only worn-out assets are replaced. In this case, it approaches Marx's notion of 'simple commodity production', which does not know any capitalists or any produced surplus value, but only surplus value extorted through forced labour or tribute. On the other side, there is a capitalist economy which has just reached the (unstable) equilibrium between prosperity and recession or its reverse, or an imaginary future (socialist?) society which has reached the optimum point of saturation of the means of production.

With regard to the economy without growth, it must be emphasised that no produced surplus value can arise. Peter is right in arguing (1934, p. 121), 'In reality an equilibrium situation, in which the law of labour value prevails and surplus value simultaneously exists is a contradictory idea.' A labour value scheme implies that a price calculation will be exclusively

based upon labour input and not on capital input. If, however, a surplus in
the capitalist sense exists, it presupposes in essence a capital relation. One
cannot very well expect, in such a case, that capital owners will not relate
this surplus as 'profit' to their stock of capital. The alternative is a feudal
power relationship, in which no surplus value derived from commodity
production occurs.

In any case, the vision of a world without net investment appears
exaggerated. If in the case of gross investment there exists the opportunity
to introduce technical progress, because replacement investment serves as
the 'vehicle', disinvestment must give rise to the opposite effect: there must
be technical losses of know-how.

It is, however, a moot point whether a petering-out of net investment, if
we leave aside the possibility of verifying it statistically, can impair
technical progress. This is a question which can be answered only within
the framework of a general assessment of the relationship between
investment and technical progress.

THE IMPORTANCE OF INVESTMENT FOR THE GROWTH PROCESS

It is a fact that the older theoreticians, amongst them Marx, took the
connexion between investment and growth for granted. These older
theories simply identified growth and investment: 'A doubling of the rate
of investment, so it was believed, would lead to a doubling of the growth
rate. Newer analyses based on macroeconomic production factors lead to
quite different results.' This statement by Bombach and von Weizsäcker
(1968, p. 481), which dates from 1962, assumes that growth cannot be
directly derived from investment, but this bypasses what were then the
newest developments in this field.

In *Capital*, Marx sees technical progress as being directly related to a
permanent increase in depreciation as compared with the wage bill,
though it is true that it looks, from some passages, as if he considered not
gross but rather net investment to be the carrier of technical progress.

Marx was by no means alone in assuming that there was a close link
between an increase in the capital stock and turnover and an increase in
the ratio of capital costs to total costs. On the contrary, there is a long chain
of theoreticians who think that 'capital deepening' is synonymous with
technical progress. Ultimately, this thesis overlaps the theory of the
'roundaboutness' of production, as advanced by such an eminent
opponent of Marxism as Böhm-Bawerk. As early as a few years before the
turn of the century, the first timid objections to this thesis were uttered:

Sidgwick . . . (1883) seems to have been the first to question the
traditional idea that technical change is necessarily capital-using.

Taussig . . . (1896) suggested that the inventions of the future might save capital by 'shortening the period of production', and J. B. Clark, a decade later, made the point that many capital-using innovations do ultimately release capital after their gestation period is over. . . . But none of them doubted that technical change had been overwhelmingly labour-saving in the past . . . .

Blaug, who wrote this passage (1963; 1971, p. 99), adds that the growing influence of Austrian capital theory reinforced the conviction that technical progress would lead to an increase not only in the capital intensity per worker, but also in capital per unit of output. This idea was still dominant in the 1930s, when Joan Robinson could still write (1937, p. 135),

It appears obvious that the development of human methods of production, from the purely hand-to-mouth technique of the apes, has been mainly in the direction of increasing 'round-aboutness', and that the discovery of short cuts, such as wireless, are exceptions to the general line of advance . . . .

This thesis, to which Marx had adhered, was then seriously questioned in the 1950s, as Phelps recalls in a survey (1962, 1969, p. 172): 'In 1956 appeared the first in a series of papers disputing the traditional thesis that capital deepening is the major source of productivity gains and conjecturing that we owe our economic growth to our progressive technology.' Phelps refers to path-finding articles by Abramovitz (1956), Kendrick (1956) and Schultz (1956).

Solow, the father of neo-neo-classical growth theory, then joined their ranks in an epoch-making article (1957). Ever since then, neo-classical authors have tended to under-estimate investment. Hand in hand with that has gone a vilification of all those theories, including Harrod's, Domar's and implicitly Marx's, which look at investment as the engine of growth; and these same authors have been rebuked for employing 'rigid coefficients' in their growth theories. Many, as we shall see later, were hopeful that the use of flexible coefficients would open up new worlds.

In 1962 Phelps remarked that it seemed that a compromise was being reached in this controversy. He was here referring partly to later work by Solow (1959) and partly to certain studies undertaken by institutions like PEP (1960) and ECE (1959). He drew (1962, p. 548) the following conclusion: 'Thesis and antithesis were synthesized by 1960. Investment has been married to Technology. In the new view, the role of investment is to modernize as well as deepen the capital stock. Now investment is prized as the carrier of technological progress.'

It remains an open question, however, whether gross or net investment is of more importance for technical progress. If net investment is more important, this may be owing to the fact that an integrated realisation of technical progress is as a general rule possible only in completely new plants. The partial renewal of older equipment would seem to be sub-optimal and in most cases represents only patchwork.

Neo-neo-classical theory laid great stress on the importance of flexibility and variability of the capital–output ratio or of capital-intensity; this was its *deus ex machina*. In general, however, the theory was inclined to consider investment as unimportant. Denison in particular showed a tendency, as early as 1964, to consider 'embodied' technical progress as unimportant. This is an element which for him is effective only through the age structure of fixed assets, and in this he finds only very limited changes.

By contrast, Nelson (1964) explains the changes in productivity in the USA in the twentieth century almost exclusively through the fluctuations in the age structure of capital goods.

The continuing existence of old assets alongside new ones raises a number of problems. As a general rule, obsolescence occurs when the variable costs of keeping old assets in service exceed the variable plus fixed costs of new assets from a technological point of view; the installations which are scrapped because of obsolescence could in many cases remain in service for a long time. They will be kept in service, if, for instance, their owners do not have the financial resources to replace them with new ones. Furthermore, monopolistic practices may entail the maintenance of over-capacity – in order, for instance, to strengthen a firm's claim to a certain market share in cartel arrangements. For this purpose, it is enough to bring into use equipment that has been temporarily disused. Finally, it can happen that a sudden increase in demand for machinery that takes a long time to manufacture makes it necessary to reactivate old machinery.

A change in the attitude of economists has, however, taken place recently, as indicated by Kennedy and Thirlwall (1972, pp. 32, 34–5):

> We are still left with the practical policy question of what is the relative importance for growth of increases in the quantity, compared with increases in the quality, of investment? . . . a possibly more important question is whether it is appropriate to regard the flow of new knowledge as independent of the rate of gross investment. If gross investment is not only necessary to put new knowledge to effect but also itself enhances the flow of new knowledge, then clearly much greater importance must be given to gross investment as a promoter of growth than Denison would allow.

This seems to confirm that Marx was right in identifying technical progress with gross investment. On the other hand, this leaves open the question of what is the function of net investment. After all, Marx based his schemes of extended reproduction on net investment, and this also plays a decisive part in his theory of technical progress in connexion with the increase in the 'organic composition of capital'.

The idea that net investment is most important for technical progress is in vogue with some modern authors. For instance, Eltis says (1971, p. 502),

> it can be argued that the rate of technical progress will be influenced by some aspect of an economy's investment activity. It may be influenced by the rate of growth of the capital stock, or the share of the National Product invested, or the period of time over which the capital stock is replaced, or the accumulated sum of past investment. Technical progress will be endogenous to the processes analysed by growth models . . . .

Even the doyen of the neo-neo-classical school, Solow, reckons in two later studies (1962, 1963) with a rate of 'embodied progress' of the order of 4–5 per cent per annum.

It is especially paradoxical that authors such as Peter and Zinn, who are well disposed towards Marxism, believe that 'disembodied' technical progress is dominant, while for Marx himself capital formation and progress were synonymous, which meant that capital was quasi-productive, as it were! On the other hand, neo-classical authors such as Denison have come very near to establishing a new version of the labour theory of value by putting the emphasis on 'human investment'! Finally, Solow seems to incline more towards the Marxian emphasis on (gross) investment.

9 The 'Law of the Tendency of the Rate of Profit to Fall' as a Trend Phenomenon

It was volume III of *Capital* that roused interest in a thesis which had remained alive in classical economics up to the time of John Stuart Mill and by which Marx, who presented it in a new garb, set great store. He gave the law of the tendency of the rate of profit to fall a new twist by introducing the problem of capital-intensity, or, as it is known in modern analysis, the problem of the capital–output ratio.

THE EARLY HISTORY OF THE LAW

To Ricardo this 'law' appeared as a warning of the cataclysm imminently to befall the new-born capitalism and stemming from the relative rise in ground rent. In his view, scarcity of land and consequent decreasing returns hit industrial capitalists in the same way as workers; capitalism was partly shackled by pre-capitalist elements, which would bring it to the ground together with its slaves. Exorbitant prices for urban land in our era could be seen as weak reflection of the Ricardian spectre, which seems to enjoy a happy return in the guise of the fashionable ecological debate.

In the *Grundrisse* (p. 752), Marx speaks of the Ricardian concept as a 'one-sided mode of conceiving . . . which elevates a historical relation holding for a period of 50 years and reversed in the following 50 years to the level of a general law, and rests generally on the historical disproportion between the developments of industry and agriculture'.

In the *Theories of Surplus Value* (III, ch. 21, p. 301) Marx explains this disequilibrium by saying that 'in order to be exploited really in accordance with its nature, land requires [did he not mean "required"?] different social relations. . . . Capitalist production turns towards the land only after its influence has exhausted it and after it has devastated its natural qualities.'

Marx derides Ricardo for 'flee[ing] from economics to seek refuge in organic chemistry' as the source of decreasing returns in agriculture

(*Grundrisse*, p. 754), and he remains optimistic since he believes that, once a certain level of industrial development has been reached, productivity will increase more rapidly in agriculture than in industry. (*Theories*, German Kautsky edition, part 1, p. 281).

John Stuart Mill's *Principles of Political Economy* had been published in 1848. It contained a summary of classical tenets, with some vestiges of the influence of Malthus. Mill considered the tendency of the rate of profit to fall inherent in capitalism – 'The rate of profit is habitually within, as it were, a hand's breadth of the minimum, and the country therefore on the verge of the stationary state' – (1848, Bk IV, ch. 4; 1965 ed., p. 281) but he thought that this tendency did not follow from Ricardo's 'law of diminishing returns', but, rather, resulted from a combination of rising accumulation (i.e. increasing capacity) caused by competitive pressure, and decreasing returns to investment generally. As counter-tendencies raising the rate he mentions inventions and innovations, 'over-trading' and capital exports.

THE MARXIAN VERSION OF THE LAW

Marx's formulation of the law of the tendency of the rate of profit to fall makes it more precise. In the *Grundrisse* (1857–9) he had already called it 'in every respect the most important law of modern political economy', and, prior to the drafts of volume III of *Capital*, in which the law gets its ultimate formulation, he had also referred to it in the *Theories of Surplus Value* (1861–3).

One could very well say that this law, which was supposed to be decisive for the decline of capitalism, held from the very beginning a prominent position in Marx's economic studies, and that he wanted to keep it in reserve to crown his work in the final volume of *Capital*. Here he imparts to it (*Capital*, III, ch. 13, pp. 212–13) its classical formulation:

Now we have seen that it is a law of capitalist production that its development is attended by a relative decrease of variable in relation to constant capital. . . . It is likewise just another expression for the progressive development of the social productivity of labour. . . .

. . . growth of the real mass of use-values . . . corresponds [to] a progressive cheapening of products. . . . the actual tendency of capitalist production . . . produces a . . . continuously rising organic composition of the total capital. The immediate result of this is that the rate of surplus-value, at the same, or even a rising, degree of labour exploitation, is represented by a continually falling general rate of profit. . . . This does not mean to say that the rate of profit may not fall temporarily for other reasons. But proceeding from the nature of the capitalist mode of production, it is thereby proved a logical necessity that in its development the general average rate of surplus-value must express itself in a falling general rate of profit.

It is a well-established fact that the bulk of Marx's drafts of volume I of *Capital* originated after most of volume III had been written. One therefore need not be surprised to find a rough sketch of the law in chapter 23 of volume I. There Marx talks about the 'relative diminution of the variable part of capital'. At the same time, he refers to 'counter-effects', and he hints at the possibility that constant capital may diminish in value: 'not only does the mass of the means of production . . . increase, but their value compared with their mass diminishes'. He goes on to say, 'As arts are cultivated . . . fixed capital bears a larger and larger proportion to circulating capital'. (Ibid., I, ch. 25, pp. 582, 584, and 591, note 2.)

The latter point concerns not constant capital, for Marx always considered it to be sacrilegious to confound this with fixed capital, but the relative importance of fixed-capital consumption as part of constant capital. Since Marx speaks elsewhere of 'economy in capital', arguing that it would be easier to save fixed capital than to save raw materials, this passage in volume I is of considerable interest, for it shows that he sometimes thought the very opposite might happen.

In volume III Marx grants wide scope to counter-effects. There he talks of the 'rise in the rate of surplus value', a phenomenon one must see in relation to the microeconomic phenomenon of the 'extra profits' of entrepreneurs who enjoy technical advantages. Furthermore, he mentions the 'cheapening of elements of constant capital' (i.e. cheapening of raw materials, auxiliary materials and fixed assets), pressure on wages, relative over-population (i.e. mass unemployment, which may serve to explain such pressure) and foreign trade (which leads to a cheapening of the prices of raw materials and to capital exports as a safety valve). He concludes that

the same influences which produce a tendency in the general rate of profit to fall, also call forth counter-effects, which hamper, retard, and partly paralyse this fall. . . . The latter do not do away with the law, but impair its effect. . . . Thus, the law acts only as a tendency. And it is only under certain circumstances and only after long periods that its effects become strikingly pronounced.

In addition to perceiving the general tendency towards a cheapening of constant capital, Marx distinguishes its various components: on the one side, savings in machinery and raw and auxiliary materials, owing to the cheaper methods of producing them; and, on the other, savings that result from a sparing use of these inputs: 'Another rise in the rate of profit is produced, not by savings in the labour creating the constant capital, but by savings in the application of this capital itself.' (Ibid., III, chs 14–15, pp. 234, 236, 239; and ch. 5, p. 82)

Here we may point to the dichotomy which results for the reduction of variable and constant capital. On the one hand, a reduction in variable capital occurs through a diminution of labour inputs into the production process – i.e. through the substitution of capital for labour, or through a cheapening of wage goods or victuals – but there is no question of effecting 'economies in nourishment'. This would occur only where forced by pressure on wages. On the other hand, in the case of constant capital it may first be possible to lower its price, owing to a cheapening of methods of production, and savings in the quantities of inputs may be brought about through rationalisation.

MICROECONOMIC CONSIDERATIONS

From a microeconomic point of view, the Marxian argument may be interpreted as follows. Basically, Marx examines three different processes: first, technical progress in the production of capital goods and in the 'reproduction' of labour (= consumer goods); secondly, a process of organisational technical progress in the application of capital and labour inputs; and, thirdly, a substitution effect.

In the first case, the essential point is that, through new inventions (mechanisation), the production costs of labour and capital goods (expressed in labour hours) at their various levels of production are lowered. A given number of labour hours serves to produce more victuals, machines and raw materials in the widest sense. The production function undergoes a scale change.

In the second case, it is a matter of the more rational use of labour and capital goods, not in supply industries but in the sector producing finished goods. In Marx's view, the consumer-goods industries seem to enjoy a productivity advantage.

In the third case, labour hours are replaced by machinery, or *vice versa*: there is a substitution effect, with a movement along the production function. Substitution of capital for labour does not represent a *shift* in the function, but only a movement to another point on the *given* function.

Now, the distinction between fixed assets, raw materials and semi-finished or finished products is of interest only at the microeconomic level (of the firm or industry); for Marx, from a macroeconomic point of view, only labour is saved. There is then the problem of distribution.

The third case depends on relative costs, which in turn are determined by the class or distribution struggle. If real wages grow too fast, this happens because the distribution claims of the workers, the 'sociological minimum', rise more rapidly than the consumption claims of capitalists, because they started from a lower level.

Marx's viewpoint is mainly microeconomic, for he gives particular emphasis to the 'rising organic composition of capital' in various plants of a given industry. Here technical progress appears as 'relative surplus value', which is realised by individual capitalists through the application of new methods. For Marx, relative surplus value originates whenever 'the increase in the productiveness of labour [seizes] upon [the] branches of industry whose products determine the value of labour-power' (*Capital*, i, ch. 12, p. 299). In other words, he is here interested in technical progress only in so far as it lowers the 'value' of the labour force (v).

The other side of technical progress, i.e. capital-saving, is investigated by Marx only in connexion with the law of the tendency of the rate of profit to fall. Because in this context Marx concentrates on the lowering of the prices of consumers' goods, he does not examine the problem of the 'stickiness' of nominal wages, but postulates at the outset constant real wages.

At this point, his business-cycle analysis and his analysis of competition merge. We do not here examine the importance of his analysis for wage theory, but consider only his analysis of technical progress and its repercussions on the firm which applies it in advance of its competitors.

When Marx postulates that a capitalist succeeds in doubling the productive force of his labour, he anticipates in volume i of *Capital* the analysis of volume iii, by assuming an increase in productivity through the use of additional machinery (and of raw materials), which leads to an increase in c.

We here refer to what has been said above in Volume i, Chapter 18. As soon as the profit rate falls, because all firms in the industry have become more mechanised, over-capacity will occur, which will lead to a further fall in profits and capital values and finally to a crisis in the industry, if not to a general depression, which would in turn lower capital values. Although 'capitalist production' aims at preserving 'the value of the existing capital' and at promoting 'its self-expansion to the highest limit (i.e. [at promoting] an ever more rapid growth of this value) . . . [the] methods by which it accomplishes this include the fall of the rate of profit, depreciation of existing capital. . . . The periodical depreciation of existing capital . . . disturbs the given conditions' (*Capital*, iii, ch. 15, p. 249).

MACROECONOMIC CONSEQUENCES

Increased net investment, which results from an increase in labour productivity in the earlier stages of production, expresses itself in Marx's value scheme partly in increased requirements for machinery and raw materials, and partly in increased surplus value, but not in higher real wages – at least, not immediately.

The increased surplus value may lead to an increase in capitalists' consumption. To cope with this, the number of workers in the consumer-goods industry may have to be increased, if increased productivity does not suffice. On the other hand, increased productivity in c may be partly offset by increased purchases of machinery and raw materials. In all these cases, increased productivity does not, so long as there is no increase in labour inputs, appear in the value scheme.

THE DISCUSSION OF THE LAW BY MARXISTS

From early on, grave objections to the 'law' have been raised, even in the Marxist camp. For instance, Natalie Moszkowska declared in 1929 (pp. 72 ff.) that a general increase in productivity must of necessity lead to a decrease in the prices of investment goods. The increase in the 'organic composition' would, therefore, be mitigated, and the rate of surplus value could be increased all the more.

In a later study the same author adds (1945, p. 18),

It is therefore always possible under capitalism to maintain the rate of profit. If all technical innovations were marginal cases, the rate of surplus value would indeed have to rise in proportion to productivity; but, even if only marginal cases were involved, the rate of profit would not need to fall absolutely. . . . If technical progress led to a decrease in the rate of profit, this rate would have had to decrease continuously in the course of capitalist development, which has after all been character- ised by continuous and rapid technical progress. . . . The rate of profit would, then, have fallen to zero long ago . . . .

Natalie Moszkowska next enters upon a discussion of the problem of the business cycle (ibid., p. 20): 'If the rate of profit really shows a tendency to fall, it must decrease ever more slowly, over longer periods, or at a declining rate . . . .'

At the same time, she adds a new idea favourable to Marx's thesis. She thinks that the 'organic composition of capital' may increase through monopolies and cartels or through an artificial appreciation of capital values owing to price maintenance schemes, which imply the preservation of reserve or surplus capacity. One must also consider whether a higher degree of cartelisation and oligopolisation in supply industries might not impede technical progress in these sectors.

Rosa Luxemburg was even more sceptical than Natalie Moszkowska. She thought that if capitalism were to collapse because of the fall in the rate of profit, it would 'still have a good while to live, perhaps until the sun is extinguished'.

Long before this, Tugan-Baranowsky had flatly denied the fall in the rate of profit, while Hilferding and even the critical Charasov had tried to maintain Marx's thesis. These apologetics were followed by a similar attempt by Grossmann, who tried, somewhat inadequately, to underpin

the law, and came very near to accepting a longer-run 'Kuznets cycle'. In
the 1930s, the Japanese professor Shibata, who was otherwise positively
inclined towards Marxism tried to disprove the law – an attempt which
later earned him a rebuke from his compatriot Tsuru. In 1931, Grossmann
was exposed to the scathing criticism of Neisser, who behaved exactly in
accordance with his dictum, 'Any two Marxists will kill a third.' However,
he did at least make a positive contribution by pointing out (1931, pp. 79–
80), as Croce had done several decades before, that what Marx calls the
'depreciation of constant capital' is not simply a counter-tendency, but
could imply that there need be no fall in the rate of profit at all.

Natalie Moszkowska, still trying to justify the law, argued (1945, p. 33)
that 'over-accumulation' could cause what she calls *faux frais*, or 'dead-
weight costs':

> One need only think of the under-utilisation of capacity in industry, of
> costly advertising, etc. Whenever necessary costs fall, owing to technical
> progress, dead-weight costs simultaneously rise, so that commodity
> prices and the prices of means of production cannot fall sufficiently. This
> makes the composition of capital appear higher than it actually is.

Here we find quite a number of arguments. The idea that cartels might
impede price decreases for fixed assets must be dropped, for it can equally
well happen that such cartels prevent the prices of consumption goods from
falling, which would cushion or compensate for a fall in the prices of wage
goods (v) as compared to machinery and suchlike (c). Furthermore, if the
under-utilisation of capacity creates a tendency for prices to rise, this may
apply only to raw-material prices, in so far as these are produced in the
home (capitalist) country or in other industrial countries. It is hardly
probable that in the long run international commodity agreements or
cartel-type arrangements will succeed in raising the prices of raw materials
exported from underdeveloped countries in relation to the prices of those
produced in industrial countries, especially as the elements of 'imperfect
competition' will be relatively stronger in the latter.

On the other hand, the under-utilisation of productive capacity is a
typical phenomenon of industrial cartels, which may carry this dead
weight for a long time, since such capacity constitutes a reserve held with a
view to obtaining higher quotas in the next round of cartel negotiations or
as a standby in the event that the cartel breaks down. One must beware of
confounding this with the under-utilisation which occurs in a slump, and
which leads to abrupt increases in the marginal capital–output ratio. This
cannot be taken into account in long-run analysis.

The reference to advertising is somewhat problematical, for advertising
costs will only rarely produce an increase in the costs of fixed assets, and still
less will they lead to an increase in raw-material costs. Advertising will in
most cases lead to an increase in labour costs, i.e. of variable capital, which

would run counter to the supposed law. These costs would matter only if they represented the expenses of hiring outside advertising agencies, which would then appear under 'purchases' (of advertising activities) in c. What is interesting here is the similarity of Natalie Moszkowska's reasoning with that of Gillman when, subsequently, he attempted to deduct dead-weight costs from surplus value instead of adding them to c.

Other leading Marxists too have been very reticent with regard to the law: for instance, Sweezy thought (1942, p. 103) that it would be somewhat exaggerated to rely on a rapid increase in the 'organic composition of capital'.

In Marx's works, the cause of the fall in the rate of profit is neatly determined. At the microeconomic level, it is conditioned by the relative rise in depreciation costs for fixed assets and stocks, as compared to value added (including 'surplus value'). In this context, it would appear advisable to leave aside the particular complications introduced by value theory. This can be done in two ways. If one considers the tendency of asset costs to rise in individual industries, one may assume that the 'organic composition' is the same everywhere. Alternatively, at the macroeconomic level, according to Marx, the sum of profits coincides in any case with the sum of surplus values, and so do the sums for values and prices, if one leaves aside inflationary price rises.

If one thus assumes that depreciation or replacement costs rise, while value added remains unchanged and its division the same (i.e. the rate of surplus value does not change), the importance of surplus values must of necessity shrink relative to the sum of costs; and the rate of profits in the flow of costs, seen as a percentage of turnover, will inevitably fall. Meek expresses this concisely (1960, pp. 36–7).

It can then easily be shown, by simple manipulation of these ratios, that the rate of profit is functionally connected with the rate of surplus value and the organic composition of capital in the following way:

$$\text{Rate of profit} = \frac{\text{Rate of surplus value}}{1 + \text{Organic composition of capital}}$$

It follows logically from these premises that if the rate of surplus value remains constant, a rise in the organic composition of capital will bring about a fall in the rate of profit.

After all, Marx initially assumed a constant rate of surplus value, as is shown by his definition of the 'organic composition of capital' in volume 1 of *Capital* (ch. 25, p. 583), where Marx speaks of the relative increase in the share of constant capital in proportion to the share of variable capital. This assumption frequently reappears, both explicitly and implicitly.

The first condition for a fall in the rate of profit is therefore the constancy of the rate of surplus value; macroeconomically speaking, this is equivalent to an unchanging division of net social product between workers and capitalists. This division may change a little – for instance, in favour of the capitalists – but for the law to be valid the change must proceed more slowly than the relative increase in the 'organic composition'.

Marx was here led astray by the pitfalls of value theory or by his limited mathematical training, for he believed (ibid., III, ch. 15, p. 247) that 'compensation . . . by intensifying the degree of exploitation has . . . insurmountable limits. It may, for this reason, well check the fall in the rate of profit, but cannot prevent it altogether.'

In Volume I we have attempted to show that one cannot attribute to Marx a theory of a decreasing share of wages in the social product, i.e. a 'relative increase in poverty'. To the extent that Marx thought that the fall in the rate of profit was decisive for the collapse of capitalism, it was not necessary for him to postulate a decreasing share of wages in the net social product.

Be this as it may, mathematically speaking a progressive adaptation remains possible, whereby the increasing rate of surplus value compensates for the increase in the 'organic composition', provided that the ratio of purchases (c) to value added remains unchanged. Dickinson, an author who was prepared to accept the general implications of Marx's theory, saw (1956–7, p. 122) the essential logical flaw in the mathematical reasoning:

> It is true that an increase in any of the quantities κ, λ_1 or λ_2 will reduce ρ. But only if σ is constant, or at least does not increase faster than $\lambda_1 \kappa + \lambda_2$. Marx assumed, in most of his discussions of the rate of profit, that σ was constant – usually he assumed a 100% rate of surplus value ($\sigma = 1$).

(Where ρ = rate of profit; σ = rate of surplus value; κ = 'organic composition'; λ_1, λ_2 = increase in average economic life of assets or the 'durability' of c and v.)

Joan Robinson, who, of all 'academic' economists, was the most sympathetic towards Marx, did not relish the law. She thought that it was tautological and explained nothing. A theory of falling profits along the lines of Keynes's decreasing marginal efficiency of capital appeared to her more plausible, provided the problem of effective demand were given proper attention. (Robinson, 1949, pp. 36, 38, 42.) The eminent Marxist Sweezy concurred in this view. This fact may seem astonishing if one considers the importance which Marx attributes to the law:

> Simple as this law appears from the foregoing statements, all of political economy has so far had little success in discovering it, as we shall see in a later part. The economists perceived the phenomenon and cudgelled

their brains in tortuous attempts to interpret it. Since this law is of great importance to capitalist production, it may be said to be a mystery whose solution has been the goal of all political economy since Adam Smith . . . . (*Capital*, III, ch. 13, p. 213.)

A Polish Marxist, Minc, has offered the criticism that neither Sweezy nor Joan Robinson has established the conditions which must prevail if the increase in the rate of surplus value is to prevent the fall in the rate of profit. Minc attempts to remedy this deficiency by arguing (1962; 1967, p. 436),

If *y* is the decrease in variable capital and the increase in surplus value, and *p* the rate of profit after technical progress has been introduced, . . . the increase in the rate of surplus value can . . . stop the fall in the rate of profit only if the following condition is fulfilled:

$$\frac{y}{\Delta c - y} > p$$

Minc further argues that the rate of profit must finally fall if technical progress is of a 'capital-using' character and if 'the increase in using-up the wear and tear of the means of production, expressed in physical terms, is important' so that 'the magnitude of constant capital (*c*) per unit of product is increased'.

THE PROBLEM OF THE CHARACTER OF TECHNICAL PROGRESS

Thus it results that the decisive question for testing the theory is that of the character of technical progress.

The essential condition for Minc's theory is 'the increase in the magnitude of constant capital per unit of product', i.e. $c/(c+v+s)$. As long as this ratio is not modified, but only the ratio c/v, any decrease in v must automatically lead to an increase in s; s can compensate for the decrease in v indefinitely. If, however, the decrease in v is tantamount to a relative increase in c in relation to value added, an increase in s cannot, of course, indefinitely counterbalance a decrease in v. The gist of the problem is: if technical progress leads to an increase not only in the ratio c/v, but also in $c/(v+s)$, what can be the underlying reasons? In macroeconomic terms, it will be necessary to employ a greater proportion of the labour force in the production of raw materials and fixed assets. Will this be so because raw materials become scarce (more inputs being required for prospecting) or for repairing ecological damage? At this point the modern debate about the problem of the increasing scarcity of raw materials becomes relevant.

Now, in a general sense, it is surely true that the main subject of economics under capitalism is the rate of profit, the variations of which reflect the cycle as well as long-run development. At the same time, profit is the main source of business finance and the engine of growth. In whatever way one looks at this, it is certain that Marx regarded this tendency in the rate of profit as an element of real economic life. This is true in spite of the fact that he conceived his theory in terms of values, which Joan Robinson regrets because she considers this to be a source of obfuscation. Marx's realism runs counter to the attitude of modern Marxists such as Mattick, who argues (1959) that no statements on the actual situation could be derived from the abstract value scheme of capital development.

THE PROBLEM OF OVER-CAPACITY AS THE CAUSE OF HIGH (MARGINAL) CAPITAL COEFFICIENTS

Natalie Moszkowska's arguments regarding dead-weight costs have been taken up by Fellner, especially in an addendum to his article of 1957. Fellner declares that, in a world of imperfect competition, over-capacity could lead to a simultaneous decrease in wages and profits. This would mean that the rate of profit falls because of a low mortality among firms, and that over-capacity persists in each industry because each of these firms retains a loyal nucleus of customers, or because cartels maintain inefficient firms in business. Dewey has shown (1969, p. 56) that in such a case the establishment of a monopoly would lead to rationalisation and the disappearance of over-capacity. This would signify that a 'rational' process of concentration would eliminate over-capacity and the resulting fall in the rate of profit.

There is still another point. Marx categorically declares (*Theories*, II, ch. 17, p. 497, note),

When Adam Smith explains the fall in the rate of profit from an over-abundance of capital, an accumulation of capital, he is speaking of a *permanent* effect and this is wrong. As against this, the transitory over-abundance of capital, over-production and crises are something different. Permanent crises do not exist.

In other words, Marx by no means believed that permanent over-production was possible. Does this mean that in his view no over-capacity could exist in the long run? This remains obscure, unless one assumes that Marx thought protracted crises in individual industries impossible. After all, long periods of recession have occurred in modern times, for instance in coal mining, although they might have been shorter and more painful if state intervention had not mitigated them. However this may be, the meaning of Marx's lapidary remarks will have to be examined later. Marx further says (ibid, ch. 16, p. 469), 'Over-production does not call forth a *constant* fall in profit, but *periodic* over-production recurs constantly. It is followed by periods of under-production etc.' From this Preiser draws the concrete conclusion (1924, p. 53): 'The fall in the rate of profit is the final driving power of development, which culminates in crisis. The basic "agent" is the fall in the rate of profit.'

SECULAR PHENOMENON OR 'WAVES' OF TECHNICAL PROGRESS?

We thus arrive at the explanation of the law as a business-cycle phenomenon.

One might be tempted to conclude from the remark of Marx quoted above that he, like John Stuart Mill, considered the law largely as an empirical fact in the sense of a secular tendency. One might then object that we shall have to evaluate the 'pure' rate of interest. As a matter of fact, rates of interest were very high under early capitalism, because they contained high risk premiums. This was a hangover from the feudal era and the usury that then accompanied loans to consumers. The decline in the rate of interest in the course of capitalist development could then give rise to the erroneous impression that it expressed a tendency towards a decline in the 'pure' rate of interest, when really it only reflected the decreasing importance of the risk element.

Thus we ought to re-examine the law primarily from an empirical point of view. In this context, however, fundamental objections arise to an analysis based on historically ascertained rates of interest. Fellner has stressed (1956, p. 248) that the rate of interest remained relatively low in the period of classical economics:

> We know that the rate at which the British Treasury could borrow during the eighteenth century was at times, though not always, lower than the present long-term rate. Adam Smith, for example, tells his readers that at the time of the publication of *The Wealth of Nations* (1776) the government could borrow at 3 per cent, while the ceiling set by the usury laws was 5 per cent. At present, the rate is close to 4 per cent. The series shows no secular downtrend since the late part of the eighteenth century (although the diagnosis becomes less certain in this regard if we assume that the present rate is appreciably influenced by the expectation of rising commodity prices, and that it thus corresponds to a lower 'real rate of interest').

Here arises the dilemma: if one takes the rate of interest as a yardstick, one must eliminate not only the risk factor, but also inflation or deflation in the respective periods.

Now, one can by no means reproach Marx for having confounded profits and rates of interest. After all, he was one of the first authors who clearly distinguished the various classificatory items, i.e. interest, entrepreneur's salary and risk premium, as opposed to profit in the narrower sense. The level of the rate of interest does not allow any direct conclusion as to the level of the rate of profit, and the movement of neither permits conclusions as to the movement of the other. It is true that, in the long run, high rates of growth are accompanied by high rates of interest, because of the implied inflationary tendencies. In the short run, conditions are more complicated. The banking crisis of 1932 saw a steep rise in interest rates, as also occurred in the inflationary European boom of the 1970s, but in the 1930s the rise was largely owing to a temporarily increased risk. Before escaping into empirical considerations, one will first have to find out what is to be understood in economics and specifically in Marxian economics by a tendency for the rate of profit to fall.

It is essential to note that Marx sees a very specific cause for this fall. He does not think of a general pressure exercised by wage increases, in the course of a business-cycle upswing or of secular growth. In his 'harbinger theory' he sees such a way of looking at a deterioration in profits as a periodic phenomenon, and it does not feature in the forefront of his reasoning.

Nor does he adopt a stagnation theory – for instance, the idea that a decline in rates of profit could be caused by a general weakening of business dynamics or by a sequence of weak growth periods, which may be caused by a lack of effective demand, or by a weak propensity to invest, or by both.

Finally, his primary interest does not lie in changes in the ratio of depreciation (of fixed assets and stocks) to the wage bill, as would be the case if over-capacity existed. His law of the increasing 'organic composition' means (*Capital* 1, ch. 25, p. 589) 'with the growth of the total capital, its variable constituent . . . also does increase, but in a constantly diminishing proportion'. This law operates with 'increasing accumulation and centralisation' (i.e. concentration by merger), and it turns into 'a source of new changes in the composition of capital, of a more accelerated diminution of its variable, as compared with its constant constituent' (ibid.).

For Marx, net investment is decisive: 'The additional capitals formed in the normal course of accumulation . . . serve particularly as vehicles for the exploitation of new inventions and discoveries, and industrial improvements in general' (ibid.). This is imaginable only in the long run, i.e. in Kuznets or Kondratieff cycles, if not indeed secularly.

At this point, Marx unmistakably says that for him technical progress arises not so much from gross investment as from net investment, i.e. in new equipment. This opinion may have been based on the consideration that the replacement and restoration of old plant must of necessity be piecemeal, since the requirements of existing plant means that the newest methods cannot be fully applied.

At this point, we must ask how far the Marxian thesis of a relative expansion of constant and shrinkage of variable capital is really in keeping with the assumption that technical progress always has a labour-saving character. If the two things do go together, it must further be ascertained whether Marx was right in supposing that labour-saving progress dominated his epoch, or in recognising a cyclical, wavelike movement of technical progress. These questions cannot be fully answered in this context, and the author deals with them elsewhere (Kühne, 1975). If, however, one accepts Burchardt's reasoning that at the macroeconomic level one should leave aside raw and auxiliary materials, the law remains restricted to successive changes in the ratio of gross investment to wage costs, so that investment nevertheless becomes the vehicle of mechanisation and renewal. Here there is an approximation to the modern 'vintage' approach, which employs several ages of machinery, the younger of which are always more efficient, because they incorporate the results of the most recent technical progress.

Marx expresses this concept of stage by stage renewal in the following way (*Capital*, 1, ch. 25, p. 589): 'But in time the old capital also reaches the moment of renewal from top to toe, when it sheds its skin and is reborn like the others in a perfected technical form, in which a smaller quantity of labour will suffice to set in motion a larger quantity of machinery and raw materials.'

To that extent, for him the law does not consist in a shift in cost relations with unchanged installations that are too large, as Natalie Moszkowska, who concentrated on changes in capacity utilisation, assumed. Marx thinks of longer periods, in which the law pertains in a more pronounced manner the greater the gross investment undertaken.

BASIC CONDITIONS FOR THE WORKING OF THE LAW

It is doubtful whether the law can be identified with a labour-saving tendency in the full sense. It would be preferable to speak of a tendency to economise on the wage bill, which is to be explained in terms of three conditions:

- firstly, a tendency to reduce the physical labour inputs;
- secondly, a tendency to reduce the price of the labour inputs (per working hour or rather per efficiency unit) through a cheapening of the means of livelihood or subsistence (this presupposes that technical progress is greater in consumer-goods industries, perhaps including construction, and that the general price level and real wages remain unchanged);
- thirdly, and principally, labour must not become relatively scarcer than capital, thus provoking wage rises, either autonomously, through entrepreneurs out-bidding each other, or through trade-union pressure,

i.e. within the institutional framework. (In this case, the 'historical minimum' or average real wage will be raised, even with less physical input, so that the ratio *c:v* may remain unchanged. Briefly, real wages must not rise so rapidly that the first two conditions are nullified, leaving wage bills unchanged.)

The first tendency, the decrease in physical input, can be taken for granted. The second one is doubtful, unless one refers, as Seton and others do, to the middle period of capitalism, in the nineteenth century, when artisans tended to produce means of production rather than consumption goods. The third condition cannot very well be maintained: real wages increased continuously during the second half of the nineteenth century, although they stagnated in the early years of the twentieth century and in Europe during and shortly after both world wars. Marx actually incorporated this rise into his theory, as we have demonstrated in Volume I, Part VI. But did the increase in real wages outweigh all other factors?

TECHNICAL AND VALUE COMPOSITION

When Marx speaks of *c:v* as the 'organic composition', he sharply distinguishes between the 'technical composition', i.e. the ratio of the volume of fixed assets and raw materials to the quantity of labour hours (or consumption goods produced), and the 'value composition', which comprises price movements.

This distinction is essential, the more so as it is often blurred by later authors and sometimes even by Marx: in his definition of the organic composition in volume I of *Capital*, he expressly says (ch. 25, p. 574) that the volume composition must be reflected in the value composition:

> The composition of capital is to be understood in a two-fold sense. On the side of value, it is determined by the proportion in which it is divided into constant capital or value of the means of production, and variable capital or value of labour-power, the sum total of wages. On the side of material, as it functions in the process of production, all capital is divided into means of production and living labour-power. This latter composition is determined by the relation between the mass of the means of production employed, on the one hand, and the mass of labour necessary for their employment on the other. I call the former the *value-composition*, the latter the *technical composition* of capital. Between the two there is a strict correlation. To express this, I call the value-composition of capital, in so far as it is determined by its technical composition and mirrors the changes of the latter, the *organic composition*. Wherever I refer to the composition of capital, without further qualification, its organic composition is always understood.

The term 'technical composition', which seems so simple, nevertheless gives rise to a number of problems. For instance, Zinn has written (1972, pp. 64, 114) that, 'in the literature, the Marxian term "technical composition" is in most cases avoided, so that its ambiguity has not become evident. . . . The differing definition of the technical and organic composition leads to difficulties. . . . ' The following question must be answered. How far does the value composition, alias organic composition, of capital reflect the technical composition? In modern terms, how far does the ratio 'quantity of capital:quantity of labour' appear in the quotient 'total value of capital:wage bill'?

Marx measured the latter in 'values' *sui generis*, i.e. in 'socially necessary' labour time expressed in money units. However, apparently he could not do without a sort of production function in volumes or physical units (machinery of a certain productivity, raw-material volumes, number of labourers). He apparently thought that the value composition must somehow reflect at least the direction in which volumes were shifting. Indeed, he recognises that the volume shift in favour of (constant) capital proceeds much more slowly in value terms, and he goes on to say (*Capital*, 1, ch. 25, pp. 583–4):

> This change in the technical composition of capital, this growth in the mass of means of production, as compared with the mass of the labour-power that vivifies them, is reflected again in its value-composition, by the increase of the constant constituent of capital at the expense of its variable constituent. . . .

What he means is that 'this law of the progressive increase in constant capital, in proportion to the variable, is confirmed at every step . . . by the comparative analysis of the prices of commodities'.

The reflection of volume movements in values is damped: there is a

> diminution in the variable part of capital as compared with the constant, or the altered value-composition of its material constituents. . . . The reason is simply that, with the increasing productivity of labour, not only does the mass of the means of production consumed by it increase, but their value compared with their mass diminishes.

From here it is only a short step to Croce's assumption in his Marxist era that the movement in volumes would be exactly compensated by the movement in values, so that no shift or 'reflection' of technical processes would occur in the field of values.

Marx early understood that a cheapening of constant capital could compensate for the technical shift. But in the *Grundrisse* (p. 390), he says that he wants .

to avoid the *nefarious presupposition* that [the worker] continued to operate with a constant capital of 60 and a wage fund of 40 – after a doubling of productive force, which introduces false relations; because it presupposes that, despite the doubled force of production, capital continued to operate with the same component parts, to employ the same quantity of necessary labour without spending more for raw material and instrument of labour . . . .

And in a footnote he adds that 'this is so for every industrialist if the force of production doubles not in his branch, but in the branch whose output he uses'.

In volume III of *Capital* (ch. 13, p. 230) he also recognises the possibility of value relations remaining the same:

Considered abstractly the rate of profit may remain the same, even though the price of the individual commodity may fall as a result of greater productiveness of labour and a simultaneous increase in the number of this cheaper commodity, if, for instance, the increase in productiveness of labour acts uniformly and simultaneously on all the elements of the commodity, so that its total price falls in the same proportion in which the productivity of labour increases, while, on the other hand, the mutual relation of the different elements of the price of the commodity remains the same. The rate of profit could even rise if a rise in the rate of surplus-value were accompanied by a substantial reduction in the value of the elements of constant, and particularly of fixed, capital. But in reality, as we have seen, the rate of profit will fall in the long run.

Well-meaning critics such as Güsten have pointed out that

there is nothing to justify Marx's statement 'as we have already seen', for in the foregoing text, we find only the ever-repeated assertion that the value composition increases. . . . It ill becomes a theorist of Marx's rank to appeal to 'reality' at the decisive moment of his abstract analysis. Whoever appeals to reality risks being contradicted by reality . . . .
(Güsten, 1960, p. 56.)

Many Marxists, however, have followed him in this appeal to the judgement stool of reality. For instance, Halbach says (1972, p. 39):

When constant-capital values decrease, it depends on how the value composition of capital $(c:v)$ changes, as compared to the technical composition. . . . This 'it depends' indicates how difficult it is to handle this case. It depends upon which sector shows the greater increase in labour productivity. This is a problem which cannot be solved by mere calculation; . . . we must consider the real course capitalist production has taken.

The present author has elsewhere (Kühne, 1976) assembled some of the facts that may be expected to shed some light on this problem and so help us to answer the question of whether the Marxian law of the tendency of the rate of profit to fall really contains a germ of truth, if we look at it from a secular view-point. It is true that Marx sketched the law very cursorily, did not find conclusive proof for the prevalence of certain tendencies, and therefore, as he often did, relied on his intuition, which gave him a glimpse of certain wave-like variations in the character of technical progress.

ATTEMPTS AT VERIFICATION

A number of attempts at verifying the theorem have been undertaken. Such a near-Marxian as Latouche has objected to all such attempts, arguing (1973, p. 164) that it is 'not an empirical, but a theoretical, law' and that it would be 'absurd to disprove it by quoting an alleged lesson from the facts'. On the other hand, such an avowed Marxist as Gillman thought the test of facts indispensable. He reached the conclusion (1957) that the law had held until about 1919–20, and that since then the 'organic composition' had fallen and the 'pure' rate of profit had risen. He nevertheless attempted to introduce the notion of a fall in the rate of profit in the broader sense, by deducting 'unproductive expenses' (advertising, the salaries of office staff, and so on) from surplus value. This provoked Joan Robinson's ironic comment that it was absurd that Marxists should assert that such advertising costs should be borne by capitalists and not passed on by them to the consumer.

Other Marxists have rashly tried to combine the theoretical approach with an attempt at verification. Thus Halbach suggests (1972, p. 88) that 'the value composition . . . increases if productivity increases with equal speed in the production- and consumption-goods sectors, because [!] the technical composition (means of production per worker) increases'. Halbach commits the same mistake as Güsten by erroneously identifying the 'technical composition' with capital intensity (capital per worker). As a matter of fact, Marx's ratio $c:v$ compares two quantities of goods: the quantity of production goods and the quantity of consumption goods, expressed in average social labour hours. The number of workers appears nowhere in this ratio!

It is a non-Marxist, Schmitt-Rink, who defines this ratio most clearly (1967, pp. 133ff.). He divides both sides of the ratio, which he conceives as consisting of sums of prices for given volumes, by the number of workers: $(c:w)/(v:w)$. This is then clearly the ratio between capital intensity and the real wage. He opposes to this another macroeconomic ratio: if one divides both sides by value added, the resulting ratio, $(c:[v+s])/(v:[v+s])$ gives the relation between the capital–output ratio and the share of wages in national income. All one can say against this interpretation is that c represents a flow, i.e. possibly an investment–output ratio, not a genuine capital–output ratio.

If one adopts Hicks's formulation (1965; 1969, p. 182), the first ratio could be made even more homogeneous if $v:w$ were to be defined as 'capital in consumption-goods terms: capital in labour-terms'. This interpretation certainly makes statistical verification easier than does Gillman's method.

Dickinson has succeeded in mathematically underpinning the 'general correctness' of the Marxian thesis by eliminating raw materials from the 'organic composition'. He is of the view (1956–7, pp. 124ff.) that a lower productivity in the consumption-goods sector would lead to an earlier fall in the rate of profit, even at a lower ratio of $c:v$.

DIFFERENT SECTORS – CAPITAL-INTENSITY AS A DESTABILISING FACTOR

It is true that the Marxian ratio is related to the notion of capital-intensity, and this fact leads us back to modern growth theory. In his first example, Marx assumed a higher ratio in the capital-goods industry, and it is fitting that Uzawa discovered a century later (1961, p. 40) that a higher capital-intensity in the capital-goods sector would in principle lead to instability. Solow (1961) thought it paradoxical that equilibrium should depend on an accident of technology. He objected to Uzawa's findings that they depended on the assumption that all wages are consumed and all profits are saved, an assumption which is generally (though not quite correctly) called the Marx–Kaldor hypothesis.

Uzawa then showed, in a second article (1963), that, even if one dropped this hypothesis and assumed that everyone saved in the face of increasing rates of interest and income, equilibrium would not prevail in the opposite case, where the consumer-goods industry is more capital-intensive – a condition which in his first example guaranteed stability!

One may well ask whether it is not true that in inflationary periods the savings of workers will be zero (because of capital losses). In that case, the reasoning in Uzawa's first essay would apply. Now it is true that in real life the differences in capital-intensity between the two sectors taken as a whole are not so pronounced. Nevertheless, if one overcomes the difficulty of drawing a clear line of demarcation between the sectors, it would seem that the capital–goods industries are more capital-intensive, if one includes basic products in this sector. This seems to be confirmed in studies by Kuznets (1966), Krengel (1962, 1975/76), Mertens (1964) and others. Here, as in the case of the long-run rate of profit, we hit on factual problems the analysis of which must be left to separate studies, in view of the vast literature on this subject.

What is essential is this: Marx thought he had found in a technological factor, i.e. the increase in capital costs in relation to wage costs (both expressed in real terms), the reason for the instability of capitalism. He did introduce different ratios for the two departments, but did not elaborate upon this. Later calculations, by Bauer and Grossmann, stress the relative increase in c, but do not introduce a differentiation as such. In this field, there remains work for Marxists to do. It is strange that Marxism has found an ally in a neo-classical author such as Uzawa. Ott has noted that it was the latter who took up the daring pioneer work done by Marx in studying two-sector models. The gist of the matter lies in the fact that instability would prevail owing not to a failure of (Keynesian) policy measures, but to inexorable structural conditions. It was Marx's purpose to discover this inner structural logic of capitalism, and Uzawa's reasoning would suit him well.

CONCLUSIONS

Modern Marxists, as for instance Maarek (1975, p. 255) are prone to reject 'Marx's law', suspecting that he might have confounded capital intensity and an increase in the 'organic composition', as indeed some of his followers did (e.g. Halbach).

This author believes that Marx was not guilty of such an elementary error, but was actually discovering the labour-saving branch of a secular cycle in the character of technical progress, which seems to have been followed by a period of predominantly capital-saving technical progress since the early twenties and by a further labour-saving swing since the mid-sixties, both reflecting changing scarcities. This hypothesis seems to be confirmed by the movement of the capital–output ratio. Such swings in the character of technical progress may be linked to longer-term cycles of the 'Kondratiev' or 'Kuznets' types. (See Bibl., Addendum: Kühne, 1976, ch. III, and 1977, pp. 76–97).

Furthermore, the Marxian 'increase of the organic composition' may appear in an increase in external and more specifically environmental costs which tend to get rather slowly internalised in our times.

10 The Idea of Stagnation and the Problems of Growth

Marx thought capitalism was bound to founder on two rocks onto which its vessel would inevitably be driven, and he saw these rocks entirely from an economic point of view (*Capital*, III, ch. 15, p. 259):

> It comes to the surface here in a purely economic way – i.e., from the bourgeois point of view, within the limitations of capitalist understanding, from the standpoint of capitalist production itself – that it has its barrier, that it is relative, that it is not an absolute, but only a historical mode of production corresponding to a definite limited epoch in the development of the material requirements of production.

In Marx's view, Ricardo had been the first to see the barrier, which, he thought (ibid.), at the same time foreshadowed a new form of society:

> Development of the productive forces of social labour is the historical task and justification of capital. This is just the way in which it unconsciously creates the material requirements of a higher mode of production. What worries Ricardo is the fact that the rate of profit, the stimulating principle of capitalist production, the fundamental premise and driving force of accumulation, should be endangered by the development of production itself.

In other words, capitalism is an indispensable stage, a necessary purgatory, through which mankind must pass if it is to arrive at socialism. The signal indicating the transition towards the new system could be the fall in the rate of profit. This, i.e. a fall in the rate of profit because of inflated capital values, perhaps reflected in artificially increased share prices, would be one of the two 'rocks' mentioned above. The second danger that could lead to the downfall of capitalism is, in Marx's view (ibid.), an exaggerated process of concentration:

> As soon as formation of capital were to fall into the hands of a few established big capitals, for which the mass of profit compensates for the

falling rate of profit, the vital flame of production would be altogether extinguished. It would die out. The rate of profit is the motive power of capitalist production. . . . Hence the concern of the English economists over the decline of the rate of profit.

Does this indicate a stagnation theory in Marx? In this case, the fall in the rate of profit would be brought about through fossilisation or bureaucratisation (cf. Kühne, 1977).

The analysis of the process of concentration has already acquainted us with the problem of stagnation. Stagnation tendencies in modern economies are caused, in the view of the protagonists of stagnation theories, more or less 'autonomously' – that is, by the tendency for monopolistic firms to put a brake on investment and to maintain surplus capacity. One might be inclined to believe that the two tendencies would counteract each other, for, if investment is held back, this should help to reduce the underutilisation of capacity. This effect need not follow if the expansion of capacity takes place despite progressively decreased net investment. This is possible if technical progress is introduced *via* gross investment.

Gross investment does indeed seem to be the main determinant for the impact of technical progress. To start with, depreciation funds feed investment long before replacement is needed. This part of gross investment represents net investment from the outset. Only later, when old equipment is withdrawn from use in a 'hump', is this matched by disinvestment, so that in the long run net investment need not appear. This extension of capacity in anticipation of replacement is the vehicle of technical progress, so that in practice capacity is increased. Marx repeatedly pointed out the importance of replacement investment for the business cycle. Joan Robinson has underlined the role of gross investment as a vehicle of technical progress.

Thus we may conclude that a continuous expansion of capacity is certainly compatible with a throttling of net investment by oligopolies, so that the outcome may very well be a permanent under-utilisation of capacity. It may even happen that investment is throttled because firms know that technical progress increases capacity in any case, even without deliberate expansion of structures and equipment.

Stagnation theorists seem to think in other terms: for them, it is not the throttling of investment that matters, but the sheer weight of over-capacity, which implies two consequences. First, there is the reduction in net investment, especially where, as is likely, in view of the vast amount of research work undertaken in oligopolistic industry, technical progress takes place. Secondly, over-capacity is deliberately maintained, for in oligopolies or quasi-cartels quotas or sales areas are distributed on the basis of existing capacity. Furthermore, over-capacity may be a weapon used by oligopolies in order to fight off outsiders, which makes its existence 'rational'.

Here is the link with the Marxian theory of the fall in the rate of profit. This tendency actually presupposes that capacity expressed in capital values grows more rapidly than profit rates. We dealt with it first of all as a long-run phenomenon; the business-cycle aspect is discussed later (see chapter 17). The question to be answered is this: is this tendency – which Marx saw – compatible with the propensity to restrict investment which other authors believe they have discovered in oligopolistic systems?

THE ORIGIN OF THE STAGNATION THESIS

Schumpeter points out (1959, p. 740) that Malthus developed an early version of the stagnation thesis in his business-cycle analysis. At the same time, he notes that Marx rejected all under-consumptionist theories, especially that of Rodbertus. It so happens that the latter's theory has a stagnationist aspect, for it assumes long-run poverty as a cause of persistent over-production. In rejecting Rodbertus's version, Marx rejected stagnationist theory.

Both Malthus and Ricardo based their sombre predictions of future stagnation upon the population explosion or upon the scarcity of land (including raw materials). For Ricardo, the secular fall in the rate of profit was a symptom of the overpowering and growing monopoly power of landlords. Today's forebodings of a secular scarcity of raw materials and energy bear the same stamp. John Stuart Mill tried, on the other hand, to interpret the tendency of the rate of profit to fall, which thesis he embraced wholeheartedly, in a positive way, for he thought that a stationary state of capital and population would allow for an even higher 'quality of life', as we should say today, i.e. cultural, moral and social development and a higher 'Art of Living'.

> It is scarcely necessary to remark that a stationary condition of capital and population implies no stationary state of human improvement. There would be as much scope as ever for all kinds of mental culture, and moral and social progress; as much room for improving the Art of Living, and much more likelihood of its being improved, when minds ceased to be engrossed by the art of getting on.
>
> (Mill, 1848; 1965, p. 754.)

Thus Mill, in his vision of the stationary state, assumed the opposite of what Malthus envisaged, i.e. a stationary population. If Mill further hoped that the stationary state would favour education, the arts, religion, sports, social contacts and scientific research, one could agree with de Finetti that this attitude is profoundly optimistic, in contrast to the lurid predictions of Malthus and Ricardo. Mill's stationary state resembles the 'state of bliss' or 'golden age' of modern growth theory and boils down to the assumption that it would be possible in that age to have technical progress without net investment. It remains an open question why the profit rate should still fall in such a 'stationary' state. According to modern growth analysis, it should in this case tend to coincide with the growth rate and thus approach zero.

Marx rejected every demographic stagnation thesis. This rejection applied not only to Malthusianism, which taught that the population explosion would bring about misery, but also to Mill's version, in which a stationary population entails economic stagnation. Since Marx considers capitalism to be essentially dynamic, a loss of dynamics can for him only be equivalent to a negation of capitalism. The 'progress in science' postulated by Mill would for Marx be completely incompatible with a stationary condition. His theory of the (periodically recurring) creation of an 'industrial over-population' is based on the assumption of technological unemployment as described by Ricardo in his *Principles*, in the chapter 'On Machinery'.

It is not easy to derive a stagnation theory from this thesis. The 'freeing' of labour occurs at intervals and can be compensated by counteracting forces, especially by more net investment. Sylos-Labini has summarised this possibility as follows (1970, p. 26):

Neither Marx nor Ricardo denied that it might be possible for redundant labour to be absorbed, if additional (variable) capital were available . . . nor that the formation of additional capital might be stimulated by a decrease in the prices of goods which are produced by machinery, for this makes part of the capitalists' income available. Marx points out, however, that this is quite a far cry from what the protagonists of the compensation theory maintain.'

Thus it is made abundantly clear that Marx never believed that the number of employed would continually decrease in relation to the unemployed. If ever he thought that such a tendency might for a while prevail, he knew that it would be at least partially reversed through new bursts of investment.

Sylos-Labini declares in his lapidary style (ibid., p. 22), 'For Marx, capitalist society is not stationary and can never be stationary.' This throws into relief the distinction between Marx and Mill.

Mill not only held that a stationary state was possible in a capitalist system, but thought it desirable. In addition to a tendency towards a fall in the rate of profit, as a result of increasing accumulation, he saw 'counteracting forces' analogous to those quoted by Marx: the transfer of capital in crises to the successful speculator, improvements in production, the cheapening of goods through imports, capital exports, and so on. (See Mill, 1848, Bk ɪᴠ, chs 4 and 5.) Marx has often been rebuked for his methodology, because he contrasted the 'tendency of the rate of profit to fall' with 'counter-forces', but here it becomes clear that in so doing he is in excellent company, for this is in the best classical tradition.

A real stagnation thesis in the modern sense did not appear until in the wake of Keynes. Schumpeter says (1959, p. 1172),

> Keynes must be credited or debited, as the case may be, with the fatherhood of modern stagnationism. In itself stagnationism is practically as old as economic thought. . . . But so far as our own epoch and scientific literature are concerned, this attitude can be traced as we have seen to Keynes's *Economic Consequences of the Peace*. . . . A group that might almost be called a school . . . rose to scientific importance under the brilliant leadership of Professor Alvin H. Hansen, who amplified and expanded the doctrine of the mature or stagnating economy in part on different grounds than Keynes.

Roll (1953; 1961, p. 504) proposed to talk in this context of the theory of declining investment opportunities.

Hansen has elaborated his theory in a number of articles and at least two books (1938, 1941). This theory was then further developed in the work of the Anglo-Austrian Steindl, who argued (1952) that even before the First World War fossilised oligopolistic capitalism had led to paralysis of the propensity to invest, and that this was the underlying reason for the near-collapse of capitalism in the 1930s.

A conservative German historian, Kesting, who died at an early age, gives (1959, pp. 239–40) an excellent résumé of Hansen's teachings, stressing their similarity to certain theories developed by Hobson:

> Hansen maintains that an economy which has reached maturity will be marked by an expansion of savings and surplus and a dwindling of investment opportunities, and this essentially for three reasons. First, population growth, which had caused more than 50 per cent of real capital formation in England and America during the nineteenth century, reached a standstill. Furthermore, territorial expansion was more or less at an end; neither from new areas nor from capital exports to under-developed areas could any impulses for investment be derived, for this presupposed unfettered capital movements. Finally, Hansen asserts that intensive growth or technical progress as an opportunity for large-scale investment is out of the question, since inventions are nowadays both capital- *and* labour-saving. The structural lack of investment opportunities only appeared in 1929 because of the destruction wrought in the First World War and the resulting capital scarcity. Since then under-investment and unemployment have been endemic, and no expansion in the nineteenth-century sense can any longer be expected.

Today, these theories have fallen into oblivion. This is to be explained primarily by the high growth rate that world capitalism achieved after the end of the Second World War and which for two decades considerably surpassed the average growth rates of the nineteenth century, contrary to Hansen's expectation. It remains to be seen whether his theory will become fashionable again in face of the slow-down in growth and the 'stagflation' of the 1970s.

Kesting added the comment, 'Hansen's theory expresses the pessimism regarding the capitalist system which prevailed in wide circles, especially among the intelligentsia, in view of the continuing depression.'

It is a moot point whether recent disturbances may cause a long-run flattening of the growth rates, or chains of deeper recessions and depressions, which could give rise to similar pessimistic tendencies, coloured by the additional virus of inflation.

THE STAGNATION THESIS AND THE MARXIAN BELIEF IN PROGRESS

It is not possible to identify such theories with the Marxian standpoint. Marx expressly wished to sever the link between population growth and economic growth, all the more so because this may work in two directions, and he stresses that capitalism creates its own surplus population *via* predominantly labour-saving progress. Furthermore, what matters for Marx is not the population increase as such, but only the increase in 'effective demand'. Finally, technical progress appears to him as profoundly favourable to, if not synonymous with, investment, for he considers it to be 'capital-using'. To this extent, Marx's concept coincides with Kaldor's 'technical-progress function'. For Marx, technical progress occurs in one action with gross investment, the flow of which is for him identical to a 'stream of new ideas'.

Kaldor calls this (1957, p. 597) a functional relationship between the proportional growth of capital and the annual proportional increase of productivity. For Marx too, increases in productivity and investment are synonymous, and this excludes the notion that there may be a lack of investment opportunities, as Hansen and his disciples think. To this extent Marx's global view of capitalist growth is of an intensive character and that of Hansen of an extensive character, although this is not directly apparent in the structure of Marx's growth models.

On the other hand, Klein has maintained (1947; 1968, p. 154) that 'the Marxian theory of the falling rate of profit is one of the first, and probably one of the best, tools for analysing the stagnation theory'. He goes on to assert (ibid., pp. 168–71) that the foundations of the stagnation thesis might be found in this Marxian theorem. He sees its essence in the accumulation or over-capacity thesis – 'It was the capital accumulation of the twenties which led to the fall in the rate of profit and the consequent stagnation of the thirties' – and he states that his own statistical investigations have led him to the conclusion that 'the stock of fixed capital is negatively related to investment. The more capital there is, other things unchanged, the less is the desire for new capital.' He admits, however, that the consequences of capital accumulation have never been thoroughly examined. Keynesian theory assumes a given stock of fixed assets in the short run; long-run analysis assumes investment to be zero. In saying this, Klein alludes to modern growth theory, which maintains that investment is of no consequence for growth. He says, 'The real world falls between these extremes, and the Marxian model . . . is a representation of the compromise.' However, he has to admit that, even if Marxian theory is interpreted in this way, this does not indicate that 'the stagnation or maturity is permanent'. If this is so, there would seem to be no evidence of a genuine stagnation thesis in Marx's work.

This is not to say that such theories do not exist in the Marxist camp. Indeed, in taking up Otto Bauer's schemes (1912–13, pp. 831–8, 862–74) intended to provide a basis for refutation of Rosa Luxemburg's theory, Grossmann tried to prove (1929), shortly before the great crisis of the 1930s, that capitalism must inexorably lead to crisis and stagnation. Both authors left technical progress completely out of account, and one is tempted to classify them as stagnation theorists.

Nevertheless, the Marxian interpretation is firmly based on one condition – the vitality of enterprise and the readiness to invest which represent the dynamic engine of the system, in analogy to those 'animal spirits' which for Keynes are the essence of capitalism. Keynes did not believe that it would matter much if the 'normal' rate of profit dropped from 15 to 10 or even 5 per cent, for he thought that these 'animal spirits' were largely bound to irrational mental forces combined (if one follows recent management research) with hunting and prestige instincts.

In modern times, Drucker has actually conceived of a theory of 'spiritual stagnation'. He thinks (1970) that the type of capitalist *homo oeconomicus* that has been responsible for economic expansion since the eighteenth century is beginning to disappear. A new type of man is in the ascendant who no longer gives priority to materialistic and economic factors, and this implies the death sentence for capitalism, but also for a socialism which attaches too much importance to economic aspects. The collapse of society became inevitable at the very moment when, as Drucker has it, Marxism proved unable to found a free and equal society. Drucker's side-swipe at Marxism raises a new problem – namely, the return to the early philosophical manuscripts of Marx, with their search for a new image of man.

One can see a further version of the stagnation thesis in theories which place in the foreground the mechanism of the compulsion to consume and the saturation of modern society with 'unnecessary' consumer goods, the so-called 'gadgets'. For instance, Bataille actually states (1949) that the problem of the modern economy is not poverty but abundance. This brings him into the territory of zero-growth enthusiasts.

Galbraith's slogan 'the affluent society' (1958/62) represents a similar attitude, although it onesidedly reflects the United States atmosphere. He tried to relieve this lopsidedness by contrasting private affluence and public squalor.

If we leave aside Bauer's and Grossmann's theses, there are three theoretical concepts that should be mentioned in the context of the stagnation thesis.

First, there is the theory of 'long' or 'secular' waves, which was conceived by two Marxists – the German Helphand, alias 'Parvus', and the Dutchman van Gelderen – at the turn of the century. This idea could be considered as a theory of temporary stagnation. The theory was refined by the Russian Kondratieff in the intellectually stimulating Marxist climate of the 1920s in the Soviet Union, and by another Dutch Marxist, de Wolff. In the Soviet Union, after a heated debate, it was declared to be politically heretical. Kondratieff was shot as the alleged leader of a peasants' party. He has, however, found his apotheosis in Schumpeter's proposal to give his name to the long-run swings of around half a century, and more recently in the fact that his theory appeals to such Marxists as Mandel, who seems to take it over lock, stock and barrel in one of his recent publications (1972, pp. 101, 115ff.).

We have already mentioned the second theory in connexion with Hansen's thesis and also within the framework of the debate on concentration and oligopolistic instability. It culminates in the concept developed by Steindl, who saw in oligopoly capitalism a major reason for the stagnation of investment.

The third theory has been developed above in Volume 1, part V. It draws heavily on Steindl and was not uninfluenced by Hansen's ideas, for it holds that a growing 'surplus' is confronted with a lack of investment opportunities. This is the thesis of Baran and Sweezy. Their basic approach seems to show that it is in contradiction to Marx's original concept. As a matter of fact, Baran and Sweezy see rather too much and not too little surplus value, while Marx derived his tendency for the rate of profit to fall from an increase in constant capital, which would be counteracted by growing surplus value.

Part III
Marx's Theories of
Business Cycles

11 Interpretations of Marxian Business-Cycle Theories

It has been said that Marx did not work out a coherent theory of the business cycle, but offered rather a series of fragments, on which various theories could be based. This opinion has been voiced by Guitton in particular (1951; 1971, pp. 125ff.) and it certainly possesses a seductive appeal.

On the other hand, it may be pointed out that Marx's entire work should be considered as a theory of the evolution of capitalism as a whole, and that the business-cycle concept is just one element of this. In Marxian theory, the dynamic evolution of capitalism, as a growth process, already contains the germ of business-cycle conditions. There can be no doubt that Marx saw one of the main results of his analysis as being the idea that capitalism would suffer ever-more violent upheavals of its economic and social structure – albeit that this tendency is not explicitly analysed in detail in his work.

In his attack upon the 'fatuous Say' and his law, Marx indicated that he thought that the basic reason for business cycles lay in the existence of money, which permitted hoarding without the holding of stocks of goods. Although Marx generally drew heavily upon Ricardo, at an early date he severely criticised, in his *Theories of Surplus Value*, Ricardo's version of Say's law. And he added drily, 'Ricardo himself did not actually know anything of crises' (*Theories*, II, ch. 17, p. 497; see also p. 502).

As we have pointed out in Volume I, Chapter 5, for Marx the possibility of crisis lies in the separation of purchase and sale, i.e. in monetary hoarding interrupting the circular flow. For a more detailed discussion of Marx's theory of business cycles, the reader is directed elsewhere (see Kühne, 1954 and 1970).

THE ANTICIPATION OF CYCLE ANALYSIS

Very few authors have tried to give a general overview of the various Marxian explanations of business cycles. Most studies remain limited to the analysis (with exaggerations) of certain individual aspects, in which, since Marx's reasoning cannot be identified with a single determinate theory, it is not possible to do justice to the kaleidoscopic complexity of his intuitions on the subject.

In his famous article on crises, Spiethoff spoke harshly (1923; 1955, p. 161) of the state of Marxian business-cycle analysis: 'This version in Volume III of *Capital* cannot have been intended to be the final one, for it forms an unbearable hotch-potch of general tendencies leading to the ultimate collapse of the capitalist economy and of the circumstances supposed to bring about fluctuations.'

Nevertheless, Spiethoff was profoundly influenced by Marx, partly *via* Tugan-Baranowsky. This is underlined by Salin, in his preface to the reprint of Spiethoff's article, when he says (ibid., p. 3) that, 'before reading Spiethoff and Wicksell, and certainly before reading Keynes, the study of Marx is indispensable', for 'a return to the masters and a beginning with their teaching establishes more easily than anything else what is indispensable, the important and pertinent questions.'

One cannot contradict Salin when he rejects dogmatism. In his opinion, there can be no 'Spiethoffians': 'There are Marxists, and there could be Keynesians, because the works of Keynes as well as those of Marx contain dogmatic elements, but one would be unjust to both of them if one were to fossilise their contemporary ideas instead of developing and answering anew their eternal questions . . . .'

An author who did more justice to Marx is Lutz, who partially opposes Spiethoff, reproaching him for proceeding too subjectively when he said that the picture of a cyclical fluctuation 'is in decisive ways dependent on the observer's opinion and personal judgement'. Lutz says it would be 'disastrous . . . if the complexity of the business-cycle phenomenon allowed individual observers to pick out, within wide limits, what they thought appeared most characteristic, for whatever reasons'. This would mean that no scientific solution would be possible, because one would be enmeshed in subjectivism. Thus Lutz reproaches both Spiethoff and Tugan-Baranowsky with explaining nothing but giving only descriptions. (Lutz, 1932, pp. 39–40, 57–8.)

Lutz recognises (ibid., pp. 84, 86–7) that Marx had profound vision:

Marx was the first to try and derive economic development, and within its framework cyclical fluctuations, from the internal preconditions of this system. It is true that his business-cycle theory is not very articulate; in essence, he gives a number of hints which are in themselves contradictory. Consistency is missing from his argument, so that a precise interpretation of this frequently obscure wording is made difficult, if not impossible. . . . Marx's theory of crises lacks careful elaboration. . . . There can be no doubt, however, that in volume III [of *Capital*] he wanted to deduce not only the possibility of crises but also their absolute necessity. . . . In this attempt to prove that crises were the necessary outcome of the system's preconditions lies the new and important element of Marx's contribution, as compared with the classics.

Lutz apparently did not know of the more detailed exposition in the *Theories of Surplus Value*, and could not know of the comments in the *Grundrisse* on the crisis problem. Thus he could not offer a full appreciation of Marx's contribution. He was well acquainted with Juglar's writings and may therefore be quoted as a witness on the question of who really discovered the medium-term cycle that Schumpeter baptised the 'Juglar cycle'.

Lutz reminds us that Juglar wrote a number of articles in the 1850s and published his main work in 1860 (new edition 1889). He declares that Juglar tried 'to refine the form of the business cycle by comparing individual cases, in order to distinguish the general problem'. He points out that Juglar offered some empirical work, but concentrated on an analysis of the essence of business cycles, in the manner of the classics, as contrasted with the more descriptive approach of his contemporaries. (Lutz, 1932, pp. 32ff.)

Nevertheless, it is clear from Lutz's studies that even Juglar did not analyse the cycle as a whole and as part of the capitalist process – 'Even Juglar concentrated his attention on the crisis . . .' (ibid., p. 41) – and this remained essentially the approach of Tugan-Baranowsky, Aftalion and others, until Cassel developed an integral concept of the cycle. On the other hand, one may claim with justice that, by the time he wrote the manuscripts of the *Grundrisse*, i.e. in the years 1857 to 1859, Marx already understood the cycle as part of the capitalist process. At that time, he paid almost as much attention to the upswing as to the downswing, since he saw in the former the germ of the crisis.

GENERAL COMMENTS ON MARX'S CYCLE THEORY

'Academic' economists began to comment on Marx's contributions to cycle theory relatively late. That notwithstanding, certain elements of Marxian thought entered into economic literature *via* Tugan-Baranowsky. Only in a few cases was Marx's cycle theory directly analysed, and this did not happen before 1910.

In his great work of 1927, Mitchell stated (1927; 1932, p. 232) that 'of the numerous speculations of this type, those of Karl Marx are of especial interest here, because they include the increasing frequency and increasing severity of business crises among the secular trends which are to usher in the socialistic state'. Mitchell talks of a 'preface' that Marx wrote for the 1873 edition of volume 1 of *Capital*, and in which he presents in a rudimentary fashion 'the role of crises in the schema of economic revolution'. It seems that Mitchell here means the Postscript to the second edition, published in January 1873. In the Postscript, however, Marx does not say a word about crises, but quotes a review in the May 1872 issue of the Russian journal *Wjestnik Ewropi*, which says that Marx developed the 'laws which govern the origin, existence, development and death of a given social organism and its replacement by a new one'.

Many authors who discuss Marxian crisis theories see them almost entirely through the spectacles of Marxist epigones. Marie Hirsch, for instance, in her book of 1929 (pp. 54ff.), hardly examines Marx's own ideas, but resorts to Rosa Luxemburg's interpretation, which is not a business-cycle theory at all but a growth analysis.

One of the first full presentations of Marx's cycle theory by a non-Marxist was made shortly before the first World War by the Russian author Bouniatian who lived in the West. He discovers (1921; 1930, pp. 22ff.) five main theories in Marx:

(1) the tendency towards an intensive deployment of productive forces (which may overshoot?);
(2) the propensity towards excessive net investment, or 'over-capitalisation';
(3) 'the difficulty of keeping proportionate production';
(4) 'the limitation of the power of consumption of the society through antagonistic conditions of distribution', and
(5) the theory of the tendency of the rate of profit to fall.

Early in the 1920s, Preiser devoted a study to Marx's cycle theory. The larger part of this has unfortunately not yet been published. In his main work on business cycles (1933), Preiser contented himself with saying (1, pp. 5–6) that, for Marx, 'crisis theory was really the last chapter of his total theory'. Preiser even finds fault with 'the analysts' group represented by Spiethoff', since, whereas they consciously base their approach on empirical facts, Marx deliberately chose a purely theoretical approach, for he was the typical representative of those economists who derive the cycle endogenously from the basic structure of the capitalist system.

In his *magnum opus* on business cycles, Schumpeter builds his analysis on the fact that, for Marx, cycles are endogenous phenomena integrated into the economic sphere and originating in it. At the same time, Schumpeter stresses (1939, 1, p. 10) Marx's emphasis on technical progress: 'we hold . . . (in this respect entirely agreeing with Marx) that technological progress was of the very essence of capitalistic enterprise and hence cannot be divorced from it'.

The relationship between Schumpeter's and Marx's views on business cycles was the subject of a perspicacious study by the Japanese economist Tsuru, who pointed out, in a work written at Harvard (1941, published 1956), that the two approaches are quite distinct. Whereas Marx sees business cycles as part of the essence of capitalism itself, Schumpeter initially assumes an equilibrium situation and progresses, as it were, 'from business cycles to capitalism'. Tsuru summarises his approach by saying (1956, pp. 25–33), 'Professor Schumpeter works on the hypothesis of an intermittent "force" impinging on the otherwise stationary process, whereas Marx leaned more on the hypothesis picturing cycles as akin to self-perpetuating waves of adaptation.'

Tsuru's hint of an element of *perpetuum mobile* in Marx's business-cycle theory, is all the more important in that Schumpeter himself ascribed this idea (1939, 1, p. 48, note 1) to Pantaleoni, who spoke of 'phenomena which perpetuate themselves indefinitely'.

The idea that Marx developed a number of different business-cycle theories was advanced by Bartoli in an article (1954), in which he traces the notion back to Joan Robinson's *Essay on Marxian Economics* (1949). In this, however, she only states that there are two diametrically opposed strains in Marx's cycle analysis: 'a theory of crises which would apply to a world in which Say's law was fulfilled', and a 'theory which arises when Say's law is exploded' (ibid., p. 51). Considering Marx's violent diatribes against Say's law, it is rather doubtful whether it is possible to talk of such a dichotomy, and Bouniatian's thesis looks much more convincing and plausible. He argues that there are various germs of cycle theory in Marx's works. This idea has been taken up in modern times by Dupriez and Guitton.

Dupriez declares that Marxism did away with liberal quietism when he established the 'deterministic thesis of a catastrophic end to the capitalist régime'. Marx saw 'in the capitalist system itself the inherent reasons for instability. . . . He considers it to be fundamentally unstable.'

Dupriez quotes the following reasons outlined by Marx: disturbance of equilibrium, owing to unequal distribution; technical progress in the process of accumulation; lack of effective demand as a consequence of under-consumption; disturbances to growth within the reproduction schemes, because 'investment blindly follows saving, without reference to profits and risks'; and, finally, disturbances in the equilibrium between the consumption- and production-goods industries. (Dupriez, 1951, 1, pp. 472, 120–3.)

Shortly after the publication of the first edition of Dupriez's work there appeared Vito's essay in which at least three business-cycle theories are attributed to Marx: first, a theory of under-consumption, in which Vito calls him 'a successor to Lauderdale, Malthus and Sismondi' and states that in Marx's work there are 'frequent passages in which he asserts that the distribution of wealth in a system based on private property is responsible for general disequilibria' (Vito, 1942; 1954, pp. 41, 49–50). As we shall see, such passages are by no means frequent! Secondly, Vito attributes to Marx a theory of replacement investment; and, thirdly, he mentions a theory of over-investment, which, he reminds us, was Tugan-Baranowsky's point of departure. Both remarks are pertinent.

Lescure, who stresses mainly the 'ingenious' theory of lags in replacement investment, quotes several other 'crisis theories' which Marx is supposed to have held. For instance, he counts Marx as an underconsumption theorist (although only *en passant*), alongside Sismondi, Bouniatian and the Marxist Grossmann. However, he also points to the theory of the 'tendency of the rate of profit to fall as a business-cycle theory, and to the over-investment elements in the Marxian theory'. (Lescure, 1906; 1932, pp. 415, 420ff.)

The latter elements are especially emphasised by Guitton, who finds three main theories in Marx. With regard to the first, he says that 'all modern theories of over-capitalisation have a common ancestor, who thought first of what he saw as inescapable contradictions and what we could call more objectively the "burden of capitalist technology": Karl Marx'. Guitton calls this theory a 'flash of genius' and says that Tugan-Baranowsky and in his wake Spiethoff expanded this into the modern theory of the cycle. Guitton then mentions also the theory of replacement investment or the 'echo principle', so that he finally arrives at a tally of four theories. The two others are the under-consumption theory and the theory of the tendency of the rate of profit to fall, both of which he accepts as fully-fledged cycle theories. (Guitton, 1951, pp. 312, 329, 331.)

MARX'S GLOBAL CONCEPT

Marx approached the problem of the business cycle from an analysis of the function of money. One might almost be tempted to the view that the monetary component is foremost in his cycle theory. It represented for him only the potential source of disturbance, because it made possible the hoarding of purchasing power or the temporary spontaneous shrinking of effective demand. In spite of that, the real processes underlying the business cycle remained the primary element for Marx. 'The industrial cycle is of such a nature that the same circuit must periodically reproduce itself, once the first impulse has been given' (*Capital*, III, ch. 30, p. 489). Marx refuses to see in the credit cycle, which is nothing but a symptom of the real cycle, anything more than a reinforcing factor.

The idea of hoarding of money leads on to one of the cycle theories which can be identified in Marx's work, within the context of simple reproduction. He thinks it possible that depreciation funds may not be used, because replacement is delayed. This would bring about a divergence between monetary receipts and their transfer into effective demand. Marx then tried to support this 'depreciation theory' of the cycle by examining the connexion between the technical or economic life of assets (especially in the railway sector) and the duration of the business cycle. In this context, he thought of the presumed ten-year cycle which Schumpeter christened the 'Juglar', although, as Schumpeter occasionally admitted, the French engineer wrote his essays after Marx had set out his early analysis on the periodicity of the cycle.

In 'academic' economics, the Marxian theory has received special attention from Lescure (1906; 1932, pp. 313ff.) and Piettre (1959). Lescure joined Guitton in calling the 'replacement-lag investment theory', as it might be called, 'ingenious'.

The depreciation complex is linked to an aspect of Marx's business-cycle analysis to which none of the theorists dealing with the analysis has paid any attention. In a passage in the *Theories of Surplus Value*, (II, ch. 17, pp. 530ff.), Marx analyses the links between the growth rate of final demand for a product and the induced investment in earlier stages of production. One may consider this an anticipation of the accelerator principle by half a century. Furthermore, the accelerator aspect appears also in the emphasis Marx lays on the importance of what he calls 'leading articles of trade' for the process of the business cycle.

It cannot be denied that Marx did not follow up these points. This is true for the entire Marxian *oeuvre*, in which there are scattered a great number of remarks which point to these aspects. The Marxist theorists who took up the cycle problem did not see the accelerator aspect, which was due to gain paramount importance in the theories of Harrod and Hicks, and was not rediscovered until after the turn of the century, by Bickerdike, Carver, Aftalion (who alone was perhaps inspired by Marx) and John Maurice Clark. Nor did the Marxists develop the 'replacement-lag investment theory' conceived by their master.

In discovering the accelerator element, Marx did not limit himself to the consumption-goods sector. On the contrary, he was fully aware of the fact that the real origin of business fluctuations was to be found in the investment-goods sector. It was Tugan-Baranowsky who, in this respect still the disciple of Marx, gave this idea (1894; 1901) its real prominence in business-cycle theory. Hansen praised in enthusiastic terms (1951, p. 226) the importance for business-cycle theory of this decisive turn, which is ultimately traceable to Marx, *via* Spiethoff's pioneer work (1923; 1955), which was essentially influenced by Marx, as will appear in our discussion of 'over-investment theories' (see Chapter 16).

In spite of the fact that Marx saw the core of fluctuations not in the consumption-goods but in the investment-goods sector, so-called 'under-consumption' elements in certain (actually very few!) passages in *Capital* were accorded exaggerated importance in Marxian exegesis. This is as true in the case of 'academic' economists as in that of those Marxist epigones who refer to an 'under-consumption theory' in Marx. This is all the more surprising as the repudiation by Marx and Engels of Rodbertus's under-consumption theories should be a clear-enough indication that they followed the opposite line. The idea of establishing a link between Marx's cycle analysis and under-consumptionist attitudes suited those who wanted to give pre-eminence to the concept of redistribution. Thus a

version of under-consumption theory which had nothing to do with Marx
became very popular, although it was in fact an outgrowth of the economic
underworld of Major Douglas, Foster and Catchings, and similar popular
authors of the 1930s, whose work Keynes reviewed in his amusing manner
in an appendix to the *General Theory*.

Schumpeter was right when he stated (1947, p. 39) that Marx never
yielded to the temptation to accept 'under-consumptionist theories of the
most contemptible type'. However, this did not prevent a large number of
his adherents from preferring such theories!

Over and over again, protagonists of Marxism have turned their
attention to the 'under-consumptionist theory', attracted by its apparent
affinity with emotional appeals to mass misery. Thus Émile Burns and
Léon Sartre, and to a certain extent also Ardant, Bouvier-Ajam, Strachey
and even Sweezy have found the theory attractive. In spite of Lenin's
rejection of it, it found much favour in many popular publications in the
Soviet Union. It is only recently that more refined theories gained new
stature even there. (In Poland and Hungary, where Marxist economists
have not yielded so much to popularising tendencies, the level of scientific
discussion has remained higher.)

It may be possible to consider as a special version of consumption
analysis the theory of the variability of 'luxury' consumption, recently
developed by Zinn (1970, pp. 202ff.). This may be linked to Duesenberry's
'ratchet effect' and Friedman's notion of 'permanent income'.

Marx undoubtedly laid stress on the accumulation process and on the
dynamics which technical progress, for him synonymous with capitalism,
introduces to it. Here two aspects should be mentioned: first, the theory of
the tendency of the rate of profit to fall; and, secondly, the theory of
disproportionalities in capitalist growth. Both theories can be linked to a
long-run concept of growth and to the business-cycle problem, but the
second is particularly important for business-cycle analysis. It rests on the
assumption that the growth process provokes disequilibria, which in turn
lead to crises in particular industries and then to general business
fluctuations.

Right from the outset we must beware of the error committed by Tugan-
Baranowsky, who thought that Marx, in his reproduction schemes in
volume II of *Capital*, sought to describe a frictionless growth process. On the
contrary, he tried to show how many conditions were required for smooth
growth, which was imaginable only as an extreme possibility. With the
growing complexity of capitalist structures, the preconditions become
more complicated, so that the probability of structural disparities in the
growth process grows as well. Marx's prediction that the amplitudes of
business cycles would tend to increase rests on this assumption.

As with all Marx's 'laws', this one must not be assumed to be of a
mechanistic character. Marx's dialectics already lead to the conclusion
that countervailing forces must be at work.

Around the turn of the century, it may have seemed that business fluctuations had become milder than previously, given the depression and stagnation of the 1870s to the 1890s. Yet the amplitudes were undoubtedly increasing in the recessions of 1907–8, 1920–1 and 1929–32, a feature which Marx might have considered as confirmation of his intuition. Again, 1950s and 1960s seemed to show a lessening of fluctuations; but in the 1970s the trend has again swung sharply in the opposite direction.

The theoretical possibility of general and increasing instability has been confirmed by Robertson in his discussion of the 'Domar' equation, in which, after saying that he himself had discovered it, in *Banking Policy and the Price Level* (1926), he concedes Marx's priority (1954; 1966, pp. 238–40):

Heaven forbid that I should claim, in my most deluded moments, to have invented the Domar Equation. Mrs. Robinson, for all I know, may well be right that it had lain for years wrapped up in the tangled phraseology of Marx before being brought to light by Domar and Harrod.

These periods being determined by entirely different sets of forces, I came to the conclusion that the preservation of even a stationary equilibrium would be something of a miracle.

Kalecki started from the Marxian equations in working out a theory of the cycle that anticipated Keynes's analysis. Where this was a short-run theory, the social upheavals of our times seem to reflect a slow-down of growth and an increase in the amplitude of business fluctuations. It may be that Hick's study at the beginning of the 1950s was an epoch-making event, for he seemed to have discovered in the cycle explosive forces resembling nuclear reactions, although there are brakes at work, functioning rather like graphite in reactors. (Hicks, 1950; 1951, pp. 70, 83ff.)

At any rate, if there exist basic explosive tendencies in the cycle, this would confirm the macroeconomic instability theory as it was developed, at very nearly the same time, by Harrod and Domar. It was Marx who first spoke of the 'explosive nature' of the cycle, when discussing (*Capital*, III, ch. 4, p. 79) the great multitude of economic crises in the first half of the nineteenth century. We now proceed to discuss those various theories in detail.

12 The Under-Consumption Component

In economics, certain misinterpretations seem to pop up again and again in the cyclical fashion described by Pantaleoni. For a misinterpretation to go on living indefinitely, it seems to suffice that it should once have been advanced by a prominent member of the profession. This has happened in the case of the so-called 'under-consumption' strand in Marx's works. 'Academic' theorists who point to this may be excused on the grounds that numerous Marxists speak of it, basing their interpretation on a single statement in *Capital*, heedless of all protests by Marx and Engels.

The alleged under-consumption thesis of Marx is mentioned in almost all histories of economic doctrine. A typical example of this occurs in the work of Mitchell, who goes so far as to claim (and Marx would have been much annoyed to hear this) that Marx went on to develop the theory of Rodbertus, whom, in fact, Marx bitterly attacked:

> The germ of this theory also is found in Sismondi and Robert Owen. Wages form but a fraction of the value of the product and increase less rapidly than power to produce. Since the masses dependent upon wages constitute the bulk of the population, it follows that consumers' demand cannot keep pace with current supply in seasons when factories are running at full blast. Meanwhile the capitalist-employers are investing their current savings in new productive enterprises, which presently add their quotas to the goods seeking sale. This process of over-stocking the market runs cumulatively until the time comes when the patent impossibility of selling goods at a profit, or even at cost, brings on a crisis. (Mitchell, 1927; 1932, pp. 8–9.)

Nowhere does Mitchell directly refer, in this regard, to statements by Marx himself. His sole authority is the Austrian Marxist Leichter (1924, pp. 45–100).

If one reads Leichter's essay, one cannot help feeling that Mitchell must have read it very cursorily, for in this rather eclectic and descriptive study Leichter does not advance the rather primitive under-consumption theory that Mitchell attributes to him, in a negligent way that is unworthy of that great business-cycle analyst. On the contrary, Leichter reaches the conclusion that several different business-cycle theories are to be found in the Marxist system: he talks (ibid., p. 99) of the 'universality of Marxian crisis theory, which is nowhere in the great work represented *ex professo*, but which runs through it like a red thread, because each chapter of *Capital* considers also, in cases of weaknesses in the economy, the appropriate crisis phenomena'.

Mitchell's ill-judged interpretation of Leichter's essay is a glaring example of the grandiose manner which eminent economists sometimes employ in quoting their authorities, and above all of the superficial way in which Marx is treated in this context.

This has not prevented innumerable other authors from slavishly repeating this argument, without making the slightest attempt to check its truth. One must respect an anti-Marxist of Röpke's calibre for his cautious formulation (1932, p. 67) of the alleged identity of the business-cycles theories of Rodbertus and Marx:

> There is the further question of whether it might be possible to explain the crisis by assuming that in the course of high prosperity there might occur a weakening of consumers' purchasing power which would make part of the production unsaleable at prices which cover costs. This question has been answered time and again in the affirmative, especially by socialists who hold that the unequal distribution of income is prejudicial to the broad masses, and constitutes in their view an inherent structural flaw characteristic of capitalism, and one which is responsible for a shrinkage of effective demand which would again and again entail a collapse of production (e.g. Rodbertus, and in a certain sense [!] also Marx and his epigones).

MARX'S REJECTION OF RODBERTUS'S THEORY

What was Marx's real attitude towards this under-consumption theory?

The standard explanation of the Marxian 'under-consumption theory' points to a single, rather isolated passage in *Capital* (III, ch. 30, p. 484): 'The ultimate reason for all real crises always remains the poverty and restricted consumption of the masses as opposed to the drive of capitalist production to develop the productive forces as though only the absolute consuming power of society constituted their limit.'

Here Marx only wants to establish a contrast between the real consumption needs of the masses and the extent to which they are met under capitalism, which recognises only demand backed by money and leaves unsatisfied all wants that do not promise to be profitable. Earlier in *Capital*, Marx mentions a number of reasons for crises – namely, price movements, credit troubles, 'speculation', (forestalled) replacement investment, and so on – that he wishes for the time being to leave aside. In chapter 15 of volume I, these 'other grounds' prevail. In general, the statement by Schumpeter (1947, pp. 38–9) is true that Marx, 'showing excellent sense, expressly repudiated . . . an underconsumption theory of the most contemptible type . . . concluding that the exploited masses cannot buy what that ever-expanding apparatus of production turns out or stands ready to turn out'.

Marx undoubtedly thought Rodbertus's theory 'despicable', for Rodbertus held that in periods of high prosperity the share of wages in national income dropped, and this led to a fall in purchasing power and therefore to a crisis. It is true that some such phenomenon seems to be borne out by modern statistics which show *Angstsparen* ('savings out of fear') in crises, but Marx's analysis is much more sophisticated.

Marx does not directly mention Rodbertus in the passage (*Capital*, II, ch. 20, pp. 414–15) in which he rejects an under-consumptionist approach, but talks of 'advocates of sound and "simple" commonsense'. Engels adds a short note underlining the relevance to 'possible followers of the Rodbertian theory of crises', but even without this it would be clear that it is Rodbertus's theory that Marx has in mind.

> It is sheer tautology to say that crises are caused by the scarcity of effective consumption, or of effective consumers. The capitalist system does not know any other modes of consumption than effective ones, except that of *sub forma pauperis* or of the swindler. That commodities are unsaleable means only that no effective purchasers have been found for them, i.e., consumers (since commodities are bought in the final analysis for productive or individual consumption).

Marx then attacks the thesis of the declining share of workers in national income:

> But if one were to attempt to give this tautology the semblance of a profounder justification by saying that the working-class receives too small a portion of its own product and the evil would be remedied as soon as it receives a larger share of it and its wages increase in consequence, one could only remark that crises are always prepared by precisely a period in which wages rise generally and the working-class actually gets a larger share of that part of the annual product which is intended for consumption. It appears, then, that capitalist production comprises conditions independent of good or bad will, conditions which permit the working-class to enjoy that relative prosperity only momentarily, and at that always only as the harbinger of a coming crisis.

In Volume I we refer to Steindl's discussion of this theory. Steindl did not see that Marx spoke of the workers' share in *consumption* only and at the top of the boom.

We know today that Marx early on pronounced himself against under-consumptionist theses. In the *Grundrisse*, which dates from 1857–8, he opposes Proudhon, who defended a naïve version of such a theory:

> Proudhon, who certainly hears the bells ringing but never knows where, therefore sees the origin of overproduction in the fact 'that the worker cannot buy back his product'. By this he understands that interest and profit are added on to it; or that the price of the product is an overcharge on top of its real value. This demonstrates first of all that he understands nothing about the determination of value, which, generally speaking, can include no overcharge. . . . From all the profits made by capital, i.e. the total mass of capitalists, there is deducted (1) the constant part of capital [the sum of all depreciation costs in the economy]; (2) the wage, or, the amount of objectified labour time necessary in order to reproduce living labour capacity. They can therefore divide nothing among themselves other than the surplus value. . . . if the capitalist, say, out of consideration for Mr. Proudhon, sold his commodities at the production costs [it follows that] his total profit . . . would be limited to that part of the wage which he consumed in the depreciated commodity. . . . Since they are, as capitalists, at the same time large consumers, and can in no way live on air . . . they have nothing to exchange or to consume apart from other peoples' products. That is, for their own consumption they exchange . . . surplus labour time. . . . But capitals . . . can realize their value in this case only through exchange among one another, i.e. through the exchange of capitalists among themselves.

In other words, workers buy consumption goods and capitalists consumption or replacement goods (in simple reproduction) or investment goods for expansion in the growth process. With regard to both groups, Marx says: 'We must always presuppose here that the wage paid is *economically* just, i.e. that it is determined by the general laws of economics. . . . The capitalist class . . . distributes the total surplus value . . . in accordance with the *size* of its capital.' (*Grundrisse*, pp. 424, 426, 435, 439, 440.)

Marx could even less speak of a fall in effective demand, as in his theory of the tendency of the rate of profit to fall he expressly considered increasing replacement needs and specifically postulated an absolute and relative increase in net investment ('accumulation') in the boom. He speaks of 'the production of additional virtual money-capital on a large scale' as 'expression of multifarious production of virtually additional productive capital', which leads 'to over-production of capital'.

Here he adopts the very opposite of an under-consumptionist attitude by deliberately developing a theory of over-capitalisation. This surplus capital is only partly transformed into 'productive' (constant) capital, i.e. into replacement investment; part of the surplus is 'converted into capital', i.e. represents net investment. At any rate, for Marx the idea that 'accumulation should take place at the expense of consumption' is 'an illusion'. (*Capital*, II, ch. 21, pp. 501–2, 507.) Marx therefore expressly rejects the idea that consumption would shrink at the top of the boom. One must weigh his words carefully: far from saying that the workers' share in national income shrinks, he stresses that their real *share in consumption* increases.

This assumes not that investment will suffer but only that the capitalists' share in consumption will suffer in the top phase of the boom, while they maintain investment at the expense of their consumption. Here we are reminded of what we called the 'Riviera theorem' in Volume I. There is an important difference: whereas Dobb thinks that capitalists might be willing to give up part of their *increase* in consumption in the long run, Marx believes that they might do so only in the short run, and he foresees the ensuing slump. Dobb believes that towards the end of Volume II of *Capital* there are hints that capitalists over-save, so that the sales of the (luxury) goods they consume shrink. We shall deal with this in the next chapter. Here we encounter the notion of 'hoarding' which is part of the 'disproportionality' thesis. (Dobb, 1942; 1966, pp. 197–8.)

If it is thus evident that Marx does not espouse the under-consumption theory, it remains to be seen how it could have been attributed to him in the first place.

The assumption that Marx advanced such a theory is sometimes based on certain passages in the *Communist Manifesto*. There Marx only says that the 'social epidemics of crises' and 'over-production' mean that there is 'too much civilization, too much industry, too much commerce', that the 'workers are exposed to all the vicissitudes of the market', and so on, but nowhere do we find a trace of a genuine under-consumption theory. It is thus understandable that Engels too draws a negative conclusion when he says in his *Anti-Dühring* (*Mega*, xx, p. 266) that the under-consumption of the masses is a necessary condition of all societies based on exploitation, and thus also of capitalism – but only the capitalist form of production leads to crises. Thus under-consumption is one of the conditions of crises and plays some part in them, but does not reveal anything about the existence or absence of actual crises today.

VULGAR MARXIST UNDER-CONSUMPTION THEORY

The real roots of refined under-consumption theory are thus not to be found in Marx or Engels, but in a number of later Marxists. There are under-consumptionist strands in the writings of Rosa Luxemburg and Sternberg, and Léon Sartre, Tsuru and others have attempted to take them up, without specifically referring to international exchange. Sweezy finally tried to develop a new version of the theory, based upon Otto Bauer: this brings the accelerator into play and therefore goes beyond the framework of pure under-consumption. Finally, there are traces of under-consumption theories in Eaton (1949), Gillman (1965) and others. The same story is repeated over and over: Marx's reputation as an under-consumption theorist is essentially owing to the fact that a number of his followers saw him or wanted to see him in this light.

We must distinguish between primitive and refined under-consumption theories. Examples of the primitive version are to be found in many popularising works, such as Baby's (1949), and in some Soviet publications. But traces of what can be called 'primitivism' in this field can also be found in a number of specialised works by Marxist authors who claim to be more sophisticated analysts of business-cycle theory.

It is, for instance, astonishing to read the following assertion by the (belatedly converted) French Marxist Bouvier-Ajam, although his statement is perhaps typical of such misinterpretations: 'Karl Marx more than once adhered to the explanation of crises which says that they are caused by under-consumption. . . . Workers receive back only part of their product in wages and therefore cannot buy back all of their product[!].' In his eclectic work, Bouvier-Ajam quotes various crisis theories, but in his synthesis he indicates the following as the essential causes: 'First, the lack of adaptation of production to demand under the capitalist régime; and, secondly, the non-adaptation of credit to production, which prevents a durable compensation for the first disequilibrium . . . .' (Bouvier-Ajam, 1948, pp. 136-7, 227.)

Another author, Ardant, says: 'The prime reason for over-production lies in the fact that the capitalist class devotes a decreasing fraction of its surplus value to consumption. . . . The second one is to be seen in the fact that the working class consumes a shrinking fraction of total production in the form of consumption goods. . . . ' Ardant admits that these circumstances do not yet explain the periodicity of crises. He therefore appeals to disequilibria: 'It is the more rapid growth of the production of investment goods in relation to consumption goods which explain that over-production is a periodic rather than constant phenomenon.' Ardant's reasoning thus tends to make him appear as an adherent of the theory of 'disproportionality'. (Ardant, 1948, pp. 136-7.)

SCIENTIFICALLY RIGOROUS MARXIST UNDER-CONSUMPTION THEORISTS

Serious attempts to construct a well-founded theory of under-consumption have been undertaken by five authors: Léon Sartre, Tsuru, Sweezy, Eaton and Lederer.

Léon Sartre, to whom many later theorists refer (as does Ardant!), sets out, in his 1937 study, from the idea that the real cause of crises is to be found in the 'contrast between production and consumption'. Ardant's theses have almost been lifted entire from Sartre's book. Here we find the statement that the main reasons why crises arise are to be found in the fact that in the upswing capitalists use an increasing part of their surplus for accumulation, while the working class consumes 'a shrinking fraction of the consumption goods which are being produced'. The latter thesis boils down to the idea of Rodbertus that the workers' share in the social product decreases. This is a view that seems to be confirmed for the earlier phases of the boom, but which was hotly contested by Marx for the decisive final phase of the boom.

Now, Sartre believes that the transfer of purchasing power to 'productive demand' in Marx's terms must mean that not enough means of production, but too many consumption goods, appear on the market. So ultimately, according to his thesis, over-production should begin in the consumption-goods industries. The recession would set in before capacity in the investment-goods sector could be sufficiently enlarged. At any rate, towards the end of his work Sartre himself indicates that he thinks he has developed an under-consumption theory. (Sartre, 1937, pp. 6, 28, 36, 43, 145.)

On the other hand, Tsuru argues that Sartre's formal proof of under-consumption served to show its very impossibility, for he had modified only individual variables (for instance, the rate of saving). Tsuru includes a decrease in the 'organic composition of capital' in the consumption-goods industry in his mathematical–graphical analysis and concludes that the increasing volume of surplus value would probably be divided between consumption and investment in such a way that the relative share of consumption would decrease. The range of possible equilibria would thus be narrowed, and a final collapse would become inevitable. (Tsuru, 1956, pp. 38, 44, 48.)

Sweezy constructed his theory in the wake of Otto Bauer. He calls it an under-consumption theory, but it contains essential accelerator elements and will therefore be examined under that heading (see Ch. 15).

Similar features are also to be found in Eaton's work, which seems to follow Sweezy, although it is more strictly under-consumptionist. For instance, he declares that in capitalism 'mass consumption is "restrained" relatively to total production. . . . The consumer market . . . inevitably proves itself restricted and inadequate to sustain the general level of the market. . . . It cannot compensate for a falling-off in the demand of capitalists for producer goods.' At this point Eaton departs from the under-consumption framework, for he argues that the recession generally begins in the production-goods sector.

Then he talks again in traditional 'vulgar Marxist' fashion of 'the contradiction between the expansion of production and the relative restriction of the mass market for consumer goods' and of the 'constant tendency for capitalist society to undermine its own mass market'. In his view, in the boom mass purchasing power, though higher in money terms, in real terms remains somewhat restricted, at all events relatively restricted. The longer the expansion continues, the stronger these inflationary trends become; but once the expansion and the inflation stop, employment and wage payments are reduced and mass purchasing power in money terms shrinks.

In order to explain the slump and the 'inevitability of the capitalist crisis', Eaton repeats the old slogan of the 'contradiction between the social character of production and the private appropriation of the values produced by the capitalists'. (Eaton, 1949; 1963, pp. 154–6.)

The most sophisticated under-consumption theory is that of Lederer, which at the same time marks the transition to disproportionality theories. Lederer's starting point is the transfer of income, which occurs in the boom to the detriment of wage earners and old-age pensioners. This causes a shift of demand in favour of the production of investment goods, while the basic demand for consumption goods cannot absorb the increased production. The pivot for the shift in income is credit: 'Credit is the lever which guides the means of production to those firms whose prices develop faster than wages. . . . One is thus compelled to conclude that credit creates or makes possible business cycles. . . . '

According to Lederer, the turning point comes when an inordinate increase in profits leads to excessive demands upon the production-goods industries. Investment goes beyond what would have been justified by the evolution of consumer demand. On the other hand, high profits give rise to additional credit creation, which contributes to still further overheating.

Lederer's theory contains the germs of forced saving. He sees elements of this even in collective bargaining, to the extent that it prevents an immediate increase in real wages whenever there is a shortage of labour. (Lederer, 1925, pp. 354ff., 390–1.)

On the other hand, he sees in monopolistic rigidities, and especially cartels, additional elements making for disturbance. These lead in the boom to more rapid accumulation, shorten the upswing and lengthen the downswing. Their inherent tendency to raise the share of profits must further increase the disproportionalities in income. Discrepancies between price and income changes are for Lederer the real source of the cycle, which tends to become more and more jerky, through a combination of credit creation by the banking sector and of the underlying tendencies of technical progress (see Lederer, 1927, pp. 25ff). Lederer's theory then leads on to the disproportionality thesis.

13 The Luxury Consumption Theory

In modern times, Zinn has taken up an aspect of Marxian business-cycle theory which may be considered a special case of under-consumption, but seems to represent an independent factor. This is the behaviour of the production of luxury goods, which, according to Zinn (1970, p. 309), is not an independent source of business fluctuations but 'a kind of endogenous reinforcing factor'. Zinn refers to passages in *Capital* where Marx says (as at II, ch. 20, p. 414) that the capitalist class converts 'a considerable portion of their surplus-value for articles of luxury' and 'each crisis momentarily diminishes luxury consumption'. Zinn considers these reinforcing tendencies all the more important the more unequal is the distribution of income. He argues (1970, p. 315) that

> the existence of specific layers of luxury consumption, the main focus of Veblen's 'leisure class', conveys particular importance to this aspect of the Marxian system. In the process of concentration, the upper class, destined for a luxurious life, is formed and enlarged. Marx points out that a big capitalist, as opposed to lower middle-class savers, considers luxury as a proof of his creditworthiness . . . .

This would be Veblen's 'conspicuous consumption' (1960, pp. 60ff). Zinn's juxtaposition of Marx and Veblen is not quite satisfactory. It is true that Marx sometimes mentions the possibility that the number of capitalists may increase in the process of concentration, and this would appear less paradoxical if one assumes that the eradication of large numbers of independent artisans and shopkeepers makes possible the creation of new capitalist firms. Nevertheless, a relative increase in the number of capitalists is not likely to be the rule and cannot be of great importance. After all, it is not the decrease in demand for expensive motor cars or yachts which matters in a recession.

It might have been better if Zinn, whose theory contains some interesting elements, had analysed the variability of 'luxury consumption' for the population as a whole in the course of the business cycle. Unfortunately, he chose (1970, pp. 305–6) a very narrow definition of 'luxury': 'The production of luxury goods . . . takes place only for capitalists. . . . To the extent that capitalists consume more and, in particular, different goods, compared with workers, we encounter luxury consumption. . . . What workers consume, i.e. the consumption goods they buy for variable capital *v*, is essential.'

Of course, any economist may choose as he pleases the assumptions to underlie his model, but it is a serious misinterpretation when Zinn claims (ibid.) that Marx took 'as a criterion for luxury and essential consumption only the material difference between workers' and capitalists' consumption'. Zinn adds, to boot, that this assumption is 'realistic'.

Later, however, he circumscribes this statement by quoting in a note Marx's own definition: 'by luxury articles we here mean all production that does not serve the reproduction of labour-power' (*Capital*, III, ch. 6, p. 106). Zinn remarks quite pertinently that every definition of 'luxury' which contains a value judgement – and this, he says, applies in the case of Marx – will remain vulnerable; he demands (1970, p. 306) the formulation of a 'value-neutral definition of luxury, i.e. an operational one. . . . One must separate this definition in principle from a judgement of what is good or bad!'

Zinn would have done better to follow his own advice to be 'value-neutral', i.e. to separate the two notions of 'luxury' and 'capitalists', however emotionally related they may appear to be. This would have been all the more justified as Marx expressly says (*Capital*, II, ch. 20, p. 414) that in the boom 'the working-class (now actively reinforced by its entire reserve army) also enjoys momentarily articles of luxury ordinarily beyond its reach. . . .'

A reasonable definition of 'luxury' would perhaps be one that takes in anything which is variable in household expenditure, especially durable consumption goods which one might consider as household investment goods. If Zinn had adopted this definition, he would have transformed his 'luxury' theory into a theory of the variation of consumer expenditure, possibly linked to instalment credit, which also has a strong bearing on the amplitude of business cycles. A theory of this kind was developed by the present author in the 1950s, (Kühne, 1954). It must be reinforced by a theory of 'over-saving'; this 'oversaving' may result from a curtailment of 'luxury consumption', which was certainly of great importance in the last recession (1973–5). The autonomous consumption decisions of households, linked to a certain general restraint on the part of consumers whenever recession or unemployment has loomed large on the horizon, have tended to become a more important destabilising element in post-war recessions.

Thus the German Council of Economic Advisers stated (1967, p. 76) in its annual report at the end of the recession year 1967: 'It seems that the consumers, in their decisions on durable consumer-goods, are beginning to behave more and more like entrepreneurs in their investment decisions'. In addition, expenditures on certain services, leisure activities and holidays are becoming more and more variable over the business cycle (see Andreae, 1970).

All the same, Zinn's contribution is a valuable reminder that Marx saw certain elements of instability in the sector of goods the consumption of which may be postponed.

14 Cycles in Replacement Investment, the 'Echo Principle' and Depreciation

Marx points out in various passages that investment 'humps' are liable to occur in certain years: 'so a host of fixed capitals expire annually and must be renewed in kind out of the accumulated money-fund'. Here it seems that he was still convinced 'that the money necessary for this replacement was accumulated in former years' (*Capital*, II, ch. 20, p. 457). This idea of the hoarding of liquid funds or of 'renewal funds' in cash on the asset side of balance sheets seems to have persisted in the minds of many economists well beyond the turn of the century; some traces of it may be found in the railway legislation of the time.

MARX AS THE DISCOVERER OF DYNAMIC DEPRECIATION POLICY

Marx overcame such ideas at an early date. In his correspondence with Engels, he began, from the end of the 1850s, to develop the idea that depreciation funds could be currently used within the business and could thus be used to finance net investment and not just replacement.

Ott points (1967, p. 637) to a letter Engels addressed to Marx in 1867 in which the notion was advanced, and Hickel has said (1971, p. 890) that 'Marx and Engels discovered dynamic depreciation financing or what is known in [German] industrial economics as the Lohmann–Ruchti effect'. In rereading the correspondence, it becomes clear that Engels, in 1867, only took up and exemplified an idea which had been developed by Marx in his letters from 1862 onwards.

The 'Lohmann–Ruchti effect', or dynamic depreciation financing, bears the name of its presumed discoverers in Germany in the 1940s (Ruchti, 1942, 1953; Lohmann, 1949). It boils down to the idea that depreciation funds that will be needed in future years to replace assets that at present are still functioning are currently reinvested in new assets. These funds thus become a source of finance for net investment in rapidly growing firms.

In Europe, this idea had been rediscovered in 1926 by the Dutch author Polak, who wrote in German, but his discovery (1926, pp. 92 ff.) did not receive much attention. Hax, who pointed out the priority of Polak in this field without knowing anything of the contribution by Marx, characterised the effect as follows (1955, p. 141):

> In firms with a large amount of fixed assets, it was found at an early date that liquid reserves showed a tendency to increase from one year to another. This is to be explained by the fact that receipts contain amounts for the depreciation of assets which need not be paid out, as contrasted with profits. . . . This has led to the idea that it is possible to increase the efficiency of equipment by currently reinvesting liquid depreciation funds, without having to attract new capital from outside the firm.

Schäfer states (1955, pp. 138 ff.) that in the last resort this represents a lack of coincidence between the lifetime and turnover of capital, i.e. a distinction between finance and real depreciation, since 'for finance, the turnover of capital is decisive'. Depreciation is 'based on the real lifetime of an asset'.

In *Capital*, Marx examined in detail the problems of capital turnover. It is curious, however, that he did not take up in this work the crystal-clear analysis which is to be found in, for instance, his letter of 20 August 1862 to Engels, where he says that, if a machine could serve for ten or twelve years, the firm would not have to replace one tenth of it every year. The fund built up for replacement purposes was in fact 'an accumulation fund for extended reproduction'. This consideration, he thought, explained the more rapid development of nations that own much capital, as contrasted with poorer nations. (See also *Capital*, I, ch. 23, and II, chs. 8 and 21.)

In *Capital*, Marx's treatment of the problems of capital turnover is limited to the periodic renewal of railway equipment and so on; he thought the average life of engines would be ten to twelve years, and of wooden sleepers twelve to fifteen years. It may be presumed that he saw here a link with the 'ten-year cycle of modern industry', which he mentions in various passages. He formulated this link most clearly in a passage in the *Grundrisse*, (p. 608) where he quotes Babbage, according to whom the life cycle of machinery in England is five years; and he guesses that the 'real' cycle may have something to do with the length of economic life of *Capital fixe*, which is more or less ten years.

In the literature in English, Terborgh pointed in 1945 (pp. 99–115) to the role of depreciation in an economy the growth rate of which declines. This problem has been dealt with extensively only by Eisner, who (1952, p. 826) underlines its importance for the growth process:

The amount of the 'excess' of depreciation allowances over replacement requirements varies directly with the rate of growth. Where the rate of growth is positive, the greater is the rate of growth the greater is the ratio by which depreciation allowances exceed replacement requirements. Where the rate of growth is negative, the smaller is the rate of growth (the faster gross investment is declining), the greater is the ratio by which depreciation allowances fall short of replacement requirements.

In growing economies or in growing firms the 'excess' of depreciation allowances is greater as the life of assets is longer. In declining economies or in shrinking firms the proportion by which depreciation charges are less than replacement requirements is greater as the length of life of assets is greater.

Later on, Eisner expressly refers to Marx, admitting that in his discussion of innovations and technological change he perceived phenomena which show typical aspects of the internal contradictions of capitalism.

About ten years later, the same idea was formulated by Edwards (1961, pp. 79, 106):

[in] the growing firm . . . growth creates annual depreciation charges that are well in excess of the cost of physical replacement. . . . A firm that is declining in size is faced with a deficiency of depreciation charges according to the running physical replacement criterion. . . .

We have seen however, that growth by itself tends to make historic cost depreciation excessive with respect to running physical replacement. It stands to reason, then, that given some rate of inflation there is some real rate of growth which will just compensate for the inflation-induced deficiency. A more rapid rate of growth would yield excess funds.

A résumé of the literature on dynamic depreciation policy, with detailed quotations from Marx's letters etc., is presented in Kühne (1979).

DEPRECIATION AND BUSINESS CYCLES

What is the link between the provision for depreciation and business cycles? This is to be found in two elements. First of all, shrinking firms slide into difficulties over finance, and the same must apply to shrinking industries or economies. Admittedly, this is a secondary effect, which presupposes that the downswing has already set in.

Secondly, for growing systems, the danger of distortions arises. The mere fact of growth favours self-financing, no matter whether firms growing today will still have the same sales outlets tomorrow. Firms which abound in depreciation funds tend to reinvest them, which leads to a weakening of the control function of the capital market and favours the building-up of over-capacity. This has been pointed out by von Hayek in particular.

Expansion has cumulative effects. On 29 October 1954, the then-fashionable 'Lohmann–Ruchti effect' was discussed at a conference of German auditors. One of the speakers, Krähe, reminded the meeting that the 'earlier use of depreciation funds for new investment instead of replacement will again generate new depreciation funds' (Krähe, 1954).

If this is coupled with accelerated depreciation, the danger of excesses leading to over-capacity looms large. Macroeconomically speaking, Domar's capacity effect (1946, 1953) appears.

Expansion as it were draws itself out of the swamp by its own bootstraps. Expansion accelerates and must end up in a slump. Here Marx's 'ingenious' depreciation analysis, as Lescure and Piettre call it, becomes relevant. The sudden recognition of over-capacity in an industry can bring about a cumulative fall not only in net investment, but even in replacement investment, as Marx was quick to point out in his discussion of simple reproduction. It is a possible reason for the slump.

Marx says with regard to these problems (*Capital*, II, ch. 20, pp. 471–2):

> A greater part of the fixed element of II_c expires than did the year before, and hence a greater part must be renewed in kind, then that part of the fixed capital which is as yet only on the way to its demise and is to be replaced meanwhile in money until its day of expiry. . . .
>
> More money would have flown from II to I, as mere means of purchase, and there would be fewer commodities II in relation to which I would have to function as a mere buyer. A greater portion of I_s [surplus value of department] . . , would not therefore be convertible into commodities II, but would persist in the form of money.

Here he describes an inflationary process: high replacement requirements in the consumption-goods industry over-strain capacity in the investment-goods sector and lead to inordinate price increases.

> In the other case, if the size of fixed capital II to be reproduced in kind [grow proportionally] . . . then the quantity of the circulating component parts of constant capital II reproduced by I would remain unchanged, while that of the fixed component parts to be reproduced would decrease. Hence either decrease in aggregate production of I, or surplus . . . and surplus that is not to be converted into money.

In this case, depreciation and reinvestment shrink, and thus a recession occurs. •

INVENTORY CYCLES

In talking of 'circulating' capital, Marx clearly saw the inventory cycle as a phenomenon of the total cycle. Thus he speaks of 'involuntary supply formation' (the involuntary investment of Keynesians!), which arises because of the 'sales resistance offered by the conditions of the process of circulation itself . . . which thwarts [the producer's] will'. Normal stock-building is proportional to production: 'The commodity supply . . . grows of itself concomitantly with capitalist production . . . ' To that extent 'the stagnation of commodities counts as a requisite condition of their sale'.

There are several factors which lead to an expansion of stocks: for instance, the proletarisation of the masses 'who live from hand to mouth, who receive their wages weekly and spend them daily', and the increase in the quantity of intermediate products because of 'the need of continuity and expansion of the process of production'. There are also the factors, especially concentration, that bring about a reduction in the costs of storage: 'The more concentrated socially the supply is, the smaller relatively are the costs.' Furthermore, the development of transport and credit facilities favours the holding of stocks, which is transferred from the consumer to retailing and wholesaling. Such structural shifts can contribute to an intensification of cyclical fluctuations. Once

commodities remain in stock unsold, then we have a case of not only the stagnation of the process of self-expansion of his capital-value . . . . The costs of preserving this supply in buildings, of additional labour, etc., mean a positive loss.

It does not make any difference whether this jam occurs in the warehouses of the industrial capitalist or in the storerooms of the merchant. . . . As soon as the commodities lying in the reservoirs of circulation do not make room for the swiftly succeeding wave of production . . . the commodity supply expands in consequence of the stagnation in circulation just as the hoards [of money] increase when money circulation is clogged.

The hoarding of money is followed by the accumulation of stocks, and 'the bulging size of the commodity-supply, for which stagnant circulation is responsible, may be mistaken for a symptom of the expansion of the process of reproduction'. (*Capital*, II, ch. 6, pp. 147–9, 151–4).

Here the problem merges with net investment. Modern authors have thought that Marx's reasoning anticipated inventory cycles as analysed by Metzler (1941) and Abramovitz (1950). For instance, Nagels says (1970, pp. 201–2) that Marx's analysis culminates in the conclusion that the inventory cycle undergoes a shift in relation to the main cycle, i.e. becomes *déphasé*.

Inventory cycles thus constitute a link with accelerator processes and with disturbances leading to 'disproportionalities'.

THE ECHO PRINCIPLE AND THE CONSTRUCTION ('KUZNETS') CYCLE

Marx saw an even closer link between cycle and replacement in the so-called 'echo principle'. For example, the ten-year life of railway sleepers suggested that there might be 'humps' of replacement investment a decade after the original investment, which would represent an 'echo' cycle. Robertson, Matthews and others have underlined the importance of Marx's intuition (Robertson, 1948, pp. 36–7; Matthews, 1959, p. 67).

The 'echo principle' has been elaborated by Einarsen (1938) for shipbuilding and by Isard (1942), who discovered the so-called 'transport-building' cycle. Both expressly referred to Marx. Their results have been generalised in the twenty-year 'Kuznets cycle', which has been related to housing. A number of authors have examined this longer cycle – among them Kuznets himself (1950), Burns (1934), Abramovitz (1961), and O'Leary and Lewis (1955). This cycle must not, however, be confounded with the 'long waves' analysed by Parvus and Kondratieff, which the present author discusses elsewhere (Kühne, 1968, pp. 9off.).

Sombart admitted (1930) that Marx's intuition which led him to link business cycles and the life cycles of durable equipment represented 'extraordinary progress'. Lescure followed up Sombart's remark and spoke (1906; 1932, p. 428) of a 'spark of genius' on the part of Marx; he quotes Tugan-Baranowsky, who, in spite of his criticism of Marx, remained his faithful disciple on this point.

In his work on economic doctrine (1959), Piettre recalled Lescure's praise; and von Haberler, who cannot be said to be kindly disposed towards Marx, also pointed out (1943, p. 84) his priority: 'This idea that, given an initial boom in capital construction, replacement tends to assume a cyclical pattern, that reinvestment moves in cycles, can be traced back to Karl Marx'.

It seems that the term 'echo principle' was introduced into economic theory by a Marxist, the Dutchman de Wolff, who wanted it to be understood as a general term covering also Kondratieff's 'long waves'. According to de Wolff, (1929) the average life of durable equipment is some forty years, and he thought that 'long waves' were nothing but a reflection or 'echo' in replacement or 'humps' in reinvestment. To that extent he refined Marx's theory.

Tinbergen (1935, p. 128) attributed the theory of the 'echo principle' to de Wolff, Tugan-Baranowsky and Cassel. In his later works, he enumerates the difficulties of attempting to ascertain the technical and even more the economic life of equipment. He rightly concludes (Tinbergen and Polak, 1950, p. 179) that the applicability of this idea is thus considerably limited in business-cycle theory: 'The simple echo principle . . . must be replaced by a much more complicated system of fluctuations in reinvestment. A number of echoes overlap, as it were: the result is a damped movement . . . .'

Thus, the echo principle can only be considered a secondary factor in business cycles. Marx's replacement theory is mentioned in modern works on business-cycle theory – for instance, by Matthews (1959, p. 67), who refers to his examples regarding machinery in the cotton industry. The relationship between replacement waves and the Kuznets cycle plays a prominent part in modern analysis. In Matthews's work, the latter appears as the fundamental cycle, to which the 'Juglar' is a subordinate element.

O'Leary and Lewis found (1955, p. 551) Kuznets upswings in Great Britain in 1875–83 and 1894–6 and in the USA in 1880–92 and 1901–13. Abramovitz identifies (1961, p. 54) fifteen- to twenty-year waves for the USA, and Wagenführ found Kuznets peaks for Germany in 1899, 1904–6 and 1911 (Kühne, 1968, p. 95).

O'Leary and Lewis tried (1955, p. 550) to combine the Kuznets cycle with Marx's classical cycle of seven to ten years by assuming that the former was caused by one Juglar cycle getting out of control every twenty years. They hinted at the possibility that this might happen again towards the end of the 1960s, when construction cycles in various Western countries became synchronised. Matthews, who gives pride of place to the Kuznets cycle, thinks it possible (1959, pp. 210 ff.) that a synchronisation of Kuznets cycles might lead to shorter Juglars and not the other way round.

Be that as it may, Marx's replacement theory provided the impetus for the elaboration of these various cycles. In relation to the future of capitalism, the Kuznets cycle seems likely to maintain its primacy – all the more so as it may possibly be connected with wave-like technical progress, recognised by Marx's theory of the tendency of the rate of profit to fall. At any rate, the Kuznets cycle seems to stand a better chance than the secular Kondratieff, which can be ascertained clearly only in the price sector. (Schumpeter, 1939, 1, pp. 164–9).

It must therefore remain doubtful whether there is much to be hoped for from attempts by modern Marxists such as Mandel (1972, pp. 101 ff.) to construct, on the basis of Kondratieff's theory (which was anticipated by Parvus and van Gelderen), a new theory of capitalist instability. On the other hand, it is strange that the Marxists have made no attempt to take up the Kuznets or transport-building cycle in this context.

15 The Concept of the Accelerator in Marx's Work

It is generally stated that the first hint at the existence of the accelerator principle is to be found in Carver's work in 1903. As a fully-fledged component of business-cycle theory, it is supposed to appear first in Aftalion's main work (1913), although that author had already developed it in an essay in 1909. Mitchell and Robertson took the idea up shortly after that, but John Maurice Clark was the first to devote a detailed study to it (in 1917).

In the meantime, it had been discussed by other authors – for instance, Bickerdike (1914) and Bouniatian (in the first edition of his great cycle study, in 1921). In the 1920s, it found full recognition in the standard theories of Fanno and Pigou, and in the 1930s Kuznets and Harrod relied on it in their general explanation of the cycle. (Von Haberler, 1943, p. 97; and Mieth, 1954, p. 12, note 1.)

In a special study, Mieth (ibid., p. 9) has summarised the principle in an example which he seems to have taken from a study on finance by Polak (1926, p. 92):

> We assume that an economy requires annually 1000 units of cargo space, which represent 100 ships, of which five are to be scrapped each year to be replaced by new carriers. If, now, demand for cargo space rises by 10 per cent in one year, shipyards will have to build not five, but fifteen ships, five for replacement and ten for additional cargo. This means the demand for ships rises by 200 per cent. The accelerator principle explains the construction of these additional ships by the 10 per cent rise in demand for cargo space.

The principle works also in downswings to the extent that in the next year demand for ships would have to fall to 5·5 units. Over and above, there are 'humps' in replacement; but here a floor prevails since construction cannot fall lower than zero, while there is no limit for an increase. All complicated models rely on the simple basic idea that variations in the rate of growth or decrease in demand are reflected in much bigger fluctuations of production in earlier stages (in investment industries).

Von Haberler explains the principle by saying (1943, p. 96) that slight variations in demand for consumption goods result in pronounced swings in demand for production goods, so that demand-swings in the final stages of production are intensified in earlier stages, a fact which, together with other elements, helps to explain the increasing strength and durability of the upswing.

'DEGREE, MEASURE AND PROPORTION' IN EARLIER AND FINAL STAGES

Marx gave an early presentation of an analogous character in his *Theories of Surplus Value*, in the context of his discussion of Ricardo's accumulation theory:

> For a crisis (and therefore also for over-production) to be general, it suffices for it to affect the principal commercial goods. . . . then it can be understood how over-production in these few, but leading articles, calls forth a more or less general (*relative*) over-production on the whole market. For the phenomenon of general over-production is derived from the interdependence not only of the workers directly employed in these industries, but of all branches of industries which produce the elements of their products, the various stages of their constant capital. In the latter branches of industry, over-production is an effect.

Marx states that during the upswing 'the constantly expanding production . . . requires a constantly expanding market and . . . production expands more rapidly than the market'. In the wake of technical progress, 'small improvements are continuously building up . . . a piling up of improvements, a cumulative development of production powers'.

Marx unmistakably formulates the accelerator principle: 'The market expands more slowly than production; . . . there comes a moment at which the market manifests itself as too narrow for production. . . . If the expansion of the market had kept pace with the expansion of production [which means demand with expansion of capacities], there would be no glut of the market, no over-production.' (*Theories*, II, ch. 17, pp. 505, 523–4.)

Marx then speaks of a relative over-production in earlier stages as opposed to the final product ('yarn as compared with cloth, iron as compared with machinery etc.'). In the case of

> articles which belong directly to [other] spheres of production and [cannot be] subsumed under the leading articles of commerce which, according to the assumption, have been over-produced, because they

supply the *intermediate product* for the leading articles of commerce, production must have reached at least the same level as in the final phases of the product, although there is nothing to prevent production in those spheres from having gone even further ahead, thus causing an over-production within the over-production.

As a general rule, Marx thus postulates the maintenance of a certain proportionality between earlier and later stages, but he admits that it will never be maintained.

He then gives other examples for such earlier stages: coal, for instance, 'was produced only in proportion to the production of iron and yarn'. He thinks that a relative over-production is always possible in this case. He then proceeds to the decisive statement: 'For *the production of coal and yarn* and of all other spheres of production which produce only the conditions or earlier phases of a product to be completed in another sphere, is governed not by the immediate demand, by the immediate production or reproduction, but by the *degree, measure, proportion*, in which these are expanding.' (Ibid., pp. 530–1.)

Indeed, the accelerator represents nothing other than the degree or the proportion of the growth of final demand on which production in the earlier stages will be based. It seems, therefore, that Marx fully grasped the basic idea of the accelerator principle.

It is certain that by stressing the importance of investment goods, he gave a decisive clue not only to Tugan-Baranowsky and his successor Spiethoff, but especially to Aftalion. It is doubtful whether the latter was familiar with the *Theories of Surplus Value* and thus Marx's notion of the accelerator, but he certainly was profoundly influenced by Marx. Thus, Hansen and Clemence, in their introduction to a reprint of the article of 1927 in which Aftalion summarises his theory, say (1953, p. 129),

> Professor Aftalion, like Cassel and Spiethoff, owes a good deal to Marx and to ideas derived from Marx by others. Marx himself did not, of course, work out an explicit theory of cycles in detail, but his writings are full of suggestions that have influenced much non-Marxist thinking about cycles, despite the fact that more orthodox writers have not always acknowledged or even realized the extent of their indebtedness to Marx.

One of these suggestions, to which nobody, except perhaps Aftalion, paid any attention, seems to have been this suggestion of the basic principle of the accelerator. In spite of all the objections to the principle that have been raised by econometricians such as Tinbergen (1938, p. 164; 1939, p. 207), it has remained up to the present, especially in Harrod's analysis and that of his followers up to Hicks (1951, pp. 37ff.), an essential stepping stone in modern cycle analysis. Its importance for the link between rates of variation in final and secondary demand touches upon many subsidiary problems – for instance, on inventory cycles and the link between house construction and industrial prosperity, which remains so important within the context of the Kuznets cycle.

SWEEZY'S ACCELERATOR–UNDER-CONSUMPTION THEORY AS A CONTINUATION OF OTTO BAUER'S IDEAS

It therefore was tempting to try to give a new theoretical foundation to under-consumption theory. This was to be based no longer on a low absolute level of consumption, but on a flattening out of its growth rate, which appears to bring about the downswing. In that sense Otto Bauer, in his last book, *Zwischen Zwei Weltkriegen?* (Between Two World Wars? – 1936), touched upon some elements of accelerator theory.

Sweezy, in his Marxist classic (1942, pp. 186ff.), developed Bauer's ideas into a new theory of under-consumption based upon the accelerator. It is curious that this authority on Marxism does not refer anywhere in his book (for instance, in the annex to chapter 10 in which he develops his principal thesis) to the relevant passages in the *Theories of Surplus Value*.

Sweezy starts from national income, in which w is the wage bill, l is consumed surplus value, and k is accumulated surplus value, which is transformed into constant capital only. National income is $1 = w + l + k$; 'k is essentially the rate of growth of the total stock of means of production. In other words, if K is the total stock of means of production, then $k = dK/dt$.'

When income increases, an increasing part of the capitalists' revenue is invested. Sweezy strangely says, 'an increasing proportion of accumulation tends to be invested'; but, in any case, the consumption of workers and of capitalists will now grow more slowly.

Sweezy assumes that 'the output of consumption goods must be proportional to the stock of means of production'. Thus the capital stock (= investment) must grow in proportion to the output of consumption goods.

If the latter increase is $\lambda (dw + dl)$, an additional investment of c will be necessary. ' . . . λ is essentially the relation described in modern business cycle literature as "the acceleration principle" or simply as "the relation"' (ibid., p. 187, note).

Now, if growth is to proceed undisturbed, c, i.e. the investment rate required by the growth of consumption, must be equal to K, the rate of investment which would result 'from typical capitalist behaviour'.

Sweezy then goes on to demonstrate that dc/dt cannot equal dk/dt if national income keeps growing at a constant or declining rate. Here is the contradiction (ibid., pp. 188–9):

Capitalists tend to increase the rate of investment ($dk/dt > 0$), but the way they allow consumption to grow warrants only a declining rate of investment $(dc/dt < 0)$. Hence if the rate of investment actually does increase, the output of consumption goods will display a continuous tendency to outrun the demand. It will be noticed that this conclusion is reached on the assumption that national income in value terms is growing at a constant or declining rate.

In other words, according to Sweezy, undisturbed growth in the upswing requires an exponential growth of national income. Here one may ask whether this is still a genuine under-consumption thesis. It looks rather like a variant of a disproportionality theory underpinned by the accelerator principle.

LERNER'S CRITICISM OF SWEEZY'S THEORY

Lerner, an authority with socialist inclinations, has severely criticised Sweezy's theory, complaining (1945, p. 83) that it was 'very sad' that he insisted on giving his own version. He thinks the gist of it is that relatively increasing savings will increasingly be invested in additional equipment, and that there is a rigid ratio of consumer goods to equipment. The latter assumption seems to be based on Snyder's statistical investigations. Lerner argues, however, that Sweezy has incorrectly identified output and consumption. There is no rigid technological ratio, and, if there were, it could be altered.

Now it is surely no decisive objection to a theory to say that it could be counteracted by policy. Nevertheless, it must be admitted that Sweezy's reasoning is unsatisfactory. It reminds us of the fact that 'the first pioneers of the accelerator principle almost accepted this discovery with a sort of business-cycle fatalism', as Mieth remarks (1954, p. 25).

It must also be asked whether Marx did not trace the accelerator elsewhere: that is, in his analysis of capital turnover. As Mieth says (ibid., p. 23) the 'accelerator is indeed the reciprocal value of the capital turnover coefficient and represents . . . the durability of capital goods, the amount of capital input per unit of product and the intensity of capital use'.

Problems of this kind lead us on to the general question of proportionality in the development of individual economic sectors.

In a recent valuable study, Steitz (1977, p. 215) indicated that Bauer's and Grossmann's work incorporated the accelerator hypothesis; the author does not, however, refer to Marx's own earlier allusion to the accelerator principle.

16 The Theory of Disproportionality

The disproportionality element in Marx's business-cycle concept was the favourite subject of Marxist economists around the turn of the century. Sweezy comments (1942, p. 158) that Marx never examined competition among capitalists in detail, and quite naturally treated disproportionality rather cursorily. He thinks early commentators neglected this aspect, and that this continued until, around the turn of the century, the German Social Democrats began to extol it as if it were Marx's only theory. He then quotes Borchardt's analysis in the postscript to his popular edition of *Capital* (1919) and hints at the ideas of Hilferding and his friends. These German authors were not so isolated as Sweezy wants us to believe.

Most of the socialist publications which appeared in the 1930s after the initial shock of the depression relied on disproportionality, often combined with the view that this was reinforced by monopolistic rigidities. Lederer (1927), whom one might mention here rather than amongst the under-consumption theorists, held this view. Among German authors, we may further mention Gurland (1931), Decker (1931), Löwe (1931), Naphtali (1931) and Hermberg (1931). There were also Frenchmen such as Duret (1933), Russians such as Tugan-Baranowsky (1894), Bulgakov (1897) (a partisan of whose was Lenin!) and von Struve (1894), and Italians such as Arturo Labriola (1933).

This wide range of adherents and their different political shades (from revisionism to Bolshevism) show that the disproportionality theory not only prevailed among the German Social Democrats, but, in addition, was the dominant strain in Marxist thought prior to World War I.

THE RUSSIAN QUARRELS OVER THE ISSUE OF HARMONY

The most comprehensive review of the controversies of this epoch has been given by Rosdolsky. He states (1968, II, p. 553) that Tugan-Baranowsky was the first to 'derive economic crises exclusively from disproportionality between various sectors of industry'. In addition, Sweezy admits (1942, p. 160) that the position of disproportionality theory was assured when such a leading Marxist as Hilferding espoused it. Rosdolsky tries to prove (1968,

II, p. 565) that there were no essential differences between Tugan-Baranowsky, Bulgakov and Lenin on this point:

> Like Bulgakov, Tugan also proclaims the absolute self-sufficiency of capitalist production and its alleged independence of social consumption. . . . And he too explains crises exclusively by disproportionalities between sectors of industry. . . . It is clear that Lenin's postulate that the relationship between production and consumption is to be subsumed under the notion of proportionality is bound to bring him into the suspicious neighbourhood of Bulgakov's and Tugan's disproportionality theory . . .

It is paradoxical that Rosdolsky condemns all three authors: the 'revisionist' Tugan – of whom Sweezy said (1942, p. 159) that he never claimed to be an orthodox Marxist! – the orthodox Bulgakov and the revolutionary Lenin. He dubs all three of them (1968, II, p. 553) 'predecessors of the later neo-harmonic current in Marxist economics'. We cannot follow Rosdolsky in this respect, in spite of his achievement in reviewing these quarrels in Russian Marxism.

First, Rosdolsky's charge (ibid., p. 546) against the 'legal Marxists and their most gifted representative', Bulgakov, that they 'continuously confound abstract . . . analysis with capitalist reality' redounds on himself, for, while in his reproduction schemes Marx himself treats of frictionless growth, he indicates a number of reasons why this would not occur. Here we may recall that Robertson, who also fixed the conditions for the stability of the system without becoming a 'harmonist', thought (1954; 1956, p. 240) that the preservation of an equilibrium would be 'something of a miracle'. It is therefore quite possible to establish conditions for harmony without falling an easy prey to the belief that it will actually prevail.

Secondly, while Rosdolsky thinks that Tugan and Bulgakov were of the same mould, such an astute critic as Lenin was of the contrary opinion and saw a deep contrast between these authors. Whereas Bulgakov saw the importance of constant capital or macroeconomic depreciation for simple reproduction, Tugan did not. Thus, while Bulgakov kept an open mind on a depreciation theory of the cycle, i.e. as an essential factor of disturbance, this remained a closed book to Tugan. Furthermore, Lenin (1898) agreed with Bulgakov that a certain level of consumption is one of the elements of proportionality. It is true that department I must expand faster than II, but the former can in no way develop independently of basic consumption. Productive consumption (consumption of the means of production) always remains linked to individual consumption, and disturbances can arise between them.

Thirdly, if one says that any presentation of the conditions of frictionless growth is already tantamount to preaching harmony, this reproach can be levelled even against Marx! We have, however, already pointed out in Part II of this volume how unjustified this would be. Marx had to explain the conditions of frictionless growth in his schemes in order to demonstrate its precarious character. These Marxist quarrels are in the last resort owing to the fact that Marx places the disproportionality thesis at the centre of his theory of the potential disturbances affecting capitalist development, but his concrete statements on this subject remain tantalisingly laconic and general.

It may be true, as Dobb states (1937; 1950, p. 102), that through his schemes Marx wanted to reply to the under-consumptionist theories to show that capital accumulation could proceed unhindered in the sphere of exchange, provided that the right ratios were preserved, although he intimated that this could happen only by accident. This is the central point of his theory and coincides with the problem of instability. Incidentally, Dobb's statement reflects Robertson's view.

Marx's statements on disproportionality are few. For instance, he says in the *Theories of Surplus Value* (II, ch. 17, p. 532): 'If production were proportionate, there would be no over-production. . . . Since, however, capitalist production can allow itself free rein only in certain spheres, under certain conditions, there could be no capitalist production at all if it had to develop *simultaneously* and *evenly* in all spheres.'

Turning the argument round, in capitalist dynamics, which makes investment industries advance intermittently, there lies the perpetually renewed negation of proportionality.

In volume II of *Capital*, (ch. 20, p. 473), Marx talks of the 'disproportion of the production of fixed and circulating capital' as 'one of the favourite arguments of the economists in explaining crises.' He then points to his scheme of simple reproduction, in which he develops the theory of recessions induced by varying rates of depreciation.

In volume III of *Capital*, he says (ch. 15, pp. 256–7):

Since the aim of capital is not to minister to certain wants, but to produce profit, and since it accomplishes this purpose by methods which adapt the mass of production to the scale of production, not *vice versa*, a rift must continually ensue between the limited dimensions of consumption under capitalism and a production which forever tends to exceed this immanent barrier.

This is no hint of an under-consumptionist theory, but an allusion to disturbances between investment- and consumer-goods industries. Marx continues,

To say that there is no general over-production, but rather a disproportion within the various branches of production, is no more than to say that under capitalist production the proportionality of the individual branches of production springs as a continual process from disproportionality. . . . The contradiction of the capitalist mode of production, however, lies precisely in its tendency towards an absolute development of the productive forces, which continually come into conflict with the specific *conditions* of production in which capital moves, and alone can move.

THE LACK OF CONCRETE ARGUMENTS IN POST-MARXIAN THEORY

Marx's epigones did not step in and expand his general statements with concrete data. Thus Oscar Lange is right in saying (1934-5, p. 196) that Marxist theory failed to deal adequately with business-cycle theory. He blames this on the labour theory of value, which explains prices only in equilibrium, any deviations from this being accidental, while such deviations are the very core of business-cycle theory. He criticises Marxists for dealing with reproduction and equilibrium without even using mathematical functions.

It is doubtful whether the labour theory of value was the main obstacle. It did not prevent Marx from making concrete observations, for which he has been praised by Leontief. The two main reasons why the Marxist literature has not contributed more profound arguments to business-cycle theory would rather seem to be the following point:

First, for many Marxists, the cycle was simply a phenomenon foreshadowing 'in miniature' the final collapse of capitalism. Such a fatalistic attitude did not provide any stimulus to analyse closely the evolution of the cycle. Only authors who hoped to be able to conquer the cycle without seeing in it the writing on the wall indicating collapse – i.e. from that point of view, revisionist or non-Marxist authors – could be genuinely interested in down-to-earth analysis. Among the revisionists we may count Tugan-Baranowsky, even if he himself did not do so.

Secondly, for those Marxists who did study the business cycle, the chief point of interest was the 'crisis' as a pathological symptom of everything that pointed to the inefficiency of capitalism. In this respect, Marxist thought even shows a retrograde development, as compared with what had been achieved from the times of Marx to Lederer. For instance, Altvater has pointed (1971; 1972, p. 70) to statements by Ölssner, who declares that it would be 'completely wrong to consider the (classical) four phases of the cycle, crisis, depression, recovery and upswing, as equally important. The crisis is the decisive phase of the cycle'. Altvater quotes this with approval and adds that the 'Marxian theory of crises does not understand the cycle as a conjunctural movement, but as a cycle of crises'. It is true that Ölssner's work contains such astonishing statements as (1949; 1955, 1, p. 9): 'Bourgeois economics has long since given up developing a theory of crisis. Instead, it has gone over to business-cycle research. . . .'

Such an attitude focuses on the symptoms and not on the origins of pathological phenomena and is of course unsuited to an analysis of disproportionalities, for it would mean searching for the causes of future disequilibria in the very stage of recovery!

In this book, by contrast, we advance the thesis that Marx, together with Juglar, discovered the cycle in capitalist growth and even the possibility of cyclical movements in stationary systems (which are an anomaly under capitalism!), and that this discovery was at the root of Marx's concept of the capitalist system as fundamentally unstable.

The artificial separation of Marxist 'crisis theory' and bourgeois 'cycle theory' has not only had disastrous consequences for the continuation of Marx's disproportionality analysis, but also seems to have blocked a final understanding of the internal disequilibrium of capitalism. In the meantime, however, a turn-around has taken place in the minds of economists of socialist countries.

For instance, Molnár has analysed in a rather unorthodox way the internal changes in the cyclical processes in the USA since the Second World War, stressing the importance of investment for technical progress, and also the growth in household investment by consumers and in investment by the state, as well as the growing weight of services. Molnár notes that cyclical periodicity has regained some favour with Soviet theorists. Molnár draws heavily (1970, pp. 10–11) on the works of authors such as Mendelson, who links the rate of growth in general demand with greater fluctuations in demand for investment goods, thus introducing accelerator elements. Mendelson also stresses (1954, 1) that induced investment leads to production by new factories at the very moment when demand begins to fail.

AFFINITIES WITH KEYNESIANISM

The critical movement in the ranks of Marxist theoreticians becomes clear when one reads the book of another Hungarian author, Erdös, who points out (1967, p. 59) that Marxists originally held a theory of economic crises, but that there was no real Marxist theory of irregular fluctuations. In his main work, Erdös tried to make up for this by discussing business-cycle analysis of a Keynesian type, emphasising the cycle as a cumulative process.

The disproportionality thesis can assume a concrete shape only if it is linked to the notion of effective demand. Here we enter Keynesian territory, which was for a long time taboo not only for orthodox economists of the Eastern bloc, but also for many moderate socialists of the West. A good example of this is the violent attack by Robert Mossé, who misunderstood (1949, p. 13) Keynes's unfortunate terminology relative to the alleged identity of savings and investment – a problem that was later solved by Swedish economists, who distinguished between voluntary and involuntary investment. Incidentally, the pseudo-Keynesian term 'surplus savings' is analogous to the concept of abstention from buying or of the hoarding of liquid means, as developed by Marx in his criticism of Say.

The affinities between the Marxian disproportionality theory and Keynesian economics were finally recognised even by Eastern orthodoxy. Lenin thought very highly of Keynes's analysis of the Treaty of Versailles, and the references to Keynes in the first edition of the *Great Soviet Encyclopaedia* of 1936 were soberly factual.

After the publication of the *General Theory*, criticism was at first very unsystematic, but it culminated in 1953 in the assertion that Keynes was an enemy of the working class and an apologist for the fascist–imperialist bourgeoisie (Letiche, 1971, pp. 493–4; Turner, 1969). Until the end of the 1940s, Keynes's main work remained unknown to most Soviet economists; not until 1948 was it translated into Russian. It is true that a somewhat factual review by Blyumin had appeared in 1946, but even this author talked rather abstrusely of Keynes in 1953 as a 'cynical intriguer and loyal servant of imperialism'.

It was only after the Stalin era was over that the thaw of co-existence began to work. In his introduction to the Hungarian translation of the *General Theory* in 1959, Erdös pleaded for scientific objectivity even towards non-Marxist works. The tolerance towards Keynesian concepts was then furthered by Russians such as Alter (1964), Czechs such as Osadchaia (1963) and many other authors, mainly from central Eastern Europe. The thaw finally culminated in a review of Sweezy's book by Oscar Lange (1943).

THE HOARDING THEORY

An excess of saving over investment, in the Keynesian sense as improved by the Swedish terminology, comes very near to Marx's critique of Say's Law. As has been pointed out in Volume I, Part VIII, for Marx the basic process of the business cycle – namely, a break in the chain of the current transformation of money into commodities and again into money, coupled with a freezing-in of commodities in an involuntary build-up of inventories, i.e. involuntary investment – has a monetary character. This process is counterbalanced by the rise in the hoarding of money, or by the destruction of money.

Joan Robinson, in her analysis of hoarding (1951; 1966), has given (p. 63) six different interpretations of the term, of which the third one – money stock minus the active circulation, or idle balances – comes nearest to this Marxian notion. Such hoarding seems to be synonymous with a decrease in income and business activity and a decrease in the average velocity of circulation of money.

In his analysis of hoarding, Marx starts from a discussion of Say's Law. If a fall in the rate of profit occurs because the 'stimulus of profit' is weakened, it can lead to a 'repeated, one-sided sale of commodities without a supplementing purchase' and to a 'successive transformation of this virtually additional productive capital into virtual money-capital [hoard]', i.e. to a lack of reinvestment. What happens is a 'repeated withdrawal of money from circulation and a corresponding formation of a hoard . . . a change in the function of money previously circulating. A while ago it functioned as a medium of circulation, now it functions as a hoard . . . .' (*Capital*, ii, ch. 21, p. 501.)

In other words, hoarding takes place, and cash holdings increase at least temporarily at certain points, while the velocity of circulation of money and the effective amount of money decrease. Here Keynes's 'liquidity trap' is anticipated. Now the disproportionality aspect prevails, investment decreases, and a recession begins.

The condition for all this is the fall in the rate of profit, however this may be explained. The theory of hoarding touches upon the theory of the tendency of the rate of profit to fall. In hoarding,

> the surplus-product . . . is . . . absolutely unproductive in its chrysalis stage of money – as a hoard and virtual money-capital. . . . It is a dead weight of capitalist production. The eagerness to utilise this surplus-value accumulating as virtual money-capital for the purpose of deriving profits or revenue from it [which, from the standpoint of entrepreneurs, means either to eliminate existing hoards or to utilise liquid means of investment] finds its object accomplished in the credit system and 'papers'. Money capital thereby gains in another form an enormous influence on the course and the stupendous development of the capitalist system of production. (Ibid., p. 502)

In other words, as soon as dishoarding sets in, such liquid means or inactive bank accounts can be mobilised to enable the rate of investment to rise by leaps and bounds. But then

> the entire credit mechanism is continually occupied in reducing the actual metallic circulation [read, 'amount of liquid money'] to a relatively more and more decreasing minimum by means of sundry operations, methods and technical devices. The artificiality of the entire machinery and the possibility of disturbing its normal course increase to the same extent. (Ibid.)

To put it another way, alongside the hoarding process, 'normal' cash stocks held for transaction purposes are currently reduced, and this offers a further possibility for a sudden increase in the active quantity of money. Marx does not mention any actual destruction of (bank) money through debt repayment, unless one wants to interpret in this sense his remark that 'only balances are to be squared so far as the mutual purchases and sales do not cover one another'.

Incidentally, Marx makes it quite clear that he speaks of a 'metallic circulation' only in order to present the matter in its simplest, most 'primitive' form instead 'of the later, reflected form . . . under the credit system as consciously regulated processes'. Behind these monetary phenomena, there are real expansionary or contractionary processes as illustrated by Marx in his reproduction schemes.

The Keynesian notion of an increase in liquidity preference is not quite identical with Marx's concept of 'hoarding'. In Robinsonian terminology, the first propensity is an increased desire to hold money instead of assets, while the second one represents a decrease in the velocity of circulation of money.

The Marxian notion becomes fruitful for the disproportionality theory only if one considers that hoarding leads to a fall in investment demand, as Marx shows in his analysis of 'crises' in simple reproduction, where replacement is postponed. It cannot be denied that the parallels of Marxian hoarding with the schemes of extended reproduction are not quite clear. Here Marxist business-cycle analysis still has a task to undertake.

ATTEMPTS TO EXTEND THE DISPROPORTIONALITY THESIS: FROM HILFERDING TO VON HAYEK

In the Marxist camp, a large-scale attempt to extend the disproportionality analysis was made by Hilferding, in particular. He starts, in the same way as Tugan-Baranowsky and Bulgakov, from the assumption that proportionality would assure smooth growth. He rejects the thesis of under-consumption. The credit-fed expansion of investment-goods industries, accompanied by price rises, disturbs proportionality. Hilferding then introduces Marx's 'rising organic composition', which is for him synonymous with technical progress. This leads to more capital expansion in the investment sector, but more fixed capital means longer periods of production, less adaptability to consumption, rising prices and accumulation, and over-accumulation in the sectors with the highest organic composition. 'The disproportionality appears when the products of the earlier spheres appear on the market. Sales are blocked by the fact that production in the spheres of lower organic composition . . . is not as rapidly . . . increased . . . .' The latter phrase reminds us of the accelerator theory, but in general Hilferding's analysis (1910; 1947, pp. 341–58) remains largely descriptive.

At any rate, Marxist theory and over-capitalisation theories overlap. The true heir to this theory is an arch-conservative, von Hayek, who paradoxically and honestly recognised (1931; 1949, p. 103) Marx's paternity:

> In the German literature similar ideas [to those formulated by von Hayek in the present text] were introduced mainly by the writings of Karl Marx. It is on Marx that Tugan-Baranowsky's work is based which in turn provided the starting point for the later work of Professor Spiethoff and Professor Cassel. The extent to which the theory developed in these lectures corresponds with that of the two last-named authors, particularly with that of Professor Spiethoff, need hardly be emphasised.

Von Hayek's work has been summarised, with his approval, by Hansen and Tout (1933, p. 183):

> Depression is brought about by a shrinkage in the structure of production (i.e., a shortening of the capitalistic process). . . . The leading cause . . . is the phenomenon of forced saving. An elongation of the process of production caused by voluntary saving tends to remain intact. . . . An increase in money supply (bank credit) . . . would cause an increase in the demand for producers' goods in relation to consumers' goods, and this would raise the prices of goods of the higher order; . . . a reversal in the price relationship of higher and lower order goods would appear as soon as the money supply ceased to increase . . . [and] a shrinkage in the artificially elongated process of production would inevitably occur. . . . An increase in consumer demand occasioned by an increase in the supply of money . . . inevitably brings about a shortening in the process of production, and so causes depression. . . . Excessive public expenditure and taxation, by increasing the ratio of spending to saving, will force a shortening in the process of production and so cause prolonged depression or business stagnation.

If this analysis strongly resembles the Marxian one (and partly even Hilferding's reasoning), von Hayek's recommendations certainly do not correspond to Marx's ideas. Whereas von Hayek thinks that 'neutral' money and an avoidance of an extension of bank credit might prevent a recession, Marx, in his criticism of Proudhon and Darimon, strongly denied the possibility of manipulating the economy through monetary policy, arguing that bank credit must largely follow transaction needs. The essential point is to be found not in von Hayek's conservative conclusions, but in his analysis of the causes of the boom and the depression, which, as he himself admits, strongly resembles the Marxian one.

This has also been recognised by Marxists such as Strachey (1932; 1933, pp. 111–18), who even discovered a further similarity with the early work of Keynes in the *Treatise on Money*: both von Hayek and Keynes argue that increased savings make the productive structure 'longer and narrower', or, in von Hayek's Viennese language, open it up like a fan. His lengthening of the production structures represents an increase in demand for investment goods, somewhat like Marx's 'higher organic composition'.

Keynes emphasises in addition the credit cycle. Entrepreneurs are induced to produce capital goods in larger quantities than is warranted by a constant saving rate. Investment and risks increase. If for some 'leading goods' prices no longer rise, investment suffers a shock, and a cumulative decline sets in. Strachey draws the conclusion that ruinous crises are owing not to monetary misdemeanours, but to the anarchy of market production.

Bankers should have prevented investment while savings were insufficient to sustain it. Strachey thinks that von Hayek may be right in demanding this, but this would mean that crises under capitalism could be prevented only by hindering the development of capitalism. Strachey himself adheres rather to the theory of the tendency of the rate of profit to fall.

In the 1930s, Henry Smith stressed falling profits and rates of interest in a similar way (1937, pp. 192–201); but for him disturbances occur because accumulation is carried on without paying attention to profitability. This was contested by Wilson, who (1938, pp. 107–13) thought Marx's theory was much more eclectic. Wilson stresses misallocation in production and circulation, the hoarding and over-expansion of some 'leading articles' favoured by credit, which in turn provokes disproportionality in the distribution of resources, a feature reinforced by replacement cycles.

He too sees a similarity between the schemes of Marx and von Hayek. A liquid capital market can induce long gestation periods; investment-goods industries attract labour and bid up prices and wages until there occurs Marx's unavoidable 'crash', which he did not describe in detail, although volume II of *Capital* contains some tools for such an analysis and for describing inventory cycles.

According to Wilson, Marx thought rising surplus value would lead to increased savings-seeking investment outlets, which in any case are dwindling. He thus comes near to the Baran–Sweezy theory, although he thinks that crises may occur because the rate of profit fluctuates independently of accumulation.

For Marx, technical progress is synonymous with the tendency of the rate of profit to fall, which we shall now consider.

17 The 'Law of the Tendency of the Rate of Profit to Fall' as a Business-Cycle Theory

We have already indicated that there are serious doubts as to whether the theory of the tendency of the rate of profit to fall has a long-run aspect, in so far as it is based on a relative increase in the costs of fixed capital, combined with a constant division of value added.

One may, however, consider it also as a business-cycle theory. Quite a number of authors have seen it in just this light. Strachey (1935, pp. 237 ff.) gives a rather orthodox explanation, although he considers the increase in the 'organic composition' to be a short-run phenomenon. For him, the crisis is a 'collapse of the rate of profit'. He does not, however, distinguish between average and marginal capital–output ratios, in the manner of modern theories.

In the first edition of his history of economic doctrines (1948, pp. 118–9), Kruse bluntly writes of the entire theorem as a business-cycle theory. He does not ask himself whether one can assume that the capital–output ratio rises in the short run, although he could have pointed to the large swings in the marginal ratios, conditioned by varying rates of capacity utilisation. He wholly maintains his opinion even in later editions of the same work (see, for instance, 1953, p. 120–1).

Another author who considered the theorem as a business–cycle theory was Schmölders (1961, p. 61).

Such an interpretation raises statistical problems. In the meantime, even Marxists, as Gillman's work shows, have started working with capital stocks instead of flows measuring the 'organic composition', by relating the capital–output ratio to the share of wages (see above, ch. 9). If the theory is now to be interpreted as a business-cycle theory, it would seem appropriate to use a marginal coefficient. According to Helmstädter (1969, pp. 31–3), this is indicated 'by how many years the additional unit produced in one period would have to continue in order to bring about the accumulation which was realised in that period'. Normally, the average coefficient is used, i.e. the 'ratio of capital stock to net product'. The distinction is crucial, for marginal coefficients show extreme variations from 1 to 10, while average coefficients fluctuate only from 3 to 5 in most countries. It appears reasonable to use the average coefficient also for measuring movements in the capital–output ratio in cyclical fluctuations, all the more so as capitalists normally calculate their rate of profit in relation to capital stocks and not the rate of investment of the relevant year. Admittedly, such an interpretation does not correspond to the Marxian notion, which measures the rate of profit as a mark-up on costs or as a profit margin, as Ullmo emphasises (1973, p. 125).

Since the depreciation of fixed assets holds a prominent position in this theory, but since it can be valued only if capital stocks are employed, it seems reasonable to choose the average capital–output ratio, particularly as Helmstädter, on the grounds that 'there is no reasonable theoretical connexion between investment and the growth of production in the same period' (1969, p. 36), has rejected the marginal coefficient.

THE LINK WITH THE 'RICARDO–EFFECT'

Marx foresees that productivity will be increased by an increase in capital input. His reasoning is thus already concerned with the medium term. This can be explained by the assumption that other short-run measures of rationalisation (the better use of existing capacity, economies in raw-material consumption, better labour organisation) are exhausted, so that rationalisation through investment is inevitable.

In this context, von Hayek's so-called 'Ricardo effect' (von Hayek, 1942/1948, pp. 220–38; see also Neisser, 1932), which is implicit in Marx's reasoning, becomes relevant. In real terms, wages may rise considerably more towards the end of the boom than do the prices of machinery. This benefits the consumption-goods industries.

The 'Ricardo effect' postulates that a rise in real wages will curtail the profits of labour-intensive industries, and prod them into substituting machinery for labour. In a certain sense, one may call Marx's theorem an inverse Ricardo effect. Here substitution occurs autonomously and leads to pressure on wages. In both cases, rates of interest may be driven up, which in turn discourages long-term investment and may provoke a recession.

On the other hand, it may happen that labour costs rise dispro-portionately only during the initial stages of the boom, since price increases for raw materials and investment goods may, in view of unused capacity in these industries or of unfavourable 'terms of trade' for overseas suppliers, be slower. At the same time, investment goods may be relatively cheaper than consumption goods, because of greater over-capacity in the former sector. This would mean that, in the initial stages of the upturn, constant capital would not be inflated in relation to variable capital.

In view of the relative expensiveness of labour, the Ricardo effect would, once the economy approaches full employment, be marked by a more pronounced substitution process. As the rate of profit does not yet suffer from the increase in the capital stock, but keeps rising, investment funds are available. In the meantime, the consumption-goods industries run up against the ceiling of full capacity, and their productivity rises more slowly than that of investment-goods industries. The latter's prices rise more slowly at first, and the continuing boom leads in the investment-goods sector to profits which begin to attract labour from the consumption-goods sector.

ANALOGIES WITH FRITZ SCHMIDT'S THEORY OF 'ERRONEOUS CALCULATION'

Now the Hegelian 'cunning of the idea' is brought to bear. A wave of mechanisation and net investment leads to a shift in value relations. Relatively more labour is required for the production of constant capital, and fixed assets are inflated, a development that Marx thought would later lead to a fall in the rate of profit. At first, in view of the presumed increase in profitability, stock-exchange speculation drives up share prices.

This now brings about the effect that the German industrial economist Fritz Schmidt foresaw in his thesis that the business cycle was the result of erroneous calculations. Receipts, for instance, dividends, are related to inflated values, profitability appears to decrease, and decreasing share prices lead to a bearish scare, which in turn really brings profits down. Schmidt saw this 'error' in real terms (1933, p. 106):

In times of increasing values, entrepreneurs consider the increase in asset prices from the day of purchase to the day of production as a profit and therefore as income, thus transforming assets into income and increasing purchasing power in such a way that it results in excessive demand, which in turn begets new increases in asset values. An excessive extension of capacity and production leads to a price fall, in which the apparent costs of apparently indispensable depreciation result in profits which are apparently lower [than they really are]. This again provokes a fall in profits and income, so that purchasing power in the market decreases, which in turn leads to an excessive price fall, which is reversed only very slowly by the increasing liquidity of money.

This resembles the Marxian theorem where entrepreneurs in the upswing base their calculation of costs on the cost price of assets and thus believe they are making high profits. Later, they find out that the replacement costs of assets and raw material stocks have increased. If competition keeps the sum of surplus values (or profits) at the same absolute level, and this sum has to be compared with inflated capital values, the rate of profit must fall. As soon as the slump sets in, assets and stocks lose their values, and replacement costs fall until the rate of profit is restored. The present author

first described these correspondences between Marx and Fritz Schmidt in
an essay in 1955 (Kühne, 1955; 1973, pp. 314 ff.).

There are three reasons why the rate of profit may fall. First, there may
be an accelerator effect because the rate of growth in the consumption-
goods sector slows down earlier and this provokes a downswing in the
investment-goods sector. This is the theory of Harrod and Hicks, and was
anticipated by Marx in the *Theories of Surplus Value* where he speaks of the
'degree, measure and proportion' of the growth of production in the
consumption-goods sector. Among Marxists, a similar theory has been
advanced by Otto Bauer and Sweezy.

Secondly, if labour is attracted into the investment-goods sector, its
assets increase in proportion to the consumption-goods sector, and at the
same time over-capacity appears. Marx expressed this as an increase in the
ratio $c:v$. The rate of profit will fall as soon as consumption-goods
industries, the labour costs of which have risen, experience a slower rate of
growth.

Thirdly, productivity may develop differentially. As long as there is a
pool of unemployed, labour-saving tendencies, which are to a point
synonymous with Marx's mechanism of the tendency of the rate of profit to
fall, do not prevail. As soon as full employment is reached, the labour-
saving bias in technical progress becomes dominant and the rate of profit
tends to fall. Considerations of finance reinforce this analysis, for a drop in
the rate of profit is reflected in the capacity for self-financing; investment
drops and labour becomes unemployed. Now, the desperate struggle for
survival may so increase productivity, particularly in the investment-
goods industry, that capital-saving technical progress prevails. In spite of
idle capacity, investment in new machinery may again be undertaken, in
view of its better performance.

REFORMULATION OF THE THEORY BY PREISER AND HENRY SMITH

In an early article, Preiser summarised Marxian business-cycle theory thus
(1924; 1970, p. 54):

> Capitalist production is like a pot of boiling water sitting on the fire. The
> fire is labour productivity. As fire transforms water in the pot into
> vapour, the water being as it were thinned and extended, so pro-
> ductivity creates a mass of products which are simultaneously de-
> preciated or thinned. The lid on the pot is the immanent limit to
> production: the fall in the rate of profit. Then the crisis occurs: there is
> too much vapour in the pot, it boils over, and calms down again: the
> contents of the pot are 'depreciated' for some time, until it boils over
> again. So it is in Marx's analysis: over-accumulated capital blows up the

intolerable fetter of the low rate of profit by depreciation and idleness. Immediately the lid is placed on the (less full) pot again, the productivity of labour, the fire flaming under the pot, makes a new attempt to overcome the immanent barrier.

Preiser cites a number of non-Marxists who have tried to analyse the theory of the falling rate of profit.

The modern socialist economist Henry Smith seems best to have grasped the Marxian ideas. In his essay of 1937 (pp. 195–203), he first eliminates the under-consumption elements, arguing that Marx understood the interaction between saving and investment too well to fall into such a trap. After discarding value analysis, he argues that technical progress may very well raise wages and interest rates together, while distribution relations remain unchanged. He tries to explain the fall in the rate of profit by the behaviour of entrepreneurs: if they invest without heeding profitability, the rate of profit must fall. If capital accumulation goes on with greater speed than technical progress raises profits from marginal investment, profit expectations will prove false, investment will stop, and the economy will be 'strewn with the rotting corpses of stillborn white elephants'.

Smith believes that many of Marx's remarks permit one to conclude that the fall in the rate of profit occurs as a consequence of wrong expectations and over-investment, and one need not rely on value theory. High oligopoly profits lead to the construction of rival plants when the rate of interest is low, thereby increasing instability, and finally leading to capital depreciation in depression. This recalls Natalie Moszkowska's cartel analysis.

In the final analysis, Marx's cycle occurs because 'the rate of accumulation exceeds the rate of technical progress' (Smith, 1937, p. 203).

GOODWIN'S MODERN VERSION OF THE GROWTH CYCLE

There is an increasing trend towards the development of a coherent Marxist business-cycle theory. Varga, a Hungarian who in the Stalinist epoch espoused unorthodox theses and thus became an *enfant terrible* of Soviet economics, has sketched (1967, pp. 232–5) what he calls the new features of capitalist cycles since 1945. For him, these are high gross investment, instalment credit, military expenditure and inflation, accompanied by a desynchronisation of cycles between the English-speaking countries on one side and Europe and Japan on the other, where he finds practically no crises at all. Thus he paves the way in Marxism for a transition from a spectacular crisis theory to growth-cycle analysis. (See also Domar, and his discussion with Sweezy, 1950.)

This step has been completed by Goodwin, who officially introduced into Marxist analysis the growth cycle, which had meanwhile become fashionable in business-cycle analysis, in the sense of fluctuations in growth rates. Goodwin tries (1967, pp. 57–8) to render the growth cycle compatible with Marx's theory. A slow-down in growth reduces employment in order to re-establish profits. Productivity then rises faster than wages. This is the temporary solution to capitalism's contradiction in Marx's theory. Improved profitability, however, leads to a vigorous expansion of output and employment, doing away with the reserve army and strengthening labour's bargaining power.

Goodwin thinks that crises may be replaced by slower growth, which would leave 'crisis theorists' bereft of their subject-matter. In another context, Goodwin has developed his own disproportionality-*cum*-rate-of-profit theory. Capitalism proceeds by fits and starts. If the economy grows too fast, wage rises slow it down, and *vice versa*. The slow-down leads to over-rapid expansion. It forever lacks a sustainable and moderate rate of growth, either over- or under-shooting it.

Goodwin then refers to the Phillips curve, according to which the rate of wage-change depends on the level of unemployment, but he thinks that money and real wages evolve in the same direction. Higher real wages and labour scarcity slow down the growth rate, as in Marx's 'harbinger' theory.

There is no permanent fall in the rate of profit, but it fluctuates over the growth cycle. The substitution of machinery prevents real wages from impairing the rate of accumulation. Contradictions are put off into the future, but they must break through, for otherwise the rate of profit would not fall, as it must to stimulate the economy into efforts to increase productivity.

Technical progress affects only the input coefficients of new ventures and therefore relies on gross investment. Real wages show a rising secular trend, while profits do not, but the relative shares of workers and capitalists tend in the long run to remain the same. The productivity of capital remains constant or declines and labour productivity increases. Goodwin returns to the falling rate of profit after a detour:

> We get roughly constant distribution shares, a well-substantiated fact. But whereas the constant share of wages consists of a falling labour–output ratio and a rising wage rate, profits consist of a constant π and capital–output ratio. At this point the model is unsatisfactory, for the profit rate is falling (it must fall to force the rise in productivity) . . . . (Goodwin, 1970, p. 126.)

18 Business-Cycle Theory and Marxism

Judgements on Marxian business-cycle theory run to extremes. On the one side, we find such a Marxist as Altvater asserting (1971; 1972, p. 71) that 'crisis theory will have to analyse the fundamental contradictions of capitalist society, deriving from their periodic sharpening the possibility and necessity of the crisis'. He goes so far as to say: 'The adequate Marxian crisis theory is nothing other than the three volumes of *Capital*. Any isolated culling of quotations in which the term "crisis" occurs cannot do justice to Marx's methodology'. For Altvater, then, Marx's 'crisis theory' is monolithic.

The other extreme is represented by authors such as Wilson, who thinks (1938) that Marx's comments on the business cycle prove that, if he had developed a coherent theory, it would have looked rather eclectic.

The truth will be found somewhere in between these two extreme positions. Surely the cycle was for Marx the logical outcome of the capitalist system. Tsuru was right to say (1956, pp. 32–3) that, if Schumpeter proceeded from cycles to capitalism, Marx, by contrast, derived the cycle from capitalism. To that extent, Altvater may be right. But surely this does not imply that one must read all three volumes of *Capital* in order to understand Marx's cycle theory. One will have to rely willy-nilly on the relevant passages, and, after all, one would be justified in saying that the *Theories of Surplus Value* are of primary importance in this respect.

It is certain that the first, so-called 'raw', draft of *Capital* looked towards a volume treating the subject of the world market and crises. Unfortunately, large parts of Marx's manuscripts of 1861–3 have not yet been published; Rosdolsky (1968, 1, pp. 27–9) estimates the unpublished material at some 1000 pages. So long as this material remains unavailable, one must rely, if not on the 'selection' of passages in which the word 'crisis' occurs, then on the chapters dealing with cycles. One thing seems to be certain: if Marx's work as a whole is still not accepted by the main body of 'academic' theory, Marx's contribution to business cycles seems to have been tacitly absorbed even by the conservative wing. We have cited the example of von Hayek. In order, therefore, to accept this contribution, it obviously is not necessary to accept everything that Marx had to say.

As to the wide recognition of Marx's work in this field, the testimony of another conservative, Recktenwald, is worthy of mention. It is true that he talks of the *membra disjecta* of Marxian business-cycle analysis, but he then goes on to recognise (1973, p. 248) that 'one finds therein all the elements which have ever been the ingredients of any serious analysis of business cycles, and as a whole very few errors'. He admits that Marx anticipated Juglar's work and that his achievement consisted in going beyond the mere notion of a 'crisis' to the analysis of the cyclical movement as such and even of minor cycles *à la* Kitchin. Why then should Marxists be the only ones to belittle his achievement and try to banish him to the pathological depth of the cycle, to an antiquated 'crisis theory'?

To do this would be all the more regrettable in that Marxists would thus make it more difficult for themselves to analyse recent cyclical phenomena. After all, it cannot be denied that, for a long period following the Second World War, the cyclical movements in a number of Western European countries and Japan took place without any visible 'crisis', but formed a clear-cut 'growth cycle' – until, that is, the great recession of 1974–5.

Moreover, even in Marx's analysis, the 'crisis' appears not purely as a kind of agony but rather as a remedy. Dobb stresses (1955, p. 196) that 'a crisis was often, not merely the expression of a rupture of equilibrium, but itself the process by which the broken equilibrium asserted itself'. If so, it is all the more important to study not only the eventual crisis, which would be followed by equilibrium, but also the process of disturbance, which begins in the phases of the cycle long before the crisis sets in, i.e. during the upswing. There Marx saw the real contradictions arise, and here is to be found the proper task of business-cycle theory, and especially of Marxist analysis!

MARXIST FEAR OF THE UNKNOWN IN BUSINESS CYCLE ANALYSIS?

It looks as if many Marxists suffered from a fear of the unknown, a sort of *horror vacui*, in entering the realm of detailed business-cyle analysis, perhaps because this smacks to them of treatment to prolong the patient's life, by means of such medicaments as cycle technology, and of giving him some modest measure of contentment. Behind this attitude there seems to lurk resentment, which has also played the role of godfather at the christening of such slogans as 'state-monopoly capitalism'.

On the other hand, it seems that in some Marxist circles the feasibility of Keynesianism was more easily accepted than in 'academic' circles, which regarded Keynesian policy management with scepticism.

As an example of such a belief in the possibilities of successful state business-cycle management, we may quote the *Analyse der Ökonomischen Verhältnisse in der Bundesrepublik* (Analysis of Economic Conditions in the Federal Republic of Germany), published by the Executive Committee of

Young Socialists of the Social Democratic Party of Germany in 1971: 'It cannot be denied that the potential for stabilisation of capitalist society has been considerably reinforced through Keynesian theory which has been elaborated and refined for thirty years. Today, governments have at their disposal a vast array of instruments for directing the economic process . . . .'

The same text says that 'It is necessary to stress this increased stabilisation potential of capitalist societies in the face of socialists who believe that the classical cycle of crises is soon to reappear', but it also warns that 'this must not give rise to the illusion that modern capitalism is immune from crises' (cited in Duve, 1973, p. 19). Such an illusion seems, however, difficult to avoid if one has to accept that the relative damping-down of business fluctuations between the end of the Second World War and 1973 was owing to Keynesianism, and their reappearance owing to its non-application.

There is a danger that the achievement and potential of business-cycle or growth policy inspired by Keynesianism may be overrated. We shall quote some examples of how uncertain the successes of Keynesianism appear to some of the authorities of 'academic' economics.

STATE INTERVENTION AS A STABILISING OR DESTABILISING FACTOR?

In December 1962 Samuelson declared (1966, pp. 1697–8) that he would not consider private investment to be the main source of instability in post-war America. Contrary to textbook economics, federal expenditure had been a disturbing factor in most post-war recessions, which were often provoked by the reduction in expenditure. He asked if there were a law 'grimmer than Parkinson's', by which governments mishandled fiscal policy as soon as economists had taught them how to use it for stabilisation purposes, or whether monetarists were right in saying that lags thwarted the efforts at 'fine tuning'.

Samuelson based his approach on studies by Brown (1960) and Fromm (1960). Fromm had declared that fluctuations in federal expenditure seemed to be the main source of instability.

Numerous studies in other countries reached similar conclusions. In 1968, a group of OECD experts, comprising Heller, Hansen and Dow, stated (OECD, 1968, p. 87) that automatic stabilisers succeeded in reducing fluctuations in the USA and France by one-half, but in other countries by only one-quarter. Only in Sweden had fiscal policy un-doubtedly been successful; but even there the forecasts for the booms of 1959 and 1963–4 had proved wrong. Such forecasting errors, although frequent in the United States and Great Britain, did not constitute the main problem, which was really that in Belgium, Italy and Federal

Germany the fiscal manipulation of global demand was not consciously undertaken. Fiscal policy tended to reinforce fluctuations in Great Britain from 1955 to 1967, while the OECD report says (ibid., pp. 65, 82–3) that things were better in France, where fiscal policy was not quite so systematically pursued.

Later studies have proceeded in the same direction, Carl Snyder states that for the period 1955–65 the extent to which the gap between actual and potential output was filled was two-thirds in Sweden, 29 per cent in France, 25 per cent in Great Britain, 21 per cent in Italy and 17 per cent in the United States (Snyder, 1970a, p. 933), and only 13 per cent in the Federal Republic of Germany and 10 per cent in Belgium (Snyder, 1970b, p. 316).

In 1972, Adolf Wagner confirmed these results for Germany in his monumental study of growth cycles (1972, pp. 160–89). He says that, 'contrary to the rules of compensatory fiscal policy, variations in state consumption in 1953, 1962 and 1963 reinforced downswings and in 1969 the upswing. . . . In 53 per cent of the cases, state investment increased cyclical fluctuations . . . .' For aggregate state outlays on consumption and investment, 'egregious sins were committed . . . in the downswings of 1953 and 1963 and in the upswing of 1969'. From Wagner's tables 13 and 26 it can be seen that state investment had anticyclical effects in only eight out of nineteen cases and was procyclical in ten cases, including the recession of 1967, in spite of Schiller's celebrated investment programme. Wagner remains sceptical for the future: 'One may doubt whether a generally anticyclical effect can be realised from state expenditure in the near future'.

Scalfari states in an essay of 1972 (p. 8) that it was 'a hundred times confirmed that it is impossible in Italy to direct the economy *via* public expenditure'. He reminds his readers that the President of the Central Bank had pointed out in his latest report that public expenditure might have reduced rather than increased total effective demand. Shortly before this, the Italian economist Masera had made a similar statement in an international symposium on Demand Management (Giersch, 1972).

These examples could be multiplied. One might be tempted to conclude that Keynes-inspired fiscal policy can hardly have been the underlying cause of the post-1945 prosperity of world capitalism. Classical monetary policy is exposed to similar doubts, which have been uttered not only by its notorious critic Friedman but also by American experts such as Gurley and Okun. (See the discussion in the *American Economic Review*, LXII, May 1972.)

Thus modern Marxism has the triple task of ascertaining the phenomena of the living cycle, of finding the fundamental reason for the relative post-war prosperity in other long-run forces and of examining whether capitalism will prove viable without far-reaching structural transformations, or whether it requires a systematic overhaul from top to bottom.

Part IV
Marx and Keynes

19 The Analogies between Marx and Keynes

Keynesians were quick to discover numerous analogies between the initiator of neo-capitalist demand management, John Maynard Keynes, and Karl Marx.

Superficially, these analogies appear striking. Both saw capitalism as moribund, infected by endogenous mortal diseases; both saw in concentration 'the end of *laissez-faire*'; both recognised that slumps and mass unemployment menaced the very existence of the system; both assume that the danger exists for capitalism of long-run stagnation, which would be accompanied by a fall in the rate of profit and of the marginal efficiency of capital; and both saw the bogey of insufficient global demand.

In his history of macroeconomic analysis (1953), Antoine comments (p. 74): 'Marx understood very well what we call today the principle of effective demand, according to which there is a circular relationship between income and production, at a macroscopic level. . . .' For both Marx and Keynes investment was the decisive lever of the cycle, which Marx thought would show increasing swings, while Keynes feared that the swings might intensify and induce long-run stagnation.

THE MINIMUM RATE OF PROFIT, ALIAS 'LIQUIDITY TRAP'

The first analogy between the two authors may be seen in their analysis of the rate of profit, the shrinkage of which heralds for them the outbreak of recession.

Marx tried to prove that Say's Law was absurd, because the circular flow money – commodity – money might break at the last stage, which would mean that liquid means would be hoarded. Marx spoke here of 'treasures' and referred to a slowdown of the velocity of circulation of money. Here is the analogy with Keynes's 'liquidity trap', which in effect furnishes a logical reason why the economy may continue to stagnate at the bottom of a depression, and which foreshadows a possible paralysis of monetary policy. Keynes says (1936; 1949, p. 207) that 'there is the possibility, for the reasons discussed above, that, after the rate of interest has fallen to a certain level, liquidity-preference may become virtually absolute, in the sense that almost everyone prefers cash to holding a debt which yields so low a rate of interest.' Patinkin concludes (1966, p. 349) that, if such a minimum level (of what Marx would have called the rate of profit) existed, monetary policy would be unable to stimulate business activity.

Thus we see from the very outset a curious identity of views. Marx thought in effect that the goad of profit might be lacking, and Keynes saw the same possibility if the minimum rate were reached. In the view of both, private investment would break down, and recession would set in.

A modern interpretation of Marx's business-cycle theory begins here. Eagly(1972, p. 534) starts from the postulate that there is a minimum rate of profit which is still acceptable. Below it, capitalists stop net investment, consuming (or hoarding) their surplus value. Eagly thinks that Marx's endogenous cycle exists in spite of Say's Law.

This may be doubted, for then the abrupt cessation of investment would hit only investment-goods industries, and a sectoral crisis could affect the entire economy only if capitalists increase their consumption insufficiently, or after a lag. If so, we should encounter a typical disproportionality. It seems, however, that Eagly believes that a shift in demand from investment to consumption goods might be possible, thus averting a recession. For Marx, it is not a question of flexibility in restructuring demand, for he sees a partial destruction of purchasing power through hoarding or through a slowing-down of velocity of circulation of money.

In Keynes's language, this would mean that entrepreneurs want to hold more cash because investment in assets is not interesting. This would lead to a slow-down or decline in the credit-creating activities of banks. A lowering of bank rate would be of no avail, because 'the horses will not drink', i.e. entrepreneurs do not wish to become more indebted.

Patinkin says (1966, p. 351): 'No matter how large the value of their initial money holdings, individuals will never agree to hold bonds at a rate of interest below r_1 [the minimum rate of interest]. At such low levels, they will always prefer to hold money instead'

This boils down to hoarding. Incidentally, if no one wants to become indebted and everyone tries to accumulate liquid assets, it is only natural that the state should be the debtor in the last resort. This is a conclusion which Keynes (and Stützel) drew but which was unknown to Marx. Modern Marxists such as Mattick (1969, p. 21) wholeheartedly recognise such affinities and assert that Marx anticipated Keynes's criticism of neo-classical theory as well as the decline in capital formation.

As Joan Robinson points out, however (1948; 1968, p. 115) there is no trace in Keynes's work of Marx's 'organic composition of capital', of a rising capital–output ratio or of increasing depreciation at the macro-economic level, for the simple reason that Keynes dealt with the short run, ignoring also the problems of the bias of technical progress.

At best, one might quote Keynes's decreasing marginal efficiency of capital. This concerns expectations, which react on the propensity to invest. The capacity problem, which is important for Marx, does not reappear prior to Harrod and Domar.

Incidentally, Marx was not so sceptical as some of Keynes's disciples about the ability of capitalism to escape from the 'liquidity trap'. He saw in the crisis an equilibrating process from which capitalism emerged like the phoenix from the ashes, with slightly singed feathers. One might perhaps be inclined to consider a secular version of the Marxian theory of the tendency of the rate of profit to fall as a stagnation theory. Kurihara compares this (1956, p. 55) to Ricardo's and Keynes's ideas, but seems wrongly to attribute to Keynes the assumption of the rise of long-run over-capacity.

Schumpeter thought that Marx and Keynes developed different 'theories of collapse', but agreed (1946, p. 512) that both believed in an inherent instability of capitalism, for 'in both theories, the breakdown is motivated by causes inherent to the working of the economic regime, not by factors external to it'.

Joan Robinson confirms this in saying (1949, p. 67) that Keynes had shown that in *laissez-faire* there is no equilibrating mechanism securing full employment, nor even wage adjustment. Keynes showed that it was a fallacy of composition to believe that, if one worker could get employment by accepting a lower wage, all workers could do so as a body. Marx also distinguishes between individual and collective wage situations by emphasising the class character of wage-fixing.

But neither of the two authors, and this is a negative similarity, had a clear-cut formula for determining the distribution of income. For Marx,

> the rate of exploitation, at any moment, is determined by the difference between real wages and total output. But, apart from a general presumption that the rate of exploitation will increase with increasing productivity of labour, there is no law which governs its movement. The academic theory . . . is in no better case. If there is any law governing the distribution of income between classes, it still remains to be discovered. (Ibid., p. 34.)

Joan Robinson's scepticism was perhaps not quite justified. Other neo-Keynesians, such as Kaldor, were to offer such a theory, though harking back to the Marxist pre-Keynesian Kalecki, for whom investment is the agent and wages are a residual.

Incidentally, in volume II of *Capital* Marx came very near to such an interpretation in stating that the capitalists themselves throw into circulation the money that they get out of it as profits. A contrast remains: for Keynes and his followers wages are the residual, for Marx it is profits.

Furthermore, for Marx there is an upper limit to wages, in a sort of minimum profit, at which level Charasov's 'investment strike' (1910) begins. Keynes, likewise, admits that there is a ceiling for wages. At the same time, however, there seems to be a ceiling for investment, compatible with a minimum of paid-out dividends.

THE WORLD ECONOMY AS A STIMULANT

Finally, one may see an analogy in the fact that in his theory of the tendency of the rate of profit to fall Marx referred to foreign trade as a 'counteracting' force. This is paralleled in the Keynesian system by the foreign-trade multiplier, which stimulates business activity and holds an autonomous role for employment. In countries whose currency is under-valued for some length of time, the manipulation of the exchange rate is actually a kind of employment therapy. Because it would mean losing this policy instrument, such countries are not in favour of flexible exchange rates (although these would contribute towards an elimination of world disequilibria), despite the fact that such countries suffer, as it were, a kind of under-consumption, because they sell their goods too cheaply abroad.

Marx sees in early capitalism 'original accumulation' based on robbery and conquest. Here is another analogy. In the *Treatise on Money*, Keynes calculated that Sir Francis Drake's spoils from piracy would at Eliz-abethan compound rates of interest have amounted by the 1920s to approximately Britain's national wealth at the time.

Analogies between Keynes and Marx culminate in the former's pragmatic–curative approach, as Mattick stresses (1969, p. 130): 'In the Keynesian formulation, Marx's findings are silently accepted and simul-taneously "remedied" by conscious interventions in the market mech-anism.' Underlying this pragmatism, however, is Keynes's assumption that capitalism might really collapse if his therapy were not applied.

FORMAL ANALOGIES

Klein pointed out that the formal analogies between Keynes and Marx would have gone further if Keynes's analysis had been expressed entirely in observable aggregates, as had Marx's. Klein regrets that Keynes instead derived all his important results from schedules of economic behaviour. Nevertheless, he had at least mentioned some historical trends, and here his results dovetail with Marx's ideas.

Klein goes so far as to assert (1947; 1968, p. 167) that a simple version of Keynesian theory, in which the quantity of money and the rate of interest do not appear as variables, is a special case of the Marxian model, for investment can be considered as a function of the capital stock and of income, and consumption as a function of income. In short-run analysis,

Keynes took the capital stock as given. Klein believes that the Marxian system offers more information: it indicates demand for consumption and investment goods and employment, while Keynes does not indicate the latter.

20 The Contrasts between Marx and Keynes

It is true that Keynes himself did not acknowledge these analogies or even want to consider them. For him, *Capital* was 'an obsolete, uninteresting and incomprehensible textbook'! He banished it to the economic underworld, together with Major Douglas and Silvio Gesell (the former Munich Soviet minister!), whose 'dwindling money' theory he praised, anticipating a better future for his doctrines than for Marxism. Nevertheless, he deigned to take a leaf out of Marx's book by dubbing his (self-styled) adversaries, from Ricardo and Mill to Marshall and Pigou, 'the classics'. There are very few passages in which Keynes discusses Marx's theses seriously. He complains, for instance, that Marx built up his theories on an acceptance of the classical hypothesis. Marx's rejection of Say shows that this is not quite true. Keynes also rebuked him for assuming 'unbridled competition', instead of its disappearance, overlooking the numerous elements of imperfect competition in Marx's work and his concentration theory. (Keynes, 1936; 1949, pp. 32, 355.)

The neo-Keynesians did not follow their master in under-estimating Marx. On the contrary, they tried to establish certain links, but they could not overlook numerous contrasts or the different basic approach. Keynes considers capitalism defective but curable and wants to preserve it; for Marx, the defects are the justification for overturning it and the lever with which to do so.

DICHOTOMY IN MONETARY POLICY

The contrasts are most sharply apparent in the monetary sector. As Patinkin says (1966, p. 349), Keynes did not accord a prominent position to his 'liquidity trap', but admitted (1936; 1949, p. 207) that the monetary authorities would lose control if it ever existed. Patinkin (1966, p. 354) thinks such an event improbable, but foresees dire consequences if ever this nightmare is realised, for the government (being obliged to borrow) would tend to become the sole debtor, upsetting the liberal creed of minimum intervention.

In other words, if the liquidity trap existed, monetary policy would be ineffective, and without an institutional transformation (the nationalisation of investment?), there would be hardly any hope of a recovery. Marx, in his criticism of Proudhon's disciple Darimon, declared from the outset that monetary policy would not succeed. Darimon completely identifies

> *monetary turnover with credit* , which is economically wrong . . . . the bank is made to share Darimon's illusion that its monopoly really allows it to regulate credit. In fact the power of the bank begins only where the private 'discounters' stop, hence at a moment when its power is already extraordinarily limited. . . . In order to secure for itself a share, and a growing share, of the discount business during the periods of easiness on the money market, the Bank of England was constantly forced to reduce its rates not only to the level adopted by the private bankers but often below it. [Here he comes very near to the 'minimum rate of interest' notion!] Its 'regulation of credit' is thus to be taken with a grain of salt; Darimon, however, makes his superstitious faith in its absolute control of the money market and of credit into his point of departure.
>
> (*Grundrisse*, pp. 123-4.)

We must not forget that Marx wrote at the beginning of the Free Trade era!

Modern authors – for instance, Friedman, and in Germany Pohl and Blochowitz – view equally sceptically the chances of central banks exercising effective control under conditions of free trade and fixed exchange rates. Blochowitz says that 'under convertibility and fixed exchange rates, bank rate policy which permits differences between internal and foreign interest rates cannot succeed'; and Pohl says, in even more drastic terms: 'In the future . . . it will be possible for the bank rate and liquidity policy of the central bank to be solely or almost solely a balance of payments policy and no longer a cyclical or price policy . . . .' (Zeitel and Pahlke, 1962, pp. 101, 121.)

PHYSICIAN VERSUS GRAVEDIGGER

Thus, at the very outset, the dominant contrast between Keynesians and Marxists appears. The latter are convinced that the evils of capitalism and above all the business cycle cannot be overcome by monetary policy. Many Keynesians see in it at least an important instrument, although they and Keynes put much more emphasis on fiscal policy.

The fundamental contrast between the two groups remains, as Klein has expressed it (1965, p. 131), that Marx analyses why capitalism will not and cannot work, and Keynes tries to show why it sometimes does not work, but argues that it can be made workable.

This is the contrast between the gravedigger and the physician, which may be partly explained by the prominence of the class struggle in Marx's system. Keynes undoubtedly underrated the struggle for higher wages by assuming that labour was subject to a 'money illusion'. This shows a lack of realism. Marx realistically saw that workers fight for higher real wages, if not for a higher share in the national income, and he even thought that, at the top of the boom, they temporarily obtained both. Marx saw in trade unions a sort of institutionalised class struggle, an embryonic revolution which, however, might be stopped once technical progress had replenished the 'industrial reserve army'.

A NEW VERSION OF THE 'IRON LAW OF WAGES' IN KEYNES?

Kaldor stresses (1957, pp. 265–6) that Marx saw in the 'industrial reserve army' and the quest for profits, which replenishes the reserve *via* rationalisation, a basic contradiction in capitalism. The quest for profits destroys the profit system, for increasing investment makes the reserve army disappear, wages rise and profits fall, and the ensuing recession lasts until the reserve is re-established. The reserve army maintains profits. Without it, they might even disappear altogether.

This interpretation of Marx is actually popular with certain young Marxist economists, such as Glyn and Sutcliffe, who think (1972) that capitalism might be ground to pieces between the millstones of over-employment and trade-union pressure. Kaldor points out that Keynes had a different view. Rising money wages are not identical with rising real wages and, therefore, need not threaten real profits. Price rises may exceed wage rises. There must be a distribution of the social product which leads to equilibrium between aggregate demand and aggregate supply.

Even if profits suffer, capitalists can raise their share by investing, and Kaldor repeats (1955–6; 1968, pp. 371–2) Kalecki's saying, 'capitalists earn what they spend, and workers spend what they earn . . . given the wage-earners' and the capitalists' propensities to save, the share of profits in income depends simply on the rate of investment to output.'

He assumes that this investment is financed by bank credit. In the meantime, however, Kalecki himself had had qualms (1949–50), as Robertson points out (1954; 1956, p. 244): 'Mr Kalecki, than whose no brow is higher, had been struck by this same thought that the induced saving might walk away and generate investment on its own'.

Kalecki indeed declares (1949–50) that high income generates high saving, which stimulates investment without indebtedness. Otherwise, an inflationary process might be unavoidable, for it is unlikely that labour would accept 'forced saving', *via* lower real wages and bank credit, that benefits only profits and investment. In times when labour has become inflation-conscious and pays attention to the price index and real wages, the Marxian analysis appears to be much more realistic than the

Keynesian, and it is accepted even in employers' circles.

The Keynesian concept recognises profits as the primary factor and wages as a residual, suggesting that wages would tend to be kept down in real terms, almost as in Lassalle's 'iron law of wages'. Marx and modern employers, however (though generally implacable adversaries), believe that wage rises keep pace with inflationary movements.

CONTRASTS IN INTEREST THEORY

In practical economics, Marxism sometimes gets the upper hand over Keynesianism, as for instance in interest theory, where Mattick suggests (1969, p. 21) that Keynesian monetary theory overrates the rate of interest: 'A decade of falling interest rates after 1929 did not affect investment decisions seriously. . . . It was not the point of view of Keynes but that of Marx which found its verification . . . .' Mattick thus joins Joan Robinson (1949, p. 70) in thinking that Marx was right to neglect the rate of interest.

On the other hand, Marx went too far in neglecting the rate of interest at the microeconomic level, as we pointed out in discussing the depreciation problem. At the macroeconomic level, Joan Robinson suggests (ibid., p. 28) that, 'when the most obvious needs have been met, it might be convenient to take a leaf out of the capitalist book, and require the socialist enterprises to earn a rate of interest on all capital allotted to them, so as to insure that trivial investment demands of one are not pressed before more urgent demands of another'.

In his revival of classical value theory, Sraffa reintroduces the rate of interest *via* the external rate of profit, for purposes of calculation, in his system of 'dated labour'.

THE 'TROIKA' MARSHALL–KEYNES–MARX: APOLOGIA, THERAPY, APOCALYPSE AND REVERSAL

In an essay comparing Marshall and Keynes with Marx, Joan Robinson contrasts (1955; 1960, II, pp. 1 ff.) their intentions and achievements. Marx represents revolution, Marshall complacency and Keynes disillusioned defence. Marx wants to understand capitalism to help to destroy it, being convinced that it will destroy itself. Marshall wants to make it acceptable and defends it in spite of its shortcomings, while Keynes sees deep faults and looks nevertheless for remedies. Marx's frugal capitalists favour accumulation and increase productivity, preventing workers from consuming more, and this shows capitalism's strong side. Marshall shows that inequality in consumption is necessary for saving, an expensive way of doing the job, which gives rise to the idea that it would be cheaper to expropriate the capitalists. Keynes believes that capitalism will lead to instability, stagnation and unemployment, and he thus justifies interventionism, compensatory therapy and state investment, although he saw a danger that this might discourage private investment. Thus Keynesianism may lead to the overthrow of private rationality, upon which the system's superiority seemed to rest, and ultimately pave the way for Marx's objective of handing over all investment to society.

FORMAL CONTRASTS

In spite of Keynes's attack on the 'classics', Klein asserts, (1965, p. 131) that Keynes inherited their methodology, while Marx was unorthodox. This may seem to be surprising, since Marx took over their value analysis.

In a formal analysis, Tsuru has tried to show (Sweezy, 1942, pp. 372-3) that Marx's $v + s$ does not correspond to Keynes's net national income. He asserts that Keynes's national income, which consists of gross turnover (A) minus user cost (V) would correspond to Marx's $v + s$ plus another item, *sav* (surplus value invested in variable capital). Bettelheim has proved (1948, p. 205) that Tsuru was misled by overlapping period analysis; *sav* is not added until the next period and is then contained in v.

It must be admitted that we here encounter the weaknesses of value theory when combined with period analysis, because the accumulated surplus value is transformed into consumption or investment in the next period. In a later publication (Ed. Kurihara, 1955), Tsuru recognises (p. 338) that Keynes's abstractions contain direct reality, which Marx approaches only successively, but this means that Keynes's approach remains static, while Marx's is dynamic.

DIVERGENCIES IN THE NOTION OF INVESTMENT

Tsuru points out (Sweezy, 1942, p. 372) another great divergence. For Keynes investment is the difference between (net) fixed assets and stocks at the beginning and the value of means of production at the end of the period, while for Marx investment consists of accumulated surplus value spent on additional assets and consumption goods in the next period. Tsuru does not, however, make it clear that, while Keynes considers stocks, i.e. physical assets expressed in monetary units, Marx reasons in flows, expressed in 'socially necessary' labour time. For him, this labour time has been spent in phase 1, and is transformed into new assets, raw materials and accumulated consumption goods in phase 2. He says: 'Surplus value is convertible into capital solely because the surplus product, whose value it is, already comprises the material elements of new capital' (*Capital*, 1 ch. 24, p. 545). In fact, he seems to imagine that capitalists hoard these commodities in phase 1 before selling them to each other and to their workers in phase 2, thereby transforming them into income.

Utta Gruber analyses in detail the problem raised by Tsuru and Bettelheim, the controversy between whom contained two elements: first, the delimitation of periods and, secondly, the 'inclusion of the labour force in the available capital and thus of additional labour for net investment and therefore for the national income'. Utta Gruber thinks that Marx solved the problem of periods by considering them as telescoping circuits, the first one leading like a spiral over into the next one. She refers to Marx's statement (*Capital*, II, ch. 4, p. 104): 'In a constantly revolving circle every point is simultaneously a point of departure and a point of return.' She concludes that Marx pointedly distinguishes between saving and investment. (Gruber, 1961, pp. 322, 325, 329.) If this is true, Marx's view would avoid Keynes's troublesome insistence on their identity and would anticipate Robertson's more realistic terminology.

Marx, however, encounters the difficulty that what appears as surplus value in the first period is spent in the second period on consumption goods (*sav*) and investment goods (*sac*); this surplus value is 'created' in the first period, but it is not until the second that it is 'realised' i.e. transformed into money. Undoubtedly, a contradiction appears here in Marx's reasoning, for the surplus value is crystallised labour value spent in the first period and taking the form of concrete stocks, which in turn will enter the process of consumption in the next period. Utta Gruber assumes that 'net investment and consumption of capitalists . . . is financed by credit'.

What, according to her, is essential in Marx's analysis is that 'the notion of investment . . . includes . . . investment in variable capital. An increase in stocks is not in every case considered to be an investment.' The latter point may be seen to represent an improvement upon Keynes, for Marx 'does not count involuntary increases in stocks as investment'. This facilitates business-cycle analysis, for involuntary stockbuilding leads to recession and inventory cycles. Utta Gruber sees in this the superiority of Marx's terminology:

> What is important for investment is not stockbuilding as such, but the fact that investment decisions have been taken. That Marx recognised this clearly means that his investment notion is not so antiquated as it seems to be at first sight, but, on the contrary, may provide fertile impulses for modern investment theory. (Ibid., pp. 331–2.)

That Marx considered wage payments for additional workers to be an investment may be explained by the fact that this is based on a renunciation of consumption by capitalists. It must be asked whether the workers spend this money on goods other than those that capitalists would have consumed. If so, wage payments may lead to new net investment and stockbuilding, while other stocks may prove redundant.

Marx's reasoning is tantamount to saying that the productive potential of society is increased by the mobilisation of new labour, i.e. 'human investment'. This must be true if this labour comes from abroad or from pools of unused manpower. Modern theory is in any case inclined to consider the training and education of labour as 'investment in men', which would correspond to Marx's ideas. Thus the mass of workers becomes a kind of 'capital stock', which, in capitalist logic, must give rise to interest.

Utta Gruber states (ibid., pp. 339–40) that Marx's notion of investment corresponds to its dual nature, the employment effect and the capacity effect, as Tsuru had already emphasised (1955, pp. 338, 342). Marx's notion is, however, more differentiated, and it is strange that none of the participants in the debate recognised this. Strictly speaking, net national income in Marx's extended reproduction equals $v + s + sav + sac$, because inventories of consumption and investment goods are built up in the first period; both of these represent 'intended' investment, but only *sac* represents investment in the Keynesian sense, because *sav* enters into consumption. *sac* then signifies an increase in the capital stock, which *sav* is not, for even Marx does not consider 'human investment' as giving rise to a capital stock. Here are the seeds of Domar's growth analysis, which takes into account capacity changes and effects, while Keynes's investment notion was primarily related to multiplier effects in short-term analysis.

The Marxian instruments seem, therefore, to be better adapted to growth analysis and, for that matter, even to development economics, for which, as Leibenstein has pointed out (1957, p. 119), Keynesian definitions do not distinguish the essential elements.

Bronfenbrenner (1967, p. 625) called Marx a 'synthesiser' in economics who combined, like Keynes, tattered pieces to make up a whole system which was more than the sum of its parts. Nevertheless, between the two authors fundamental, formal contrasts persist, which Kurihara has characterised (1956, p. 55) as the opposition of Marx's 'organicistic' approach, which sees capitalism as an organic whole, and Keynes 'mechanistic' equilibrium analysis, which in modern times has led to what has been dubbed 'hydraulic Keynesianism'. These apparently methodological divergencies hide a profound antagonism. Marx saw capitalism as a living and aging body which gives birth to a new society, while Keynes saw it as an imperfect machine breaking down occasionally, but which could be repaired and survive indefinitely.

THE QUINTESSENCE OF KEYNESIANISM: SHORT-TERM ESCAPISM?

Thus the divergence lies not in the formal apparatus, but in Keynes's desire to act as a physician and Marx's desire to dig capitalism's grave. Keynes leaves out the class problem, but for Marx this provides the clue. The 'industrial reserve army' and the wage struggle are stepping-stones to the transformation of society, and in this sense distribution theory is relevant for Marx. It was not for nothing that Samuelson, when asked what distinguishes Marxism and is not to be found in other textbooks, declared: 'The class struggle' (Hymer and Roosevelt, 1972, p. 646).

The deepest contrast between the two systems is to be found in their judgement on the adaptability of capitalism. Can it be transformed from a society based upon dynamic irregularity and variability into one in which exploitation is kept well enough in check to keep those who are exploited happy?

The alternative has been formulated by Vigor, who reminds us (1969, p. 171) that, in the wake of the Second World War, governments felt obliged and were able to abolish the 'boom–slump' cycle and mass unemployment. Marx might argue that stop–go policy is a form of suppressed cycle, and he might point out that the rift between capitalists and workers has deepened.

Dörge states (1964, p. 199) that the theory of increasing poverty, which we have seen to be a misinterpretation, was superseded by the problem of wage earners' falling share *per capita* in the social product. This is a measure for which the Marxian term the 'rate of exploitation' would be a good terminological formula, the more so as no fixed term has been found for it as yet.

Marx and Keynes tackle distribution quite differently. For Marx, class antagonism is reborn again and again through capitalist dynamics, which lead capitalists to create finance by having recourse to banks, so as to finance investment and push up profits. Thus, inequality of income is immanent in capitalism in a diabolically inevitable way, even where capitalists do not consume their income but reinvest it, for, the faster the system grows, the more unequal will income distribution become. Tugan-Baranowsky's nightmare of investment for investment's sake, while consumption is throttled, may be inherent in the most prosperous capitalist societies.

On the other hand, for Keynes any attempt to reduce inequality through government intervention has a double purpose. First, this represents a sort of safety net below which production cannot fall, while, secondly, overheating and therefore disproportionality crises are avoided, and along with them mass unemployment and concomitant gross disparities of income. Thus, redistribution remains a keynote for Keynesians.

Curiously enough, Marx finds an ally in Pareto, who affirmed that the inequality coefficient remains secularly unchanged, in spite of all efforts.

21 Neo-Keynesian Interpretations

The neo-Keynesian with the closest affinity to Marx is, without doubt, Joan Robinson. The French Jesuit economist Calvez (1956, p. 642) and recently Cuyvers (1978) classified her outright as a neo-Marxist.

JOAN ROBINSON'S IMPERFECT MARXISM

For Joan Robinson, Marx's analysis is fundamentally macroeconomic. Thus she consistently rejects his microeconomic peculiarities, especially his value theory, which she considers a mystification and as offering only a very crude approach to modern price theory. (Robinson, 1949, p. 22, and 1966.)

She thinks that Marx was fully conscious that the labour theory of value would never suffice for the purpose and that it is inapplicable to the Soviet economy, because it will not lead to a rational allocation of scarce resources. On the other hand, 'if capitalists have to be bribed to keep their capital intact, they ought rather to be expropriated'. Joan Robinson rejects the orthodox idea that interest and profit are indispensable to bring forth capital as its 'supply price'. According to Keynes, 'animal spirits' would suffice to supply capital, even at a low rate; the level that would suffice is determined by conventional notions. Capitalism, however, depends on continuing accumulation and could not survive long periods of disinvestment, such as in the 1930s. Joan Robinson does not rely on orthodox equilibrium theory: 'The man on the bicycle is the moving long-period position of equilibrium. The short-period situation follows the path of the dog running after him. But the resources of mathematics fail us if the dog is liable to bite through the tyres of the bicycle when the man slows down his pace.' This, she thinks, is exactly what Marx foresaw. (Robinson, 1949, pp. 17, 21, 28, 56, 60–1.)

On the other hand, she does not accept Marx's 'law' of the tendency of the rate of profit to fall, partly because she erroneously thinks that Marx thought that real wages must remain constant. She sees this law partly as a business-cycle phenomenon, for she interprets the 'organic composition' as denoting the marginal capital–output ratio. Here she draws a parallel with Kalecki's business-cycle analysis, which foresees a lower degree of capital utilisation, because monopolistic firms reach Chamberlin's 'tangential situation'. This argument was to be used later by Fellner in his reply to Samuelson's criticism. Joan Robinson recognises a certain affinity between Marx's theories and the theory of imperfect competition, but she does not see the analogy with the law of the falling rate of profit. At the same time, she thinks that Marx did not succeed in combining his law with the notion of 'effective demand', though she thinks his term 'realisation of surplus value' comes near to filling this gap. (Ibid., pp. 36–42.)

Marx refutes Say's Law by referring to the possibility of hoarding. Joan Robinson analyses his reproduction schemes in her introduction to the English edition of Rosa Luxemburg's *Accumulation of Capital* and points out that he saw the possibilities of crises even under conditions of simple reproduction, and the key to fluctuations in investment, and that, while he rejected a monetary explanation of crises, he anticipated the foreign-trade multiplier. Joan Robinson thinks that Marx, who rejected a crude theory of under-consumption (which could be cured through redistribution!) saw the ultimate cause of crises in a disequilibrium of consumption and production. He developed no straightforward business-cycle theory, but gave at least some clues to it, emphasising capitalism's fundamental instability. His reproduction theory was meant to show not the possibility of steady growth, but, on the contrary, the precariousness of such growth, although his sketches are more or less scattered notes. (Ibid., pp. 43–9, 64–8, 71–2.)

Long-run dynamic analysis is Marx's primary objective, and this field is still largely untilled. The laws of motion of capitalism still remain to be discovered, and hope of progress resides in the use of academic methods to solve these problems (ibid., p. 95). Some socialist authors, such as Guihéneuf and Rosdolsky, are antipathetic to Joan Robinson's analysis just because of her rejection of Marxist methodology; others would rather claim her for Marxism.

At any rate, Marxists would be well advised to accept the intellectual armoury of the English Cambridge School as an ally against neo-classical harmony theories. Joan Robinson's short *Essay on Marxian Economics* is certainly the most profound analysis of the subject. She thinks, as Kalecki did, that 'Marx's theory, or at any rate some theory on the questions which Marx discussed, is as much required to supplement Keynes as Keynes's theory is to supplement Marx' (ibid., pp. 80–1).

KLEIN'S INTERPRETATION OF THE 'KEYNESIAN REVOLUTION'

Klein not only wrote a book on the 'Keynesian revolution' but also offered an evaluation of the Marxian system as an independent achievement. He drew analogies in stagnation theory, but for him 'the primary advantage of the Marxian model is that it provides more information than does the Keynesian system' – namely, on the conditions of employment.

Klein emphasises (1947; 1968, pp. 154, 167–8) that Marx based his analysis of effective demand on the behaviour not of individuals but of classes. Here he joins Joan Robinson in suggesting that trade-union power may just have counterbalanced increasing exploitation. When Joan Robinson quotes the alternative theory that a secular increase in the degree of monopoly may have been counteracted by improving terms of trade for raw materials as an 'academic theory', she forgets that it was also Kalecki's explanation of the 'mystery of the constant relative shares'. In any case, both explanations seem to her (1949, pp. 80–1) 'somewhat lame'.

Klein calls any attempt to cure unemployment by a redistribution of income from profits to wages 'old-fashioned' and reminds us that Marx emphasised cost aspects and did not consider that redistribution would solve business-cycle problems – especially as it was not clear what would happen to the marginal propensity to save. Here Keynesian reformers encounter Marxist incredulity. (Klein, 1947; 1968, pp. 171–5.)

Klein stresses the importance of the reproduction schemes and thinks that business cycles can be introduced into the models, if capitalist consumption in department II is considered a function of surplus value. He joins Rosa Luxemburg in talking of the passive investment reaction of the capitalists in II. He builds a model which is meant to extend Marx's analysis and to show the complexity of the equilibrium growth conditions, although he starts from the erroneous assumption that Marx relies on a subsistence wage level. (Ibid., pp. 160–1, 168.)

KALDOR AS THE FALLEN ANGEL OF MARXISM?

Kaldor's standpoint is much more varied. In various passages in his numerous articles on growth and business cycles, he has judged Marx correctly, but there are a number of misinterpretations. On the whole, G. L. Bach is right in advising the left (Hymer and Roosevelt, 1972, p. 641) to look for stimuli in the work of neo-Keynesians, among whom Kaldor and Balogh (the 'Hungarian twins') hold important positions; Kaldor (1954) spoke positively of Marx's accumulation theory and confirmed that Marx, though a disciple of the classical economists, saw profits as the main source of investment – a position contrary to that of Ricardo. Kaldor also anticipated the as yet unknown *Grundrisse* by assuming that Marx would consider the growth of scientific knowledge the most important independent variable in economic growth. Elsewhere (1957a, p. 263), he emphasises his belief as a Western socialist that mankind could control the endogenous forces of society in the same way as science is able to control the forces of nature.

Incidentally, Kaldor (1954) agrees with Marx that the business cycle is not just a by-product of growth, as it might occur in a stationary system. For him, it is the cycle that determines the growth trend, which means that one cannot neglect the cycle in growth theory. Kaldor does not wish to apply the 'echo principle' directly, but he gives an example of a replacement cycle by relating the length and amplitude of boom and depression periods to the ratio of investment industry capacity to the normal depreciation of the capital stock.

Kaldor is not immune from some of the current misunderstandings. For instance, he thinks Marx held a theory of increasing poverty and did not believe in the growth of real wages. In contrast to Marx, he believes that capitalism could be free from cycles and growing concentration, but Heilbroner has questioned (1955, p. 136) whether this would still be capitalism. What is fascinating is Kaldor's brief summary (1957a, pp. 265–6) of Marx's theories: Wages are determined by the reproduction cost of labour and profit is a residual, being the difference between production and consumption per head. Labour supply always exceeds the demand for it, although the 'industrial reserve army' may temporarily disappear. The attempt to increase profits may destroy the basis of the profit system, for growing accumulation will exhaust the reserve army and make profits fall. This leads to a crisis, which restores profits through the restoration of the reserve army.

This description of classical Marxian theory agrees with modern conservative analyses and neo-Marxist interpretations, which see trade-union wage pressure as the lever for a new theory of 'collapse'. (Glyn and Sutcliffe, 1972, pp. 50ff.)

KALDOR'S AFFINITIES WITH KALECKI

Kaldor thinks that one of Keynes's chief merits lies in emphasising that, while money wages are directly determined by the availability of labour, real wages are determined by macroeconomic demand and the supply of goods. Capitalists can reduce their demand for investment goods. Their expenditure is not related to their income, while that of workers is.

Kalecki's and Kaldor's slogan that 'capitalists earn what they spend, while workers spend what they earn' is essentially the idea in volume II of *Capital* where Marx concludes that capitalists themselves throw into circulation the money which makes up their profits. Kaldor is not quite conscious of this analogy, otherwise he would not have tried to draw a contrast on this point.

Nowadays Keynes's 'money illusion' no longer exists in trade union circles, for they reason in terms of real wages. Kaldor and Keynes believe that an optimum distribution of income would tend to prevail. If wages rise above an equilibrium level, prices rise and the real share of wages falls, and *vice versa*. Full employment is to be based on an equilibrium relation between prices and wages. The inflationary tendencies of the 1970s have certainly upset any belief in the existence of a self-equilibrating process in this area. Marx's analysis, which ignores price movements and runs in terms of social tension, seems to be nearer to reality. In his article published in *Économie Appliquée* (1957a), Kaldor says (pp. 267, 272) that it is a

> normal feature of the capitalist system that capacity increases faster than production – which must sooner or later . . . lead to an interruption of the investment process. This is what I consider the main reason why progress proceeds by fits and starts – in cyclical fluctuations and successive upswings and depressions in capitalist societies . . . .

He did not perceive that this periodic reappearance of over-capacity resembles Marx's theory of a periodic relative increase in the ratio of constant capital to value added.

Kaldor erroneously believes that Marx thought wages would always remain at the subsistence level, and states in his defence that this might be true for early capitalism. In that period, capital productivity would have been low, and the capital–output ratio would have risen. As soon as the capital stock reaches a certain level, the propensity to invest determines the share of profits. Real wages grow in proportion to productivity, and distribution shares remain constant. (Kaldor, 1957b, p. 619.)

Kaldor's weakness is that he always appeals to the facts, and this being so he must also accept their evidence. The constancy of relative shares seems to be typical of the nineteenth century, but Kaldor claimed (1957a, pp. 264, 274) that it should apply to the later stages of capitalism. In fact, however, during the twentieth century the share of wages has started to grow. In view of these misunderstandings, which make him appear as a fallen angel of Marxism, showing reverence and dissension at the same time, Kaldor's interpretation is not entirely satisfactory.

NEO-KEYNESIAN AFFINITIES AND AVERSIONS

Certain basic characteristics seem to be common to all neo-Keynesians. They esteem Marx's early rebuttal of Say's Law, his anticipation of the notion of effective demand, and his opposition to the quantity theory. They recognise that Marx saw in investment the key to the business cycle and to technical progress, which was for him 'embodied' in accumulation. Here they see in Marx an ally against the neo-classicists, for whom technical progress is 'manna from heaven'.

Neo-Keynesians further recognise that Marx went beyond Keynes's short-period analysis, refused to recognise a 'supply price' for capital, and saw the possibility of business cycles in the stationary state, and not as a by-product of growth. On the other hand, the neo-Keynesians reject Marx's value theory as a mystification and attribute to him, mostly through misunderstanding or as a result of doubtful interpretation, a certain number of (mostly factual) errors, such as a subsistence theory of wages and a theory of increasing poverty.

Neo-Keynesians go beyond Marx's 'real' cycle theory in attributing great importance to monetary factors, but admit that it was his chief purpose to discover the inner workings of capitalist growth and instability.

Joan Robinson once remarked (1937, pp. 254-5) that 'the Marxist rightly distrusts the intellectual', because 'a belief in scientific truth is enervating' and 'an untenable belief that leads to a successful revolution is to be preferred to a correct argument that allows a fetid society to rot undisturbed'. She was thus prepared to forgive Marx's 'errors' and thought that 'a belief in Marxism leads to wished-for results'. This, however, was not Marx's attitude, for he did not believe in the well-foundedness of a revolution of a 'voluntarist' kind, but believed in a transformation that arose from the logic of historical development.

22 Post-Keynesian Interpretations

Post-Keynesians share some of the misinterpretations usually found among neo-Keynesians. Thus Fellner seems to attribute to Marx the theories of the subsistence wage, of growing poverty, of chronic crises and a stagnation theory, although Marx steadfastly denied that there could be 'permanent crises'.

FELLNER'S CONSERVATIVE APPRECIATION OF MARX

Fellner, when in his discussion of the movements in the capital–output ratio (1958) he remarked (pp. 131–2) that Marx might be right in describing what might happen if investment became chronically unprofitable, took seriously the theory of the tendency of the rate of profit to fall. In an earlier article (1957, pp. 16ff.) he had interpreted Marx's theory to mean that relatively more capital may be required to produce the same quantity of natural resources or to feed the same number of workers, i.e. that 'a mechanism of automatic maladjustment' occurs. In other words, workers may not profit from technical progress, because it is labour-saving, and capitalists may not benefit, because it induces too high a rate of capital formation.

This thesis was opposed by Samuelson, who tried to prove (1957, p. 893) that either labour or capital or even both would have to benefit from technical progress. For a translation (prepared by the present author, unpublished) of his article of 1957, as yet unpublished, Fellner modified his argument in such a way that it became exclusively based on Chamberlin's 'tangential situation': If all firms under conditions of imperfect competition operate with low capacity utilisation, profits and wage rates may decline simultaneously – the nightmare of a semi-cartelised world in which price maintenance has collapsed.

In his analysis Fellner finally rejects the thesis of the falling rate of profit. It is not possible to explain the decline in the capital–output ratio by an increasing importance of wage-intensive sectors, for capital-intensity in the Western world has increased. Fellner sees, paradoxically, 'a mild, but not very consistent downtrend in rates of return on capital (before taxes)', because 'they had not been so labour-saving as to prevent a significant uptrend in real wage-rates'.

Fellner also thinks (1957, pp. 23–5) that capital-saving innovations and increases in capacity have led to a mild secular decline in the marginal productivity of capital: 'Temporary insufficiencies of the innovational process' could even lead to business cycles, although these have been mitigated, thanks perhaps to Marx's dire forebodings, reinforced by trade-union and egalitarian initiatives. Fellner closes on a very sceptical note, arguing that it is not safe to assume that these tendencies make it easier for Western economies to stay at or near full capacity. These social trends have tended to reduce not merely the amount of investment, but also the willingness to engage in it; they have reduced the propensity to save primarily by way of tax policies. While the egalitarian policies of recent decades presumably have diminished the degree of cyclical instability around the long-run path of the economy, economic analysis provides no basis for a similarly favourable or secure evaluation of the effect of these policies on the long-run path itself. In his book of 1960, Fellner showed (pp. 135–6) even more sympathy for what he sees as the Marxian thesis:

In the Marxian system, unfavorable trends in real wage-rates and unfavorable trends in profit rates, as jointly observable trends, presumably have this explanation: technological progress is exceedingly labor-saving, new capital formation proceeds at a very rapid rate, and monopoly power is rising significantly. Without the rise in 'monopoly power' one would have to conclude that technical progress would raise either the real wage-rate or the profit rate (unless the essence of the matter was that rents from natural resources are rising greatly, which was hardly the crucial Marxian assumption). In a system with enough monopoly power . . . built into it, the Marxian double downtrend could conceivably come through . . . .

The essential Marxian hypotheses have not so far been confirmed by facts. In the United States, and in other Western economies, technological-organizational improvements have been sufficiently plentiful to prevent a decline of output per unit of capital-input, even though the capital-input has been rising in a much higher proportion than the other factor inputs . . . .

SAMUELSON'S NEO-CLASSICAL QUALMS

The ill-conceived disqualification of Marx as a 'minor Ricardian' is to be found in Samuelson's lecture of 1961 (1966, II, pp. 1510–12). At that time, his general conclusion was that Marx's analysis of technical progress was right regarding the cycle, but wrong in the long run. He tauntingly asked how many Marxists really read the whole of *Capital*, but he himself can hardly have done so, otherwise his attack would not be built upon so many wrong premises. Hunt and Schwartz are right to point out (1972, p. 26) that his textbook falsifications are generally aimed at a dummy.

Samuelson's wrong premises appear clearly in his article (pp. 884ff.): While making the usual assumption that Marx believed in decreasing real wages, he states that Marx's production functions were based on fixed proportions and constant returns, and he dubbed him a 'Ricardo without decreasing returns'. Apparently he was thinking of the reproduction schemes of volume II of *Capital*. On the contrary, it is typical of Marx to refer again and again to increasing returns.

Most of these errors have been pointed out by Gottheil (1960, pp. 715ff.). Heertje (1972, pp. 33–45) extended the latter's criticism by pointing out that Marx emphasised increasing productivity in mass production, and that he assumed 'Harrod-neutral' technical progress. Heertje especially criticises Samuelson's contention that Marx assumed perfect competition, for the truth is that he assumed an oligopolistic environment, as Fellner recognised. Heertje admits that Marx assumed a specific (capital-using) kind of technical progress, but says that he was actually the first economist to see its all-embracing importance for development.

Samuelson must have felt that he had not done full justice to Marx, for he felt prompted to publish two studies on the transformation problem. In an essay (1971, pp. 399ff.), he described this as an 'algorithm' and compared value theory to the famous 'phlogiston', arguing that a theory of competitive pricing could do better.

Then, surprisingly, he developed (ibid., pp. 410, 418) an alternative theory of exploitation, based on a two-commodity comparison between maximum production and the subsistence level. Once profits are positive, exploitation appears as the graphical difference between what maximum production would be at zero profits and what can actually be produced with profits.

Lerner reacted violently (1972, pp. 50–1) against what he considered an upgrading of the labour theory of value, thus preventing sophisticated Marxists from divesting themselves of it. He quotes, among others, Soviet economists such as Lurje who try to get rid of this methodology.

BRONFENBRENNER'S OPEN QUESTIONS

Bronfenbrenner joined in (1973, pp. 58–69), summarised Mattick's, Wolfson's and Lerner's positions, and concluded from the last that Samuelson only wanted to stress once more that net investment or technical progress or both must necessarily increase profits or real wages or both.

Bronfenbrenner thinks that Samuelson's analysis leaves many open questions. Did Marx postulate that, for money prices as for labour values, the rate of surplus value was the same for different industries? Did he want to equate macroeconomically an adjusted sum of values and prices or of surplus values and profits? Was 'alienation' for him a consequence of capitalism or of commodity production? What mattered to him, the increasing subjective alienation or a decreasing share of wages? Did Marx measure the 'organic composition' by $c:v$ or $c:(c+v)$? (Actually, Peter thought of a further possibility $c:(v+s)$!) Did Marx consider the rate of accumulation to be given technically or institutionally? Is it influenced by relative prices or by rates of profit? Do 'hoarding crises' and 'realisation crises' coincide? Were they for Marx a lever for revolution or a stimulus, or was revolution triggered off subjectively, through the self-consciousness of the proletariat?

Bronfenbrenner's questions, which were a by-product of the debate over Samuelson's contributions, are certainly inherently more interesting than the latter.

BLAUG'S ATTEMPT AT A SOBER REAPPRAISAL

Blaug (1962; 1968, pp. 227ff.) in most cases grasps Marx's premises correctly, limiting himself to economics, which still leaves an 'enormous picture'. He fully understands that Marx saw the labour theory of value as relevant only if there are no divergencies in capital-intensity. The transformation problem, which is an attempt to approach reality, remains of an 'incredibly restrictive character'. Marx never thought that in real life the rate of surplus value would be the same in all industries.

Marx never intended to furnish a detailed theory of pricing. His distinction between 'paid' and 'unpaid' labour refers only to aggregate output. His 'value' is no exchange ratio, but a postulated ratio which appears if one credits each labourer with an average share in output. While admitting that Marx's works teem with 'provocative hypotheses', Blaug rightly considers macroeconomic dynamics to be Marx's most fertile contribution. He is wrong, however, in assuming that Marx thought that capitalists invest without paying attention to profits, an assumption which would destroy his cycle theory. Marx often spoke of the 'sting of profit'.

In an essay devoted to the tendency of the rate of profit to fall, Blaug analyses (1963) "the myth of a labour-saving bias" and a rising capital output–ratio and does not see the more complex ratios given by Schmitt-Rink. He admits the theorem's relevance for business-cycle theory and Marx's attention to capital-saving efforts.

For him, Marx's reproduction schemes provide a growth analysis, anticipating Harrod and Domar and raising the question of whether 'hitchless expansion' is possible. Blaug makes the criticism that Marx did not indicate the growth conditions explicitly and examined only constant rates with an unchanged 'organic composition'. He reminds us, however, that Marx hinted at the possibility of avoiding deadlock even with increasing growth rates, provided savings increase or capital is exported.

It is interesting that Blaug considers Harrod's equations to be less illustrative than Marx's, but both suffer from a common weakness, for they do not show what happens if growth conditions are vitiated.

The 'catharsis' of the cycle raises for Blaug the most profound problem in Marx's system: what determines investment? Capitalists may save and invest to maintain their status, but in the face of declining profits, they react by cutting investment. Blaug emphasises that Marx's rate of profit (as a percentage on costs) is not the same as the current notion.

Blaug follows Lange's criticism of the Marxists, but states that they at least give a systematic view of capitalism's evolution (including 'imperialism'), though they have stuck too rigidly to its institutional framework and have not seen that equilibrium and growth give rise to similar problems under socialism as under capitalism.

Blaug offers the further criticism that Marx believed that in the short run money wages would change inversely to the rate of profit, and he seems to think this is the assumption which underlies Sraffa's and Samuelson's 'factor-price frontier', which shows, in Wan's definition (1971, pp. 102–3), for each wage rate the maximum rate of profit compatible with existing technology. This notion presupposes what Marx did not assume: namely, smooth growth and perfect competition. Furthermore, Marx was interested not in substitution, but in the development of technical progress.

Part V
The Dynamics of the
Marxian System

23 Bronfenbrenner's Synthesis of Growth and Cycle Theory

Bronfenbrenner has ingeniously tried (1965; 1968, pp. 205ff.) to combine Marx's contributions to cycle and growth theory. He thinks that Marx anticipated Keynes in devising a system of moving equilibrium, but that this gets bogged down in continually deteriorating employment conditions.

Bronfenbrenner accepts the Marxian schemes with a uniform rate of surplus value and of profit for both departments. This assumption, which Blaug says Marx only once thought of justifying, in volume III, where he explained it by competition among workers, can perhaps be explained by equal degrees of unionisation. Bronfenbrenner then introduces a uniform growth rate g, which may increase if mass consumption or profits increase. Now, if the rate of surplus value (Kalecki's 'degree of monopoly') rises, unemployment will increase and *vice versa*. When capitalists invest more and raise the 'organic composition', the rate of surplus value must rise and unemployment must increase, or the rate of profit falls, hoarding throttles growth and unemployment increases even more. In the first case, 'under-consumption crises' such as Rosa Luxemburg and Sweezy envisaged occur (Blaug denied that Marx thought this possible!). In the second case, there arise 'hoarding' crises (as envisaged by Dobb) and these are reminiscent of Keynes's 'liquidity trap'.

Capitalism moves between Scylla and Charybdis. Either the rate of profit falls and provokes liquidity crises, or it remains constant, which leads to realisation crises. Bronfenbrenner thinks (ibid., p. 220) that in real life events may fluctuate between the two extremes. At any rate, the system is doomed, for no unemployment level, however high, can be preserved forever.

Bronfenbrenner illustrates his interpretation with a diagram measuring the movement of the rate of profit over time (see Fig. 1). In this diagram the minimum rate is a horizontal line, below which is the area of 'liquidation' or 'hoarding crises', and above which is the area of 'realisation crises'. The diagram shows curves of profit rates compatible with certain rates of unemployment. Since they cut the minimum profit line, Bronfenbrenner concludes that even high rates of unemployment do

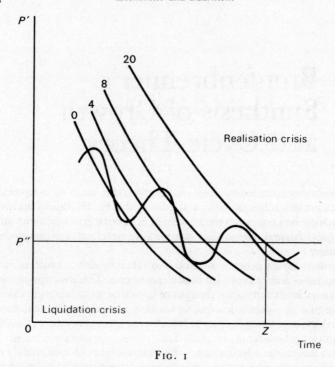

FIG. 1

not prevent the economy from sliding time and again into worse crises. He thinks that Marx thus preached stagnation of a worse kind than Keynes, Hansen or Schumpeter ever envisaged.

Bronfenbrenner then fixes a 'revolution limit', say at the point where the 20 per cent unemployment profit-rate curve cuts the minimum line; to the right of this point, Z ($= \mathit{Zusammenbruch}$, 'collapse'), capitalism cannot survive, for it falls into permanent stagnation.

Now this raises two questions. First, Marx repudiated the idea of permanent crises. Secondly, it is doubtful whether Marx ever held a theory of collapse.

Bronfenbrenner then criticises the theory, which he attributes to Marx: Marx saw possibilities for monetary and fiscal policy 'only partially', underrated the possibility of capital-saving innovations, postulated fixed technical coefficients within his rigid value system, did not consider services as part of the social product, and did not think of the possibility that labour might become scarce. Bronfenbrenner quotes Murad, who said (Kurihara, 1955, pp. 248ff.) that the last factor might only delay the 'collapse'.

We must emphasise that Marx did analyse capital-saving tendencies extensively, in the chapter 5 of volume III of *Capital*.

24 The Thesis of Fundamental Instability: Marx, Harrod and Domar

The idea that capitalism is fundamentally unstable has been presented by Marx in various versions, which are not devoid of obscurities. Marx speaks of ever-recurring crises, but presents them as if they were at the same time a means of overcoming contradictions. He leaves it open as to how far such temporary breakdowns can go. In his criticism of Say's Law, Marx does not verify these tendencies in detail.

The idea of fundamental instability has been taken up by Keynes, who went beyond Marx by conjuring up the nightmare of a depression equilibrium. Marx at least conceived of the cycle as a *perpetuum mobile* with automatic escape from depression and even some degree of convalescence from price distortions.

Harrod formulated his theory of the fundamental instability of the capitalist system (1939; 1970, pp. 53ff.) by examining various kinds of growth, 'natural', 'warranted' and 'actual'. He describes the tendency towards instability as follows.

If actual growth (G) exceeds warranted growth (G_w), the capital stock will not grow as desired; there will be a shortage of stocks and equipment, and expansion will be induced. The more actual growth exceeds the warranted rate, the more it will increase. If, on the other hand, actual growth falls below the warranted rate, the capital stock will be excessive, and recession will lead to depression. 'A departure from equilibrium, instead of being self-righting, will be self-aggravating. G_w represents a moving equilibrium, but a highly unstable one. Of interest this for trade-cycle analysis!'

Harrod's analysis is based on two fundamental equations. The warranted growth rate will be determined by the savings propensity and the capital–output ratio. Only when this rate is maintained will entrepreneurs not be disappointed. 'On either side of this line is a "field" in which centrifugal forces operate. . . . Departure from the warranted line sets up an inducement to depart further from it. The moving equilibrium of advance is thus a highly unstable one.'

Here we find a certain similarity with Marx, who also postulated a rate of saving determined by the rate of surplus value, which in turn depends on the class struggle over distribution. Marx's 'organic composition of capital' is a sort of capital–output ratio combined with the class struggle *via* the wages share, i.e. partly technically and partly sociologically determined. It is true that in his reproduction schemes Marx did not elaborate upon the precarious character of the equilibrium. He had already demonstrated in his example of simple reproduction how small deviations in replacement investment could induce cyclical movements. In contrast to Harrod, Domar referred several times to Marx's works and the models of Marxists, who, in his opinion, 'come closest to developing a substantive theory of economic growth, and they might have succeeded had they given less time and effort to defending their master's virtue', i.e. his somewhat antiquated methodology (Domar, 1957, pp. 17, 70, 87).

Domar's famous equation $r = \alpha \times \sigma$ (equilibrium growth rate = propensity to save multiplied by potential social average productivity of investment or the ratio of potential output to capital) is a formalisation of Harrod's G_w. Domar also pointed out that it was possible to construct a theoretical model in which investment and income continuously reinforce each other. Such a model is highly unstable, through the acceleration principle, and the growth path which winds its way between the two extremes inflation and depression is narrow. (Ibid., pp. 89–97, 112, 125.)

At the same time, Domar reminds us (ibid., p. 167), through his reference to the Soviet economist Notkin (1948, pp. 104–8), that Marx discovered the principle of the dynamic investment–replacement relationship.

THE PROBLEM OF GENERAL OVER-PRODUCTION

Harrod and Domar raise the problem of general over-production, as formulated by Marx. Harrod calls it (1939; 1970, pp. 54–5)

a condition in which a majority of producers . . . find they have produced or ordered too much. . . . This state of things can only occur when the actual growth has been below the warranted growth, i.e. a condition of general overproduction is the consequence of producers in sum producing too little. . . . Overproduction is the consequence of production below the warranted level . . .

This plainly recalls Marx's words (*Theories*, II, ch. 17, pp. 532, 506):

There are, however, also cases where the over-production of non-leading articles is not the result of over-production, but where, on the contrary, *under-production* is the cause of *over-production*. . . . This explanation of over-production in one field by under-production in another field therefore means merely that if production were proportionate, there would be no over-production. The same could be said if demand and supply corresponded to each other, or if all spheres provided equal opportunities for capitalist production and its expansion – division of labour, machinery, export to distant markets etc., mass production. . . .

What after all has over-production to do with absolute needs? It is only concerned with demand that is backed by ability to pay. It is not a question of absolute over-production – over-production as such in relation to the absolute need or the desire to possess commodities.

For Marx as for Harrod, the essential point is a comparison between actual production, which appears as over-production, and potential production, which compared to the former appears as under-production.

It is often argued that the model of Harrod and Domar is based on the assumption of a fixed capital–output ratio. This is not quite accurate. Although Harrod does not assume variability of the average capital–output ratio in the short run and thinks it improbable that it will decrease in the long run, because 'it may often stand below the level appropriate to the technological conditions of the age', he leaves open (1939; 1970, p. 56) the possibility that it may rise. This would imply a tendency towards a decreasing warranted rate of growth. If actual growth tended to remain below the latter, inflationary tendencies might result, as has been the case in the 1970s. This represents one side of Harrod's 'pair of scissors'.

Marxists have tended to emphasise the other side, the tendency towards depression. Thus, for completeness, inflation should be incorporated into the Marxian system. The Marxian term the 'rate of profit' is certainly related to Keynes's 'marginal efficiency of capital', although the latter contains an element of expectations.

In his theory of the 'organic composition of capital', Marx makes an assumption similar to that of Harrod. He points to the probability of increasing capital–output ratios, although his 'organic composition' goes beyond that ratio. The two are equivalent only if the share of wages remains constant; as, since 1945, the wage share has tended to increase, it is not certain that Marx's coefficient moves in the same direction as Harrod's. One might assume that Domar's σ is nearer to the Marxian term, since it indicates (Domar, 1947; 1957, p. 95) 'the annual increment in capacity of the whole economy per dollar invested'. This does not coincide with Keynes's term, for I_σ is the potential increase in production. Domar thus emphasises the capacity effect neglected by Keynes. For Marx, investment, capacity expansion and productivity increases are synonymous.

A positive savings rate is necessary; for Domar, savings are no longer a by-product of investment. Oppenländer sets out (Gahlen and Ott, 1972, p. 252) Domar's conditions for equilibrium growth:

Voluntary savings must be equal to planned investment. . . . The marginal savings rate remains constant in time and corresponds to the average rate of savings. . . . The marginal capital–output ratio k' remains constant in time and corresponds to the average ratio k. . . . Equilibrium growth prevails whenever the increment in income brought about by net investment is just sufficient to bring about the full utilization of additional capacity created by net investment, when this grows at the constant rate s/k. . . .

These are more or less the conditions of Marxian growth! Harrod allows (1939; 1970, p. 57) for a greater variability in the propensity to save, but stresses that 'for any normal warranted rate of growth and level of saving' the instability principle holds.

In his article of 1947 in which he discovered his affinities with Harrod, Domar stresses (1947; 1957, p. 92) that it is not sufficient for yesterday's savings to be invested today, for today's investment must always exceed yesterday's savings, which means an increasing injection of money. This is the credit expansion which caused Marx such a headache when he asked where the additional money comes from. At the same time, this exponential expansion implies its own interruption and hence the instability principle.

Harrod thought (1939; 1970, pp. 61–2) this might be mitigated through long-term investment. His warranted rate of growth is not fixed. It may diminish through depression or increase through inflation and may even remain above its 'proper' level throughout a series of booms. Thus long periods of prosperity, as in the 1950s and 1960s, are compatible with Harrod's instability principle. The warranted rate of growth has been temporarily raised. Since the warranted rate depends on the rate of saving and the feasible investment rate, it can be considered identical with the concept upon which Marx's model is built: Harrod's 'natural rate' is represented in Marx's scheme by the shadow 'reserve army', while the actual rate of growth is related to Marx's realisation problem.

RECENT FORMULATIONS OF THE INSTABILITY THEOREM

A Young Italian economist, Cozzi, has compared (1972, pp. 185–7) Harrod's instability principle to the Marxian conception:

> One starts from an equilibrium situation: if investment and income grow at the warranted rate and productive capacity and demand at the same rate, entrepreneurs will be happy about their own decisions, and the system will remain in equilibrium. . . . Then the capital stock desired by entrepreneurs always equals the actual one. . . . In Marxian terms, one may say that they are happy with the conditions required for the realisation of their surplus value.

Cozzi next assumes that entrepreneurs desire to carry out more investment. Demand grows more rapidly:

> The available productive capacity is less than what is required to satisfy demand. Here we encounter a paradox. Because the entrepreneurs invested more than they had to, they now find out that they have less productive capacity than they desire. . . . Demand for goods exceeds the quantity of goods that can be produced. There is too much demand and a capacity gap; entrepreneurs are being induced to invest more and more rapidly, and they thus push the system into situations marked by more acute inflation . . . .

Cozzi's example characterises Domar's concept of the cumulative process and at the same time fits the inflationary situation into which the Western world stumbled in the 1970s.

Cozzi then analyses the opposite case,

> where entrepreneurs earn less than is required to maintain equilibrium. . . . They then have a larger productive capacity than desired. Thus entrepreneurs will carry out less investment than they would have done otherwise. Demand is correspondingly less, and the system enters into a phase of cumulative depression. . . . The economic system is in Harrod's view highly unstable. It is said, even if Harrod does not like the term, that it is on a knife edge when it moves along the (warranted) growth rate . . . .

More than twenty years after the publication of Harrod's epoch-making book on dynamics and about thirty years after his first path-finding article, Joan Robinson referred to the 'knife edge' by saying (1970, pp. 731 ff.) that no one would object if Harrod had said that uncontrolled capitalism was unlikely to maintain a steady growth rate, but that it was surprising that he had declared it a logical impossibility.

Since the savings rate is given, as a result of the propensity to save (and she should have added 'of the income distribution'), and the capital–output ratio is dictated by technology, the warranted rate is determined, while 'God and the engineers' dictate the 'natural rate'.

Leon (1965, pp. 54 ff.) and others have in the meantime dissolved Marx's uniform rate of profit into a scale, giving rise to a whole series of possible growth rates. This widens or blunts the 'knife-edge'. Neo-classical authors have tried to make the capital–output ratio v inversely proportional to the actual rate of growth g, but Joan Robinson seems to think that an increasing growth rate would be more likely to entail an increased v.

Joan Robinson relies on Leon, but this author explicitly refers to Marx in arguing that consumption is by no means autonomous in the long run, as the marginalists, in upholding subjectivist traditions, had assumed it to be. Leon thinks that consumption is a creature of capitalism, which uses it to lower the savings rate required for its own long-run evolution. This would imply that, if v rises, the warranted rate of growth will come under pressure from both sides. If, as Joan Robinson is inclined to think, the capital–output ratio rises, this will suffice to put a brake on growth if the savings ratio remains constant. There is in fact a further argument. In a footnote, Joan Robinson refers to Pasinetti's analysis of workers' savings. As workers' propensity to save is lower, an increasing share of wages may lead to a decrease in the rate of saving in the long run, and the warranted rate would be crushed between the two millstones of an increasing capital–output ratio and a declining savings rate. This points to a new version of the stagnation theory, and, in so far as the warranted rate of growth indicates the rate of profit, as neo-classicists such as von Weizsäcker say, to Marx's falling rate of profit.

Incidentally, Joan Robinson fears an under-consumption situation if savings out of wages increase more rapidly than investment, especially if profits suffer. Under Marx's basic assumption that entrepreneurs alone save, the rate of profit equals $\pi = g/sp$ ($=$ savings ratio out of profits). Now the rate of profits exceeds the warranted rate of growth, and this remains below the natural rate. The more capitalists consume, the lower will the warranted rate be.

Joan Robinson retains two cases where the 'knife-edge' appears: where in the long run workers' savings equal capitalists' savings, and, in the short run, when the rate of profit reacts on the capital–output ratio. She points out that Harrod thought that one could not expect equilibrium growth if there were no conscious control of the growth process. 'The point of Harrod's argument was that actual economies cannot be expected to grow at a steady and desirable rate without conscious control and direction.' (Robinson, 1970, pp. 731 ff.)

Joan Robinson starts from the premise that the marginal and the average capital–output ratios are identical. She concludes that, if all profits are saved and workers do not save, the equilibrium rate of growth must be equal to the rate of profit. If capitalists save less than their entire income, the equilibrium rate of growth must remain below the natural rate.

In his reply, Harrod agrees (1970, pp. 737–41) that there may be more than one equilibrium rate of profit, but he does not believe that the degree of monopoly is decisive. There would be a minimum rate of profit which is still just acceptable to entrepreneurs. For him, the decisive problems are: 'Given the dynamic determinants, will there sometimes, or even usually, be more than one equilibrium growth rate consistent with them?'; and is equilibrium for all such rates unstable?

He answers the first question by saying that the number of such rates would in any case be less than in microstatics. For him, an identity between the marginal and the average capital–output ratios is 'highly unlikely', and so is Joan Robinson's 'unacceptable assumption that $g = i/k$'. If technical progress is capital-saving and not too important, 'quite a small proportion of profit income might . . . finance my "natural" growth'.

As to the second question, Harrod thinks that the

> knife-edge . . . is an unwarranted description for his argument that an equilibrium growth path is quite unstable. . . . If it is on a knife-edge, a very tiny push would serve to move it away; but it would also be in unstable equilibrium if it were at the top of a shallow dome. Then a much larger push would be needed to set it moving. . . . All depends on the gradient . . . and friction.

At any rate, there is a time lag of at least six months, 'illustrated by experience in the USA'.

In his book of 1973, Harrod quite unrepentantly defends (pp. 32–5) his instability principles. He quotes

> a better example: a ball lying on a grassy slope. It might take quite a hard kick to move it. But, once moved, it might go further, especially if the hill was steep. . . . It requires a fairly large deviation, such as might be caused by a revision of assessments across the board in some important industry, like the motor car industry . . . .

He goes on to mention as possible sources of disturbance 'substantial regional or industrial disparities in growth rates'. In this case, 'the feasible overall increase in actual growth may drop and fall below the warranted growth before full employment is reached'.

Harrod's important industry reminds us of the Marxian 'leading trade articles', his motor-industry example of the oil crisis of 1973.

ANALOGIES WITH HARROD IN MORISHIMA'S INTERPRETATION OF MARX

Morishima has pointed out (1973, pp. 144–50, 157–9) the analogies between the instability principles of Marx and Harrod. For Morishima, the Marxian models of extended reproduction correspond to Harrod's 'warranted' growth paths. 'Marx, like Harrod, was also concerned with temporary or more persistent deviations of the actual path from the corresponding warranted path.'

Analysing the value compositions of Marx's departments i and ii, Morishima arrived at the conclusion that

> this balanced growth path is definitely unstable, so that, if the economy

is initially moved off the balanced growth ray, it will diverge further from it as time goes on; we have explosive oscillations around the balanced growth ray if the value-composition of capital is higher in department II than in department I, and monotonic divergence from the ray in either direction if the capital intensity is reversed . . . .

Morishima then introduces a formula similar to that used by Joan Robinson. Here the warranted growth rate of the capital stock is $g_k^*(t) = s_s \pi$, i.e. the savings propensity of capitalists multiplied by the rate of profit.

Marx built his accumulation rate a on the assumption that it could be based on an observable propensity of capitalists to save. Morishima shows, however, that the two may diverge, which in the last resort can be attributed to Marxian hoarding, i.e. to a version of the disproportionality thesis, for Morishima argues that 'without restrictive conditions on technology and capitalists' consumption, s_c can equal a only in the case where (i) capitalists do not consume and (ii) a balanced growth of output prevails in the economy. . . . Condition (ii) is problematic, because the balanced growth equilibrium has been proved to be unstable . . . .' Difficulties arise from the Marxian value formula, because 'Marx's transformation formula, that the ratio of the surplus value to the aggregate total capital equals the rate of profits, holds true as a relationship along the Marx–von Neumann golden equilibrium path, but it must be replaced in all other circumstances' by other growth formulas.

Marx's instability principle contains certain variants which touch upon his business cycle analysis. Taking into account the long-run tendency of the rate of profit to fall, we get an instability theory based on a 'bias' in the sense of a one-sided trend of technical progress. Güsten describes this as follows (1960, pp. 133–4): a tendency towards instability results 'once the trend of primarily or exclusively labour-saving progress ceases', for in this case 'department I is over-developed; in a non-harmonic society of this kind, therefore, there is always a latent danger of crisis'.

In her principal work (1956, pp. 171 ff.), Joan Robinson declares this 'bias', in the sense of a permanent one-sidedness in technical progress, improbable. Nevertheless, she admits, in the sense of our analysis in Part II, that it would be 'possible that a bias should persist, in one direction or the other, for a considerable period, phases of one bias, perhaps, alternating with phases of the other'. If this is so, the instability linked with the theory of the falling tendency of the rate of profit can prevail over long periods, during which the propensity to invest will be depressed and recessions will recur. Conversely, in periods with a high propensity to invest, high profits may lead to social unrest, so that sociologically conditioned instability will be present.

Marx's instability principle may be understood in yet another way. In Marx's model of extended reproduction, growth goes on because additional labour, the 'shadow' of which appears in the value system under the guise of an increase in variable capital, is always available.

This source may be exhausted for a country if a capital-saving bias persists for a long time. If the growth process is not to be interrupted, wages must be increased to attract either people who were not willing to work before or foreign workers. If production goes on in the same proportions and capitalists are not prepared temporarily to reduce their consumption in favour of wage earners, there will be a temporary shortage of consumption goods and, therefore, a price rise in department II, which will attract workers from department I. Once capacity is fully employed, it will have to be enlarged, which will lead to price increases in department I as well.

The shortage of labour entails inflationary tendencies. If an accelerator effect now operates in the investment-goods industry, the extension of department II goes beyond the level which corresponds to Harrod's warranted rate of growth.

Once the accelerator effect becomes negative, investment-goods industries sack workers, the consumption-goods industry declines, and recession sets in, because entrepreneurs had in the upswing tried to remedy the labour shortage by an over-extension of capacity, which cannot be maintained. Such a process can come about only if a rather rigid relationship between capital and labour inputs prevails. Harrod's model has been criticised on this score. At any rate, it is related to the Marxian model in so far as it sees a fundamental instability in capitalism. Harrod himself still staunchly maintains his basic thesis (1977 p. 45):

> I am confident that the theory that the 'warranted' equilibrium growth rate of *laissez-faire* capitalism, without management or interference, is unstable, stands firm. . . . There is the further question of whether *laissez-faire* capitalism tends to bring the economy to a full employment position. It was the central doctrine of Keynes, with which I agree, that this was not so. . . . But even if it were so, that would not guarantee growth in accordance with potential.

HARROD – A CRYPTO-MARXIST?

One might suppose that Harrod's theory was welcomed by Marxists. Curiously, it was not. It is true that the East German economist Meissner states (1972, pp. 31 ff.) that 'Harrod's considerations contain a correct nucleus. This is the opinion that there is no automatic mechanism in modern capitalism which would become effective once deviations from equilibrium occur, and which would restore the economy to equilibrium'; but the same author criticises many aspects of Harrod's model. He raises the objection that it is 'inadmissible to calculate growth rates equally on production and income, because that presupposes an unlimited realisation of the total product'. In other words, Harrod, who takes instability for granted, is accused of ignoring business cycles, which are its consequence!

Meissner goes on to criticise Harrod's assumption of a constant savings ratio, which implies that the marginal capital–output ratio C_r must exceed the average ratio if the actual growth rate G is larger than the warranted growth rate G_w. He argues that it is not evident that, if $G > G_w$, $C < C_r$. This, however, follows from Harrod's assumption of a decreasing efficiency of marginal investment. Finally, Meissner protests that Harrod 'wants to infer directly from a high utility effect of investment high realised profits'.

One is tempted to suspect that this somewhat unsympathetic treatment of Harrod is owing to some displeasure in the possibility that a non-Marxist economist has succeeded in finding the proof of the Marxian intuitive thesis that capitalism is fundamentally unstable. This is short-sighted. One may suppose that Engels would have been more magnanimous. After all, he accepted wholeheartedly the 'academic' author Lexis, dubbing him a 'crypto-Marxist' because of his reformulation of the theory of surplus value in circulation terms. Why should not Engels similarly have admitted Harrod to the Parnassus of Marxism?

The reticence of official Marxism in the face of Harrod is all the more curious as Meissner invokes as witnesses against Harrod and Domar other 'academic' economists – for instance, Bombach, who said (1965, p. 777) that Harrod's model allowed no statements on concrete dependencies. Another 'academic' economist, Rose, thinks (1953, p. 340) that Harrod 'sacrifices reality on the altar of an elegant closed model'.

Such objections seem irrelevant in face of Harrod's concern in his 1973 study to remain close to the reality of the 1970s. One must acknowledge that he saw capitalism as walking a tightrope (although perhaps not so narrow as to justify the expression 'knife-edge'), off which it might slip at any time. After all, capitalism did slip into depression in the 1930s and into recession coupled with inflation or 'stagflation' in the 1970s. It seems that so far it has not attained that degree of control that would eliminate instability. If this cannot be attained, a thoroughgoing transformation of the structure and essence of our society becomes unavoidable.

25 The Antithesis of the Potentially Stable Growth Path

The instability theorem of Harrod and Domar remained isolated and was hotly contested. Neo-neo-classical authors argued that Harrod and Domar's premises were too rigid, and they pleaded for a flexible capital-intensity, which, they conceived, like a *deus ex machina* would reintroduce equilibrium. Neo-Keynesians counter-attacked by questioning the measurability of capital, and neo-Ricardians supported them by showing, in the 'reswitching' debate, that increasing capital-intensity is by no means synonymous with decreasing rates of profit, and that it is not necessarily a monotonic function of the wage–interest ratio. In the upshot, all the contestants in the fight were injured.

Tugan-Baranowsky (1894) and Bulgakov (1897), whom Rosa Luxemburg challenged, were to some extent predecessors of the neo-neo-classical thesis, but they believed in a one-sided rise in capital-intensity. Neo-classical authors, by contrast, believe in the variability of capital-intensity and in infinite possibilities of substitution.

Curiously enough, neo-classical authors no longer consider capital or investment to be decisive. Solow, in his analysis of US growth over the period 1909–49 (1957), ascribed only 12·5 per cent of the increase in output per head to capital, and the rest to technical progress, although he later (1960), like Marx, recognised gross investment as a vehicle of technical progress.

EQUILIBRIUM THROUGH SUBSTITUTION?

Sen (1970, pp. 20–3) has described the Solow–Swan adjustment mechanism, upon which neo-classical authors rely, in the following terms: once the warranted rate of growth is higher than the natural rate, the economy tries to break through the full employment barrier, making labour more expensive and encouraging labour-saving methods. This increases the capital–output ratio and lowers the warranted growth rate until it coincides with the natural one, on the assumption that there are no wage and interest constraints. If the warranted rate falls below the natural rate, labour becomes redundant, real wages fall relative to the rate of interest, labour-intensive techniques are chosen, the capital–output ratio falls and the warranted growth rate increases. Movements of the capital–output ratio perform single-handedly the feat of re-equilibrating the economy.

Sen also defines the limits to this approach. It is based on the assumption of flexible factor prices and labour-augmenting ('Harrod-neutral') technical progress, for other kinds of progress are incompatible with steady growth. Finally, entrepreneurial expectations are ignored, and there is no investment function.

Harrod based his instability theorem precisely on expectations, and, as soon as an independent investment function is introduced into the Solow–Swan model, the instability problem reappears, as has been shown elsewhere by Eisner (1958), Hahn (1960) and Sen (1965). The neo-classical substitution theorem does not, therefore, seem to disprove the instability thesis. Besides, there are a number of arguments against the assumption of a high degree of substitutability between capital and labour:

- historical evidence does not show a high variability in average capital–output ratios;
- the 'switching' theorem shows that there is no well-determined relationship between techniques and profit rates;
- the measurability of capital is doubtful; and
- an analysis of multi-sector systems shows that simple variability in factor proportions is insufficient, because the further condition of a higher capital-intensity in the consumption-goods industry must be fulfilled, and this is considered unrealistic, as Beckmann has emphasised (Gahlen and Ott, 1972, p. 317).

THE PROBLEM OF THE EXPLOSIVE CYCLE

Morishima has considered (1973, pp. 135–6) just this aspect of a higher value composition in Marx's department II, and he argues that this must lead to increasing oscillations around the equilibrium path and that these oscillations will finally turn out to be explosive.

This would indeed justify the Marxian hypothesis of increasing amplitude. As a matter of fact, almost at the same time as Harrod developed his instability principle, Hicks enunciated (1951, pp. 68, 90–1) the possibility of explosive cycles: he employs an 'investment coefficient' or accelerator v, i.e. the ratio of induced investment to output variations. If v exceeds a certain value, the upturn will not be reversed and the system moves inexorably away from equilibrium. Hicks does not explain this explosiveness by erratic shocks from outside the system, but envisages the possibility of an inherently explosive cycle bound by certain constraints.

He even tries to prove that this hypothesis is compatible with elementary statistical facts!

It seems that a neo-Marxist theory of increasing amplitudes in the cycle must start from a combination of Harrod's, Hicks's and Morishima's contributions, taking into account numerous other aspects of neo-Keynesian growth theory.

THE ROLE OF THE INVESTMENT FUNCTION

The main weakness of neo-classical authors seems to lie in the fact that they have no investment function and that for them technical progress falls like manna from heaven, while Marx saw it embodied in gross fixed-capital formation. Technical progress appears as a residual in the macroeconomic production function, i.e. as production growth minus factor growth. Ott points out (Gahlen and Ott, 1972, pp. 282–3) that it has been asked whether this is really justified and whether the difference could not be explained by, for instance, the degree of concentration, the competitive situation, foreign trade, or simply reduced waste.

Winfried Vogt has tried to explain (1968, p. 73) why a real investment function is missing. Saving is supposed to explain capital formation, because growth theory assumes equilibrium will always be preserved, so that saving equals investment. This had already been assumed in Walrasian models.

It is curious that the neo-classicists turned Keynes's identity between saving and investment upside-down. He argued that (active) investment would produce (passive) saving, while in neo-classical growth models it is the other way round! In neo-classical systems, investment no longer matters, for the growth rate is independent of the rate of investment, which, as Krelle points out (1964, p. 6), cannot influence the growth rate in the long run. This is confirmed by Oppenländer (in Gahlen and Ott, 1972, p. 255): 'If one assumes constant growth of labour potential and unchanged technical progress, the growth of the gross national product goes on independently of the rate of investment, provided that the latter is positive.'

In this the neo-classical system certainly appears somewhat unrealistic. It represents exactly the opposite point of view to that which Marx tried to demonstrate in his reproduction schemes: for him, growth and investment are synonymous, and, in his criticism of Say's Law as well as in his examples of fluctuations under conditions of simple reproduction, he states that investment processes may be interrupted by autonomous hoarding tendencies.

The neo-classical denial of the importance of investment went so far that Krelle could say (1964, p. 6),

The communist states are damaging themselves by the artificial increase of the share of investment; they reach a higher level of production, but at lasting cost to consumption. Since the growth rate remains finally unaffected, there can be no question of overtaking the Western world, least of all in consumption, as long as population growth and technical progress, which alone determine the natural rate of growth, are the same in both systems.

Another author, Gahlen (Gahlen and Ott, 1972, p. 316) thought it 'a joke' that, in general, 'multi-sector models show that, if any implications are to be drawn from these theories for economic policy, they must be drawn for a totally planned economy'. Neo-classical growth theory ignores fluctuations. It examines growth by assuming that it will not be disturbed. Here it is at loggerheads not only with Marx, but also with business-cycle theory in general, which cannot renounce an investment function short of losing its *raison d'être*. Winfried Vogt says (ibid., p. 74): 'In practical life, one cannot of course work without an investment function. . . . Market disequilibria occur, the phenomenon of business cycles must be analysed, and it is precisely in business-cycle theory that the investment function holds a central place.'

The neo-classical authors reached their conclusions on the basis of a number of very specific assumptions: savings invariably find investors in the long run, labour and technical progress are external factors and cannot be influenced, an unchanged part of the gross national product is invested, and the capital stock grows at the same rate as income (Oppenländer, ibid., pp. 255–6). In this way, the volume of investment is simultaneously institutionalised and made to disappear as a problem, and it is assumed that growth will take place without net investment, a thesis too rashly accepted even by Marxist authors such as Zinn.

Domar flatly contradicts the neo-classical contempt for investment. His opinion is paraphrased by Krelle, who states (1964, p. 6) that Domar thinks that

the volume of investment will have to be made as great as possible, and the present generation will have to sacrifice as much as they are prepared to do on behalf of future generations. Under this assumption, the stepping-up of investment by the communist states would be a rational economic policy, and it would then be certain that these states, although their absolute level is still low, would overtake the West not only in production, but also, finally, in consumption, because of their higher investment rates and, therefore, growth rates.

The outcome of all this is the following confrontation. On the one side we find Marx, Harrod and Domar, with the latter two not only reinforcing the instability principle, which in Marx's reasoning is exclusively based on intuition, but also confirming the policy of states whose philosophy is the Marxian creed. On the other side, we find the neo-classical authors, who deny that capitalism must be unstable and who consider investment unimportant and technical progress as disembodied, having, as it were, an 'astral body'. The first group finds allies in two other groups: the neo-Keynesians, led by Kalecki and Joan Robinson, for whom investment matters because, together with capitalist consumption, it determines the share of profits, as Marx also indicated; and the 'vintage theorists', who, influenced by Marx, consider technical progress to be 'embodied' in successive age groups of equipment.

SAMUELSON'S SURROGATE PRODUCTION FUNCTION

Samuelson tried (1962) to justify the use of a production function by introducing Sraffa's notion (1960) of the ratio of wages to the rate of profit under the new term 'factor-price frontier'. This shows the decrease in the rate of wages as a function of an increase in the rate of profit. Samuelson thought that this ratio could indicate a sequence of production techniques of higher or lower capital-intensity. With higher rates of profit, less capital-intensive techniques would be chosen, without the necessity of quantifying capital values for heterogeneous capital goods. In this way, he believed, a useful 'parable' was substituted for the 'production function', which had been devastatingly criticised by neo-Keynesians. His argument, however, was shattered by Garegnani (1970), Pasinetti (1969) and others, who pointed out that falling rates of profit and increasing wage rates need not always automatically entail an increase in capital-intensity. This is the so-called 'return of techniques' or 'reswitching', of which Jaeger says (Gahlen and Ott, 1972, pp. 149-50) that 'the rate of interest [or of profit] can in this case even less than in the case of one technique serve as an indicator of relative capital scarcity'.

This seems to torpedo Samuelson's parable and defence of the production function. It is true that it has been argued that the 'reswitching' analysis is a pure imaginative possibility seldom encountered in life, and that its chances are less the more technical change occurs over time (discussion of Jaeger's paper, ibid., pp. 176-7). It has been pointed out by Cozzi (1972, pp. 224-5) that

> the same capital value per worker can be compatible with several rates of profit, even where the return of techniques does not occur, and that the value of capital per worker depends on the system's growth rate, in such a way that, for a given rate of profit, the same capital value per worker can appear, in an economic system, with several rates of growth.

Cozzi refers to a symposium on capital theory in the *Quarterly Journal of*

Economics in 1966 and to the work of Spaventa (1968) and Nuti (1970), both of whom may be considered to be unorthodox Marxists. From all this he draws (1972, pp. 225–6) an ironic conclusion:

> Neo-classical theory will only be fully valid in the case where a single good is produced or where all goods are produced by techniques of the same capital-intensity, so that the goods are therefore economically indistinguishable. As is well known, the principle on which neo-classical theory is based had its origin in a reaction against Marx's (and Ricardo's) theory according to which the value of commodities is represented by the quantity of labour embodied in them. It has been said that the labour theory of value can serve to explain relative prices only in the special case where capital is used in the production process of different goods of the same organic composition, but not in the general case. One may perhaps allow oneself the ironic remark that neo-classical theory will not be valid either if this condition is not fulfilled!

In other words, the irony of the history of economic doctrines has willed it that the neo-classicists have been equally condemned to represent a 'special case'. It thus seems that the validity of Harrod's instability theorem, and with it Marx's intuition, has not been decisively disproved.

INVESTMENT VINDICATED?

If technical progress is embodied, in the long run an investment function will be indispensable for a realistic analysis of growth.

Several empirical studies have been undertaken to check the correlation between investment and growth. Hill (1964) examined investment (excluding construction) for only a short period (1953–61). Kromphardt (1971) studied the models of Domar and Phelps for fourteen countries for the period 1953–1967. Neither study was conclusive, but it is true that the neo-classical variant was nowhere justified.

Schatz (1971) examines growth in fifteen OECD states from 1950 to 1968 and maintains that investment is capable of explaining 5·9 of 6·5 points of the average growth rate. Krelle (1962b) has found for the period 1950–60 in eleven countries a 'positive, although not very close correlation between the volume of investment and the growth rate' and has emphasised at the same time that Harrod's approach was by no means outdated by Phelps's model.

Oppenländer reviews all these studies (Gahlen and Ott, 1972, p. 263) and reaches the conclusion that 'Investment as an explanatory factor is getting more important. . . . Only by investment can the vehicle be introduced which stimulates technical knowledge.'

It is Kaldor's investment function and Arrow's 'learning by doing' which point in a direction that is compatible with Marx's point of departure.

THE NEO-KEYNESIAN EQUILIBRIUM VARIANT

Neo-Keynesians were the allies of Harrod and Domar in rejecting the idea that equilibrium could be restored by varying the capital–output ratio or capital-intensity, though they did not share their belief in the instability principle. Instead, they believed that it would be possible to establish an equilibrium situation by way of redistribution.

If the natural rate exceeds the warranted one, unemployment results, which sets off the mechanism of the 'Phillips curve'. Wages tend to level off, and income distribution turns against the workers. The savings rate rises with rising profits. If they are reinvested, the actual growth rate rises, and the warranted rate is pushed up to the level of the natural rate.

This idea has been most concisely summarised by Kaldor (1955–6; 1968, pp. 373 ff.). Investment exceeds savings and leads to excess demand. Full employment brings about price increases; income is redistributed in favour of capitalists. Saving increases, and equilibrium is restored. Once saving exceeds investment, equilibrium is restored by way of falling prices.

This neo-Keynesian theory presupposes price flexibility and appears as a new version of harmony theory, but not one that operates well from the point of view of the workers. Rising profits are justified by the consideration that indirectly they will create jobs, *via* a rising growth rate. It is strange that this school derives from Keynes; for, whereas in its view saving is the active factor, and the tail wags the dog, Keynes saw things the other way round, with investment creating savings.

Incidentally, Marx's theory of a relative growth of the pauper-class may be interpreted as meaning that he thought that the natural rate would remain above the warranted one in the long run.

At any rate, Kaldor recognises that

> this does not mean that there will be an inherent tendency to a smooth rate of growth in a capitalist economy, only that the causes of cyclical movements lie elsewhere . . . in a disharmony between the entrepreneurs' desired growth rate, which governs the rate of increase of output capacity (G) and the natural growth rate (G') . . . . It is the excess of G' over G – not the excess of s [the volume of savings] over G_w – which causes periodic breakdowns in the investment process through the growth in output capacity outrunning the growth in production.

Kaldor's cycle theory is thus not directly built on Harrod's instability theorem. It seems that the neo-Keynesians also have not found a satisfactory solution to Harrod's problem. Neo-classical and neo-

Keynesian authors both rely on a policy of stabilisation of the business cycle to make growth possible, and not the other way round. It is Harrod alone who thinks that growth policy can stabilise the cycle.

The neo-classical conception has been very aptly described by Cozzi, who argues that savings and investment could be equilibrated by monetary policy and 'direct intervention aimed at regulating in an appropriate way the investment activities of public enterprise and of firms through state participation'. This would lead to the paradoxical consequence that the neo-classicists would have to rely on a certain degree of nationalisation, in order to guarantee that private enterprise functioned well.

On the other hand, Cozzi characterises the neo-Keynesians by saying (1972, pp. 215, 230–1) that they rely on monetary and fiscal policy together with the manipulation of public investment. For them it is thus not the capital–output ratio but the volume of savings, that re-establishes equilibrium. Cozzi disputes this: 'The hypothesis that larger savings are invested is particularly restrictive. It is in fact very likely that, if wages are reduced through unemployment, the demand for consumption goods will fall. Entrepreneurs may then decide not to increase investment.' In that case, G_w would not be raised to G_n, for entrepreneurs would rather reduce investment, and we should be confronted again with Harrod's instability. Kaldor's *deus ex machina*, the savings ratio, would thus not function.

Harrod intended to show that the system is fundamentally unstable. If both schools insist upon the necessity of counteracting these inherent tendencies through active policy measures, they equally acknowledge the validity of this thesis; for neither of the two schools has proved the system to have the capacity to re-equilibrate itself. Both presuppose a self-equilibrating force only for the growth process, provided that short-term fluctuations can be avoided. Both thus assume what needs to be proved: 'that the system can grow in equilibrium. In order to maintain this assumption, we must drag in the public authorities and charge them to re-establish equilibrium between savings and investment . . . ' (ibid., p. 231).

One may certainly consider the state as a sort of *deus ex machina*, but the question then arises of the 'technical' viability of capitalism. Harrod also postulates public intervention – not in order to eliminate short-term fluctuations, which oscillate round a basically stable trend, as the neo-classicists assume, nor in order to avoid pathological distortions outside the growth and saving process, as neo-Keynesians believe, but to stabilise growth, which he thinks all-important. He believes that such stabilisation is possible. Marx, on the other hand, believes that structural transformations are inevitable, because of the ever-recurring – and, he believes, increasing – fluctuations in the growth process.

26 Marx and the Theory of the 'Collapse' of Capitalism

At least seven different theories of 'collapse' have been based, or purport to be based, on Marx's works.

First there is the old-fashioned Marxist *Zusammenbruchstheorie* (collapse theory). Its existence in Marx's works is somewhat controversial. It has been propounded by Marx's adversaries, and its only clear formulation, dating from the end of the nineteenth century, is to be found in Cunow's works.

Second, following upon the theory of the tendency of the rate of profit to fall, there is the theory that Grossmann formulated shortly before, as it happened, the great world depression of 1929.

Third, before this Rosa Luxemburg had given a particular twist to a long-term under-consumptionist growth theory, which lives on in the theory of imperialism.

Fourth, there is the theory developed by Schumpeter, who thinks the idea that capitalism must collapse, because of its internal contradictions, basically correct, but argues that these contradictions are not of an economic, but of a sociological and cultural–morphological character. Schumpeter thinks, as he often does, that Marx was right but for the wrong reasons. This theory comes near to negating itself. Many voluntarist tendencies of our times support it; for instance, it is argued by Marcuse that capitalism deserves to die, that we must work towards this, and that its breakdown will not come about automatically or through economic forces, but only through intellectual forces. The 'intelligentsia' replaces a complacent 'proletariat'.

Fifth, Baran and Sweezy have developed a theory which assumes that capitalism will be suffocated by its excessive surplus.

Sixth, an eclectic choice of older and newer Marxist theses has been transformed into a neo-Marxist web of condemnation of capitalism. It has been soberly formulated by Tsuru (1961).

Seventh, there is a theory that exists only in embryo, as a combination of Harrod's and Domar's instability principles, which were intuitively anticipated by Marx. Contributions have been made by Sraffa, Garegnani, Pasinetti, Joan Robinson, Kaldor, by 'academic' independents sympathetic to Marx, such as Bronfenbrenner and Morishima, and, paradoxically, even by neo-classical authors such as Hicks. The last word on this matter has not yet been said.

DID MARX HOLD A THEORY OF COLLAPSE?

It remains questionable whether Marx ever held a theory of the collapse of capitalism. He used the term 'collapse' only incidentally and in connexion with the conditional tense, in the context of concentration processes and of the tendency of the rate of profit to fall: 'This process would soon bring about the collapse of capitalist production if it were not for counteracting tendencies, which have a continuous decentralising effect alongside the centripetal one' (*Capital*, III, Ch. 15, p. 246).

In an almost synonymous passage in the *Theories of Surplus Value* (III, Ch. 21, p. 311), he says: 'This process would soon bring capitalist production to a head if it were not for the fact that, alongside the centripetal forces, counteracting tendencies exist . . . .'

This seems to be very scanty for a theory of collapse. It is Engels who uses the term somewhat more positively. In the Preface to Marx's anti-Proudhon pamphlet *The Poverty of Philosophy*, Engels says in 1884 that

> the above application of the theory of Ricardo, which shows to the workers that the totality of social production, which is their product, belongs to them because they are the only real producers, leads direct to communism. . . . Marx has never based upon this his communist conclusions, but rather upon the necessary overthrow, which is developing itself under our eyes every day, of the capitalist system of production.

Even Engels never developed a 'theory' on such a slender foundation. The term 'collapse' in this context remains a metaphor of the essence of the two authors' conception of historical evolution.

One and a half decades later, Bernstein, the leading revisionist, set out to disprove what he calls the 'theory of collapse' (1898; and 1899/1909, pp. 47 ff.). The arguments are the same as those employed in his main work, which appeared one year later. He sees a consistent improvement in the situation of the working classes, a slow-down in the process of concentration, an enlargement of the class of shareholders and of the middle class, and a mitigation of crises. In short, he sees a *détente* in capitalism contradicting any breakdown theory. Cunow then wrote his essay in reply to Bernstein. He takes the 'theory of collapse' for granted, is convinced that Marx held such a theory, and defends it. The 'conflict between the consumption capacity of the market' and the 'increase in capitalist accumulation' must lead to a sharpening of crises and to a collapse. If capitalism has not yet collapsed, this is to be explained by an extension into foreign markets, 'which will create a channel for an ever recurrent plethora', and which 'will also diminish the tendency towards crises'. This cannot go on forever: one can 'already see a certain end to an extension of the export markets'. Once they shrink, the breakdown must inexorably occur. (Cunow, 1899, pp. 356, 396, 424–7.)

Grossmann was not altogether wrong in saying (1929; 1970, p. 42) that Rosa Luxemburg took up Cunow's basic ideas. The doyen of the American Marxists, Boudin, took them up somewhat earlier, in an article of 1905, and later in a counterattack against Simkhovich's ideas (Boudin, 1912, p. 150), though he does not quote exact titles. Simkhovich held (1908–12; 1912/19) that Marx's value theory had nothing to do with his communist vision, and that the latter had to be understood within the framework of his theory of collapse, as developed by Engels. Boudin argues (1907; 1912, pp. 150–65): 'This inevitable breakdown can only be understood and explained with the aid of the Marxian theory of value.'

He refers partly to the mechanism of the falling rate of profit, which is based on the idea of labour-saving technical progress. In addition, he develops a consistent Marxian accumulation theory. Accumulation depends on the existence of an 'elastic working-class'. Capitalism must go on creating technological unemployment. This tends to hold down wages; the working-class reacts by becoming organised, so as to raise its standard of living. At the same time, concentration brings about an ossification of capitalism and unused capacity in cartels. These represent a kind of 'reserve army of capitalists', who hold only quotas in cartels without serving any social purpose. Over-capacity in turn leads to disproportion-ality: 'The surplus product . . . will find no purchasers, will clog the wheels of production and bring the whole economic machinery of society to a stop. . . . The purely mechanical, economic breakdown of the capitalist system will result, according to the Marxian theory, from the inherent contradictions of the law of value. . . . ' One could call Boudin a precursor of the Bronfenbrenner formula.

Before Boudin, other 'bourgeois' theorists had taken up the cue furnished by Engels: above all, the Czech philosopher Masaryk, who wrote at the same time as Cunow. Masaryk asserts that Marx 'prophesied that capitalist society will soon collapse', owing to the concentration process, which destroys small business and ruins the workers. Grossmann em-phasises (1929; 1970, pp. 34ff.) that Masaryk (1899, pp. 223, 226, 287ff.) quotes no texts of Marx to support his theory of 'breakdown'. Masaryk believes that Marx is disproved because the middle class has not disappeared and a relative increase in poverty has not taken place.

The theory of growing poverty is the subject of a whole book by Michels (1928), who goes back to its origins with Locke and to the theory of 'catastrophy', which he believes exists in Marx's works and which he traces to the particular conditions of the Industrial Revolution (pp. 194–5).

Prior to Michels, Spiethoff (1919, p. 439) tried to attribute to Marx a 'theory of collapse' based, it appears, on the forces of under-consumption. Finally, Sombart thought (1924, 1, p. 395) that a 'breakdown theory' is to be found in the *Communist Manifesto*, but he admits that an explicit thesis of this kind 'has not since been developed, either by Marx–Engels or their successors'.

Hilferding tried in vain to counteract these misinterpretations by denying that such a theory was held by Marx. For instance, he declared at the 1927 Kiel Congress of the German Social Democratic Party (1927; see also Grossmann 1929/1970, p. 57):

> I have always refused to accept a theory of economic collapse. In my opinion, Marx also showed that such a theory was wrong. . . . There has been no such breakdown. We have no reason to regret this. We have always been of the opinion that the collapse of the capitalist system must not be awaited in a fatalistic mood, that it will not be triggered off by the inner laws of this system, but that it must be brought about by the conscious will of the working-class.

Thus Hilferding appears as a protagonist of 'voluntarism', and the fatalism thesis of the Second International seems barely tenable. It is true, however, that the Second International was shocked wherever real revolutions broke out and degenerated into dictatorships, as Karl Kautsky's bitter diatribes against the Bolshevik system prove. Kautsky even hoped (1931, pp. 54ff.) that there would be a peasants' revolt.

The presumed theory of collapse had deeply penetrated the consciousness of many Marxists. This is proved by the fact that Charasov (1910), Braunthal (1927) and Grossmann (1929) discuss it earnestly. However, after 1927, when the 'pope' of the Second International, Kautsky, condemned the theory, it disappeared from socialist textbooks, in spite of what appeared to be the almost complete breakdown of capitalism in the great depression.

Braunthal discusses (1927, pp. 7ff.) chiefly the Luxemburg–Sternberg version of the theory. He thinks, however, that in the 'younger Marx', i.e. the Marx of the *Manifesto*, certain traces may be found of this idea, 'as if he regarded crises as those kinds of contradictions which will increase and become ever more insoluble, bringing about the downfall of the capitalist economy'. In Braunthal's eyes, the 'mature Marx' 'did not expect the victory of socialism to arise from breakdown and increasing poverty, but, on the contrary, from an increasing polarisation of the two classes', within the framework of the concentration process. Braunthal thinks that whoever believes in a 'breakdown' from within must fall a victim to 'passivity'.

Charasov pronounces himself against a 'theory of collapse', which he appears to find in Marx's thesis of the tendency of the rate of profit to fall.

He introduces a sort of revolutionary trade-union theory. He is convinced that the fall in the rate of profit does not occur in the way Marx thinks, but rather in the manner of the 'harbinger theory'. According to Charasov, it is the working class that should bring about the downfall of capitalism, by demanding ever higher wages: 'Then the general crisis will not have to be awaited' and the workers would take over the productive system and accumulation. (Charasov, 1910, pp. 294, 316ff.) The scarcity of labour in the 1960s led modern British Marxists such as Glyn and Sutcliffe to adopt this theory; they may be called modern Charasovians.

Finally, Bukharin, who, in spite of his antagonism to Rosa Luxemburg, nevertheless espoused a kind of 'theory of collapse', says (1926, pp. 120ff.) that 'the process of extended reproduction must . . . [produce] contradictions which will of necessity blow up the capitalist system as a whole'. In another context, he explains this by a series of imperialist wars which he expects.

THE BAUER-GROSSMANN VERSION

Grossmann, to whom we owe the most comprehensive review of the 'collapse' theory, built his own version on Otto Bauer's growth schemes, which Bauer had developed (1913, pp. 838ff.) in his criticism of Rosa Luxemburg. Bauer's schemes showed a slowly decreasing rate of profit. Grossmann took up this hint, extended it, and tried to show that the rate of profit would decline from the eleventh year onwards and would finally, once the fortieth year was reached, tend towards zero. The accumulation rate, which is contained in Bauer's schemes, must eventually have the consequence that from the thirty-fourth year onwards capitalists would no longer be able to consume anything.

Grossmann thought (1929, p. 122) that such a situation would be 'synonymous with a decomposition of the capitalist mechanism, and with its economic end'. Grossmann's critics, above all Hans Neisser, had a relatively easy task. Neisser showed (1931, p. 73) that Grossmann's results were but a tautology, if one takes his premises for granted. If the rate of profits keeps falling, 'the moment must come when surplus value will no longer suffice to continue accumulation . . . at the required rate', even if the capitalist class keeps cutting its consumption.

Neisser criticises above all the condition of a 'proportional extension of the various productive branches', by which Grossmann, as it were, assumed away the disturbance which might have made his approach fertile, independent of the 'fall in the rate of profit'. Furthermore, Grossmann looks at technical progress in a one-sided way and cannot imagine that it may be capital-saving. Lenin's dictum that arithmetical tricks do not prove anything seems to fit Grossmann's reasoning.

Grossmann struck opposition everywhere, and, although he wrote on the eve of the great depression, his scheme soon fell into oblivion, and with it also the 'theory of collapse'.

Since 1945, this idea has been revived in Georgescu–Roegen's criticism of the Bauer–Sweezy under-consumption scheme, which we have already analysed in chapter 15 of this volume. In Georgescu–Roegen's account (1960; 1966, p. 399), one statement is remarkable: 'Surprising as this may seem, the Marxist scheme of extended reproduction cannot be cast into a mathematically correct model'.

By and large, this author agrees with Howard and King (1975, p. 210) when they say that Marx 'does not use his theory of the falling rate of profit to argue for any mechanical "breakdown" theory of Capitalism, for Marx has no such theory. . . '.

But Marx seems indeed to view his theory of the falling rate of profit – in its long-run version as well as in its cyclical version – 'as a vindication of his general theory of historical materialism by showing that Capitalism faces a barrier to accumulation which in turn implies that it is not an absolute mode of production, but is historical and relative' (Howard and King, ibid.).

27 The Debate on the Future of Capitalism

The global debate on the future of capitalism was resumed in the 1950s by Marxists outside the Eastern bloc, above all in Japan. There a discussion developed among economists such as Goto, Kawa and Tsuru, of whom the last two could be considered Marxists. This discussion remained unknown outside Japan, since it was carried on in Japanese. Then in 1961 Tsuru published a collection of essays on this subject, in English. In this collection a number of leading Marxist economists, and along with them Galbraith, discussed the problem.

THE ESSENCE OF THE TSURU DEBATE 1956–61

Tsuru raised four central issues:

(1) Has capitalism changed, and is it now immune from severe depressions?
(2) What economic difference is there between capitalism and socialist states?
(3) What are the prospects for the future? Will there be mass unemployment again?
(4) What is the future of capitalism? Can it slowly transform itself into socialism?

Questions (1) and (3) are almost synonymous. The Frenchman Bettelheim repeated orthodox arguments, stating (in Tsuru, 1961, pp. 93ff.) that capitalism could not develop enough mass purchasing power. He thinks that oligopoly capitalism puts a brake on technical progress, and under-utilisation of capacity is for him its principal vice as compared with socialism, which leads to full capacity utilisation.

The Russian Kronrod recognises (ibid., pp. 111ff.) that some measure of income redistribution underpins prosperity, but he believes that latent forces making for crises are accumulating. He thinks that militarisation and technical progress will support growth, but must also lead to inflation, over-capacity and finally depression. Strachey (ibid., pp. 67ff.) sees the main dilemma for 'late capitalism' as consisting in the fact that full employment can be maintained only if profits remain high and are not threatened by redistribution.

Baran (ibid., pp. 147ff.) did not answer the questions directly, but developed a version of the under-consumption theory. Concentration causes a shrinking number of giant firms to acquire a growing share in the social product, which leads to less desirable forms of production (advertising, selling costs, frequent changes of style, and so on) and consumption ('gadgets'), instead of resources being used for rational purposes. Besides, productivity grows faster than real wages, and the 'surplus' cannot be absorbed by capitalist consumption and investment. Not enough will be spent on collective consumption, except for irrational armaments. Capitalism must finally founder in unproductive expenses.

Dobb's contribution (ibid., pp. 139ff.) is more reticent. He thinks that the two main theses are wrong. Those who think capitalism has undergone no transformation are 'dogmatical', and those who exaggerate the transformation that has taken place, dreaming of the 'Welfare State', are revisionist Utopians. Neither armaments nor state capitalism is a new phenomenon. Lenin discovered the latter's roots before 1914. The state's control over production is still limited. What matters is only the high share of the public sector in the social product. This offers greater opportunities for anticyclical state activity, but there is no certainty that these will be used. There has been only a slight shift in favour of low incomes. Oligopoly is the main problem. It provokes over-capacity, if high profits are reinvested in the same sector; and, if invested elsewhere, rivalry grows and profits fall.

Tsuru himself reminds us (ibid., p. 4) that economists such as Clark and Betin were disappointed in their forecasts that there would be deep depressions in the 1950s. Even the synchronised recession of 1958 remained moderate, and otherwise there prevailed a desynchronisation of the international cycle. To Tsuru's way of thinking, Stalin propped up capitalism by provoking the 'cold war' after Korea, which gave rise to armament booms. These cannot maintain prosperity indefinitely, and eventually it is necessary to switch from instruments of death to instruments of life. Redistribution of income by itself will not do. It is the use of profits which has to be modified. Traditional nationalisation can contribute to the transformation of a society which has so far not changed fundamentally. The chief instrument for a gradual transformation of capitalism is, for Tsuru, a rational reinvestment of profits, which would represent a 'socialisation' of flows rather than of stocks.

Sweezy (ibid., pp. 83ff.) contests the argument that income distribution is more equal, for business expenses and fringe benefits for managers are larger than ever. Previously, business booms and recessions (for instance, the 1958 one) have been of the traditional kind, and capitalism can be transformed only through socialisation.

Galbraith emphasises (ibid., pp. 167 ff.) that liberals and Marxists agree that economic power must be counteracted; but, curiously enough, this power has been enhanced with the disappearance of competition, and trade unions represent only partially a 'countervailing power'. Tsuru cites a number of Japanese economists – for instance, Goto, who is optimistic about the future of capitalism, for he points out that prior to 1953 the USA survived two drastic reductions of military spending without deep depressions. Another optimist is Kawa, who sees capitalism's resurgence as a reaction to the challenge of the Soviet bloc, and the stabilising effects of redistribution through taxation.

Tsuru himself thinks (ibid., pp. 206 ff.) that the latter effect may be counteracted by a higher propensity to save. He reminds us that private consumption, which amounted to 75 per cent of the social product of the USA in 1937–9, has been reduced to 65 per cent. On the other hand, he thinks that an investment share of 15–16 per cent (USA, 1947–56) is too low. He comes near to Baran when he states that the growing 'surplus' must be counteracted by (possibly unproductive) spending, but goes beyond him in his view that Keynesian demand management, 'humped' technical progress and an increase in the share of services may help to stabilise capitalism.

Tsuru enumerates other positive factors: innovations (nuclear energy, automation, electronics, air transport, synthetic materials), automatic stabilisers, stable oligopolistic ('administrative') pricing, a growing public sector and intensified Keynesian demand management have underpinned prosperity. Rising instalment credit, capital exports, 'waste' of resources and more rapid obsolescence assist to the same end.

Tsuru nevertheless believes that many negative elements persist. Capitalism still relies on profit, which appears not to have changed its basic character: he quotes Meyer and Kuh, who stress the rising share of undistributed company profits. State activities remain limited, and there is a tendency to reverse the trend. Redistribution and the production of armaments cannot be intensified beyond a certain point. He sees the decisive element for a transformation into socialism in a (flexible) kind of nationalisation, which, however, is not possible in the existing political structure in the West. Oligopolies will oppose the long-run state planning of investment. He favours a policy of growing state participation.

After all, the US growth rate remained modest from 1944 to 1956: 1·8 per cent per annum as compared with 2·9 per cent for 1918–29. If recessions have become milder, other problems still exist, as follows:

- Will increased innovations lead to greater depressions later?
- Has income distribution really become more equal?
- Can the decreased share of personal consumption be reversed or counteracted by investment or collective consumption?
- Has the rate of technical progress been reduced through oligopolisation?

THE NAPOLEONI–COLLETTI VERSION

In an introduction to a collection of essays, the Italian economist Napoleoni says (Napoleoni and Colletti, 1970, pp. xxi, xxv) that Marx saw two main levers destined to bring about the downfall of capitalism: the long-run falling tendency of the rate of profit and the intensification of the business cycle. Napoleoni does not find a 'theory of collapse' in Marx, and he reminds us that even Lenin never accepted the 'idea of an unavoidable crash'.

In the same volume, Colletti confirms (p. cvii) that Bukharin was not in favour of a theory of collapse either. He thinks that the only serious representative of the 'theory of collapse' is Grossmann. Colletti summarises his own opinion by saying that 'blind alley situations never exist'.

ELEMENTS OF COLLAPSE CONCEPTS IN 'ACADEMIC' THEORY

Now, paradoxically enough, an absolute optimism about capitalism's future has not always prevailed in 'academic' economics. In his 1973 study, Harrod points out (p. 35) that in the 1930s many economists thought that capitalism 'would go pfut'. Perhaps Hansen's stagnation theory, developed in the 1930s, could also be considered in this context.

Harrod's instability principle reinforces a possible 'breakdown' conception, and so does Hicks's proof that the cycle contains explosive elements. It cannot be denied that Hicks is in general rather critical of Harrod's work, and that the general trend of neo-classical economics has played down Harrod's instability principle. Yet, even in Solow's model, traces of instability remain, as Wan has pointed out (1971, pp. 138–9):

> In a Solovian one-sector model, diminishing marginal product of capital . . . assures the uniqueness of the balanced growth path. In a two-sector model, one must assume either that the consumption goods industry is the more capital-intensive or that the elasticity of factor substitution is not less than unity in both sectors . . . .
>
> Direct generalization of the Solovian model leads to underdeterminacy of the momentary equilibrium, which is much more serious than the indeterminacy in two-sector models. . . . The crucial questions now become: Is the growth path stable? and: What is the implication of an unstable path?

Wan also emphasises (ibid., pp. 122 ff.) that in a two-sector model equilibrium will prevail only if either the consumption-goods industry is more capital-intensive or the elasticity of factor substitution in both sectors does not fall below one. This has also been stressed by Morishima, who thinks that Marx, in his two-sector model, was about to discover this kind of instability. On the other hand, Sato has stated (1964, p. 380) that the variations in capital-intensity cannot be very great; if so, the Harrod-Domar rigidity cannot be wide of the mark. Finally, Eisner has proved (1958, pp. 707 ff.) that Harrod based his reasoning not on rigid proportions as such, but on the rigidity of the rate of interest.

At any rate, Harrod has undauntedly upheld his instability principle. Thus, Marx's intuition is more or less justified, if not confirmed, by a not negligible body of 'academic' theory. After all, it was Marx who established the principle that the process of accumulation 'without constantly recurring explosions' was inconceivable (*Capital*, III, ch. 15, p. 258).

PROBLEMS NOT MENTIONED

A number of factors have not been specifically mentioned in these debates, especially those which propped up prosperity in the 1950s and 1960s:

- the temporarily mitigating effect of the desynchronisation of the cycle in Europe and America;
- the 'super-Keynesian' effect of almost permanent US balance-of-payment deficits (Tsuru still thought of dollar shortages!);
- linked to this, the credit expansion based on the Eurodollar system; and
- the possibly stabilising influence of a higher share of services in gross national product.

The last factor is contested by authors such as Gillard and Sereni, who point out (1968, p. 145) that instability is greatest in countries with a high share of services (Great Britain, USA, Netherlands), but these authors acknowledge that instability seems to be less where the tertiary sector grows fast. It is not clear what is cause and effect in this context.

Structural modifications are difficult to judge, especially as potential instability seems to be greater where investment-goods industries prevail. With the development of light industry in the less-developed countries, the investment-goods sector, including durable consumer goods, which may be considered as household investment, may loom larger in industrial countries.

The elements making for more violent fluctuations have not been considered in the debate. These include

- the exhaustion of the once-for-all effect of trade liberalisation in world trade and the reappearance of protectionism;
- the growing importance of the Kuznets (or 'transport-building') cycle;
- the reversion of growth cycles into traditional cycles in the 1970s;

– the slowing-down of technical progress and some growth industries; and
– the phenomenon of 'stagflation' in the 1970s.

THE 'NEW LEFT' AND THE FUTURE OF CAPITALISM

The analysis of the future of capitalism has been carried on by a number of authors, who have been subsumed under the title of the 'New Left'. Their views have been summarised and criticised by an 'academic' author, Lindbeck (1971, pp. 10, 32, 54ff.).

The critical attitude of these authors is directed partly against traditional economics, partly against capitalism. They rebuke 'academic' economists for concentrating too much on microeconomic problems, studying marginal changes instead of qualitative transformations. They also think that 'academic' economists neglect dynamic distribution aspects, external effects and the 'quality of life', while overemphasising the allocation of resources.

Lindbeck in turn censures the 'New Left' for thriving on nothing but negative attitudes and criticism and neglecting the new 'socialist' economics, which deals with methods of planning, though it itself threatens to become immuned in its own traditionalism.

Lindbeck's main criticism of the 'New Left' is that its attitude remains heterogeneous and muddled. It wants neither markets nor bureaucratic centralism, wants 'pure needs' to be catered for while rejecting distortions through advertising, but does not want the state to direct consumption. It desires a decrease in economic power and in inequality, but it does not deal adequately with the problems of incentives, which has led socialist states to create artificial inequalities. Thus, the 'New Left' does not clearly indicate where a transformation of capitalism may lead. Lindbeck himself thinks that a solution for a new society could be found by eliminating centralisation in many areas where it now exists and by introducing it elsewhere, where it may be indispensable.

Lindbeck's book provoked a number of violent reactions. Hymer and Roosevelt upbraid him (1972, pp. 644ff.) for having muddled the issues. They say he offered nothing but a 'bourgeois paradigm', and they refer to Keynes, who said that modern capitalism is neither intelligent nor beautiful nor just and that its worst fault is that 'it doesn't deliver the goods'. They criticise Lindbeck for not mentioning the alternative to marginal productivity analysis offered by the British Cambridge School, for not taking into account Marx's analysis of an endogenous transformation of preferences, and, finally, for totally neglecting the dynamics of historical processes.

Sweezy objects (ibid., pp. 663ff.) that Lindbeck believes the market system to be superior because it promotes 'innovation'; he thinks that it would be better to stick to quality products once reached and to concentrate on the humanisation of working conditions. He asks why the authors of the 'New Left', many of whom had been writing since the 1940s, had not found large audiences before the 1960s.

A non-Marxist, G. L. Bach, points out (ibid., pp. 634ff.) that the 'New Left' does not often enough have recourse to the dynamic theories of those who could now perhaps be called the 'Old Left', Joan Robinson and Kaldor. (see *Quarterly Journal of Economics*, 1972.)

Finally, Tobin (1972, p. 1217) justly castigates Lindbeck for not mentioning the problem of participation and joint decision-making in industry, which may be the touchstone for distinguishing the New Left's 'genuine' socialism from bureaucratic state planning. It may be that Marx himself pointed the way in his references to associations of free producers and so on.

A RETURN TO MARX'S VISION OF APOCALYPSE?

Another point which Lindbeck does not discuss in detail concerns the chances of survival of humanity in general, a topic which has been raised by some fashionable modern publications, notably that of the Club of Rome.

In this context, it must be emphasised that Marx attacked Malthus passionately, censuring him for making inadmissible comparisons between human and animal environments. He also chided Malthus for ignoring productivity increases in agriculture and industry and for transforming sociological problems into ethical ones.

The Club of Rome, in its 'Neo-Malthusianism' and 'Neo-Ricardianism', has argued that, with exponential growth, raw materials would be exhausted around 2050 (Meadows 1972). If one were to attempt to counteract this by the industrial development of new artificial materials, environmental pollution would increase to such an extent that human existence would be threatened from that side.

Marx did not ignore the tendencies towards depletion in capitalism. After all, he wrote (*Theories*, III, ch. 21, p. 309):

> Anticipation of the future – real anticipation – occurs in the production of wealth only in relation to the worker and to the land. The future can indeed be anticipated and ruined in both cases by premature over-exertion and exhaustion, and by the disturbance of the balance between expenditure and income. In capitalist production this happens to both the worker and the land.

This recalls Hicks's suspicion (1950, p. 302) that the past 200 years may be nothing but a gigantic capitalist boom, and Georgescu-Roegen's admonition (1966, p. 68) that economic progress must end in entropy, i.e. create inorganic waste in the sense of the thermodynamic law of Clausius. Marx himself was optimistic: he thought that technical progress was unlimited and might bring about an age of plenty under socialism, although he did not bother to predict the future.

This point has been taken up by Bombach and other authors who argue that dire need would provoke new responses to the challenge. Marxism here encounters neo-classical authors such as Solow, who counters the apostles of 'zero growth' by pointing out (1972; 1974, pp. 49ff.) that productivity in the use of natural resources has grown exponentially over the last century or so, for copper, lead, zinc, manganese and iron by some 2 or 2·5 per cent since 1950, and for coal by 3 per cent, though for oil it stagnated and for natural gas it actually decreased, owing to low prices prior to 1973. The present author has elsewhere (1973, pp. 111–130) tried to reconcile socialist and neo-classical attitudes on this point.

Other authors, like Herre (1973, p. 16), have pointed out that it was Rosa Luxemburg who examined the methods which would allow capitalism to stave off disaster – namely, by extending the capitalist mode of production to the entire globe, thus exploiting its natural resources and labour to the maximum.

Although 'academic' economists such as Beckerman have condemned prophecies of doom as dangerous nonsense, it nonetheless remains true that there is severe doubt about whether less developed countries can attain the standard of living of modern industrialised countries – unless, that is, the population explosion is stopped and the husbandry of resources through socialist planning is introduced.

Part VI
Synthesis

28 The Contribution of Marx to Economics

The future of the Marxian system will not depend solely on its intrinsic value as a philosophical and sociological system and perhaps even less on its critical attitude towards traditional economics. On the contrary, Marxism will be confronted by tangible economic tasks, the more so as the large part of the world dominated by its doctrine will develop. It is in this context that one has to ask what its cash value is in economic analysis.

Here we encounter two basic objections. The first is what may be called Marxist holism: this is the tradition which fights desperately for an elimination of what it calls 'economism' and which would like to transform Marxism into a science in its own rights. The protagonists of this interpretation try to justify their attitude by the argument that Marx was able to combine philosophy, history, sociology and economics into a comprehensive and apparently indivisible whole. This, however, was also true of John Stuart Mill and other contemporaries; such holism is simply no longer possible, in view of the sheer size of the literature in each of these disciplines.

If we deliberately analyse only one aspect or even parts of it, we do so because the vast literature on all these subjects together is no longer manageable not just because the master's touch is lacking. This author candidly admits that he has deliberately stuck to his (economic) guns; this renunciation of a holistic (and inevitably muddled) approach may rather be considered a virtue.

The second objection is that advanced especially by younger Italian Marxists. For instance, Botta says (1971, pp. 135, 137),

> It is quite evident that Marx was no economist, and that the economic dimension did . . . not enjoy a position of privilege in his theory. . . . Marxism is nothing but a critical social science of the working class, an instrument of theoretical criticism for the proletariat . . . which permits the discovery of the economic laws which reflect 'constraining tendencies' and indicate the path of economic evolution . . .

Such reasoning must be opposed strongly. There can be no doubt that economics is always prone to stumble into the pitfalls of class-conditioned 'wishful thinking'. The reverse, however, is also true: any economics based purely on a class point of view is self-deluding. Besides, we must not forget that Marx himself recognised the possibility that 'non-vulgar' pure economics might be possible, for he said of Ricardo that he was 'not vulgar' – in other words, no mere apologist. Science is not to be found on the shop floor. Economics has to be learnt, like any other craft, not only to enable us to criticise, but also for positive use.

This thesis must be seen in conjunction with another illusion, that of the 'withering-away of economics', which will doubtless prove as illusory as the famous thesis of the 'withering-away of the state'. A victorious working-class or the advent of socialism requires more and not less economics. Planning is impossible without planners who master economic categories.

This is by no means true only of macroeconomics. Individual plants or firms will persist under socialism, and this will give industrial economics a rather higher status than hitherto. Under capitalism, the owner can perhaps allow himself the luxury of renouncing scientific business methods; if an enterprise is owned by the nation, muddling through is no longer admissible. A planning system cannot thrive on the criticism of past institutions and theories. What, then, is the contribution of Marxism to positive economic analysis?

Jordan has complained (1971) that Marx's contribution to empirical and pragmatic sociology has been largely ignored; one dare say the same of his practical contributions to economics, which were by no means limited to a critique of capitalism's faults. Even the critical parts of his work contained positive elements, as Leontief, who praised Marx's acuity in the practical analysis of concrete phenomena, has reminded us.

SURPLUS VALUE AND 'EXPLOITATION' AS AN INPUT–OUTPUT ANALYSIS

Positive elements in this sense are even contained in what may seem Marx's most abstract theorem – his value concept.

We have pointed out that a value scheme alongside 'normal' price schemes in economics can be justified by the consideration that it amounts to a (hypothetically) different allocation of that part of value added which is not paid out in the form of wages. The sum of profits is allocated to different branches not as a mark-up on their 'total costs' (or as a percentage of turnover), but in accordance with what may be called a co-operative formula, on the basis of the manpower input.

In other words, in his 'pricing formula' in volume III of *Capital*, Marx, as is the practice of most businessmen, relates profits not to the stock of capital but to current expenses for purchases, depreciation and wages paid. Since he insists on the tendency of the rate of profit to be the same in every industry, this results in a more or less uniform mark-up on costs, assuming the absence of monopolistic distortions.

Now, provided labour is distributed among those industries in a technologically optimal fashion, a value scheme boils down to this: the sum of profits is allocated not in proportion to total costs $(c+v)$, i.e. as a mark-up on costs, but only in proportion to the wage bill (v) in each industry. In other words, every worker is credited with an equal share in the total profits of the economy, although this share need not be paid out to him. This would be tantamount to (profit and) price increases in labour-intensive industries and to corresponding decreases in capital-intensive ones (i.e. those with a high share of c).

This is our interpretation of the value scheme, which is justified as a sort of macroeconomic 'participation' scheme that considers each wage-earner as a prospective shareholder in the economy and anticipates to some extent profit-sharing schemes. That it is based on a system of 'technologically optimum distribution of the labour force' has been recognised by such authors as Zinn and Rehberg (1977, p. 421). The concept of surplus value or 'exploitation' rests on the sociologically conditioned division of value added at the macroeconomic level, i.e. on the division of national income.

Marx, in his *Critique of the Gotha Programme*, gave it the right macroeconomic flavour, depriving it of any romantic moral implications. The concept then found its most sober formulation in Joan Robinson's interpretation. The entire 'socially necessary' labour time is compared with the labour time spent on the replacement of productive assets and stocks and on the production of wage goods. The difference yields the mass of surplus value, and its ratio to wage goods the rate of surplus value. Meldolesi (in von Bortkiewicz, 1971, pp. xviii, lxxff.) calls this the birth of surplus value from a sequence of theoretical configurations, the real basis of which is the production process. He also reminds us that von Bortkiewicz, to whom so many critics refer, derived surplus value and the Marxian notion of profit in this way, after correcting the mathematical flaws.

Marx's specific achievement lies in the elaboration of the concept of surplus value, in the sense of the creation of a surplus of outputs over inputs, without relying on a price theory based upon a demand–supply concept. It is not the formula of exploitation as such which was new in Marx's reasoning, for exploitation had been directly visible in the feudal world, but it had taken on a mysterious form under capitalism and Marx wanted to demystify it by exposing its essence, which was the same as under other social systems.

A younger Italian economist, Lippi, has clearly formulated this idea (1973, p. 257):

> I do not believe that the problem for Marx was to show the existence of exploitation in the capitalist world. That part of the labour product is

appropriated by a class of non-workers without a valid title . . . was
only too obvious to Marx and had besides been enunciated with the
greatest clarity by the early (Ricardian) socialists. Marx even started
from the assumption that a 'surplus' existed over and above that part of
the product destined to replace (real) capital and to pay
wages. . . . Marx's scientific problem consisted in showing how [exploit-
ation] can proceed under social conditions where human relations are
no longer based on personal submission, and in which the laws of
exchange are not violated . . . .

Marx accomplished this by showing that the working class as a whole
spends only part of its working time in producing consumption goods for
itself and in replacing fixed assets and stocks. Thus a surplus arises in von
Neumann's sense, i.e. where one considers labour time spent for (necessary) consumption and replacement as 'input destined to reproduce
productive forces'. If one applies this reasoning to individual workers, the
phenomenon of a surplus is to be explained by the fact that, in exchange for
the use of his labour, the worker receives (*via* a money advance) the
quantity of consumption goods which corresponds to his historically and
sociologically determined standard of living, and, where he saves, possibly
more. The product, however, will fetch more on the market as long as these
historically determined claims, which reflect the relative strength of the
two classes in their economic struggle, do not exceed a certain limit. With
the introduction of the class struggle, Marx goes beyond the von Neumann
concept, which recognises consumption only as input to produce robots.

In a dynamic sense, the persistence of surplus value is guaranteed by
technical progress, which is for Marx more labour-saving than capital-
saving and, therefore, tends periodically to replenish the 'industrial reserve
army', thus fending off any serious threat that wage claims may present to
surplus value. Samuelson claims that Marx did not demonstrate this, but
one may dare say that the Phillips curve makes up for that.

THE TRANSFORMATION OF VALUES INTO PRICES

The distribution of the surplus takes place in proportion to 'capital', which
in Marx's analysis is not a stock but a flow, i.e. capital spent on
replacements, purchases and wages at plant level.

The so-called 'transformation problem' arises only if there are different
degrees of capital-intensity in various industries. In a 'value scheme',
surplus is allocated to each industry in proportion to its wage bill, which is
proportionate also to total costs if there are no differences in labour-
intensity. In a 'price scheme', surplus is allocated to each industry in
proportion to total cost, through the mechanism of the 'equalisation of the
rate of profit', which works through competition and in the absence of

excessive monopolistic distortions. We emphasise the term 'excessive', because the very existence of a profit margin proves that competition is not strong enough to compete it away.

Modern authors sympathetic to Marx's theories (for instance, Ullmo – 1973, p. 115) are inclined to consider this problem of secondary, if not negligible, importance. It may therefore appear astonishing that this theorem has become a favourite subject of mathematically inclined economists, as the exercises of Samuelson and Morishima show.

The Italian quasi-Marxist Napoleoni even thinks (1972, pp. 172–3) that the problem has disappeared since Sraffa's neo-Ricardian revolution, for in Sraffa's system 'the rate of profit and the system of production prices are simply determined by a certain production constellation, i.e. by physical quantities of goods . . . and means of production without referring to the labour quantities they contain'. Napoleoni thinks that Sraffa's results may be quoted 'to confirm the possibility of the determination of these prices and rates of profit independent of value theory'. Then one could say: 'If we tackle the transformation problem in rigorous pursuit of the line Marx sketched, it will destroy itself automatically, for one does not get a transformation of values into prices, but simply a determination of prices without values . . . .'

This reminds us of Samuelson's attempt to derive a 'rate of exploitation' from mere quantitative data. On the other hand, one may harbour some doubts with regard to Napoleoni's audacious interpretation, for most commentators on Sraffa's work seem to agree that his 'rate of profit' is externally determined.

VALUE THEORY OBSOLETE?

Some authors, such as Guihéneuf (1952, p. 166), still uphold the value theory, which Pareto ironically dubbed 'the Marxists' banner'. Guihéneuf has asserted that, 'if the labour theory of value is eliminated from Marxism, nothing remains!'. This rash statement has been contradicted by Lukacz, who states (1970, p. 58) that the essence of Marxism consists not in this or that theory, but exclusively in its dialectical methodology.

There is, however, no question of value theory being discarded altogether. It may retain a certain expository usefulness in static analysis – for instance, in an attempt to show 'the social relations in capitalism' (Guihéneuf, 1952, p. 184) – provided equal capital-intensity in all industries is assumed, and it may appear interesting to elicit the theoretical, potential 'co-operative social dividend' per worker; but value theory is certainly neither necessary for nor even useful for or applicable to dynamic analysis. After all, it would be amazing if this clumsy apparatus, which Marx had inherited from the classics, should constitute the kernel of

Marxism, which would then be Ricardian in essence.

Exploitation can be demonstrated more directly, as Graziadei has shown. Moreover, as Domar (1950, p. 140) has pointed out, modern Marxists need not insist on employing a stone axe once quality steel utensils are available. It would be strange if analytical methodology had not progressed since the times of Ricardo and Marx. Marx set great store by technical progress. Why should he have rejected it in economic technique?

Furthermore, thoughtful Marxists have always harboured doubts as to why the value scheme, which Marx saw as directly applicable only to pre-capitalist systems, should be compatible with capitalism, let alone with the higher stage of socialism. It is true that Marx seemed to hint that it might be restored in the latter. But the doyen of French Marxist economists, Denis, stated (1950, pp. 112, 115) that, 'with the disappearance of the blind and automatic market mechanism . . . value must disappear itself, for it owes its existence only to the market'. In its stead, 'thanks to the socialisation of production, social utility will play an essential part . . . in production and distribution'.

We here approach the concept of 'gross social utility' or cost–benefit analysis, which, in spite of some Marxists' ill-justified denunciation of it as a capitalist product, (Hunt and Schwartz, 1972, p. 30) has been propagated in our times by socialists such as Mansholt and 'academic' economists such as Juster (1973, pp. 25–83).

There are strong forces at work to overhaul the cumbersome apparatus of value theory, especially among Italian Marxists. Lippi (1973, pp. 247–8) concludes that the substance of Marx's exploitation theory could be maintained, and states that 'all those who do not harbour dogmatic prejudices' agree that it must be reformulated. Lippi asks himself 'why there has been . . . a refusal in Marxian theory to recognise results which are obvious and which have been reached outside and in opposition to the marginalist camp'. Here he is evidently thinking of the neo-Keynesians. Lippi believes that it was through Hilferding's influence, which helped to obscure their views, that orthodox Marxists got stuck up a blind alley, for Hilferding looked askance at 'production prices'. It may be an onset of pangs of conscience which has caused neo-classical writers to begin to discuss value theory again. This may be partly explained by the success of Sraffa's surplus concept, which is related to Marx's surplus value, but 'elevates it', in the Hegelian sense of the term. It is understandable that Samuelson should return to a study of Marx (who provides the basis of Sraffa's reasoning) after his relatively unsatisfactory 'surrogate production function'. His and von Weizsäcker's (1973, p. 263) attempt to formulate a modern version of the exploitation theory, relative to a growing economy, may be considered to represent a sort of convergence of the two schools.

It undoubtedly remains true that the main weakness of value theory consists in its clumsiness from the point of view of growth analysis: it does not show the growth in the 'volume' of 'use values'. This is all the more curious as Marx gave a decisive stimulus to dynamic analysis. It must be asked whether this weakness could not be eliminated by the use of 'compound values', i.e. productivity adjusted labour hours.

Here we encounter future tasks for Marxists who would like to develop a more extensive notion of value. It would then have to be assumed that productivity is increased by training and research; one would have to apply the so-called 'Denison hypothesis' of 'human capital'. This would agree perfectly with Marx's *Grundrisse*.

Modern Marxists (see Cutler, Hindess, Hirst and Hussain, 1977, I, pp. 51–95) tend to reject value theory, emphasising (p. 93) that 'the labour theory of value . . . must admit the crucial role of demand [and] a necessary composition of the social product'.

THE ROLE OF PROFIT

The gist of Marx's profit theory is his refusal to recognise the existence of a supply price for capital. Wicksell assumes that there would be a zero rate of interest in stationary equilibrium, and Schumpeter joins him in denying the existence of interest in a stationary economy. More recently, even neo-classical authors such as von Weizsäcker share this opinion.

The starting point for such considerations is the same as for Marx's concept, but he thought that a stationary equilibrium would be possible only at the turning points of the cycle, and that it would then be unstable. Marx recognised a 'minimum profit' below which the 'sting' for accumulation would be lacking. For him, Keynes's 'animal spirits' were not sufficient to ensure capitalism's survival. Some of Marx's most remarkable contributions are to be found in an analysis of the composition of what we today consider as gross profits, notional interest, employer's salary etc.

There is first of all the category of interest payable for loans; interest payments are recognised as an economic category by Marx, inspite of his refusal to ascribe a 'money-creating' capacity to capital as such. Now even socialist states consider a 'contribution to a Social Fund' or an interest of some kind payable on loans as indispensable to solving the problem of depreciation and the direction of investment. (Finger-Stoll, 1968, pp. 141ff.)

Marx also analysed the other 'notional' items of gross profits in rational cost-accounting: namely, risk premium, entrepreneur's salary and 'normal profit'. Even his method of calculating profits looks quite modern, for he relates gross profits not to the stock of capital, but to total costs. Ullmo formulates this (1973, p. 113) in a very pertinent manner: '$s/(c+v)$ is by no means a rate of profit, but a profit margin which is calculated "externally", as a ratio between profits and costs, and not "internally", as a ratio between profits and turnover . . . .'

Thus, the irony of the history of economic doctrine is such that Marx, who always protested against a mark-up theory and who was presented by von Bortkiewicz as the protagonist of a 'deduction theory', in fact did calculate a mark-up. One may even consider Marx's way of calculating his rate of surplus value, philosophically conditioned as it may be, as a sort of mark-up on the wage bill, as it has indeed been interpreted by such a Marxist as de Cindio, anticipating Hall and Hitch's 'full-cost principle' adhered to by many businessmen.

We must still add to this picture Marx's (and Engels's) discovery of the principle of dynamic depreciation, which Polak in the Netherlands, Ruchti and Lohmann in Germany, and Eisner and Domar in the literature in English rediscovered almost three-quarters of a century later. This brings us to the analysis of dynamic growth, investment and business cycles in Marx.

INVESTMENT IN MARX'S THEORY AND IN MODERN ECONOMICS

There is first of all a possible link between the notion of exploitation and that of investment. If the (economically) optimum level of investment is permanently exceeded, especially in the case of 'forced saving', this will mean that the nation as a whole is worse off than is necessary. This is the point where the neo-classical objections against investment superstition seem to be justified.

Ullmo has tried (1973, p. 138) to give an investment interpretation to the Marxian concept of exploitation: in the case of

over-investment, we encounter an excessive level of investment, which means that the well-being of society remains eternally below what it could get from its productive efforts, if only investment were better distributed over time. . . . Any society certainly has the right to sacrifice the present for the future, but it is of importance that this sacrifice should be efficient and that it does not result in a permanent loss of blood which is constantly repeated. Here a new version of exploitation appears: this implies a waste of human effort through the ill-conceived or the badly oriented use of [investment resources] . . . .

Ullmo is certainly thinking partly of investment idolatry in developing countries. The concept, however, is wider. An economy which largely operates below its potential, because it grows too slowly or is recession-ridden, would thus be characterised by this kind of 'exploitation'. The worst criticism of capitalism, or of any other system, would thus be that it failed to reach the 'natural growth rate' because the volume of investment was excessive.

This would then appear to be in the nature of 'self-exploitation' of the system, which would occur as a general rule at the expense of the masses, since the volume of investment and the share of profits are more or less identical. The attempt to find an 'actuarial rate of interest' corresponding to an optimum rate of growth – as it has been described by Desrousseaux (1965) and, in essence, von Weizsäcker (1973) – within, for instance, the framework of French indicative planning, is in this context of particular interest.

THE REAL ROLE OF INVESTMENT

Investment has a particular part to play in the Marxian scheme. Marx assumes that capital-using technical progress, or 'capital deepening', forms the basis for productivity increases in capitalism. This presupposes increasing investment. The irony of history becomes visible in Marx's insistence on the identity between capital formation and productivity increase, for this might be interpreted as synonymous with an assertion of the productivity of capital.

Marxism's great adversary, neo-classical theory, holds (König, 1968, p. 27) that technical progress falls like manna from heaven. It denies that capital-using progress is required to bring about an increase in productivity, for it imagines that replacement is sufficient to bring forth ever more efficient assets. In the early 1950s, Cairncross emphasised (1954, p. 234) that technical progress might operate independently of investment. This alternative seems tenable only if one assumes a permanently increasing level of training of labour and an ever improved efficacy of equipment. The emphasis on 'disembodied technical progress' seems to have reached its climax in the late 1950s.

This period of recantation was relatively brief. In 1962, Phelps enumerated the authors who argued against the identification of capital deepening with productivity increase: among them were Abramovitz, Fabricant, Kendrick and Solow. He pointed out, however (1962, p. 548), that a new synthesis of thesis and antithesis was developing. The new idea was that investment is the vehicle of technical progress. Phelps thinks that the breakthrough of the new concept came about through three publications – ECE (1959), PEP (1960) and US Council of Economic Advisers (1961) – before finding its classical formulation in Kaldor and Arrow. In fact, the new synthesis is already clearly apparent in Kaldor's famous article of 1957 (1957b, p. 596): technical progress, which had previously been considered a residual, was now considered as being 'embodied' either in gross investment generally or in successive 'vintages' of equipment (see Heubes, in Gahlen and Ott, 1972, p. 44).

Thus Marx's intuition is finally vindicated. Oppenländer says (ibid., p. 249) that 'investment as an explanatory factor is gaining in importance. . . . It is only through investment that the vehicle stimulating technical knowledge comes into being. It is in this way that we must understand Kaldor's technical-progress function and Arrow's concept of learning by doing . . . .'

Thus Kaldor's concept is linked even formally to the Marxian thesis. In Kaldor's system, the sum of annual investment is substituted for the capital stock; thus a flow replaces a stock, as does Marx's c. The rate of profit P/K is in Kaldor's system equal to $(P/Y) \times (Y/K)$. Kaldor thinks that the quotient P/Y is not very meaningful; entrepreneurs are scarcely influenced by their share in the social product, and this is a notion which is 'expectation-inelastic'. Ultimately, therefore, the rate of profit depends on the capital–output ratio only. This seems to show that there is a close link between Marx and the modern analysis of the capital–output ratio.

TECHNICAL PROGRESS AND CONCENTRATION

Marx makes the capital–output ratio, in the form $c:v$, the pivot of his theory of the business cycle. Perhaps the long-run version of his theory of the tendency of the rate of profit to fall may be linked to what we now call the Kuznets cycle, or to Kondratieff's 'secular long wave'. In that context, Marx seems to establish a phenomenology of wave-like movements in the character of technical progress, as the present author has tried to show elsewhere (Kühne, 1976, pp. 54ff.).

It was in fact Marx who saw the very essence of capitalism in technical progress. At the same time, his theory of concentration led him to link instability to this phenomenon.

Nowadays, Marx's anticipation of the modern phenomena of cartelisation and mergers is hardly contested, and the process appears to continue apace. Scherer shows for the United States (1971) that the increasing domination of the leading 100 industrial firms since 1947 is no statistical illusion: their share in value added rose from 23 per cent in 1947 to 33 per cent in 1966. Both Adelman and Samuelson err on this, and Marx is right, although the concentration process must peter out statistically the more complete it is.

Capitalist concentration and growth go hand in hand. The relatively faster growth in constant capital in proportion to wages, i.e. a growing capital–output ratio, is linked to the growth of big business.

MARX AND GROWTH THEORY

If for Marx technical progress was the lever controlling growth, the variability of the capital–output ratio was the auxiliary instrument. Here Marx raised a question which has subsequently been answered differently. He believed in a persistent bias in favour of labour-saving progress, while the neo-classical authors, who took their cue from Marx, recognised the pivotal character of the capital–output ratio, but insisted on its equilibrating character through alternating movements in the coefficient.

Marx certainly sketched the first (two-sector) model of equilibrium growth, but not in order to demonstrate that growth must inevitably be well-equilibrated. He wanted instead to establish the precariousness of capitalist growth.

He denied the neutrality of technical progress, thought that it occurred in swings and that it made the system thoroughly unstable. He tries to demonstrate this basic contradiction, remaining faithful to his dialectical method. Here he reaches the instability principle of Harrod and Domar, without being able to expound it explicitly.

MARX'S BUSINESS-CYCLE ANALYSIS

Marx tried to demonstrate his intuition about instability less in growth terms than in terms of the increasing amplitude of the business cycle. He discovered the eight- to ten-year cycle which Schumpeter dubbed the 'Juglar', although one can find elements of the Kuznets or 'transport-building' cycle in his theory of replacement cycles. Thus, half a dozen variants of cycle theory appear in a nutshell in Marx's theory, which relied heavily on the 'disproportionality' thesis. Marx inspired Tugan-Baranowsky, who in turn influenced Spiethoff; so Hansen and von Hayek were right to see in Marx one of the fathers of modern business-cycle analysis.

MARX AS AN ECONOMIST

This author agrees, by and large, with an interpretation given by Angus Walker in an unpublished manuscript (1977, p. 1): 'Karl Marx is more commonly thought of as a political theorist than as an economist. Marx's magnum opus is . . . primarily an economic study. Most of its 2000 pages are filled with the discussion of employment, price determination, income distribution, business cycles, capital accumulation and technical progress. The political theorist will find in it few answers to his questions . . . .'And the identity of capitalism and growth is forcefully stated by the Japanese Marxist Kozo Uno in an unpublished translation: 'Marx was the first economist to characterize capital as the self-augmenting motion of value' (1964/75, p. 107).

29 Marxian Economic Analysis and Socialist Systems

THE LASTING IMPORTANCE OF CYCLE AND GROWTH ANALYSIS UNDER SOCIALISM

Oscar Lange points out (1965; 1969, pp. 97, 120), in commenting upon Marx's theory of reinvestment or 'echo cycles' that these 'may appear also in a socialist economy' and that the heritage of a six year plan may thus be mirrored in the future. Notkin had somewhat earlier (1961) developed a theory of the stagelike nature of expanded reproduction, pointing out planning defects as one of the sources of cycles.

In the 1970s, Bernholz has raised (1972, I, pp. 179, 183) the general question of the stability of planned systems. He thinks that a market economy has the advantage of relying on a vast number of decentralised quantity transactions, which it transforms into information on prices, thereby acting like a gigantic computer. A market economy would on the other hand be inferior to a centrally planned system if it were more prone to instability, and the advantage of information does not exist with regard to public goods. Röpke once guessed (1932, p. 81) that instability, which under capitalism spreads from investment, would under socialism originate in the consumption sector.

Several authors – for instance, the American Nutter (1962) the Frenchman Zaleski (1962) and the Yugoslav Bajt (1971) – have examined the stability of communist systems. Zaleski states that Röpke's prediction was only partially true, for consumption and agriculture were only partial shock absorbers, and in 1932 there was stagnation in the Soviet steel industry. Staller (1964) examined the Comecon countries and Yugoslavia and concluded that they had shown bigger fluctuations since 1950 than the OECD countries, but he did not eliminate harvest fluctuations.

Economists of the Eastern countries have in the meantime demonstrated the existence of growth cycles. Goldmann (1964a,b) found for Czechoslovakia, East Germany, Poland and Hungary pure reinvestment 'quasicycles', although he suspected the existence of 'socialist speculation', i. e. the hoarding of investment goods. Pajestka (1968) discovered in the Polish construction industry what he called 'development cycles'.

Goldmann was criticised in the West by Olsienkiewicz, who thought (1969, p. 783) that expansion of investment did cause swings in consumption. The Argentine economist Olivera (1960, pp. 229ff.) partly confirmed Goldmann's views by discovering over-investment cycles, periodic 'stop–go' and concessions to consumers, which Goldmann thought were owing to a shortage of raw materials or foreign currency.

Nove investigated a longer period for the Soviet Union and pointed (1969, pp. 288, 302) to special reasons for apparently cyclical phenomena. These were the high importance of harvest fluctuations, internal and external political factors and a secular trend towards decreasing growth rates. He concludes that there were no genuine cycles in the Soviet Union. He was partially contradicted by a former Soviet economist, Levine, who thought that new technology introduced cyclical phenomena in the Soviet Union. A. Eckstein (1967) found similar phenomena for China and Gleitze (1974) for Eastern Germany. Whatever the outcome may be, it seems certain that, even for communist countries, cycle analysis retains some interest. Stability is certainly not a gift from heaven: it must be sought. It therefore seems nonsensical to talk about a 'withering away' of economics under such systems. On the contrary, macroeconomic planning will require more and not less economic science, as Marx, who inaugurated research in so many fields, would surely have confirmed.

Arturo Labriola spoke (1926; 1944) of 'the topical importance of Marx for our times'. This would seem to remain true for all aspects of economics.

THE DEBATE ON ECONOMIC CALCULUS UNDER SOCIALISM

Marx made no direct contribution to the subject of economic rationality or calculus, although he alluded to certain elements of price calculation. It was Engels who remarked that, under socialism, political economy would be banished with the state apparatus, the spinning wheel and the bronze axe to the museum.

Barone (1908) opened the debate on the political economy of socialism, which he thought would try to attain the beneficial results of the market mechanism through rational planning.

Von Mises (1920) contested the very possibility of rational calculus under socialism and Oscar Lange (1936) wanted to dedicate a monument to him for having provoked a debate among socialists on this subject. Joan Robinson declared (1949) that to introduce something equivalent to the rate of interest, for the sake of rational allocation, it was impossible not to take a leaf out of capitalism's book.

As Dobb stated in retrospect (1955, p. 57ff.), two replies were given to the attack by von Mises. First, Dickinson answered (1930) that socialism could well develop markets for the means of production, so its managers had to calculate rationally. Secondly, Lange wanted (1936) to retain markets for consumption goods only, while a system, such as exists inside trusts, of administered prices based on relative scarcity should be applied to equipment. Dobb himself cast some doubt on the rationality of consumers' decisions and stressed the growing importance of public and collective goods, for which the market mechanism does not work anyway.

Lerner emphasised (1934), in his criticism of Lange, that the rule 'marginal cost equals price' would apply also to a socialist system. Bergson's view (1948) was that von Mises's attack had lost its impetus, while Lange himself thought that moderate partisans of von Mises, such as von Hayek, had withdrawn to an intermediate position, acknowledging that rational allocation might in principle be possible under socialism, but that it would be improbable. Hesselbach (1971) has put the result in a nutshell by saying that liberals have had to recognise that private property is not the only rational system, while socialists have had to accept the regulatory function of decentralised markets.

The debate overlapped with that on 'welfare economics', the rationality of which has been contested by Little (1957) and by some socialists, such as the Weisser school in Germany (Kühne, 1963), while being upheld by other socialists, such as Pigou (1928; 1937), Bergson (1948), Lerner (1934) and Rittig (1977). In discussions during the 1960s, the last defenders of centralised budgetary socialism were Cubans such as Che Guevara (1963), while the French Marxist Bettelheim fought (1946) for a decentralised 'transitional economy'.

It remains to be seen how far, after the collapse of the 'Prague spring', the cautious reforms in Hungary and Poland and, since Liberman, in the Soviet Union will bring about this decentralisation and a 'convergence' of the systems, which would represent a 'synthesis' in dialectical terms. (Wilczynski, 1973, pp. 3ff.)

We must limit ourselves to these few remarks in this context, all the more so as the subject has been dealt with in detail in other publications, notably in Moshe Lewin's book (1974, pp. 127ff.).

30 Conclusions

In the two volumes comprising this work, an attempt has been made to subject the debate between 'academic' economics and Marxism to searching scrutiny, while translating the terminology into commonly intelligible terms. This has necessitated some, perhaps excessive, simplification.

We certainly do not want to advocate an intellectual 'convergence theory' but a dialectical confrontation can be fertile only if both sides make some concessions. The 'academic' economists must come down from the pedestal of their aloofness and recognise the similarity of certain propositions, while Marxists must acknowledge the value of analytical tools that are by no means system inspired but may help to replace antiquated weaponry.

The Marxian system was understood by its author as a critique. A critic must be fully conversant with what he criticises. Marx fulfilled this condition, for Schumpeter has certified that nothing of importance escaped his attention. This cannot be said of his epigones.

On the other hand 'academic' economists often do not read the basic texts, but are content to copy older misinterpretations.

This work is mainly intended to counteract the latter, but misinterpretations are by no means an 'academic' monopoly. It has become fashionable since Althusser to learn to read *Capital*, but one does no justice to Marx by reading his work using epistemological or historicist spectacles. Marx, in his late years, regarded himself more and more as an economist. To appreciate him as such, one must read him using current terminology while renouncing stereotype orthodox formulas and variations of the original text.

The real starting point of the Marxian system is not, as is often thought, the theory of exploitation, but Marx's criticism of the dehumanisation or 'alienation' under capitalism – in which direct human relations, between ruler and ruled, master and slave, exploiter and exploited, are replaced by indirect relations *via* commodities. Not only the workers, who no longer have an immediate relationship with their products, are alienated, but so too are the bourgeoisie: for them, domination is replaced by capital accounting.

Marx attacked this tendency. He hoped to overcome it under socialism. His research on the 'laws of motion' of capitalism undoubtedly had a teleological purpose: he hoped to establish that the evolution of the

313

economic infrastructure would bring about the overthrow of capitalism and would 'elevate it' into the higher sphere of rehumanised socialism. Marx very soon recognised that such an evolution could come about only once capitalism had fulfilled its own historical task of liberating mankind from the stagnation of traditionalism, and of launching a gigantic growth process for the forces of production, for living standards and for general intellectual development. This broadened outlook would of necessity create fissures in traditional ideology, which would permit the rise of new ideals for potentially revolutionary groups or classes. In this sense, will-power was for Marx an instrument of history.

On the other hand, he did not indulge in 'voluntarism', as did the followers of Blanqui in his time and as do the pupils of Marcuse today. Impulses at the economic level were indispensable if the old foundations were to be shattered. What mattered was not so much the question of whether violence must be the midwife by which an old society is delivered a new one as whether the birth pangs had commenced, for without them no infant could be produced. Marx therefore set out to study the process of travail in the form of disturbances of old tissues, which for him was synonymous with an investigation of the capitalist cycle. He saw in the latter not only disease, but also pulsating new life for the patient.

This led him to study macroeconomics. He soon recognised that his attack on profits was not enough and that other forms of criticism were required. The apologetic economists had made a fetish out of dead fixed capital by assuming that it could miraculously generate surplus value. For Marx surplus value was bound up with value added and the use of the labour force. Thus net product or national income appeared to him in a new light, for he emphasised the necessity of replacing used assets, including depleted stocks, which with value added constitute the gross national product.

From this vantage point, he analysed the circular flow, which contains germs of disturbance even in a stationary economy. Marx then proceeded to analyse capitalism, which he saw as essentially dynamic, and here he encountered greater deviations from the trend. He rejected apologetics, which attribute these disturbances to monetary mismanagement or other ephemeral phenomena. For Marx, the cycle is endogenous to capitalism; it gives it strength, but induces swings which make it inevitable that there will be repercussions in social life, so that new forces, conceived within society, will be the torch-bearers of the new system. These forces are for him synonymous with the proletariat, i.e. propertyless workers who are united not so much by common misery as by the feeling of being part of a new social class, based not on property but on know-how. Here the economist in Marx hands over to the sociologist, the politician and the revolutionary, whose strength derives from his economic vision, which makes him believe in an inevitable victory. It can also be said here that the normative economist gets the upper hand over the positive student of industry, in spite of his disciple Weber, who wanted to banish the former to oblivion. Positive economics, even in its Marxist garb, will be unable to follow him in the soaring flight of his overall conception; it will only be able to grasp at his coat-tails.

On the other hand, Marx's analysis of capitalist dynamics, his quest for its driving force and the innermost workings of human dynamics, must be evaluated as a contribution to positive economics.

As Adey (1977, p. 105) pointed out, further studies in this direction, while not altogether rejecting off-hand all value-based enquiries, should first and foremost concentrate on analyses based on prices of production, carrying out tests of 'falsification' and attempts to find concrete confirmation of Marx's abstract 'laws' by means of inductive methods.

It is disappointing that the most ambitious recent work, the monumental study by Cutler, Hindess, Hirst and Hussain (the last being an economist) (1977/78) which could have been a step in this direction, limits itself in its volume I to a sober reappraisal of value theory and class relationships, while bestowing a swift glance on the 'law of the tendency of the rate of profit to decline', only to reject it (as, incidentally, all other Marxian 'laws'!), and remains in its volume II restricted to a discussion of money, capitalist calculation and Sraffa's model. It concludes that 'Capitalism has no evolutionary tendencies in general, and takes the form of specific national economies . . . ' so that 'socialisms must differ . . . ' (II, p. 263). Though we do not entirely disagree with the latter statement and certainly welcome concrete studies, we nevertheless maintain that Marx laid bare some of the innermost laws of capitalist evolution that, in our view, does follow a definite pattern.

Those who see in Marx's work primarily the elements of social dynamics will appreciate mainly the revolutionary character of his work. This cannot be adequately judged without taking into account the elements of economic dynamics that underlie the social process and convey to it an internal impetus beyond the frontiers of differing social systems.

Economic dynamics is being 'elevated', in Hegel's sense, and transposed into the dynamics of historical evolution, in which capitalism, in Marx's view, is only a transitory phase in an ever-recurring process of social transformation. Marx's merit lies in his recognition of the function of this economic substratum in the transformation process. Moreover, as a thinker he contributed deeply, in manifold ways, to the formation of the social, political and intellectual structure of the modern world.

Bibliography

I WORKS OF KARL MARX*

(A) COLLECTED EDITIONS

1. *Karl Marx, Friedrich Engels: Historisch-kritisch Gesamtausgabe, Werke, Schriften, Briefe,* ed. D. Rjazanov (till 1931) and V. Adoratsky (after 1931) (Frankfurt and Moscow, 1927–35, unfinished). Divided into three parts: (1) writings of Marx and Engels, excluding *Capital,* (2) *Capital* and preliminary studies, (3) correspondence. Only scientific, fully reliable edition. Includes *all* works to 1 Jan 1849. (Referred to as *MEGA.*)
2. *Gesammelte Schriften von Karl Marx und Friedrich Engels, 1852–1862,* ed. D. Rjazanov (Stuttgart: Dietz, 1917), 2 vols. Complete only to 1857!
3. *Aus dem literarischen Nachlass von K. Marx, F. Engels, F. Lassalle,* ed. F. Mehring (Stuttgart: Dietz, 1902), 4 vols. Second edition 1923. (Referred to as *Nachlass.*)
4. *Der historische Materialismus,* ed. S. Landshut and J. P. Mayer (Leipzig, 1931), 2 vols.
5. *Die Frühschriften,* ed. S. Landshut (Stuttgart, 1953).
6. *Marx–Engels: Werke* (Berlin: Dietz, from 1956), 35 vols. Not complete, on account of Russian edition. (Referred to as *Werke.*)
7. *Marx–Engels: Ausgewählte Schriften* (Berlin: Dietz, 1954), 2 vols.
8. *Karl Marx: Werke, Schriften, Briefe,* ed. H. J. Lieber and P. Furth (Darmstadt, 1960–4), 6 vols.
9. *Karl Marx: Ausgewählte Schriften,* ed. and introduced B. Goldenberg (Munich, 1962).
10. *Karl Marx: Gesammelte Schriften 1841–1850* (Stuttgart, 1962), 4 vols.
11. *Karl Marx: Texte zur Methode und Praxis,* ed. and introduced G. Hillmann (Munich: Rowohlt, 1967).
12. *Marx–Engels: Studienausgabe,* ed. I. Fetscher (Frankfurt: Fischer, 1966), 4 vols.
13. *Karl Marx: Ökonomische Schriften,* ed. and introduced K. Kühne (Stuttgart, 1970).

---

* English editions of the principal works of Marx (as cited in the present work) are listed in the Preface to Volume 1.

(B) CHRONOLOGICAL SURVEY OF SEPARATE WORKS

1. *Differenz der demokritischen und epikureischen Naturphilosophie* (1841). (*MEGA*, I, I.)
2. Articles in *Rheinische Zeitung* (Cologne), 1842–3. (*MEGA*, I, I.)
3. *Kritik des hegelschen Staatsrechts, d. i. Hegels Rechtsphilosophie* (1843, not 1841–2). (*MEGA*, I, I.)
4. 'Zur Judenfrage', *Deutsch-französische Jahrbücher*, 1844. (*MEGA*, I, I; *Werke*, I.)
5. 'Zur Kritik der hegelschen Rechtsphilosophie. Einleitung', ibid. (*MEGA*, I, I; *Werke*, I.)
6. Economic–philosophical manuscripts, 1844. (*MEGA*, I, III.)
7. Marx–Engels, *Die heilige Familie, oder Kritik der kritischen Kritik, gegen Bruno Bauer und Konsorten* (Frankfurt, 1845). (*MEGA*, I, III; *Werke*, II.)
8. *Thesen über Feuerbach* (1845). (*MEGA*, I, V.)
9. Articles in *Westphälisches Dampfboot und Gesellschaftsspiegel*, 1845–7. (*MEGA*, I, III, IV.)
10. Marx–Engels, *Die deutsche Ideologie, Kritik der neuesten deutschen Philosophie in ihren Repräsentanten, Feuerbach, B. Bauer, und Stirner, und des deutschen Sozialismus in seinen verschiedenen Propheten* (1845–6). (*MEGA*, I, V; *Werke*, III; Dietz, 1953.)
11. *Misère de la philosophie. Réponse à la philosophie de la misère de M. Proudhon*, Foreword by Engels (Paris, 1847).
12. 'La Critique moralisante et la morale critique', *Deutsche Brüsseler Zeitung*, 28 Oct–25 Nov 1847. (*MEGA*, I, VI.)
13. Marx–Engels, *Zirkular gegen den 'Volkstribun'*, ed. H. Kriege (1846). (*MEGA*, I, VI.)
14. Articles in the *Deutsche Brüsseler Zeitung*, the *Triersche Zeitung* and *Reform*, 1847–8. (*MEGA*, I, VI.) Discourse on the Poles, writings against Grün and Heinzen.
15. 'Speech of Dr. Marx on Protection, Free Trade and the Working Classes', *Northern Star*, 1847. (*MEGA*, I, VI.)
16. *Manifest der Kommunistischen Partei* (original text in German!) (London, Feb 1848).
17. 'Lohnarbeit und Kapital' (Wage Labour and Capital), *Neue Rheinische Zeitung*, 1849. (*MEGA*, I, VI; *Werke*, VI.) Lectures by Marx to the Deutsche Arbeiterverein in Brussels, 1849.
18. Articles in *Neue Rheinische Zeitung*, 1848–9. (*Nachlass*, III; *MEGA*, I, VI; Dietz, 1928.).
19. Articles in *Neue Rheinische Zeitung, Politisch–Oekonomische Revue* (1850; re-edited as: *Die Klassenkämpfe in Frankreich*, ed. F. Engels (Berlin, 1895). (*Werke*, VII; Dietz, 1953).
20. 'Der achtzehnte Brumaire des Louis Bonaparte', *Die Revolution*, no. 2, ed. J. Weydemeyer (New York, 1852); new edition, with Foreword by Marx (Hamburg, 1859). (*Werke*, VIII; Dietz, 1953.)

21. *Materialien, Erklärungen und Schriften zum Kölner Kommunistenprozess 1851–2* (Basle and Boston, Mass., 1853); with Introduction by Engels (Hottingen, Zurich, 1885). Afterword of 1875. (*Werke*, VIII.)

22. Articles in *New York Tribune* and *People's Paper*, 1851–62; also in Engels, *Revolution and Counterrevolution in Germany*, ed. E. M. Aveling (London, 1896).

23. *The Eastern Question. A Reprint of Letters Written 1853–1856 dealing with the Events of the Crimean War*, ed. E. M. and E. Aveling (London, 1897).

24. 'Palmerston and Russia', *Political Fly-sheets*, no. 1 (London, 1853). Second edition under the title 'Palmerston and Poland' (1854).

25. 'Palmerston. What Has He Done?', *Political Fly-sheets*, no. 2 (London, 1854).

26. *Der Ritter vom edelmütigen Bewusstsein* (London and New York, 1853). Polemic against Willich.

27. Articles in *Neue Oder Zeitung* (Breslau, 1854–5).

28. 'Secret Diplomatic History of the Eighteenth Century' and 'The Story of the Life of Lord Palmerston', articles in *Free Press* and *Diplomatic Review*, 1856–8; both ed. E. M. Aveling (London, 1899).

29. *Grundrisse der Kritik der politischen Ökonomie*, first draft 1857–8, Appendix 1850–9, first published Moscow, 1939–41, 2 vols. (Also Berlin: Dietz, 1953.)

30. Articles on Bernadotte, Bolívar and Blücher for the *New American Cyclopaedia*, ed. G. Ripley and C. Dana (New York, 1858–63).

31. *Zur Kritik der politischen Oekonomie* (Berlin, 1859). (Also Dietz, 1953.)

32. Article in *Das Volk*, 1859.

33. *Herr Vogt* (in German) (London, 1860); with Appendix by Engels, Introduction by R. Franz (Leipzig, 1927). (Also Dietz, 1953.)

34. Articles in *Die Presse* (Vienna, 1861–2).

35. Articles in *The Beehive* (London, 1864–70).

36. *Address and Provisional Rules of the International Working Men's Association, Established Sept. 28th 1864, at a Public Meeting Held at St. Martin's Hall, Long Acre* (London, 1864). ('Inaugural Address') (*Werke*, XVI.)

37. Article against Proudhon in *Der Sozialdemokrat*, 1865; in Appendix to *Misère de la philosophie*, 10th ed. (German), (Stuttgart 1923), pp. xxv.

38. 'Erklärung gegen J. B. Schweitzer', *Berliner Reform*, Mar–Apr 1865.

39. *Value, Price and Profit*, address delivered to the General Council of the International (in English) (London, 1865).

40. *Das Kapital, Kritik der politischen Oekonomie*, I (Hamburg: Meissner, 1867; second edition 1872–3; third edition, ed. Marx and Engels, 1883), II, ed. Engels (1885), III, ed. Engels (1894). (*MEGA*, 3 vols. Berlin: Dietz, 1953; new edition 1969.)

41. *Theorien über den Mehrwert* (ed. Karl Kautsky, Stuttgart: Dietz, 1905–10), 4 vols; new edition by Institut für Marxismus-Leninismus beim Zentralkomitee der sozialistischen Einheitspartei Deutschlands (Berlin: Dietz, 1965), 3 vols.

42. Manifestos, programmes, declarations and statutes of the General Council of the International, (in English) (1867–73).

43. J. C. Eccarius and Marx, 'A Working Man's Refutation of J. S. Mill', (in English) series of articles in *Commonwealth* (London, 1868–70).

44. *On the War* and *The Civil War in France*, addresses of the General Council of the International (in English) (London, 1870–1).

45. L'Alliance de la Démocratie Socialiste et l'Association Internationale des Travailleurs, several reports and documents (in French) (London and Hamburg, 1873). Report on Bakunin at the wish of the Hague Congress.

46. *Zur Kritik des sozialdemokratischen Parteiprogramms*, 1875, published by Engels 1891; ed. V. Adoratsky (Zurich, 1934; Berlin, 1955). Reprinted under various titles (e.g. *Randglossen zum Programm der deutschen Arbeiterpartei*).

47. Engels, *Herrn Eugen Dühring's Umwälzung der Wissenschaft*, Part II, ch. 10 (written in collaboration with Marx).

48. Letter to Mikhailovski, 1877; repr. as 'Sur le développement économique de la Russie' in *Revue socialiste*, 24 May 1902.

49. *Resultate des unmittelbaren Produktions prozesses* (posthumous), ed. P. Weller/G. Frelich, (Frankfurt 1969).

(c) CORRESPONDENCE

1. *Karl Marx–Friedrich Engels, Briefwechsel*, (*MEGA*, III).

2. *Briefe und Auszüge von J. P. Becker, J. Dietzgen, Fr. Engels, Karl Marx und andere an F. A. Sorge und andere*, ed. F. A. Sorge (Stuttgart: Dietz, 1906 and 1921).

3. *Briefe an Kugelmann (aus den Jahren 1862–1874)*, with Introduction by Lenin (Berlin: Viva, 1927; Dietz, 1952).

4. *Die Briefe von K. Marx und Fr. Engels an Danielson*, with Introduction by G. Mayer (Leipzig: Liebing, 1929).

5. 'Briefwechsel zwischen K. Marx und Bruno Bauer, Arnold Ruge und anderen, ferner zwischen Marx und seinem Vater', *MEGA*, I, I.

6. *Briefe von Marx an Weydemeyer und Frau, Waffenkammer des Sozialismus* (Frankfurt, 1907).

7. 'Freiligrath und Marx in ihrem Briefwechsel', ed. F. Mehring, *Neue Zeit*, (1912).

8. *Die Briefe von Karl Marx und Heinrich Heine*, ed. G. Mayer (Stuttgart, 1922).

9. 'Briefwechsel zwischen Vera Zassulitsch und Marx', ed. D. Rjazanov (Moscow and Frankfurt: Marx–Engels Institut, 1931); French original of letter to Vera Zassoulitch, 8 Mar 1881, published by M. Rubel in 'Karl Marx et le socialisme populiste russe', *Revue socialiste*, no. 11 (1947).

10. Marx–Engels, Briefe über 'Das Kapital', (Berlin: Dietz, 1954).

II GENERAL BIBLIOGRAPHY

Abramovitz, M., *Inventories and Business Cycles* (New York, 1950).
——'Resource and Output', *American Economic Review*, XLVI, (May 1956).
——'The Nature and Significance of Kuznets Cycles', *Economic Development and Cultural Exchange*, IX (1961).
Adelman, Irma, *Theories of Economic Growth and Development* (London, 1962).
Adelman, M. A., 'The Measurement of Industrial Concentration', *Review of Economics and Statistics*, XXXIII, no. 4 (Nov 1951).
Aftalion, A., *Les Fondements du socialisme*, (Paris, 1923).
——Les crises périodiques de surproduction, Paris 1913.
Alter, L., 'Teorija i praktika kapitalestitschesowo regulirowanija' (Theory and practice of capitalist regulation), in: *Mirowaja ekonomika i meschdunarodnije otnoschenija*, no. 3 (1964).
Althusser, L., *Lire le Capital*, 2 vols (Paris, 1968).
Altvater, E., *Die Weltwährungskrise* (Frankfurt, 1969).
——'Konjunkturtheorie als Analyse von Widersprüchen', *Wirtschaftswoche*, 1971; repr. in *Kontaktstudium Ökonomie und Gesellschaft*, ed. R. Molitor (Frankfurt, 1972).
Altvater, E., Neusüss and Blanke, 'Kapitalistischer Weltmarkt und Weltwährungskrise', *Probleme des Klassenkampfes*, no. 1 (Nov 1971).
Andreae, C. A., *Ökonomik der Freizeit* (Rembek, 1970).
Andrews, P. W. S., *Manufacturing Business* (London, 1949).
Ansiaux, M., *Traité d'economie politique*, III (Paris, 1926).
Antoine, J. C., *Introduction à l'analyse macroéconomique*, I (all!) (Paris, 1953).
Ardant, H., *Les Crises économiques* (Paris, 1948).
Arndt, H., 'Volkswirtschaftliches Wachstum und weltwirtschaftlicher Geldkreislauf', in *Wirtschaftskreislauf und Wirtschaftswachstum, Festschrift für Carl Föhl*, ed. E. Schneider (Tübingen, 1966a).
——Mikroökonomische Theorie, II (Berlin, 1966b).
Aron, R., *La Lutte des classes* (Paris, 1964).
Aubert, Jane, *La Courbe d'offre* (Paris, 1949).
Aucuy, M., *Les Systèmes socialistes d'échange* (Paris, 1908).

Baby, J., *Principes fondamentaux d'économie politique* (Paris, 1949).
Bach, G. L., see: *Quarterly Journal of Economics*, (1972).
Bader, V. M., Ganssmann, H., Goldschmidt, W., and Hoffmann, B., 'Zur Kritik an Barans und Sweezys Theorie des Monopolkapitalismus', *Das Argument*, II, no. 51 (Apr 1969).
Bajt, A., 'A Post Mortem Note on the Transformation Problem', *Soviet Studies*, XXI, no. 3 (Jan 1970).
——'Investment Cycles in European Socialist Economies', *Journal of Economic Literature*, IX (1971).
Baldwin, R. E., 'Discussion, 71st Annual Meeting of the American

Economic Association' (27–29 Dec 1958), *American Economic Review, Papers and Proceedings*, XLIX, no. 2 (May 1959).

Balinky, A., *Marx's Economics* (Lexington, Mass., 1970).

Banfi, R., 'Probleme und Scheinprobleme bei Marx und im Marxismus', in *Folgen einer Theorie, Essays über 'Das Kapital' von Karl Marx* (Frankfurt, 1967).

Baran, P. A., *The Political Economy of Growth* (New York, 1962).

Baran, P. A., and Sweezy, P. M., 'Economics of Two Worlds', in *Marx and Modern Economics*, ed. Horowitz (1968a)

——*Monopoly Capital* (Harmondsworth, 1968b)

Barion, J., 'Die philosophischen Grundlagen des Marxismus', in *Historischer Materialismus und europäisches Geschichtsdenken* (Düsseldorf, 1954).

Barone, E., 'Il Ministero della produzione nello stato collettivista', *Giornale degli economisti*, Sep 1908; repr. in *Collectivist Economic Planning*, ed. F. von Hayek (London, 1935).

Barrault, H. E., 'Le Sens et la portée des théories antiquantitatives de la monnaie', *Revue d'histoire des doctrines économiques et sociales*, (1910).

Bartoli, H., *La Doctrine économique et sociale de Karl Marx* (Paris, 1950).

——'Les Théories des Marxistes', *Fluctuations économiques, Analyses de théories*, ed. A. Marshal, II (Paris, 1954).

Basso, L., 'Appunti sullo sviluppo della teoria rivoluzionaria in Marx ed Engels', in *Neocapitalismo e sinistra europea* (Bari, 1969).

Bataille, G., *La Part maudite, essai d'economie générale* (Paris, 1949).

Bauer, O., Review of Hilferding's *Finanzkapital*, in *Der Kampf*, (1909–10).

——'Die Akkumulation des Kapitals', series of essays in *Die neue Zeit*, XXXI, 1 (1913); repr. in *Kapital*, ed. R. Hickel, II Annex (Berlin, 1970), pp. 775 ff.

——*Der Weg zum Sozialismus* (Vienna, 1919).

——*Kapitalismus und Sozialismus nach dem Weltkriege*, I (all!) (Vienna, 1931).

——*Zwischen zwei Weltkriegen?* (Bratislava, 1936).

Baumol, W. J., Samuelson, P. A., and Morishima, M., Symposium 'On Marx, the Transformation Problem and Opacity', *Journal of Economic Literature*, XII (Mar 1974).

Bénard, J., *La Conception Marxiste du Capital* (Paris, 1952).

Bergson, A., 'Socialist Economics', in *A Survey of Contemporary Economics*, ed. H. S. Ellis (Philadelphia and Toronto, 1948).

Berle, A. A. *The Twentieth Century Capitalist Revolution* (London, 1955).

Berle, A. A., and Means, G. C., *The Modern Corporation and Private Property* (New York, 1936).

Bernal, J. D., 'Dialectical Materialism', in *Aspects of Dialectical Materialism* (London, 1934).

Bernholz, P., *Grundlagen der politischen Ökonomie*, (Tübingen, 1972), I.

Bernstein, E., 'Zur Frage des ehernen Lohngesetzes', series of essays in *Die neue Zeit*, VIII, 1 (1891).

Bernstein, E., 'Zur Zusammenbruchstheorie', series of essays in *Die neue Zeit*, XVI, (1898).

——*Die Voraussetzungen des Sozialismus und die Aufgaben der Sozialdemokratie* (Stuttgart, 1920). (First edition 1899.)

Bettelheim, C. 'Formas y métodos de la planificación socialista', *Cuba socialista*, no. 32 (Apr 1946).

——'Revenu national, épargne et investissements', in *Revue d'economic Politique*, LVIII (Jan–Feb 1948).

——*Problèmes théoriques et pratiques de la planification*, third edition (Paris, 1966). (First edition 1946.)

——'Présentation' and 'Remarques théoriques' in A. Emmanuel, *L'échange inégal* (1969).

Beveridge, W. H., *Full Employment in a Free Society*, third impression (first edition 1944) (London, 1945).

Bhaduri, A., 'On the Significance of Recent Controversies on Capital Theory: A Marxian View', *Economic Journal*, LXXIX (1969); repr. in: Capital and Growth, ed. Harcourt, Harmondsworth 1971.

Bharawaj, K. R. 'Value through Exogenous Distribution', *Economic Weekly* (Bombay), 24 Aug 1963.

Bickerdike, C. F., 'A non-monetary cause of fluctuations in employment', *Economic Journal*, XXIV, (1914).

Bigo, P., *Marxisme et humanisme, Introduction à l'oeuvre économique de Karl Marx* (Paris, 1953).

Blair, J. M., and Houghton, H. F., 'The Lintner–Butters Analysis of the Effect of Mergers on Industrial Concentration 1940–47: A Reply', *Review of Economics and Statistics*, XXXIII, no. 1 (Feb 1951).

Blanc, L., *Organisation du Travail*, ninth edition (Paris, 1850). (First edition 1841.)

Blaug, M., 'A Survey of the Theory of Process-Innovations', *Economica*, Feb 1963; repr. in *The Economics of Technological Change*, ed. V. N. Rosenberg (Harmondsworth, 1971).

——*Economic Theory in Retrospect*, second edition (London, 1968). (First edition 1962.)

Bloch, E., 'Marx als Denker der Revolution', in *Marx und die Revolution* (Frankfurt, 1970).

Blochowitz, W., 'Wirksamkeit der Zinspolitik bei Freier Konvertibilität', in *Konjunkturelle Stabilität als wirtschaftspolitische Aufgabe*, ed. Zeitel and Pahlke (1962).

Block, H., *Die Marxsche Geldtheorie* (Jena, 1926).

Bloom, G. F., 'A Reconsideration of the Theory of Exploitation', *Quarterly Journal of Economics*, LV (1940–1).

Böhm-Bawerk, E. V., 'Geschichte und Kritik der Kapitalzins-Theorin', *Kapital und Kapitalzins*, 1, fourth edition (Jena, 1921). (First edition Innsbruck, 1884.)

——'Zum Abschluss des Marxschen Systems', in *Festgabe für Karl Knies*

(Berlin, 1896); English edition by P. M. Sweezy, 'Karl Marx and the Close of his System' (New York, 1966).

Bombach, G., 'Die verschiedenen Ansätze der Verteilungstheorie', in *Einkommensverteilung und technischer Fortschritt*, ed. E. Schneider (Berlin, 1959).

——'Wirtschaftswachstum und Stabilität' (address of 28 Feb 1959), in *Wachstum und Konjunktur* (Darmstadt and Opladen, 1960).

——'Wirtschaftswachstum', in *Handwörterbuch der Sozialwissenschaften* (Stuttgart, Tübingen and Göttingen, 1965).

Bombach, G., and von Weizsäcker, C. C., 'Optimales Wachstum und Gleichgewichtswachstum' in *Wachstum und Entwicklung der Wirtschaft*, ed. H. König (Cologne and Berlin, 1968).

Borchardt, J., 'Die Marxsche Krisentheorie', annex to his popular edition of *Kapital* (Berlin, 1919).

——*Die Volkswirtschaftlichen Grundbegriffe nach der Lehre von Karl Marx*, second edition (Berlin, 1923).

Bose, A. *Marxian and Post-Marxian Political Economy*, (Harmondsworth, 1975).

Botta, F. (ed.), *Sul capitale monopolistico* (essays), collezione 'Dissensi', no. 36 (Bari, 1971).

——*Teoria economica e marxismo* (Bari, 1973).

Boudin, L. B., *The Theoretical System of Karl Marx*, 2nd ed. (Chicago, 1912). (First edition, 1907.)

Boulding, K., *The Economics of Peace* (New York, 1946).

Bouniatian, M., *Les Crises économiques*, second edition (Paris, 1930). (First edition 1921.)

——*Wirtschaftskrisen und Überkapitalisation* (Munich, 1907).

——*Ekonomitscheskije Krisisi* (Economic crises) (Moscow, 1915).

Bourguin, M., *Les Systèmes socialistes et l'évolution économique* (Paris, 1904).

Bouvier-Ajam, M., *Les Mouvements cycliques des prix et leur explication par la théorie capitaliste*, third edition (Paris, 1948). (First edition 1936.)

Braunthal, A., *Die Entwicklungstendenzen der kapitalistischen Wirtschaft* (Berlin, 1927).

——'Erwiderung' (reply to Nathalie Moszkowska, 1932), in *Die Gesellschaft*, II (1932).

Brenner, Y. S., *Theory of Economic Development and Growth* (London, 1966).

Breysig, K., *Der Stufenbau und die Gesetze der Weltgeschichte*, second edition, (Stuttgart and Berlin, 1927). (First edition 1918.)

Brinkmann, C., 'Francis Ysidro Edgeworth', *Archiv für Sozialwissenschaft und Sozialpolitik*, VI (1926); repr. in *Geschichte der Volkswirtschaftslehre*, ed. by A. Montaner (Cologne and Berlin, 1967).

Brody, A., *Proportions, Prices and Planning, A Mathematical Restatement of the Labour Theory of Value* (Amsterdam, 1970). (Hungarian original published Budapest, 1970.)

Bronfenbrenner, M., '*Das Kapital* for the Modern Man', *Science and Society*, Autumn 1965; repr. in *Marx and Modern Economics*, ed. Horowitz, (1968).

——'Marxian Influences in "Bourgeois" Economics', *American Economic Review, Papers and Proceedings*, LVII, no. 2 (May 1967).

——(ed.), *Is the Business Cycle Obsolete?* (New York and London, 1969).

——*Income Distribution Theory* (London 1971).

——'Samuelson, Marx, and Their Latest Critics', *Journal of Economic Literature*, XI, no. 1 (Mar 1973).

Brown, C. E., 'Federal Fiscal Policy in the Postwar Period', in *Postwar Economic Trends in the United States*, ed. R. E. Freeman (New York, 1960).

Bücher, K., 'Das Gesetz der Massenproduktion', *Zeitschrift für die gesamte Staatswissenschaft*, LXVI (1910).

Budge, S., *Lehre vom Geld* (Jena, 1931).

Bukharin, N., *Der Imperialismus und die Akkumulation des Kapitals* (Berlin and Vienna, 1926).

Bulgakov, S., *O rynkach pri kapitalistitscheskom proiswodstwje* (On the question of markets in capitalist production) (Moscow, 1897).

Bundesamt für Gewerbliche Wirtschart, Frankfurt, 'Report on Concentration', *Bundestagsdrucksache* IV, 2320 (5 June 1964).

Burchardt, F., 'Die Schemata des stationären Kreislaufs bei Böhm-Bawerk und Marx', II: 'Marx', *Weltwirtschaftiches Archiv*, XXXV (Kiel, Jan 1932).

Burnham, J. *Managerial Revolution* (New York, 1941).

Burns, A., *Production Trends in the USA since 1870* (New York, 1934).

Cairncross, A. K., 'The Place of Capital in Economic Progress', *International Science Bulletin*, VI, 2 (1954).

Calogero, G., *Il Metodo dell'economia e il marxismo*, fourth edition (Bari, 1967). (First edition 1941.)

Calvez, J. Y., *La Pensée de Karl Marx*, seventh edition (Paris, 1956).

Calwer, R., Article in *Sozialistische Monatshefte* (1907).

Carritt, E. F., 'Dialectical Materialism', in *Aspects of Dialectical Materialism* (London, 1934).

Cass, D., and Yaari, M., 'Individual Saving, Aggregate Capital Accumulation and Efficient Growth', in *Essays on the Theory of Optimal Economic Growth*, ed. K Shell (Cambridge, Mass., 1967).

Carver, T. N., 'A Suggestion For a Theory of Industrial Depression', *Quarterly Journal of Economics*, May 1903.

Cassel, G., *Theoretische Sozialökonomie*, third edition (Leipzig, 1923). (First edition 1918.)

Catephores, G., 'Marxian Alienation – A Clarification', *Oxford Economic Papers*, new ser. XXIV, no. 1 (Mar 1972).

Chamberlin, E. H., *The Theory of Monopolistic Competition*, fifth edition (Cambridge, Mass., 1946). (First edition, 1933).

Chamley, P., *L'Oligopole* (Paris, 1944).

Charasov, G., *Das System des Marxismus* (Berlin, 1910).

Clark, C., *The Conditions of Economic Progress*, third edition (London, 1957). (First edition 1940).

Clark, J. M., 'Distribution' in *Encyclopedia of the Social Sciences*, v (New York, 1931); repr. in *Readings in the Theory of Income Distribution* (Philadelphia and Toronto, 1946).

Cole, G. D. H., *What Marx Really Meant* (London, 1934).

——*A History of Socialist Thought*, 3 vols., II (New York, 1953).

Collins, N. R. and Preston, E., 'The Size Structure of the Largest Industrial Firms, 1909–1958', *American Economic Review*, LI, no. 5 (Dec 1961).

Conze, W., 'Vom Pöbel zum Proletariat – Sozialgeschichtliche Voraussetzungen des Sozialismus in Deutschland', *Vierteljahresschrift für Sozial – und Wirtschaftsgeschichte* (Wiesbaden, 1954); repr. in *Historischer Materialismus und europäisches Geschichtsdenken* (Düsseldorf, 1954).

Coontz, S. H., *Productive Labour and Effective Demand* (London, 1965).

Council of (US) Economic Advisers, Hearings on the Economic Report of the President, (Washington 1961).

Cournot, A., *Recherches sur les principes mathematiques de la théorie des richesses* (Paris, 1838).

Cozzi, T., *Teoria dello sviluppo economico* (Bologna, 1972).

Croce, B., *Historical Materialism and the Economics of Karl Marx* (London, 1914) (First Italian edition: Materialismo storico ed economia marxistica, Milan and Palermo, 1900.)

Cunow H., *Monopolfrage und Arbeiterklasse* (Berlin, 1918).

——'Zur Zusammenbruchstheorie', *Die neue Zeit*, XVII, (1899).

Cuyvers, L., 'Joan Robinson's "Neo-Marxist Theory of Economic Growth" ', (unpublished paper, Univ. of Antwerp 1978).

Cuvillier, A., *Manuel de Sociologie* II (Paris, 1956).

Dahrendorf, R., *Gesellschaft und Demokratie in Deutschland* (Munich, 1968).

d'Avenel, Vicomte G., *Découvertes d'histoire sociale* (Paris, 1920).

Davis, A. K., 'Sociological Elements in Veblen's Economic Theory', *Journal of Political Economy*, LIII, no. 2 (June 1945).

de Brunhoff, Suzanne, *La Monnaie chez Marx* (Paris, 1967).

——*L'Offre de monnaie* (Paris, 1971).

de Cindio, F., *Il Sistema monetario aureo* (Rome, 1962).

——*Le Ragioni di scambio in oligopolio* (Milan, 1967).

Decker, G., 'Wirtschaftskrise und Politik', *Die Gesellschaft*, VIII (Berlin, 1931).

de Finetti, B., *Requisiti per un sistema economico accettabile in relazione alle esigenze della collettività* (Milan, 1973).

de la Charrière, G., *Commerce extérieur et sous-développement* (Paris, 1964).

Deletaille, E., *Dépréciation monétaire et capitalisme* (Geneva, 1959).

Delpech, M., 'La Circulation monétaire et la théorie antiquantitative', *Annales de droit et de sciences sociales*, no. 6 (1936).

de Man, H., 'Kapitalismus und Sozialismus', in *Kapital und Kapitalismus*, ed. Harms, 1 (1931).

Denis, H., *Le Monopole bilatéral* (Paris, 1943).

——*La Valeur* (Paris, 1950).

Denison, E. F., 'The Unimportance of the Embodied Question', *American Economic Review*, Mar 1964.

Denison, E. F. and Pouillier, J. P., *Why Growth Rates Differ* (Washington, 1967).

Dennert, J., 'Bemerkungen zum Revolutionsbegriff bei Marx und Marcuse', in *Hamburger Jahrbuch für Wirtschafts-und Gesellschaftspolitik*, 1969.

Desrousseaux, J., *L'Evolution économique et le comportement industriel* (Paris, 1965).

Dewey, D., *The Theory of Imperfect Competition* (New York, 1969).

de Wolff, S., 'Prosperitäts- und Depressionsperioden', in *Der lebendige Marxismus* (Jena, 1924).

——*Het Economisch Getijd* (Amsterdam, 1929).

Dickinson, H. D., 'The Economic Basis of Socialism', *Political Quarterly*, (Sep–Dec 1930).

——'Price Formation in a Socialist Community', *Economic Journal*, XLIII (June 1933).

——'The Falling Rate of Profit in Marxian Economics', *Review of Economic Studies*, XXIV, no. 64 (1956–7).

——Review of Meek's *Studies in the Labour Theory of Value* (London, 1956), *Economic Journal*, LXVII (Sep 1957).

Dieterlen, P., 'La Relation d'insatisfaction', *Economie appliquée*, VII, nos 1–2 (Jan and June 1954).

——*L'Investissement* (Paris, 1957).

di Toro, C., 'Sviluppo economico e crisi', in *Sul capitale monopolistico*, ed. F. Botta (1971).

Djilas, M., *Die neue Klasse* (Munich, 1957).

Dmitriev, W. K., *Ekonomitscheskije studii* (Moscow, 1904).

Dobb, M., 'A Sceptical View of the Theory of Wages' (1929); repr. in *On Economic Theory and Socialism*, second edition (repr. London 1965). (First edition 1955.)

——'Economic Theory and the Problem of a Socialist Economy', in *Economic Journal*, XLIII (Dec 1933).

——*Political Economy and Capitalism* (London, 1950). (First edition 1937.)

——'A Lecture on Marx', lecture at Cambridge, 14 Nov 1942; repr. in *On Economic Theory and Socialism*.

——'A Note on the Transformation Problem', in *On Economic Theory and Socialism*.

——*On Economic Theory and Socialism*, second edition (London, 1965). (First edition 1955.)

——'A Further Comment on the Transformation Problem', *Economic Journal*, LXVII (Sep 1957).

——'The Falling Rate of Profit', *Science and Society*, XXIV no. 2 (1959).

——*An Essay on Economic Growth and Planning* (London, 1960).

——*Wages*, second edition (London, 1948).

——*Studies in the Development of Capitalism*, third edition (London, 1967). (First edition 1946.)

Dobias, P., 'Zur Struktur des Marxschen Systems', *Weltwirtschaftliches Archiv*, CV (Tübingen, 1970).

Dognin, F. D., *Initiation à Karl Marx* (Paris, 1970).

Domar, E. D., 'Capital Expansion, Rate of Growth and Employment', *Econometrica*, XIV (Apr 1946); repr. in *Essays* (1957).

——'Expansion and Employment', *American Economic Review*, XXXVII (Mar 1947); repr. in *Essays* (1957).

——'The Varga Controversy', *American Economic Review*, XL (Mar 1950), and Domar's discussion with Sweezy, ibid.

——'A Theoretical Analysis of Economic Growth', *American Economic Review, Papers and Proceedings*, XLII (May 1952); repr. in *Essays* (1957).

——'Depreciation, Replacement and Growth', *Economic Journal*, LXIII (Mar 1953); repr. in *Essays* (1957).

——'A Soviet Model of Growth', in *Essays* (1957).

——*Essays in the Theory of Economic Growth* (New York, 1957).

Dörge, F. W., 'Lohnpolitik in der wachsenden Gesellschaft', in *Wirtschafts- und Sozialpolitik*, ed. H. D. Ortlieb and F. W. Dörge (Opladen, 1964).

Drucker, P., *The End of Economic Man* (London, 1970).

Duesenberry, J. S., *Income, Saving, and the Theory of Consumer Behavior* (Cambridge, Mass., 1949).

Dunayevskaya, R., 'New Revision of Marxian Economics', *American Economic Review*, XXXIV (Sep 1944).

Dunstan, R., 'The Origins of Capitalism', in *The Case for Capitalism*, ed. M. Ivens and R. Dunstan (London, 1967).

Dupriez, L., *Des mouvements économiques généraux*, second edition (Louvain, 1951), I. (First edition 1947).

Duret, J., *Le Marxisme et les crises* (Paris, 1933).

Duve, V. F. (ed.), *Die Dokumente zur Grundsatzdiskussion der Jungsozialisten* (Reinbek, 1973).

Dyabushkin, T., 'From the History of the Balance-sheet of the USSR National Economy', in *Bulletin International de Statistique*, XXXVI, no. 2 (Brussels, 1960).

Eagly, R. V., 'A Macro-Model of the Endogenous Business Cycle in Marxist Analysis', *Journal of Political Economy*, LXXX, no. 3, part I (May–June 1972).

Earley, J., 'Marginal Policies of "Excellently Managed" Companies', *American Economic Review*, Mar 1956.

Eaton, J., *Political Economy*, third edition (London, 1966). (First edition 1949.)

ECE (Economic Commission for Europe, United Nations) *Economic Survey of Europe in 1958* (Geneva 1959).

Eckstein, A., 'Trends and Cycles in Communist China's Economic Development and Foreign Trade', paper presented at the University of Chicago, Center for Policy Study, Conference on China, (5–9 Feb 1967).

Eckstein, G., 'Die Akkumulation des Kapitals' (1913); in Rosa Luxemburg, *Die Akkumulation des Kapitals*, 1923 edition (Berlin). reprinted in Ullstein edition of 'Das Kapital', ed. by R. Hickel (Berlin 1970), Annex.

EEC Commission, *Grundkriterien für die Festsetzung der Löhne*. . . . (Basic Criteria for Fixation of Wages), Series Social Policy, no. 19 (Brussels 1967).

Edwards, E., 'Depreciation and the Maintenance of Real Capital', in *Depreciation and Replacement Policy* (Amsterdam, 1961).

Ehrenberg, R., in *Thünen-Archiv*, 1 (1910?), quoted in Pietranera (1966, p. 39).

Einarsen, J., 'Reinvestment Cycles', *Review of Economics and Statistics*, xx (Feb 1938).

Eisner, R., 'Depreciation Allowances, Replacement Requirements and Growth', *American Economic Review*, XLII (Dec 1952).

——'Technological Change, Obsolescence and Aggregate Demand', *American Economic Review*, XLVI (1956).

——'On Growth Models and the Neo-classical Resurgence', *Economic Journal*, LXVIII (1958).

Eltis, W. A., 'The Determination of the Rate of Technical Progress', *Economic Journal*, LXXXI (Sep 1971).

Emmanuel, A., 'Échange inégal et politique de développement' (paper presented at the Sorbonne, Paris, 18 Dec 1962), *Problèmes de planification*, no. 2 (Paris, 1963).

——*L'Échange inégal* (Paris, 1969).

Engels, F., *Die Entwicklung des Sozialismus von der Utopie zur Wissenschaft* (Stuttgart, 1891).

——*Herrn Eugen Dührings Umwälzung der Wissenschaft* (Leipzig, 1878).

——'Wirkung des Umschlags auf die Profitrate', ch. 4 in *Kapital*, III.

Erdös, P., 'The Application of Marx's Model of Expanded Reproduction to Trade Cycle Theory', in *Socialism, Capitalism and Economic Growth*, ed. C. H. Feinstein (Cambridge, 1967).

Eucken, W., *Kapitaltheoretische Untersuchungen* (Tübingen and Zürich, 1954).

Falkner, S. A., 'The Idea of the National Economic Balance and its Components', *Planned Economy*, no. 9 1928; and 'To the History of the Idea of a National Economic Balance', ibid., no. 10 (1928).

Fanno, Marcu, Cicli di produzione, cicli di credito e fluttuazioni industrali, *Giornale dogli economisti*, 1931.

Fan Wen-Lan, *Drjewnjaja istoriji kitaja* ('Ancient Chinese History'; Russian trans. of Chinese original) (Moscow, 1958).

Fatemi, N. S., de Saint-Phalle, T., and Keefe, G. M., *The Dollar Crisis* (New York, 1963).

Federici, L., 'Observations', in *La Monnaie*, ed. R. Mossé (Paris, 1950).

Feiwel, G. R., 'Michail Kalecki's *Introduction to the Theory of Growth*', *Journal of Economic Literature*, IX (1971).

Feldman, G. A., 'K teorii rosta narodnowo docnoda' (The theory of the rate of growth of national income), *Planowoje chosjaistwo* (Planned economy), nos 11 and 12 (Nov 1928). German edition *Zur Wachstumstheorie des Nationaleinkommens* (Frankfurt, 1969).

Fellner, W., *Trends and Cycles in Economic Activity – An Introduction to the Problems of Economic Growth* (New York, 1956).

——'Marxian Hypotheses and Observable Trends under Capitalism: A "Modernised" Interpretation', *Economic Journal*, LXVII (Mar 1957).

——*Trends and Cycles in Economic Activity* (New York, 1958).

Fenili, see Koch 1971.

Ferguson, G. E., 'Theories of Distribution and Relative Shares', *Jahrbücher für Nationalökonomie und Statistik*, CLXXVI (Feb 1964).

Finger, H.-Stoll, W., et al., *Kredit und Zins im System der Eigenerwirtschaftung der Industrie* (East German planning brochure) (Berlin, 1968).

Fisher, I., *The Theory of Interest* (New York 1930). French edition: *La Théorie de l'intérêt*, (Paris, 1933.)

Fourastié, J., *Le Grand espoir du Vingtième siècle* (Paris, 1949).

Frank, A. G., *Capitalism and Underdevelopment in Latin America* (New York, 1967).

Franklin, R. S., *American Capitalism – Two Visions* (New York, 1977).

Friedman, M., 'The Demand for Money: Some Theoretical and Empirical Results', *Journal of Political Economy*, LXVII (Aug 1959).

Friedman, M., and Anna Jacobson Schwartz, *Monetary Statistics of the United States* (New York 1970).

Fritsch, B., *Die Geld- und Kredittheorie von Karl Marx*, (Frankfurt and Vienna, 1968).

Fromm, G., 'Inventories, Business Cycles, and Economic Stabilization', in Joint Economic Committee, Congress of the US, *Supplementary Study Papers*, Part IV (Washington, DC, 1960).

Fürst, G., *Konzentration der Betriebe und Unternehmen* I, in *Die Konzentration in der Wirtschaft*, I (Berlin: Verein für Sozialpolitik, 1960).

Fullarton, J., *On the Regulation of Currencies* (London, 1845).

Fustado, C., *Développement et sous-développement* (Paris, 1968).

Gahlen, B., and Ott, A. (eds), *Probleme der Wachstumstheorie* (Tübingen, 1972).

Galbraith, J. K., *The Affluent Society* (Harmondsworth , 1962) (First edition 1958).

Garegnani, P., 'Heterogeneous Capital, the Production, Function and the Theory of Distribution', *Review of Economic Studies*, XXXVII (1970).

Georgescu-Roegen, N., 'Mathematical Proofs of the Breakdown of Capitalism', *Econometrica*, XXVIII (1960); repr. in *Analytical Economics* (Cambridge, Mass., 1966).

German Council of Economic Advisers (Bundesdeutsche Sachverständigenrat), *Jahresgutachten 1967*, Bundestagsdrucksache v, 2310 (Bonn, 4 Dec 1967).

Gestrich, H., *Die nationalökonomische Theorie* (Breslau, 1924; repr. 1970).

Gide, C., and Rist, C., *Geschichte der volkswirtschaftlichen Lehrmeinungen*, third edition (Jena, 1921). (First French edition Paris, 1909.)

Giersch, H. (ed.), *Demand Management (Globalsteuerung)* (Kiel, 1972).

Gillard, L., and Sereni, P., 'Matériaux pour une analyse structurale des mouvements courts', in *Cahiers d'analyse économique: Analyse des mouvements conjoncturels d'après-guerre*, ed. V. A. Barrère and H. Guitton (Paris, 1968).

Gillman, J. M., *The Falling Rate of Profit* (New York, 1957).

——*Prosperity in Crisis* (New York, 1965).

Gleitze, B., 'Gibt es auch in der DDR Wirtschaftskonjunkturschwankungen?', in *Die Quelle* (Berlin: DGB), xxv (Feb 1974).

Glyn, A., and Sutcliffe, B., *British Capitalism, Workers and the Profit Squeeze* (Harmondsworth, 1972).

Godelier, M., *Rationalité et irrationalité en economie* (Paris, 1966).

Goldmann, J., in *Planowoje hospodarstwi* (State planning), nos 9 and 11, (1964a).

——In *Economics of Planning* (Oslo), IV, no. 2 (1964b).

Goodwin, R. M., 'A Growth Cycle', in *Socialism, Capitalism and Economic Growth*, ed. C. H. Feinstein (Cambridge, 1967).

——*Elementary Economics from the Higher Standpoint* (Cambridge, 1970).

Gordon, D. F., 'What Was the Labor Theory of Value?', *American Economic Review, Papers and Proceedings*, XLIX, no. 2 (May 1959).

——Discussion, Centenary Meeting of American Economic Association, *Am. Ec. Review, Papers and Proceedings*, LVII, no. 2, (1967).

Gordon, R. A., *Business Leadership in the Large Corporation*, second edition (Berkeley, Calif., 1960). (First edition 1945.)

Gottheil, F., 'Wages and Interest: A Modern Dissection of Marxian Economic Models: Comment', *American Economic Review*, L, no. 4 (Sep 1960).

Gramsci, A., *Elementi di Politica*, ed. M. Spinella (Rome, 1964).

——Article in *Rinascita*, 1957, pp. 149–158.

——*Scritti Politici*, ed. P. Spriano (Rome, 1967).

Gray, A., *The Socialist Tradition* (New York, London and Toronto, 1946).

Graziadei, A., *La Produzione capitalistica* (Milan, 1899).

——*Le Prix et le surprix dans l'économie capitaliste – Critique de la théorie de la valeur selon Karl Marx* (Paris, 1925). (First Italian edition 1923.)

Grossmann, H., *Das Akkumulations- und Zusammenbruchsgesetz des kapitalistischen Systems*, (Leipzig, 1929; and Frankfurt, 1970).

Gruber, Utta, 'Wachstumstheoretische Beziehungen in der Akkumulationstheorie von Karl Marx – Bemerkungen zu dem Diskussionsbeitrag von Sigurd Klatt', *Jahrbücher für Nationalökonomie und Statistik*, CLXXII (1960).

——'Zur Frage der Gesamtgrössenbetrachtung bei Marx und Keynes', ibid., CLXXIII (1961).

Grünberg, C., 'Sozialdemokratie', in *Wörterbuch der Volkswirtschaft*, ed. Elster, third edition (Jena, 1911). (First edition 1907.)

Guevara, Che (E. C.), 'Consideraciones sobre los costos de producción . . .', in *Nuestra industria* (Havana, Cuba), June 1963.

Guiducci, M., *Marx dopo Marx* (Turin, 1970).

Guihéneuf, R., *Le Problème de la théorie marxiste de la valeur* (Paris, 1952).

Guillebaud, C. W., 'Marshall's *Principles of Economics* in the Light of Contemporary Economic Thought', *Economica*, May 1952.

Guitton, H., *Les Fluctuations économiques* (Paris, 1951).

——*Les Mouvements conjoncturels* (Paris, 1971).

Günther, E., 'Die revisionistische Bewegung in der deutschen Sozialdemokratie', *Schmollers Jahrbuch*, XXIV (1905).

Gunzert, R., *Was ist Konzentration?* (Frankfurt, 1960).

——*Konzentration, Markt und Marktbeherrschung* (Frankfurt, 1961).

Gurland, A., *Das Heute der proletarischen Aktion* (Berlin, 1931).

——'Die ökonomischen Theorien des Marxismus', paper presented at SPD Conference, Bonn, 5–6 Dec 1953 (unpublished).

Gurley, J. G., 'Have Fiscal and Monetary Policies Failed?', *American Economic Review, Papers and Proceedings*, LXII (May 1972).

Gurvitch, H., 'La sociologie du jeune Marx', *Cahiers Internationaux de Sociologie*, IV (1948).

Güsten, R., *Die langfristige Tendenz der Profitrate bei Karl Marx und Joan Robinson* (Munich, 1960).

Haberlandt, K., *Das Wachstum der industriellen Unternehmung* (Neuwied, 1970).

Hahn, F. H., 'The Stability of Growth Equilibrium', *Quarterly Journal of Economics*, LXXIV (1960).

Halbach, F., *Kapitalismus ohne Krisen? – Zur bürgerlichen Kritik des 'Gesetzes vom tendenziellen Fall der Profitrate'* (Giessen, 1972).

Halbwachs, M., *La Classe ouvrière et les niveaux de vie* (Paris, 1912).

Hall, R. I., and Hitch, C. J., 'Price Theory and Business Behaviour', *Oxford Studies in the Price Mechanism* (Oxford, 1951).

Haller, H., *Gibt es eine Lohntheorie?* (Stuttgart and Berlin, 1936).

Halm, G. N., *Geld, Kredit, Banken* (Munich and Leipzig, 1935).

Halm, G. N., *Wirtschaftssysteme*, Part III: 'Marxismus' (Berlin, 1960).

——*Economic Systems, A Comparative Analysis*, second edition (New York, 1968). (First edition 1951.)

Hamilton, E. J., 'American Treasure and the Rise of Capitalism (1500–1700)', *Economica*, 9 Nov 1929.

Hankel, W., *Währungspolitik* (Stuttgart and Berlin, 1971).

Hansen, A. H., *Full Recovery or Stagnation?* (New York, 1938).

——*Fiscal Policy and Business Cycles* (New York, 1941).

——*Business Cycles and National Income* (New York, 1951).

Hansen, A. H., and Clemence, R. V. (eds), *Readings in Business Cycles and National Income* (London, 1953).

Hansen, A. H., and Tout, H., 'Annual Survey of Business Cycle Theory: Investment and Saving in Business Cycle Theory', *Econometrica*, I, no. 2 (Apr 1933).

Harcourt, G. C., *Some Cambridge Controversies in the Theory of Capital* (Cambridge, 1972).

Harcourt, G. C., and Laing, N. F. (eds), *Capital and Growth* (Harmondsworth, 1971).

Harcourt, G. C., and Massaro, V. G., 'A Note on Mr. Sraffa's System', *Economic Journal*, LXXIV (1964).

Harms, B. (ed.), *Kapital und Kapitalismus*, I (Berlin, 1931).

Harris, D., 'On Marx's Scheme of Reproduction and Accumulation', *Journal of Political Economy*, LXXX, no. 3, part I (May–June 1972).

Harrod, R. F., 'An Essay in Dynamic Theory', *Economic Journal*, XLIX (1939); repr. in *Growth Economics*, ed. Sen (1970).

——*Towards a Dynamic Economics* (London, 1948).

——'Second Essay in Dynamic Theory', *Economic Journal*, LVV (1960).

——*Money* (London, 1969).

——'After Twenty-one Years – A Comment', *Economic Journal*, LXXX (Sep 1970).

——*Economic Dynamics* (London, 1973).

Hart, P. E., 'The Analysis of Business Concentration', *Journal of the Royal Statistical Society*, 1960. (See also under Prais and Hart.)

——Article in *Bulletin of Oxford University Institute of Statistics*, Aug 1957.

Haussmann, F., *Die wirtschaftliche Konzentration an ihrer Schicksalswende* (Basle, 1940).

Hax, K., 'Abschreibung und Finanzierung', *Zeitschrift für handelswissenschaftliche Forschung*, VII (1955).

Heertje, A., 'An Essay on Marxian Economics', *Zeitschrift für Volkswirtschaft und Statistik*, 1972.

Heilbroner, R. L., *The Great Economists* (London, 1955).

Heiman, H. 'Antikartelle', in: *Archiv für Sozialwissenschaft und Sozialpolitik*, XXVI (1899?)

Heller, W., *Die Entwicklung der Grundprobleme der volkswirtschaftlichen Theorie*, fourth edition (Leipzig, 1931). (First edition 1902?.)

Helmstädter, E., *Der Kapitalkoeffizient* (Stuttgart, 1969).

Hermberg, P., *Krisenablauf einst und jetzt* (Berlin, 1931).

Hesselbach, W., *Die gemeinwirtschaftlichen Unternehmen* (Frankfurt, 1971).

Hickel, R., 'Zur Methode der politischen Ökonomie', annex to his edition of *Kapital*, III (Berlin, 1971).

Hickman, B. G., *Investment Demand and US Economic Growth* (Washington, DC, 1965).

Hicks, J. R., *The Theory of Wages*, second edition (1966). (First edition 1932.)

——*A Contribution to the Theory of the Trade Cycle* (Oxford, 1951). (First edition 1950.)

——*Value and Capital*, second edition (Oxford, 1950). (First edition 1946.)

——*Capital and Growth*, second edition (Oxford, 1969). (First edition 1965.)

Higgins, B., *Economic Development* (London, 1959).

Hildreth, R. J., 'Some Reflections on Income Distribution Research', paper delivered at meeting at North Carolina State University, Apr 1966; in *Income Distribution Analysis* (Raleigh, NC, June 1966).

Hilferding, R., 'Böhm-Bawerks Marx-Kritik', in *Marx-Studien*, I (Vienna, 1904); English edition by Sweezy, *Böhm-Bawerk's Criticism of Marx* (New York, 1966).

——'Geld und Ware', *Die neue Zeit*, XXX (1911–12).

——'Referat auf dem Kieler Parteitag, May 1927', *Kieler Volkszeitung*, 27 May 1927.

——*Das Finanzkapital* (Berlin, 1947; Frankfurt, 1968). (First edition Vienna, 1910.)

Hill, T. P., 'Growth and Investment according to International Comparisons', *Economic Journal*, LXXIV (1964).

Himmelmann, G., 'Arbeitswert, Mehrwert und Verteilung' (Dec 1972, unpublished).

Hirsch, Marie, *Zur Theorie des Konjunkturzyklus* (Tübingen, 1929).

Hitch, see Hall

Hobson, T. A., *Imperialism* (London, 1902).

Hofmann, W., 'Verelendung', in *Folgen einer Theorie – Essays über 'Das Kapital' von Karl Marx* (Frankfurt, 1967).

Hofmann, W. and Abendroth, W., *Ideengeschichte der sozialen Bewegung des 19. und 20. Jahrhunderts*, fourth edition (Berlin and New York, 1971). (First edition 1956.)

Holesovsky, V., 'Marx and Soviet National Income Theory', in *American Economic Review*, LI, no. 3 (June 1961).

Holtrop, M. W., 'Die Umlaufsgeschwindigkeit des Geldes', in *Beiträge zur Geldtheorie*, ed. by F. von Hayek (Vienna, 1933).

Horowitz, D., Introduction to *Marx and Modern Economics* (London, 1968).

Houghton, see Blair

Huffschmid, J., 'Die Bilanzanalyse, Instrument zur Aufdeckung der Ausbeutung und des Profits', in *Betriebsfibel*, ed. B. Kelb, Rotbuch 31 (Berlin, 1971).

Hunt, E. K. and Schwartz, J. G., *Introduction to A Critique of Economic Theory*, ed. Hunt and Schwartz (Harmondsworth, 1972).

Hymer, S., and Roosevelt, F., Comment, Symposium on Lindbeck's *The Political Economy of the New Left*, *Quarterly Journal of Economics*, LXXXVI, no. 4 (Nov 1972).

Ibn Khaldun, *Discours sur l'histoire universelle* (*Al-Muqaddima*), 3 vols (Beirut, 1967). (From manuscripts of 1382–97; first printed edition (in Arabic) Bûtâq-Cairo, 1857.) First (French) translation by W. Mac-Guckin de Slane (Paris 1862–68); English translation (by F. Rosenthal): *An Introduction to History* (London, 1958).

Isard, W., 'A Neglected Cycle: "The Transport Building Cycle"', *Review of Economic and Statistics*, XXIV (Nov 1942).

Jasny, N., 'The Soviet Balance of National Income and the American Input–Output Analysis', *L'Industria*, 1962.

Jeuck, Karin, 'Währungskrise', in *Express-Zeitung für sozialistische Betriebs-und Gewerkschaftsarbeit* (Offenbach, 1973).

Jewkes, J., 'Monopoly and Economic Progress', *Economica*, new. ser., XX (Aug 1953).

Jöhr, W. A., 'Das Modell der vollkommenen Konkurrenz', in *Konkurrenz und Planwirtschaft* (Bern, 1946).

Jordan, J. A., 'Introduction: Karl Marx as a Philosopher and Sociologist', in *Karl Marx* – Economy, Class and Social Revolution (London, 1971).

Jourdan, G., and Valier, J., 'L'Échec des explications bourgeoises de l'inflation', *Critiques de l'économie politique*, no. 1 (Sep–Dec 1970).

Juglar, C., *Des crises commerciales et de leur retour périodique* (Paris, 1889). (First edition, 1860.)

Jung, W., 'Zur Frage der Anwendungsmöglichkeiten der Marxschen Theorie der Profitrate bei der Analyse der kapitalistischen Entwicklung', in *Wirtschaftswachstum*, ed. R. Schilcher (Berlin, 1964).

Justc., F. T., 'A Framework for the Measurement of Economic and Social Performance', in *The Measurement of Economic and Social Performance*, ed. M. Moss (New York and London, 1973).

Kaldor, N., 'The Relation of Economic Growth and Cyclical Fluctuations', *Economic Journal*, LXIV (Mar 1954).

——'Alternative Theories of Distribution', *Review of Economic Studies*, XXIII (1955–6); repr. in *The Labour Market*, ed. B. J. M. McCormick and E. O. Smith (Harmondsworth, 1968).

——'L'Évolution capitaliste à la lumière de l'économie Keynésienne',

Economie appliquée, x, no. 2 (Apr–June 1957a).

——'A Model of Economic Growth', *Economic Journal*, LXVII (Dec 1957b).

Kalecki, M., *Essays in the Theory of Employment* (London, 1933).

——*Essays in the Theory of Economic Fluctuations* (London, 1939). New edition 1966.

——'A New Approach to the Problem of Business Cycles', *Review of Economic Studies*, 1949–1950.

——*Theory of Economic Dynamics*, third edition (London, 1956). (First edition 1954.)

——*Zarys teorii wzrostu gospodarki socjalistycznej* (Warsaw, 1963). English edition: 'Introduction to the Theory of Growth in a Socialist Industry' in *Selected Essays on the Economic Growth of the Socialist and the Mixed Economy* (Cambridge, 1972).

Kantorovich, L. V., *The Best Use of Economic Resources* (Moscow, 1959).

Kautsky, B. (ed.), Note in abridged version of *Kapital* (Stuttgart, 1957), p. 713.

Kautsky, K., *Karl Marx, Ökonomische Lehren* (Berlin, 1930). (First edition 1887).

——*Handelspolitik und Sozialdemokratie* (Leipzig, 1901).

——'Krisentheorien', *Die neue Zeit*, xx, no. 2 (1901/2).

——'Geld, Papier und Ware', in *Die neue Zeit*, xxx, no. 1 (1912).

Kaysen, K., 'The Social Significance of the Modern Corporation', *American Economic Review*, XLVII (May 1957).

——'The Corporation: How Much Power? What Scope?', in *The Corporation in Modern Industry* (Cambridge, Mass., 1959).

Keiser, G., *Die kapitalistische Konzentration* (Berlin, 1931).

Kende, P., 'Economie et socialisme', in *Centenaire du 'Capital'* (Paris, 1969).

Kendrick, J. W., 'Productivity Trends: Capital and Labor', *Review of Economics and Statistics*, XXXVIII (Aug 1956).

——*Postwar Productivity Trends in the United States 1948–1969* (New York, 1973).

Kennedy, C. and Thirlwall, A P., 'Surveys in Applied Economics: Technical Progress', *Economic Journal*, LXXXII (Mar 1972).

Kerschagl, R., 'Was kann Marx uns heute noch sagen?', *Schmollers Jahrbuch*, LXXX (1960), rep. in *Geschichte der Volkswirtschaftslehre*, ed. A. Montaner (Cologne and Berlin, 1967).

Kesting, H., *Geschichtsphilosophie und Weltbürgerkrieg, Deutungen der Geschichte von der französischen Revolution bis zum Ost–West-Konflikt* (Heidelberg, 1959).

Keynes, J. M., *The Economic Consequences of the Peace* (London, 1919).

——*A Treatise on Money*, 2 vols (London, 1934). (First edition, 1930.)

——*Essays in Persuasion* (London, 1933).

——*The General Theory of Employment, Interest and Money* (London, 1949). (First edition 1936.)

Kindleberger, C. P., *The Terms of Trade* (London, 1956).

Kindleberger, C. P., *Foreign Trade and the National Economy* (New Haven, Conn., and London, 1962).

——*Economic Development*, second edition (New York and Tokyo, 1965). (First edition 1958.)

Klatt, S., 'Wachstumstheoretische Beziehungen in der Akkumulationstheorie von Karl Marx', *Jahrbücher für Nationalökonomie und Statistik*, CLXXII (1960).

Klein, L. R., 'Theories of Effective Demand and Employment', *Journal of Political Economy*, LV, (Apr 1947); repr. in *Marx and Modern Economics*, ed. Horowitz (1968).

——*The Keynesian Revolution* (London, 1965).

Koch, J. V., and Fenili, R. N., 'The Influence of Market Structure upon Industry Price-Cost Margins', *Rivista Internazionale di Scienze Economiche e Commerciali*, XVIII (Nov 1971).

Kolm, S.-G., 'Les Etats-Unis bénéficient-ils du "droit du Seigneur" dans le système monétaire international?', *Kyklos*, XXIII (1970).

König, H., 'Konzentration und Wachstum', in *Zeitschrift für die gesamte Staatswissenschaft*, 1959.

——'Ansätze und Probleme der Wachstumstheorie', in *Wachstum und Entwicklung der Wirtschaft* (Cologne and Berlin, 1968).

Kondratieff, N. D., *Mirowoje chosjaistwo; jewo konjunktury wo wrjemja poslje vojny* (World economy: its course in post-war times) (Vologda, 1922).

——Articles (1926–8) in *Die langen Wellen der Konjunktur*, ed. Prinkipo (Berlin 1972).

Koopmans, T. C., 'Economic Growth at a Maximal Rate', *Quarterly Journal of Economics*, LXXVIII (1964); repr. in *Growth Economics*, ed. Sen (1970).

Koppel, A., 'Für und wider Karl Marx, Prolegomena zu einer Biographie', quoted by von Bortkiewicz in *Archiv für Sozialwissenschaft*, XXIII (1906).

Krähe, see report on the meeting of chartered accountants in Dortmund on 29 Oct 1954, *Zeitschrift für handelswissenschaftliche Forschung*.

Kregel, T. A., *Rate of Profit, Distribution and Growth* (London, 1971).

Krelle, W., *Verteilungstheorie* (Tübingen, 1962a).

——'Investition und Wachstum', *Jahrbücher für Nationalökonomie und Statistik*, CLXXIV (1962b).

——'Investition und Wachstum', *Jahrbücher für Nationalökonomie und Statistik*, CLXXVI (1964).

——'Marx im Lichte der heutigen Theorie des wirtschaftlichen Wachstums' (paper delivered at a conference in Münster, 1968), in *Beiträge zur Wachstumstheorie*, ed. W. G. Hoffmann (Tübingen, 1969).

——'Marx as a Growth Theorist', paper presented to Social System Research Institute, University of Wisconsin, July 1970; published as 'Marx als Wachstumstheoretiker' in *IFO-Studien* (Berlin, 1970).

Krelle, W. and Gabisch, G., *Wachstumstheorie* (Berlin, 1972).

Krengel, R., 'Produktionskapazitäten, Kapitalintensität und Kapital-
ausnutzung der westdeutschen Industrie', *Vierteljahreshefte zur Wirt-
schaftsforschung*, 1962.

Krengel, R., *et al.*, *Produktionsvolumen und Potential, Produktionsfaktoren der
Industrie in der BRD* (Berlin, 1974/76).

Kreps, T. J., 'The Effectiveness of Federal Antitrust Laws', *American
Economic Review*, XXXIX (June 1949).

Kromphardt, J., 'Zur makroökonomischen Produktionsfunktion',
Jahrbücher für Nationalökonomie and Statistik, CLXXXIII (1971).

Krünitz, in *Ökonomische Enzyklopädie* (Berlin, 1776). (Quoted in Passow,
1927, p. 107, note.)

Kruse, A., *Geschichte der volkswirtschaftlichen Theorien*, third edition (Munich,
1953). (First edition 1948.)

Kühne, K., 'Marx und die moderne Nationalökonomie', *Die neue
Gesellschaft*, II (Bielefeld, 1955a); repr. in *Geschichte und Ökonomie*, ed.
H. -U. Wehler (Cologne; 1973). (Series of four articles, as follows:
'Arbeitswert und Mehrwertrate', Jan–Feb 1955; ' "Verelendung"
und Konzentration', Mar–Apr 1955; 'Krisen, Unterkonsumtion und
fallende Profitrate', May–June 1955; 'Investitionsproblem,
Konjunkturzyklus und Wachstumsprozess des Kapitalismus', July–
Aug 1955.)

——'Das Rätsel Reallohn', in *Gewerkschaftliche Monatshefte*, VI (Cologne,
1955b).

——'Teilzahlung-Ärgernis und Gefahr?' *Gewerkschaftliche Monatshefte*,
May 1954.

——*Funktionsfähige Konkurrenz* (Berlin, 1958).

——'Wohlfahrtsökonomie und moderne Finanzwissenschaft', *Gewerkschaftliche Monatshefte*, XIV (1963)

——*Grenzen der Konjunkturpolitik im Wachstumszyklus* (Cologne, 1968).

——'Marx im Lichte der modernen Wirtschaftswissenschaft', Introduction to *Karl Marx, Ökonomische Schriften in thematischem Zusammenhang*,
(Stuttgart, 1970).

——'Weltboom und Weltbankier', *Gewerkschaftliche Monatshefte*, XXII
(1971a).

——'Der öffentliche Sektor in säkularer Sicht', *Die öffentliche Wirtschaft*, XX
(Berlin 1971b). Includes list of articles by Recktenwald (1970–1).

——*Das gemeinwirtschaftliche Unternehmen als Wettbewerbsfaktor* (Frankfurt,
1971c).

——'Sozialistische Konzeption und Menschheitsperspektiven', in *Freiheit-
licher Sozialismus, Festschrift für G. Weisser*, ed. Flohr, Lompe, Neumann
(Bonn–Bad Godesberg, 1973).

——*Geschichtskonzept und Profitrate im Marxismus* (Neuwied, 1976).

——'Zur ökonomischen Theorie der Bürokratie', in *Neuere Entwicklungen in
den Wirtschaftswissenschaften* Verein für Sozialpolitik, XCVIII (Berlin,
1978).

——'Der kapazitätserweiterungseffekt bei Abschreibungen' in: *Finanzierung öffentlicher Unternehmen-Festschrift für Paul Münch*, ed. P. Eichhorn, Th. Thiemeyer (Baden, 1979).

Kurihara, K., 'Distribution, Employment, and Secular Growth', in *Post-Keynesian Economics*, ed. Kurihara (London, 1955).

——*Introduction to Keynesian Dynamics* (London, 1956).

——*The Keynesian Theory of Economic Development* (London, 1959).

——*Applied Dynamic Economics* (London, 1963).

Kurucz, J., 'Marx-Kult und Marxismusbegriff', *Jahrbuch für Sozialwissenschaft*, XXI (1970).

Kuusinen, Arbatov, Belgakov, Tscheidin, Makarovsky, Miljeikovsky, Sitkovskiy, Vygodsky (eds), *Les Principes du Marxisme/Leninisme* (Moscow, 1961).

Kuznets, S., *Secular Movements in Production and Prices* (New York, 1930).

——*Modern Economic Growth* (New Haven, Conn., and London, 1966).

Labriola, Antonio, *Karl Marx – L'économiste, le socialiste* (Paris, 1910).

——*Capitalismo*, second edition (Naples, 1926). (First edition 1910.)

——*La Concezione materialistica della storia* ('Collection of Essays') (Bari, 1969).

Labriola, Arturo, *L'État et la crise* (Paris, 1933).

——*L'Attualità di Marx* (Naples, 1943). Original edition (Milan, 1926) was burnt by Fascists.

Lange, E., 'Karl Marx als volkswirtschaftlicher Theoretiker', *Conrads Jahrbücher*, ser. 3, XIV (1897).

Lange, O., 'Marxian Economics and Modern Economic Theory', *Review of Economic Studies*, II (1934–5)

——'On the Economic Theory of Socialism, *Review of Economic Studies*, IV, no. 1 (Oct 1936): new edition with F. M. Taylor, *On the Economic Theory of Socialism* (Minneapolis, 1938).

——Review of Sweezy's *Theory of Capitalist Development*, *Journal of Philosophy*, XL, no 14 (July 1943).

——'Quelques remarques sur l'analyse input–output', *Cahiers de l'Institut de Science Economique Appliquée*, ser. G, no. 2 (1957). (Originally published in the Indian review *Samkhya*, 1957.)

——*Theory of Reproduction and Accumulation* (Warsaw, 1969). (First Polish edition 1965.)

Latouche, S., 'A propos de la baisse tendancielle du taux de profit', *Revue économique*, XXIV (Jan 1973)

Laurat, L., *Marxisme en faillite* (Paris, 1939).

——*Marxism and democracy* (London, 1940). (First French edition 1939.)

Lavigne, M.-L., *Le Capital dans l'économie soviétique* (Paris, 1961)

Lebowitz, M., 'Monopoly Capital', *Studies on the Left*, no. 5 (1966); repr. in Italian in *Sul capitale monopolistico*, ed. Botta (1971).

Lederer, E., *Grundzüge der ökonomischen Theorie* (Tübingen, 1922).

Lederer, E., *Konjunkturen und Krisen, Grundriss der Sozialökonomik* (Tübingen, 1925).

——'Monopole und Konjunktur', *Vierteljahreshefte zur Konjunkturforschung*, Suppl. (1927).

Lefebvre, H., *Le Marxisme*, third edition, (Paris, 1951). (First edition 1948).

Leibenstein, H., *Economic Backwardness and Economic Growth* (New York, 1957).

Leichter, O., 'Zur Analyse der Weltwirtschaftskrise', in *Der lebendige Marxismus, Festgabe zum 70. Geburtstage von Karl Kautsky*, ed. O. Jenssen (Jena, 1924).

Lenel, H. E., *Ursachen der Konzentration* (Tübingen, 1962).

Lenin, V. I., 'On the so-called question of markets' (in Russian), mimeo (1893); in *Bolshevik*, no. 81 (Moscow, 1937), and *Oeuvres*, I, (Paris, 1958), pp. 91ff.

——'Note on the Theory of Markets' (in Russian) (1898) in *Oeuvres*, I, (Paris, 1958), pp. 54ff.

——*Marx, Engels, Marxismus* (Berlin, 1947).

——*Imperialism, The Highest Stage of Capitalism* (in Russian) (Petrograd, 1916), in *Collected Works*, XXII.

——*Collected Works* (Moscow, 1964 etc.).

Leon, P., *Ipotesi sullo sviluppo dell'economia capitalistica* (Turin, 1965).

Leontief, W., 'The Significance of Marxian Economics for Present-Day-Theory', *American Economic Review*, XXVIII (Mar 1938); repr. in *Marx and Modern Economics*, ed. Horowitz (1968)

——'Domestic Production and Foreign Trade: The American Capital Position Re-examined', *Proceedings of the American Philosophical Society*, XCVII (1953).

Lerner, A. P., 'Economic Theory and Socialist Economy', *Review of Economic Studies*, I (Oct 1934).

——'Marxism and Economics: Sweezy and Robinson', *Journal of Political Economy*, LIII (Mar 1945).

——'A Note on "Understanding the Marxian Notion of Exploitation"', *Journal of Economic Literature*, X (1972).

Leroy-Beaulieu, P., *Le Collectivisme – Examen critique du nouveau socialisme* (Paris, 1884).

Lescure, J., *Des crises générales de surproduction*, fourth edition (Paris, 1932). (First edition 1906.)

Lester, R., 'Marginalism, Minimum Wages and Labor Markets', *American Economic Review*, XXXVII (Mar 1947).

Letiche, J. M., 'Soviet Views on Keynes: A Review Article Surveying the Literature', *Journal of Economic Literature*, (1971).

Lewin, M., *Political Undercurrents in Soviet Debates* (Princeton, 1974).

Lewis, A., 'Economic Development with Unlimited Supplies of Labour', *Manchester School*, (May 1954).

——*The Theory of Economic Growth* (London, 1960). (First edition 1955.)

Lexis, W., *Allgemeine Volkswirtschaftslehre*, second edition (Berlin, 1913). (First edition 1916.)

Liberman, E. G., 'Plan, Profit, Bonus' *Pravda*', 9 Sep 1962.

Lichtheim, G., *Marxism in Modern France* (New York and London, 1966).

——*Marxism – An Historical and Critical Study*, third edition (London, 1967). (First edition 1961.)

——*A Short History of Socialism* (London, 1970).

Lindauer, J. H., *Macroeconomics* (New York, 1968).

Lindbeck, A., *The Political Economy of the New Left* (New York, 1971).

Lindsay, A. D., Preface to Croce, *Historical Materialism and the Economics of Karl Marx* (1914).

——*Karl Marx' 'Capital'* (London, 1925).

Lintner, J. and Butters, J. K., 'Effect of Mergers on Industrial Concentration', in *Review of Economics and Statistics*, XXXII, no. 1 (Feb 1950).

Lippi, M., 'Questioni relative alla teoria marxiana del Capitale', in *Requisiti per un sistema economico accettabile in relazione alle esigenze della collectività*, CIME congress on Mathematical Economics, Urbino, 20–5 Sep 1971 (Milan, 1973).

Little, J. M. D., *A Critique of Welfare Economics*, second edition (London, 1957). (First edition 1950.)

Lohmann, M., 'Abschreibungen, Was sie sind und was sie nicht sind', *Der Wirtschaftsprüfer*, 1949.

Lombardini, S., *Concorrenza, monopolio e sviluppo* (Milan, 1971).

Löwe, A., 'Der Sinn der Weltwirtschaftskrise', in *Neue Blätter für den Sozialismus*, Feb 1931.

Loria, A., *Carlo Marx* (Rome, undated [1890?]).

Lukacz, G., 'Was ist orthodoxer Marxismus?', in *Geschichte und Klassenbewusstsein* (Neuwied, 1970). (First edition Vienna, 1923).

Lukas, E., *Geld und Kredit* (Heidelberg, 1951).

Lutz, F., *Das Konjunkturproblem in der Nationalökonomie* (Jena, 1932).

Luxemburg, Rosa, *Die Akkumulation des Kapitals*, Second edition (Leipzig, 1921). (First edition Berlin, 1913; recent edition Frankfurt, 1966.)

MacBean, A., *Export Instability and Economic Development* (London, 1962).

Macchioro, A., 'L'Economia politica del marxismo' (1961), in *Studi di storia del pensiero economico* (Milan, 1970).

Machlup, F., 'Theories of the Firm: Marginalist, Behavioral, Managerial', in *American Economic Review*, LVII (Mar 1967).

——'Rejoinder to an Anti-marginalist', *American Economic Review*, XXXVII (Mar 1947).

——*The Political Economy of Monopoly* (Baltimore, 1952).

Mackenroth, G., 'Der Zins in der kapitalistischen Wirtschaft', *Weltwirtschaftliches Archiv*, LXII (1949).

McConnell, J. W., in 'Papers and Proceedings, 61st Annual Meeting, Cleveland, 1948', *American Economic Review*, XXXIX (May 1949).

Mandel, E., *Traité d'économie marxiste*, 2 vols (Paris, 1962).
——*La Formation de la pensée économique de Karl Marx*, second edition (Paris, 1970).
——'Geschichte des Kapitalismus und seiner Bewegungsgesetze' (address to a congress at Tilburg, Sep 1970), in *Kapitalismus in den siebziger Jahren* (Frankfurt, 1971).
——*Der Spätkapitalismus* (Frankfurt, 1972).
Mangold, G., 'Die Strukturanalyse des wirtschaftlichen Kreislaufs', II. 2: 'Karl Marx' Analyse des gesamtwirtschaftlichen Prozesses', *Schmollers Jahrbuch*, LXXVII (1953).
Mansfield, E., *The Economics of Technological Change* (London, 1960).
Marchal, J., 'Les Facteurs qui déterminent les taux des salaires dans le monde moderne', *Revue économique*, (June 1950).
——*Deux Essais sur le Marxisme* (Paris, 1955).
Marchal, J., and Lecaillon, J., *La Répartition du revenu national*, 3 vols, III: 'Le Modèle classique – le modèle marxiste' (Paris, 1958).
Marcuse, H., *One-Dimensional Man* (London, 1970). (First edition 1964).
Marglin, S., 'The Rate of Interest and the Value of Capital with Unlimited Supplies of Labor', in *Essays on the Theory of Optimal Economic Growth*, ed. K. Shell (Cambridge, Mass., 1967).
Marshall, A., *Principles of Economics*, VIII (London, 1930). (First edition 1890.)
Masaryk, T. G., *Die philosophischen und soziologischen Grundlagen des Marxismus* (Vienna, 1899).
Mason, E. S., *Economic Concentration and the Monopoly Problem*, (Cambridge, Mass., 1957).
——'The Apologetics of "Managerialism"', *Journal of Business*, Jan 1958.
Matthews, R. C. O., *The Trade Cycle* (Cambridge, 1959).
Mattick, P., 'Value Theory and Capital Accumulation', *Science and Society*, XXIII, no. 1 (1959).
——*Marx and Keynes, The Limits of the Mixed Economy* (London, 1969).
May, K., 'Value and Prices: A Note on Winternitz's Solution', *Economic Journal*, L (Dec 1940).
Mayer, G. P., 'Die Marxismus-Diskussion in der sozialwissenschaftlichen Literatur Frankreichs, Englands und Amerikas (1933–1954)', *Die neue Gesellschaft*, I (July–Aug 1954).
Mazzini, G., *Scritti*, XVII (Rome, 1871).
——*Scritti scelti* (Florence, 1924).
Means, G. C., *Pricing Power and the Public Interest* (New York, 1962).
Meadows, D. H.; Meadows, D. L.; Runders, J.; Behrens, W. W.: *The Limits to Growth – A Report For the Club of Rome* (New York, 1972).
Meek, R. L., *Studies in the Labour Theory of Value* (London, 1956a).
——'Some Notes on the Transformation Problem', *Economic Journal*, LXVI (Mar 1956b).

——'The Falling Rate of Profit', *Science and Society*, xxiv, no. 4 (1960).

——*Economics and Ideology* (London 1967); in which reprinted 'Marx's Doctrine of "increasing pauperisation" ', *Science and Society*, Fall 1962.

Meissner, H., *Theorie des Wirtschaftwachstums* (Berlin, 1972).

Meldolesi, L., 'Il contributo di Bortkierricz', in *V. Bortkierricz* (1977).

Melotti, U., *Marx e il terzo mondo* (Milan, 1972).

Mendelson, L. A., *Teorija i istorija ekonomitschestkich krisisow i ziklow* ('Theory and history of economic crises and cycles') (Moscow, 1954).

Mertens, D., *Die Wandlungen in der industriellen Branchenstruktur in der BRD* (Berlin, 1964).

Metzler, L. A., 'The Nature and Stability of Inventory Cycles', *Review of Economics and Statistics*, xxiii (Aug 1941).

Michelet, G., *Nouvelles théories economiques: principes de valoristie* (Brussels and Paris, 1936).

Michels, R., *Die Verelendungstheorie*, (Leipzig, 1928).

Mieth, W., *Das Akzelerationsprinzip* (Berlin, 1954).

Miksch, L., *Gibt es eine allgemeine Überproduktion?* (Jena, 1929).

Mill, James, *Commerce Defended*, (London, 1808); repr. in Mill's *Selected Economic Writings*, ed. Winch (Chicago, 1966).

Mill, J. S., *Principles of Political Economy* (London, 1965). (First edition, 1848.)

Mills, C. W., *The Marxists*, third edition (New York, 1966). (First edition 1962.)

Mills, F. C., 'Opening Remarks: The Sociology and Economics of Class Conflict', in 'Papers and Proceedings, 61st Annual Meeting, Cleveland, 1948', *American Economic Review*, xxxix (May 1949).

Minc, B., *Ekonomia polityczna socjalizmu* (Political economy of socialism) (Warsaw, 1962). Italian edition: *Economia politica del socialismo* (Milan, 1967).

Mirabeau, G de Riqueti, comte de, see R. Hohoff, in *Archiv für die Geschichte des Sozialismus und der Arbeiterbewegung*, v; quoted in Passow, (1927).

Mitchell, W., *Business Cycles – The Problem and its Setting* (New York, 1932). (First edition, 1927.)

Molnár, F., *Economic Growth and Recessions in the USA* (Budapest, 1970).

Mondolfo, R., *Le Matérialisme historique d'après F. Engels* (Paris, 1917).

——*Sulle Orme di Marx*, fourth edition (Bologna, 1948). (First edition 1930?)

Montesano, A., 'Il sistema teorico dell' equilibrio economico generale e la coerenza della teoria walrasiana della capitalizzazione', *Giornale degli economisti e annali di economia*, (May–June 1971).

Morishima, M., *Marx's Economics, a Dual Theory of Value and Growth*, (Cambridge, 1973).

Morus, T. (Sir Thomas More), *Utopia* (London, 1518).

Mossé, Éliane, *Marx et le problème de la croissance* (Paris, 1956).

Mossé, R., 'Le Keynésianisme devant le socialisme', *Revue socialiste*, 1949.
Moszkowska, Natalie, *Das Marxsche System* (Berlin, 1929).
——'Zur Verelendungstheorie', *Die Gesellschaft*, II (1932).
——*Zur Dynamik des Spätkapitalismus* (Zürich and New York, 1945).
Muhs, K., 'Der Produktionsprozess des Kapitals', *Anti-Marx, Betrachtungen über den inneren Aufbau der Marxschen Ökonomik*, I (Jena, 1927).
Müller, J. H., 'Konzentration', in *Staatslexikon – Recht, Wirtschaft, Gesellschaft*, 5 vols (Freiburg, 1959).
Myrdal, G., *The Political Element in Economic Doctrine* (London, 1953). German edition: *Das politische Element in der nationalökonomischen Doktrinbildung* (Hannover, 1963).

Nagels, J., *Genèse, contenu et prolongements de la notion de reproduction du capital selon Karl Marx, Boisguillebert, Quesnay, Leontiev* (Brussels, 1970).
Naphtali, F., *Wirtschaftsdemokratie* (Berlin, 1928).
——'Der organisierte Kapitalismus in der Wirtschaftskrise', *Die Gesellschaft*, VIII, no. 5 (1931).
Napoleoni, C., *Il Pensiero economico di 1900* (Turin, 1963). Quoted from German edition: *Grundzüge der modernen ökonomischen Theorien* (Frankfurt, 1968).
——*Lezioni sul Capitolo Sesto inedito di Marx* (Turin, 1972).
Napoleoni C., and Colletti, L. (eds), *Il Futuro del Capitalismo* (Bari, 1970).
Naville, P., *Le Salaire socialiste*, 2 vols (Paris, 1970).
——*Les Echanges socialistes* (Paris, 1974).
Neisser, H., 'Das Gesetz der fallenden Profitrate als Krisen- und Zusammenbruchsgesetz', *Die Gesellschaft*, VIII (Jan 1931).
——'Lohnhöhe und Beschäftigungsgrad im Marktgleichgewicht', *Weltwirtschaftliches Archiv*, XXXVI (Oct 1932).
Nell, E. J., *A Note on Cambridge Controversies in the Theory of Capital* (Cambridge, 1972).
Nelson, R., 'Aggregate Production Functions and Medium Range Growth Projections', *American Economic Review*, LIV (Sep 1964).
Nemchinov, V. S., 'Nyekotorye voprosy ispolzovanya bilansovogo metoda v statistikie vzaimnosvyazannykh dinamicheskikh ekonomicheskikh sistem' (Some problems connected with using the balancing method in the statistics of mutually connected dynamic economic systems), in *Utschonije sapiski po statistikje*, V (Moscow, 1959).
Neumann, F., 'Der Entwurf eines Monopol- und Kartellgesetzes', *Die Arbeit*, 1930.
Neumann, J. V., 'Über ein ökonomisches Gleichungssystem und eine Verallgemeinerung des Brouwerschen Fixpunktsatzes', in *Ergebnisse eines mathematischen Kolloquiums*, no. 8 ed. Karl Menger (Vienna, 1935–1936).
Neusüss, see Altvater (1971).
Notkin, A. I., *Otscherki teorii socialističeskowo wosproisdwodstwa* (Remarks on

the theory of socialist reproduction) (Moscow, 1948).

——*Tempi i proporcii socialistíceskowo wosproisdwodstwa* (Rates and proportions of socialist reproduction) (Moscow, 1961).

Nove, A., 'Cyclical Fluctuations under Socialism', in *Is the Business Cycle Obsolete?* ed. Bronfenbrenner (1969).

Nuti, D. M., 'Capitalism, Socialism and Steady Growth', *Economic Journal*, LXXX (Mar 1970); repr. in *Capital and Growth*, ed. Harcourt and Laing (1971).

Nutter, W., *The Growth of Industrial Production in the Soviet Union* (Princeton, 1962).

OECD (Organisation for Economic Co-operation and Development), *Fiscal Policy for a Balanced Economy: Experience, Problems and Prospects* (Paris, 1968).

Okun, A. M., 'Have Fiscal and/or Monetary Policies Failed?', in *American Economic Review, Papers and Proceedings*, LXII (May 1972).

O'Leary, P. J. and Lewis, A. L., 'Secular Swings in Production and Trade 1870–1913', in *The Manchester School*, XXIII (May 1955); repr. in *Readings in Business Cycles*, ed. R. A. Gordon and L. R. Klein (London, 1966).

Olivera, J., 'Cyclical Economic Growth under Collectivism', *Kyklos*, XIII (1960).

Olsienkiewicz, H., 'Entwicklungsschwankungen und Konjunkturzyklen in der Ostblockwirtschaft', *Osteuropa*, XIX (Nov 1969).

Ölssner, F., *Die Wirtschaftskrisen*, 1, fifth edition (Berlin, 1955). (First edition 1949.)

Onofri, F., *Potere e strutture sociali nella società industriale di massa* (Milan, 1967).

Oparin, D. J., 'Das theoretische Schema der gleichmässig fortschreitenden Wirtschaft', *Weltwirtschaftliches Archiv*, XXXIX (1930).

Oppenheimer, F., *Theorie der reinen und politischen Ökonomie* (Berlin, 1911).

Osadchaia, I., 'Evoljutsija Keinsjanstwa' (Evolution of Keynesianism), *Mirowaja ekonomika i meschdunarodnoje otnoschenija* (World economy and international relations) (Moscow, 1963).

Ott, A., *Einführung in die dynamische Wirtschaftstheorie* (Göttingen, 1963).

——'Marx und die moderne Wachstumstheorie', *Volkswirt*, XXI (Apr 1967).

Paillet, M., *Marx contre Marx* (Paris, 1971).

Pajestka, J., *Życie gospodarcze* (State activities) (Warsaw, 1968).

Palloix, C., *Problèmes de la croissance en économie ouverte* (Paris, 1969).

Palyi, M., 'Ungelöste Fragen der Geldtheorie', in *Festschrift für Lujo Brentano*, 2 vols (Leipzig, 1925).

Panzieri, R., 'Plusvalore e pianificazione', *Quaderni Rossi*, no. 4 (1964).

Papi, G. U., *Principii di economia*, III, eleventh edition (Padua, 1959). (Ninth edition 1953; first edition 1930).

Pareto, V., 'L'Économie marxiste' in *Les Systèmes socialistes* (Paris, 1926). Italian edition: "L'economia marxista", in *La teoria dello sviluppo capitalistico*, ed. C. Napoleoni (Turin, 1970). (First edition in French 1898.)

'Parvus' ('A. Helphand'), *Die Handelskrisis und die Sozialdemokratie* (Munich, 1901).

Pasinetti, L., 'Switches of Techniques and the "Rate of Return" in Capital Theory', *Economic Journal*, LXXIX (1969).

Passow, R., *Kapitalismus*, (Jena, 1927).

Patinkin, D., *Money, Interest and Prices*, second edition (New York and Tokyo 1966). (First edition 1955.)

Penrose, Edith T., *The Theory of the Growth of the Firm* (Oxford, 1972).

Pentzlien, K., *Marxisten überwinden Marx* (Düsseldorf and Vienna, 1969).

PEP, *Growth in the British Economy* (London, 1960).

Perroux, F., *La Coexistence pacifique* (Paris, 1958).

——*Indépendance de la nation* (Paris, 1969).

Pesenti, A., 'The Falling Rate of Profit', *Science and Society*, XXIV, no. 3 (1959).

——*Lezioni di Economia Politica: La Moneta*, (Rome, 1962).

——*Manuale di economia politica*, 2 vols (Rome, 1970).

Peter, H., *Grundprobleme der theoretischen Nationalökonomie*, I (Stuttgart, 1933) and II (Stuttgart, 1934).

Petry, F., *Der soziale Gehalt der Marxschen Werttheorie* (Jena, 1916).

Phelps, E. S., 'The New View of Investment: A Neoclassical Analysis', *Quarterly Journal of Economics*, LXXVI, no. 4 (Nov 1962); repr. in *Readings in the Modern Theory of Economic Growth*, ed. J. E. Stiglitz and H. E. Uzawa (Cambridge, Mass., and London, 1969).

Phillips, A. W., 'Unemployment and Wage Rates', *Economica*, XXV (1958), repr. in *Readings in Macroeconomics*, ed. M. G. Mueller (London and New York, 1970).

Phillips, J. D., 'Appendix: Estimating the Economic Surplus', in *Baran and Sweezy, Monopoly Capital* (1968b).

Pietranera, 'La Teoria del valore lavoro' (1946), in *Capitalismo ed Economia* (Turin, 1966).

Piettre, A., *Marx et Marxisme*, third edition (Paris, 1962). (First edition 1957.)

——*Histoire de la pensée économique et analyse des théories contemporaines* (Paris, 1959).

Pigou, A. C., *The Economics of Welfare*, fourth edition (London, 1938). (First edition 1920.)

——Industrial Fluctuations, second edition (London, 1929). (First edition 1927).

——*Socialism versus Capitalism* (London, 1937).

Pirenne, H., *Economic and Social History of Europe* (London, 1949). (First edition 1936.)

Plekhanov, G. W., *Unsere Differenzen* (St Petersburg, 1900).

Pohl, R., 'Devisenüberschüsse – Geldpolitik – Konjunkturstabilisierung', in *Konjunkturelle Stabilität*, ed. Zeitel and Pahlke (1962).

Pöhle, V., *Der Unternehmerstand* (Jena, 1910).

Pohle, L., *Kapitalismus und Sozialismus*, third edition (Berlin, 1923); fourth edition ed. G. Halm (Berlin, 1931). (First edition 1921.)

Polak, N. J., *Grundzüge der Finanzierung mit Rücksicht auf die Kreditdauer* (Berlin and Vienna, 1926).

Popper, K. R., 'Hegel and Marx', *The Open Society and its Enemies*, II (London, 1966).

Power, J. H., 'Capital Intensity and Economic Growth', *American Economic Review*, XLV (1955).

Prais, J. S., and Hart, P. E., 'The Analysis of Business Concentration', *Journal of the Royal Statistical Society*, Oct 1956.

Preiser, E., 'Das Wesen der Marxschen Krisentheorie', in *Wirtschaft und Gesellschaft, Beiträge zur Ökonomik und Soziologie der Gegenwart* (Frankfurt, 1924); repr. in *Politische Ökonomie im 20. Jahrhundert* (Munich, 1970).

——*Grundzüge der Konjunkturtheorie* (Tübingen, 1933).

——'Kapitalexport und Vollbeschäftigung', *Jahrbücher für Nationalökonomie und Statistik*, CLXII (1950); repr. in *Theorie der Internationalen Wirtschaftsbeziehungen*, ed. R. Rose (Cologne, 1965).

——'Besitz und Macht in der Distributionstheorie', in *Synopsis, Festgabe für Alfred Weber* (Heidelberg, 1948).

——'Erkenntniswert und Grenzen der Grenzproduktivitätstheorie', (1953), repr. in *Bildung und Verteilung des Volkseinkommens*, second edition (Göttingen, 1961). (First edition 1957.)

——*Wachstum und Einkommensverteilung*, second edition (Heidelberg, 1964). (First edition 1961.)

Preston, see Collins (1961).

——Article 'Distribution I (Theorie)', in: *Handwörterbuch der Sozialwissenschaften*, II (1959), pp. 620ff., repr. in 1961 (above):

Preobrashensky, E., *Nowaya Ekonomitscheskaya Politika* (The new economics) (Moscow, 1926).

Quarterly Journal of Economics: Symposium: 'Paradoxes in Capital Theory', LXXX (Nov 1966).

——Symposium: 'Economics of the New Left', LXXXVI (Nov 1972).

Ramsey, F. R., 'A Mathematical Theory of Savings', *Economic Journal*, XXXVIII (1928); repr. in *Growth Economics*, ed. Sen (1970).

Recktenwald, H. C., 'Die Finanzwirtschaft der Bundesrepublik in der Mitte unseres Jahrhunderts', *Jahrbücher für Nationalökonomie und Statistik*, CLXXVII (1965).

——'Political Economy: A Historical Perspective', in *Karl Marx* (London, 1973). (For a list of other writings, see Kühne, 1971b.)

Rehberg, see Zinn (1977).

Ricardo, D., *Principles of Political Economy and Taxation*, ed. P. Sraffa

(London, 1951). (First edition 1817.)

Rischin, M. A., 'A Note on Trends in Industrial Concentration in the USA 1948–1956', *Antitrust Bulletin*, (July–Aug 1959).

Rist, see Gide.

Ritschl, H., *Theoretische Volkswirtschaftslehre*, 2 vols (Tübingen, 1948).

Rittig, G., *Gemeinwirtschaftsprinzip und Preisbildung bei öffentlichen Unternehmen unter volkswirtschaftlichen Gesichtspunkten* (Frankfurt, 1977).

Rizzi, B., *La bureaucratisation du monde* (Paris, 1939).

Robbins, Lionel, *The Great Depression* (London, 1935).

Roberts, P. C., and Stephenson, M. A., 'A Note on Marxian Alienation', *Oxford Economic Papers*, new ser. XXII no. 1 (Mar 1970).

Robertson, D. H., *Banking Policy and the Price Level* (1926).

——*Economic Fragments* (London, 1931); repr. under the title 'Wage Grumbles' in *Readings in the Theory of Income Distribution* (Philadelphia and Toronto, 1946).

——*A Study of Industrial Fluctuations* (London, 1948). (First edition 1915).

——'Thoughts on Meeting Some Important Persons: The Domar Equation', address at the universities of Harvard and Princeton, Apr 1953, in *Quarterly Journal of Economics*, LXVIII (May 1954); repr. in *Essays in Money and Interest* (Manchester, 1966).

——The Basic Theory of Distribution', in *Lectures on Economic Principles* (London, 1959).

Robinson, Joan, *The Economics of Imperfect Competition* (London, 1933).

——'What is Perfect Competition?', *Quarterly Journal of Economics*, XLVIII (1934).

——*Essays in the Theory of Unemployment* (London, 1937).

——'Marx and Keynes', *Critica Economica* (Nov 1948); repr. in *Marx and Modern Economics*, ed. Horowitz (1968).

——*An Essay on Marxian Economics* (London, 1949). First edition 1942, reissued with 'small alterations' 1947. Reprint (here used) 1949; second edition 1960.

——Preface to Rosa Luxemburg, *Accumulation of Capital* (London, 1951). (For German original, see under Luxemburg.)

——*The Rate of Interest* (London, 1952).

——'The Production Function and the Theory of Capital', *Review of Economic Studies*, XXI (1953–4); repr. in *Capital and Growth*, ed. Harcourt and Laing (1971).

——'The Labour Theory of Value' in *Collected Economic Papers*, II (1954).

——'The Production Function', *Economic Journal*, LXV (1955a).

——'Marx, Marshall and Keynes', *Occasional Paper No. 9*, Delhi School of Economics (1955b); repr. in *Collected Economic Papers*, II.

——*The Accumulation of Capital*, second edition (London, 1958). (First edition 1956.)

——'The Philosophy of Prices', in *Collected Economic Papers*, II.

——'The Concept of Hoarding', in *Collected Economic Papers*, II (1951).

——*Collected Economic Papers*, third edition, 2 vols (London, 1960). (First edition 1951.)

——'Solow on the Rate of Return', *Economic Journal*, LXXIV (1964); repr. in *Capital and Growth*, ed. Harcourt and Laing (1971).

——'Harrod after Twenty-one Years', *Economic Journal*, LXXX (Sep 1970).

Robinson, Joan, and Eatwell, J., *An Introduction to Modern Economics*, revised edition (Maidenhead, 1974). (First edition 1973.)

Rogers, J. E. T., *The Economic Interpretation of History* (Oxford, 1888).

Roll, E., *A History of Economic Thought*, second edition (London, 1961). (First edition 1953.)

Röper, B., 'Ansätze einer Marktformenlehre bei J. J. Becher', *Schmollers Jahrbuch*, LXIV (1949).

Röpke, W., *Krise und Konjunktur* (Leipzig, 1932).

——*Die Lehre von der Wirtschaft* (Tübingen, 1943).

Rosdolsky, R., *Zur Entstehungsgeschichte des Marxschen 'Kapital'*, 2 vols (Frankfurt, 1968).

Rose, K., 'Die Bedeutung der Akzeleratorprinzips für die Dynamisierung des Keynesschen Systems', *Jahrbücher für Nationalökonomie und Statistik*, CLXV (1953).

Rosenbluth. G., 'Measure of Concentration', in *Business Concentration and Price Policy* (Princeton, NJ, 1955).

Rostow, W. W., *The Process of Economic Growth* (Oxford 1960.) (First edition 1953.)

——*The Stages of Economic Growth*, second edition (Cambridge, 1971). (First edition 1959.)

Rothschild, K. W., *The Theory of Wages*, (London, 1954). Quoted from Spanish edition: *Teoria de los Salarios* (Madrid, 1957).

——'Theme and Variations – Remarks on the Kaldorian Distribution Formula', *Kyklos*, XVIII (1965).

——'Price Theory and Oligopoly', *Economic Journal*, LVII (1947).

Rowthorn, R., and Hymer, S., *A Study of Comparative Growth* (Cambridge, 1971).

Rubel, M., *Marx-Chronik, Daten zu Leben und Werk* (Munich, 1968). (French edition 1963.)

Rubin, W. A., 'Rabowladjenije w drjewnjem kitaje . . .' (Slavery in ancient China in the seventh to fifth centuries BC), in *Wjestnik drjewnjej istorii* (Annals of ancient history) (Moscow, 1959).

Ruchti, R., *Die Bedeutung der Abschreibungen für den Betrieb* (Berlin, 1942).

——*Die Abschreibungen – Ihre grundsätzliche Bedeutung als Aufwands-, Ertrags- und Finanzierungsfaktor* (Stuttgart, 1953).

Rudas, R., 'Graziadei, ein Ökonom und Kommunist von Gottes Gnaden', in *Unter dem Banner des Marxismus* (1926).

Saint Phalle, see Fatemi

Salvati, M., 'Lo Scambio inegale, una recensione polemica', *Problemi del socialismo*, XIII (1971).

Samuelson, P. A., 'Wages and Interest: A Modern Dissection of Marxian Economic Models', *American Economic Review*, XLVII (Dec 1957).

——'Economists and the History of Ideas', Presidential Address to the American Economic Association, *Collected Scientific Papers*, II (1961)

——'Parable and Realism in Capital Theory: The Surrogate Production Function', *Review of Economic Studies*, XXIV (June 1962).

——'Stability, Growth and Stagnation', Wicksell Lecture, in *Collected Scientific Papers*, II (Dec 1962).

——*Collected Scientific Papers*, ed. J. E. Stiglitz, II (Cambridge, Mass., 1966).

——'Marxian Economics as Economics', *American Economic Review*, LVII (May 1967).

——'The "Transformation" from Marxian "Values" to Competitive "Prices": A Process of Rejection and Replacement', *Proceedings of the National Academy of Sciences*, LXVII (Sep 1970).

——'Understanding the Marxian Notion of Exploitation: A Summary of the So-called Transformation Problem between Marxian Values and Competitive Prices', *Journal of Economic Literature*, IX (1971).

Sartre, L., *Esquisse d'une théorie marxiste des crises périodiques* (Paris, 1937).

Sato, R., 'The Harrod–Domar Model versus the Neo-Classical Growth Model', *Economic Journal*, LXXXIV (June 1964).

Say, J. B., *Traité d'économie politique*, 2 vols (Paris, 1803). (English edition based on sixth French edition, Philadelphia, 1841.)

——'Correspondances de M. Say', *Oeuvres* (Paris, 1844). Edition of letters to Malthus here used: Spanish edition of *Traité*, II, annex (Madrid, 1821).

Scalfari, E., 'Mentre lo stato perde tempo', *L'Espresso*, 3 Sep 1972.

Schäfer, E., 'Abschreibung und Finanzierung', *Zeitschrift für handelswissenwissenscaftliche Forschung, Neue Folge*, VII (1955).

Schäffle, A., *Die Quintessenz des Sozialismus* (Gotha, 1919). (First appeared as articles in *Deutsche Blätter*, 1874.)

Schatz, K. W., *Wachstumsbedingungen der Bundesrepublik Deutschland im Internationalen Vergleich* (Kiel, 1971).

Scherer, B. M., *Industrial Market Structure and Economic Performance*, third edition (Chicago, 1971). (First edition 1970.)

Schlesinger, K., *Theorie der Geld- und Kreditwirtschaft* (Leipzig, 1914).

Schlote W., *Entwicklung und Strukturwandlungen des englischen Aussenhandels von 1700 bis zur Gegenwart* (Jena, 1938).

Schmidt, C. (ed.), Introduction to: *Centenaire du 'Capital'* (Paris, 1969). (Origin in congress held in Paris, 11–20 July 1967.)

Schmidt, D., *Entschleierte Profite. Bilanzlesen leicht gemacht* (Frankfurt, 1971).

Schmidt, F., *Betriebswirtschaftliche Konjunkturlehre* (Berlin, 1933).

Schmidt, K., 'Was ist Materialismus?', *Die neue Zeit*, XVII, 1 (1898–9).

Schmitt-Rink, G., 'Kapitalintensität und Kapitalrentabilität im

Marxschen Modell', *Schmollers Jahrbuch*, LXXXVII (1967).

Schmölders, G., *Geschichte der Volkswirtschaftslehre* (Wiesbaden, 1961).

Schneider, E., *Einführung in die Wirtschaftstheorie*, I (Tübingen, 1958).

Schneider, O., 'Der Begriff der Konzentration', in *Zeitschrift für Betriebswirtschaft*, no. 10 (1960).

Schönlank, B., 'Die Kartelle', *Archiv für Soziale Gesetzgebung und Statistik*, III (Tübingen, 1890).

Schultz, T. W., 'Reflections on Agricultural Production, Output and Supply', *Journal of Farm Economics*, XXXVIII (Aug 1956).

Schumpeter, J. A., 'Zur Soziologie der Imperialismen', *Archiv für Sozialwissenschaft*, XLVI (1918), reprinted in *Aufsätze zur Soziologie* (Tübingen, 1953).

——*Theorie der wirtschaftlichen Entwicklung*, second edition (Bonn, 1926). (First edition Vienna, 1912.)

——*Business Cycles*, I vols (New York, 1939).

——'John Maynard Keynes, 1883–1946', *American Economic Review*, Sep 1946.

——*Capitalism, Socialism and Democracy*, second edition (London, 1947). (First edition New York, 1943)

——*History of Economic Analysis* (New York, 1959).

Schütte, E., 'Marx und Engels als Urheber materialistischer Geschichtsauffassung', in *Historischer Materialismus und europäisches Geschichtsdenken* (Düsseldorf, 1954).

Schwartz, Anna, see Friedman.

Schwartzmann, D., 'The Effect of Monopoly on Price', *Journal of Political Economy*, LXVII (Aug 1959).

Scitovsky, T., 'Some Theories of Income Distribution', in *The Behavior of Income Shares* (Princeton, NJ, 1964).

——'Economic Theory and the Measurement of Concentration', in *Business Concentration and Price Policy* (Princeton, 1955).

Seligman, E. R.-A., *L'Interprétation économique de l'histoire* (Paris, 1903).

Sen, A. K., *Choice of Techniques* (Oxford, 1960).

——'Neo-classical and Neo-Keynesian Theories of Distribution', *Economic Record*, XXXIX (Mar 1963).

——'The Money Rate of Interest in the Pure Theory of Growth', in *The Theory of Interest Rates*, ed. F. H. Hahn and F. P. R. Brechling (London, 1965).

——Introduction to *Growth Economics*, ed. Sen (Harmondsworth, 1970).

Seton, F., 'The "Transformation Problem"', *Review of Economic Studies*, XXIV (June 1957).

Shonfield, A., *Modern Capitalism*, second edition (Oxford, 1969). (First edition 1965.)

Shove, M., 'The Imperfection of the Market', *Economic Journal*, XLIII (Mar 1933a)

——Review (1933b) of Hicks's *The Theory of Wages*, in second edition of same.

Simkhovitch, V. G., *Marxism against Socialism* (New York, 1912; French ed. Paris 1919). Previously published as a series of articles in *Political Science Quarterly*, 1908–12.

Simmel, G., *Philosophie des Geldes* (Leipzig, 1900).

Sismondi, Simonde de, *Nouveaux principes d'économie politique* (Paris, 1950). (First edition Geneva, 1819).

Skinner, A. S., *An Inquiry into the Principles of Political Economy*, I (Edinburgh and London, 1966).

Smith, A., *Wealth of Nations*, ed. J. R. McCulloch, ch. 7 (London, 1835). (First edition 1776.)

Smith, H., 'Marx and the Trade Cycle', *Review of Economic Studies*, IV (June 1937).

——*The Economics of Socialism Reconsidered* (London, 1962).

Snyder, W., 'Measuring Economic Stabilization: 1955–1965', *American Economic Review*, LX (Dec 1970a).

——'Measuring the Effects of German Budget Policies', *Weltwirtschaftliches Archiv*, CIV (1970b).

Sofri, P., *Il modo di produzione asiatico – Storia di una controversia marxista* (Turin, 1969).

Solow, R. M., 'A Note on the Price Level and Interest Rate in a Growth Model', *Review of Economic Studies*, XXI (1953–4).

——'Technical Change and the Aggregate Production Function', *Review of Economics and Statistics*, XXXIX (1957).

——'Investment and Technical Progress', in *Mathematical Methods in the Social Sciences*, ed. K. J. Arrow, S. Karlin, P. Suppes (Stanford, Calif., 1960).

——'A Note on Uzawa's Two-Sector Model of Growth', *Review of Economic Studies*, XXIX (Oct 1961).

——'Technical Progress, Capital Formation and Economic Growth', *American Economic Review, Papers and Proceedings*, May 1962.

——*Capital Returns and the Rate of Return* (De Vries Lectures) (Amsterdam, 1963).

——*Growth Theory* (Oxford, 1970).

——'Is the End of the World at Hand?', in *The Economic Growth Controversy* (Symposium, Bethlehem, USA, 17–19 Oct 1972), ed. Weintraub, Schwartz, Aronson (London, 1974).

Sombart, W., 'Zur Kritik des Ökonomischen Systems von Karl Marx', *Archiv für soziale Gesetzgebung*, VII, no. 4 (1899).

——*Der proletarische Sozialismus* (Jena, 1924), (First edition 1922)

——'Der kapitalistische Unternehmer', *Archiv für Sozialwissenschaften und Sozialpolitik*, XXXIX (1927a).

——*Der Moderne Kapitalismus*, 3 vols in 6 (Leipzig, from 1927 (b)).

——'Bericht zur Tagung des Vereins für Socialpolitik', *Schriften des Vereins für Socialpolitik, Berlin*, CXIII (1930).

Sowell, T., 'Marx's "Increasing Misery" Doctrine', *American Economic Review*, L (Mar 1960).

Spaventa, L., 'Realism without Parables in Capital Theory', in *Recherches récentes sur la fonction de production* (Namur, 1968).

——'Rate of Profit, Rate of Growth and Capital Intensity in a Simple Production Model', *Oxford Economic Papers*, July 1970.

Spengler, O., *Der Untergang des Abendlandes* (Munich, 1972). (First edition 1923.)

Spiethoff, A., 'Einige Bemerkungen zur Lehre von der Sozialisierung', *Schmollers Jahrbuch*, XLIII (1919).

——'Aufschwung, Krise, Stockung', *Handwörterbuch der Staatswissenschaften* (Leipzig, 1923); repr. as *Die wirtschaftlichen Wechsellagen* (Tübingen and Zürich, 1955).

Sraffa, P., *Produzione di merci a mezzo di merci* (Turin, 1960).

Staller, G., 'Fluctuations in Economic Activity, Planned and Free Market Economies', *American Economic Review*, LIV (June 1964).

Stammler, R., *Die Lehre vom richtigen Recht*, (Leipzig, 1926). (First edition 1900.)

Stavenhagen, G., *Geschichte der Wirtschaftstheorie*, second edition (Göttingen, 1957). (First edition 1951.)

Steindl, J., *Maturity and Stagnation in American Capitalism* (Oxford, 1952).

Stephinger, A., *Welt und Geld* (Tübingen, 1918).

Steuart, Sir J., *An Inquiry into the Principles of Political Oeconomy*, ed. A. S. Skinner (Edinburgh and London 1966), 1. (First edition 1767.)

Stigler, G. J., 'Monopoly and Oligopoly by Merger', in *American Economic Review*, XL (May 1950).

Stoleru, L., *L'Équilibre et la croissance économique – Principes de macroéconomie* (Paris, 1969).

Strachey, J., *The Coming Struggle for Power* (London, 1933). (First edition 1932.)

——*The Nature of Capitalist Crisis* (London, 1935).

Struve, P. B., *Notes critiques sur la question du développement économique de la Russie* (Petersburg, 1894).

Sweezy, P. M., 'Demand under Conditions of Oligopoly', *Journal of Political Economy*, XLVII (1939).

——*The Theory of Capitalist Development* (New York, 1942).

——'Professor Cole's History of Socialist Thought', *American Economic Review*, XLVII (Dec 1957).

——(ed.), Introduction to *Karl Marx and the Close of His System* (New York, 1966). (See also *Quarterly Journal of Economics*, 1972.)

Sylos–Labini, P., 'Il Problema dello sviluppo economico in Marx ed in Schumpeter', in *Teoria dello sviluppo economico*, ed. G. U. Papi (Milan, 1954).

——*Oligopolio e progresso tecnico* (Milan, 1957).

——*Problemi dello sviluppo economico* (Bari, 1970).

Tangri, O. P., 'Omissions in the Treatment of the Law of Variable Proportions', *American Economic Review*, LVI (1966).

Taussig, F. W., *Wages and Capital* (New York, 1896).

Terborgh, G., *The Bogey of Economic Maturity* (Chicago, 1945).

Theimer, W., *Der Marxismus* (Berne, 1950).

Thiemeyer, T., *Gemeinwirtschaftlichkeit als Ordnungsprinzip* (Berlin, 1970).

Thornton, Judith, 'Differential Capital Charges and Resource Allocation in Soviet Industry', *Journal of Political Economy*, LXXIX, no. 3 (May–June 1971).

Tiano, A., *L'Action syndicale ouvrière et la théorie économique du salaire* (Paris, 1957).

Tinbergen, J., *De Konjunktuur* (Amsterdam, 1935).

——'Statistical Evidence on the Acceleration Principle', *Economica*, new ser., V (May 1938).

——*Les Cycles économiques aux Etats-unis d'Amerique de 1919à 1932* (Geneva, 1939).

Tinbergen, J., and Polak, J. J., *The Dynamics of Business Cycles* (London, 1950).

Tobin, J., Review of Lindbeck's *Political Economy of the New Left*, in *Journal of Economic Literature*, X, no. 4 (Dec 1972).

Toynbee, A. J., *A Study of History*, 12 vols (London, from 1934).

Tsuru, S., 'On Reproduction Schemas', annex to Sweezy, *Theory of Capitalist Development* (1942).

——'Keynes versus Marx: The Methodology of Aggregates', in *Postkeynesian Economics*, ed. K. K. Kurihara (London, 1955).

——*Essays on Marxian Economics* (Tokyo, 1956).

——(ed.), *Has Capitalism Changed?* (Tokyo, 1961).

——'Marx and the Analysis of Capitalism', in *Marx et la pensée scientifique contemporaine* (Paris, 1967).

Tucker, R., *Karl Marx – Philosophy and Myth* (London, 1962).

Tugan–Baranowsky, M. V., *Studien zur Theorie und Geschichte der Handelskrisen in England* (Leipzig, 1901). (First Russian edition St Petersburg, 1894).

——*Osnowy polititscheskoi ekonomii* (Foundations of political economy) (St Petersburg, 1915).

Turner, C. B., *An Analysis of Soviet Views on J. M. Keynes* (Durham, NC, 1969).

Ullmo, J., 'Sur quelques concepts marxistes', *Revue économique*, XXIV, no. 1 (Jan 1973).

Utton, A., *Industrial Concentration* (Harmondsworth, 1970).

Uzawa, H. E., 'On a Two-Sector Model of Economic Growth', article 1, *Review of Economic Studies*, XXIX (1961); article 2, ibid., XXX (1963). Reprinted in *Readings in the Modern Theory of Economic Growth*, ed. J. E. Stiglitz and H. E. Uzawa (Cambridge, Mass., and London, 1969.)

——'Optimal Saving in a Two Sector Model of Growth', *Review of Economic Studies*, XXXI (1964).

Vaag, L., Essay in *Pravda*, 24 Sep 1969.

Vacca, G., 'Technologia e rapporti sociali: Dahrendorf, Marcuse, Mallet', in *Marxismo e analisi sociale* (Bari, 1969).

van Gelderen, 'Spring Floed', *De Nieuwe Tije*, XVIII (1913).

van Overbergh, C., *Karl Marx – Critique de son Economie Politique*, (Brussels, 1949).

Varga, E., *Essais sur l'économie politique du capitalisme* (Moscow, 1967).

Veblen, T., 'The Socialist Economics of Marx and his Followers', *Quarterly Journal of Economics*, XX (Aug 1906).

Vigor, P. M., 'Marx and Modern Capitalism', in *Political Ideas*, ed. D. Thomson (Harmondsworth, 1969).

Vito, F., *Le Fluttuazioni cicliche*, fifth edition (Milan, 1954). (First edition 1942.)

Vogt, W., *Theorie des wirtschaftlichen Wachstums* (Berlin and Frankfurt, 1968).

von Bortkiewicz, L., 'Wertrechnung und Preisrechnung im Marxschen System', I, *Archiv für Sozialwissenschaft und Sozialpolitik*, XXIII (1906) and II, XXV (1907a).

——'Zur Berichtigung der grundlegenden theoretischen Konstruktion von Marx im 3. Band des *Kapital*', in *Jahrbücher für Nationalökonomie und Statistik*, XXXIV (1907b); repr. in *Böhm-Bawerk, Karl Marx and the Close of his System*, ed. and introduced by P. M. Sweezy (New York, 1966).

——First complete edition of his works on Marx (in Italian) *La Teoria Economica di Marx e altri saggi* ed. and introduced by L. Meldolesi (Turin, 1971).

von Haberler, G., *Prospérité et dépression*, third edition (Geneva, 1943). (First edition 1937.)

von Hayek, F., *Prices and Production*, second edition (London, 1949). (First edition 1931.)

——'The Ricardo–Effect', *Economica*, new ser., IX (May 1942); repr. in *Individualism and Economic Order* (London, 1948).

von Mises, L., 'Die Wirtschaftsrechnung im sozialistischen Gemeinwesen', *Archiv für Sozialwissenschaft*, XLVII (Apr 1920); repr. in *Die Gemeinwirtschaft* (Jena, 1922).

von Neumann, J., 'Über ein ökonomisches Gleichungssystem und eine Verallgemeinerung des Brouwerschen Fixpunktsatzes', in *Ergebnisse eines mathematischen Kolloquiums*, ed. K. Menger, VIII (Vienna, 1937).

von Struve, P., *Notes critiques sur la question du développement économique de la Russie* (St Petersburg, 1894).

von Weizsäcker, C. C., *Wachstum, Zins und optimale Investitionsquote* (Tübingen and Basle, 1962).

——'Modern Capital Theory and the Concept of Exploitation', *Kyklos*, XXVI (1973).

Wagner, Adolph, 'Staat in nationalökonomischer Hinsicht', *Handwörterbuch der Staatswissenschaften*, VII (Jena, 1911).

Wagner, A., *Die Wachstumszyklen in der Bundesrepublik Deutschland* (Tübingen, 1972).

Wagner, V. F., *Geschichte der Kredittheorien* (Vienna, 1937).

Walras, L., *Eléments d'économie politique pure* (Paris, 1952). (First edition 1874.)

Wan, H. Y., *Economic Growth* (New York, 1971).

Weddigen, W., *Grundriss der Wirtschaftstheorie* (Jena, 1934).

West, E. G., 'The Political Economy of Alienation: Karl Marx and Adam Smith', *Oxford Economic Papers*, new ser., XXI, no. 1 (Mar 1969).

Weston, F., 'Comment on Lintner/Butters' Analysis of the Effect of Mergers on Industrial Concentration, 1940/47', in *Review of Economics and Statistics*, XXXIII, no. 1 (Feb 1951).

Whittaker, E., *A History of Economic Ideas* (New York and London, 1947). (First edition 1940.)

Wicksteed, P. H., *The Common Sense of Political Economy* (New York, 1950).

Wilczynski, J., *Profit, Risk and Incentives under Socialist Planning*(London, 1973).

Wilson, J. D., 'A Note on Marx and the Trade Cycle', *Review of Economic Studies*, V (Feb 1938).

Winternitz, J., 'Values and Prices: A Solution of the So-called Transformation Problem', in *Economic Journal*, L (June 1940).

Wolfson, M., *A Reappraisal of Marxian Economics* (New York and London, 1966).

Wolfstetter, E., 'Surplus Labour, Synchronised Labour Costs and Marx's Labour Theory of Value', *Economic Journal*, LXXXIII (Sep 1973)

Wrightman, D., *Monetary Theory and Policy* (New York and London, 1971).

Zaleski, E., *Planification de la croissance et fluctuations économiques en URSS*, I (Paris, 1962).

Zeitel, G. and Pahlke, J. (eds), *Konjunkturelle Stabilität als wirtschaftspolitische Aufgabe* (Tübingen, 1962).

Zinn, K. G., 'Konsum und Krise bei Marx', *Jahrbuch für Sozialwissenschaft*, XXI, no. 3 (1970).

——*Arbeitswerttheorie* (Berlin, 1972).

Zinn, K. G. and Rehberg, K.-S., 'Marx's Theory of Value as a Basic Concept of Interdependent Structures of the Distribution in Capitalist Societies' (English title), *Jahrbücher für Nationalökonomie und Statistik*, CXCI, nos 5–6, (Apr 1977).

Zweig, F., 'The Theory of Social Classes', *Kyklos*, XI (1950).

Bibliography – Addendum

Adey, J., *Kapitalakkumulation und Krise des Kapitalismus*, Institut für Wirtschaftspolitik, University of Cologne (Cologne, 1977).

Amin, Samir, *L'Accumulation à l'échelle mondiale, Critique de la théorie du sous-développement* (Paris, 1970).

Cutler, A., Hindess, B., Hirst, P., Hussain, A., *Marx's Capital and Capitalism Today*, 2 vols (London and Boston, 1977 and 1978; repr. 1979).

Herre, G., *Verelendung und Proletariat bei Karl Marx* (Düsseldorf, 1973).

Howard, M. C., and King, J. E., *The Political Economy of Marx* (Burnt Mill, Harlow, 1975, repr. 1977).

Kühne, K., *Geschichtskonzept und Profitrate im Marxismus* (Neuwied, 1976).

——'Fall der Profitrate und Kapitalkoeffizient in ihrer langfristigen Bedeutung für das Schicksal des Kapitalismus', in *Politik und Wirtschaft, Festschrift für Gert von Eynern*, ed. C. Böhret (Opladen, 1977) (Politische Vierteljahresschrift, xviii, special ed. no. 8).

Maarek, G., *Introduction au Capital de Karl Marx – Un Essai de Formalisation*, with preface by E. Malinvaud (Paris, 1975).

Steitz, W., *Einführung in die politische Ökonomie des Marxismus* (Paderborn, 1977).

Uno, Kozo, 'Principles of Political Economy – A Theory of Pure Capitalism' (unpublished manuscript of translation by T. T. Sekine, London, 1975). (Japanese original Tokyo, 1964.)

Walker, A., 'Marx: Capitalism Transcended – An Introductory and Critical Essay on the Political Economy of Karl Marx' (unpublished manuscript, London, 1977; possibly to be published by Liverpool University Press).

Index

DATE DUE

BRODART, INC.   Cat. No. 23-221